MYRTLEFIELD
HOUSE

The Riches of
Divine Wisdom

Myrtlefield Expositions

Myrtlefield Expositions provide insights into the thought-flow and meaning of the biblical writings, motivated by devotion to the Lord who reveals himself in the Scriptures. Scholarly, engaging, and accessible, each book addresses the reader's mind and heart to increase faith in God and to encourage obedience to his Word. Teachers, preachers and all students of the Bible will find the approach to Scripture adopted in these volumes both instructive and enriching.

The Riches of Divine Wisdom (NT use of OT)
According to Luke (The Third Gospel)
In the School of Christ (John 13–17)
True to the Faith (Acts of the Apostles)
An Unshakeable Kingdom (Letter to the Hebrews)

Other books by David Gooding:

The Bible and Ethics (with John Lennox)
Christianity: Opium or Truth? (with John Lennox)
Definition of Christianity (with John Lennox)
How to Teach the Tabernacle
Key Bible Concepts (with John Lennox)
Windows on Paradise (Gospel of Luke)

The Riches of Divine Wisdom

The New Testament's Use of the Old Testament

David Gooding

Myrtlefield House

Contents

**Part One   The General Relation of the New Testament
to the Old Testament**

**Part Two   New Testament Thought Categories
for Old Testament Interpretation**

Category One – Prophetic Insights

Contents

Contents

Tables

Abbreviations

ESV	English Standard Version
EBC	*Expositor's Bible Commentary*
KJV	King James (Authorised) Version
LXX	Septuagint
MT	Masoretic Text
NASB	New American Standard Bible
NEB	New English Bible
NIV	New International Version
RV	Revised Version
scil.	*scilicet*: that is to say; namely
TSF	Theological Students' Fellowship
TWOT	*Theological Wordbook of the Old Testament*
vel sim	*vel similis*: or similar
s.v.	*sub verbo*: see under the specified word
ZAW	*Zeitschrift für die Alttestamentliche Wissenschaft*

Foreword

For many years David Gooding has exercised a remarkable teaching and preaching ministry in the United Kingdom and internationally, and many thousands have found their interest in the Bible set alight as they have listened to his expositions. The present writer recalls with uncharacteristic clarity the first occasion when in the early 1960s he heard him give a talk in a series on the book of Acts. It was then that one began to appreciate just how much attention should be given to the thought-flow and narrative development in biblical texts, obscured as these sometimes are by the otherwise helpful versification of the text in the Authorized Version and Bible translations generally.

In recent years there has been a rolling programme for the translation of David Gooding's writings into various languages, which makes the appearance of a new work in English all the more welcome. In *The Riches of Divine Wisdom* the author shares valuable insights on the interplay of the two Testaments, paying special attention to the way the Old Testament is cited and interpreted in the New Testament. As is often observed, the Old Testament was the Bible of the church's Lord, and, especially in its Greek translation popularly known as the 'Septuagint', it was the Bible of the apostles and of the early church. Clearly, in the New Testament writers' use of the Old Testament there are important clues as to how we should hold and interpret that same Old Testament and its younger companion piece, and this study brings some of this impressively to light. It so happens that David Gooding's international reputation as an academic scholar is based on his seminal published work on the 'Septuagint', which is both a primary witness to the earliest form of the Hebrew text of the Old Testament and also the earliest repository of Jewish biblical interpretation, second only to the developing biblical tradition itself.

Various features of the volume stand out, and I shall note just a few. First, it reflects the author's high view of Scripture, in which respect he is but following the example of the Lord and his apostles. For it would be a strange inconsistency to disparage the text in the study and in the lecture room and then to look to it for guidance and help when approaching it in another mode or in a different setting. Secondly, it is written unpretentiously in 'layman's language' and should therefore be accessible to a wide readership. Thirdly, it includes a number of 'worked examples' that take the reader step by step through the process of the questioning, comparing, and contrasting of texts—a harmonic progression by which further warranted meaning and significance come into view. Fourthly, we are shown how the interpretative principle 'Christ in all the Scriptures', if properly applied, need not constrict the Old Testament to a narrow range of repetitively observed Christological parallels and anticipations. The discussion of the story of David and Goliath illustrates this very nicely. Fifthly, the author's penchant for narratology—the study of the structuring and function of narrative—in both his academic and his more popular expositions, is given its head in these chapters. And a great deal of the Bible takes the form of narrative.

In this wide-ranging study we meet typology, allegory, and 'fulfilment', and the different levels at which fulfilment may take place. We are reminded that dogged adherence to either a literal-historical or a typological reading of Scripture risks selling it short. And that, whereas we must always begin our engagement with texts at the literal-historical (or grammatico-historical) level, that is often only the first step in the unfolding of what they have to convey (witness the discussion of Melchizedek, and of the symbolically rich tabernacle, or 'Tent of Meeting'). Finally, as the chapter on the Gibeonite deception in Joshua 9 well illustrates, the reading of a narrative within its larger context may significantly alter our perspective on the story, its presuppositions, and its message.

David Gooding presents this splendid volume as a kind of manual on the interpretation of Scripture, and on how consideration of the interplay of the two Testaments may help inform our own attempts at interpretation and exposition. It is, then, a manual on 'biblical mining' — a manual in which readers will find, to their great pleasure, exegetical nuggets and insights such as they themselves may hope to uncover in their study of the biblical text.

Robert P. Gordon
Regius Professor of Hebrew Emeritus
University of Cambridge

Preface

This book is written by a student of Scripture in order to share with other such fellow-students the joy of exploring God's Word and of discovering the spiritual riches that detailed study of its contents can unearth. Its special thesis is that the interplay between the two testaments, when closely examined, often brings to light depths of meaning that can easily remain unsuspected, and actually undetected, if the two testaments are simply read separately without serious study of their interconnections.

The New Testament's use of the Old is a topic much studied in the past; and in more recent decades its pursuit at the academic level has produced a flood-tide of publications. This book is not intended as a contribution to this academic discussion; hence the almost total absence of any attempt to interact with scholarly works. Readers who are not aware of the wide range of present scholarly publications on this topic are herewith alerted to their existence, and urged to acquaint themselves with them.

Meanwhile this book sets itself a humbler, more narrowly focussed, practical task. It is addressed to teachers and preachers and Bible students generally who, while not necessarily academics, find themselves attracted to the Old Testament, and particularly to its narratives, and wish to understand it better and base their teaching and preaching on it. And they find themselves in a dilemma.

They notice in themselves a certain instinctive sympathy with the typological interpretation of the Old Testament. After all, does not the New Testament itself sometimes interpret the Old Testament typologically? But then they are aware of the fanciful excesses in which typological interpreters (outside the New Testament) have often indulged, and for which such interpreters are widely criticized — and quite rightly so — by the professional expositors. They, therefore, feel bound to submit to the general rule that we must not regard anything in the Old Testament as a type, unless the New Testament explicitly says it is. The advocates of this rule will argue that the New Testament apostles had the authority to pronounce that such and such person, thing, institution or event in the Old Testament is a type. But we ourselves, not being inspired apostles, should not attempt to copy them in this matter; for we have no authority to declare something to be a type, if Scripture does not say it is.

Nowadays this rule is by no means so widely held as it used to be, and it certainly does not go unchallenged even among academic theologians. But the students, preachers and teachers I have in mind feel its weight, and are themselves afraid of the fancifulness of which much typological interpretation has been guilty. This then forms the one side of their dilemma.

On the other hand the basic rule that interpretation of anything in the Old Testament must start from its literal, historical significance as understood by its original readers, is unexceptionable. But when it adds, as sometimes it tends to do, that no further significance may be accurately derived from it, it leaves many students of the Bible uncomfortably unsatisfied. For now large parts of Old Testament narrative become for them little more than bare historical facts, of mere antiquarian interest. They absorb the facts, but then find themselves asking: 'So what? Why do we need to know these facts?' They find it difficult to see in them any lesson for themselves, and rightly feel uneasy about arbitrary attempts to bring these ancient stories up-to-date, and give them modern relevance by 'contextualising' them in the vastly different situations of our modern world. For in such attempts different teachers arrive at widely different interpretations, as seemingly arbitrary as fanciful typology is at the other extreme. And all the while our teachers, preachers and students cannot forget that the New Testament asserts that 'every-thing that was written in the past [i.e. in the Old Testament] was writ-ten to teach us, that through endurance and the encouragement of the Scriptures we might have hope' (Rom 15:4 NIV). How then can a principle of biblical interpretation be right, that makes it so difficult to perceive what valid lesson, if any, large parts of Old Testament narrative were meant to teach us? This forms the other side of their dilemma.

This present book, then, is aimed at making a contribution to the solution of both parts of this dilemma. As we study in detail the many devices the New Testament uses for extracting lessons from the Old Testament one basic fact will quickly become clear: the idea that an interpretation of an Old Testament passage must be either lit-eral-historical or else typological is far too simple. Moreover, inves-tigation of these many interpretative devices will bring to light other basic principles of Old Testament interpretation that will guide us in our ongoing study of what was 'written in the past'.

The author is under no illusion: this book will not even mention, let alone discuss, many large areas that properly belong to the study of biblical hermeneutics. But he hopes that his readers will find that even a little help is better than none.

David Gooding
Belfast, 2013

Acknowledgements

This book has been a long while in gestation. Some decades ago its major topics formed a series of lectures delivered in Spain and were translated there by Mr Eric Bermejo. Much later a revised and enlarged edition was translated and published in Russian by the generosity of Mr Michael Middleton of Cambridge. Since then I have reorganised, and added to, its contents, which were subsequently typed out by Mrs Barbara Hamilton with her usual efficiency and accuracy. Even so, the book would scarce have appeared in English had it not been for the encouragement of Professor Arthur Williamson and the diligent and extensive editorial work done on it enthusiastically by Dr Joshua Fitzhugh and Mr Peter Whyte. To one and all of these I offer my sincerely felt gratitude.

ἡ πολυποίκιλος σοφία τοῦ θεοῦ
The manifold wisdom of God
—Ephesians 3:10

ταῦτα δὲ τυπικῶς συνέβαινεν ἐκείνοις,
ἐγράφη δὲ πρὸς νουθεσίαν ἡμῶν, εἰς οὓς
τὰ τέλη τῶν αἰώνων κατήντηκεν.

Now these things happened to them
as an example, but they were written
down for our instruction, on whom
the ends of the ages have come.

—1 Corinthians 10:11

Introduction

The Plan and the Example

T he New Testament everywhere declares its indebtedness to, indeed its dependence on, the Old Testament, and accepts its divine authority. The early Christians learned their very gospel in its terms: 'Christ died for our sins according to the [Old Testament] scriptures' (1 Cor 15:3).

It is, perhaps, a pity that the canon of Christian books in the Latin versions came to be called 'The New Testament', and the Hebrew canon accordingly 'The Old Testament'. In modern English the word 'testament' is customarily heard in the phrase 'last will and testament'. Obviously, it would not make sense to think of the Hebrew canon as 'The Old Last Will and Testament', and of the Christian canon as 'The New Last Will and Testament'.

The Latin word *testamentum* (English 'testament') in this biblical context is a translation of a Greek word (διαθήκη, *diathēkē*), which has in fact a number of meanings. It certainly can mean 'a will' or 'testament'; and it is used in this sense, for instance, at Hebrews 9:16–17. The writer there argues that a will does not come into force until the person who made the will has died. So all the blessings that Christ has 'willed' to us depended on his death to bring them into effect.

Diathēkē, however, basically means 'a disposition' of one's affairs. It can, therefore—and more often than not in Scripture it does—take on the meaning of 'a covenant'. It is the word the ancient Jewish translators of the Hebrew Old Testament into Greek (the Septuagint) used of the covenant God made with Israel at Sinai (Exod 24); and similarly in Jeremiah 31:31ff, where God promises to make a new covenant with the house of Judah and Israel to replace the Sinai covenant. It is also the word used in Luke 22:20 where our Lord, on handing the cup to his disciples, says: 'This cup is the new covenant in my blood' (RV). The same is true in Hebrews 8:6 where the new covenant is said to have been enacted, that is, to have passed into law, thus rendering the Sinai covenant obsolete and ready to vanish away (8:13).

So, then, instead of calling the Hebrew canon 'The Old Testament', would it not be better to call it 'The Old Covenant'? No, for that would be inaccurate and potentially misleading. The covenant that is rightly called old and obsolete is, as we have just noticed, the covenant God made with Israel and Judah when he took them by the hand to bring them up out of Egypt (Jer 31:31; Heb 8:9). It was thus not enacted until over four hundred years after Abraham, let alone the antediluvians! Abraham never lived under it; and the covenant God made with Abraham and his seed, guaranteeing to them inheritance of the land, was legally a completely different kind of covenant from that at Sinai (see pp. 155–60). So much is that so, that the New Testament protests that it would be illegal to take the conditions imposed by the old covenant and read them back into God's covenant with Abraham (Gal 3:15–18).

Moreover, while the old covenant has become obsolete, the principle on which Abraham was justified (Gen 15:6) has not thereby become obsolete as well. It was always independent of the old covenant. It lives on still, and shall forever (Rom 4:1–8). It would not do, therefore, to call a book in which Genesis appears 'The Old Covenant'.

How then shall we refer to the Hebrew canon? The title 'The Old Testament', as we have seen, is not the best. But in the English-speaking world, at least, it would be pedantic to try at this late stage to change it. It is enough to know why it is inadequate; and then, when talking with Jewish friends to use their title, the Tanakh.[1]

1 An acronym of the Hebrew for 'the Law, the Prophets and the Writings' (see Table 1).

At the same time, if the New Testament declares that some of the Old Testament is now obsolete, what does this imply? Does it mean that Christians can safely ignore large parts of the Old Testament as now being spiritually irrelevant and therefore unprofitable? What exactly is the general relationship of the New Testament to the Old?

The plan of this book

Part One—The general relationship

We shall begin by investigating what the New Testament itself says on this topic; and we shall do so under four heads:

1. A Matter of History: the New Testament's dependence on the Old Testament
2. Continuity and Discontinuity: the New Testament is not just a continuation of the Old Testament
3. All of it Profitable: the New Testament's attitude to the Old Testament
4. Whose Intention? The New Testament's attitude to authorial intention in the Old Testament

Two things will then stand out clearly. On the New Testament's authority:

1. *The Old Testament is valid in its own right.* It was originally inspired by God. It still is. It has not ceased to be inspired since the advent of the New Testament. And since the God who originally spoke it to the fathers by the prophets, speaks it still to those who will listen, what believer would turn a deaf ear to it?

2. *The Old Testament is all of it profitable.* This follows from the fact that it is divinely inspired. 'Whatever was written in former days', says the New Testament (Rom 15:4), 'was written for our instruction, that through endurance and through the encouragement of the Scriptures we might have hope.' Who, then, would forego the hope by neglecting to take the instructions of the Old Testament seriously?

Now it is the fact that all down the centuries believers have received great encouragement from the Old Testament. Psalms have comforted their hearts. The messianic prophecies have confirmed their faith. They have felt the force of the prophets' denunciation of religious, commercial, social and political corruption. They have been guided by the pithy, practical wisdom of Proverbs, taught the sanctity and joy of married love—as distinct from its perversions—by the Song of Songs; and have been sobered by the world-weary wisdom of Ecclesiastes. And the exploits of the men and women of faith have fired their faith and courage.

That said, it remains true that there are, for many believers, difficult areas in the Old Testament, not least in its apparently straightforward historical narratives. What lessons are we meant to learn from Jacob's sheep-breeding methods (Gen 30:29–43)? Or from his sons' massacre of the Shechemites (Gen 34)? How came David's wife to have teraphim in the house (1 Sam 19:11–17)? And what of David's repeated lying to Achish (1 Sam 27:7–12)? Granted that David was the Lord's anointed, how did he fail so often to control Joab: in the murder of Abner, in inducing David to bring back Absalom, in killing Absalom against David's orders, in assassinating Amasa and resuming command of David's army after David had demoted him? How was it that the only time David insisted on having his own way against Joab was when David went against Joab's advice and numbered the people, with disastrous results (2 Sam 24:2–4)? How, too, shall we handle the last gloomy, not to say lurid, chapters of Judges (chs. 18–21)? And as for the seemingly interminable genealogies in Chronicles, where in them should we look for the promised encouragement and hope?

That is not to deny that there is encouragement to be found, even in such like passages in the Old Testament. Nor is it to cast doubt on the possibility of finding it. Far from it. We have God's own assurance that it is there to be found. But it is to confess that if we had to set about reading, interpreting and applying the Old Testament for ourselves without any guidance from the New Testament, our task would be daunting. Mercifully we are not left to ourselves. The New Testament has gone before us; and we can study, and learn from, the thought categories that it uses when interpreting the Old Testament, and the many devices it employs for harvesting its wealth.

4

Part Two—New Testament thought categories
Our investigation will progress through five categories, each one containing a number of insights, concepts, devices, or features that the New Testament uses in its interpretation of the Old.

Category One—Prophetic Insights
We shall begin by focussing on the two comings of Christ, first on the significance of our Lord Jesus' own assertion that the Old Testament had predicted two comings, and then on the relation of the two comings to the problem of evil. We shall then need to consider the concept of 'fulfilment' more generally as the New Testament understands it, both in its primary meaning as the fulfilment of predictions and also as the final, higher expression of basic principles.

Category Two—Legal Concepts
On some occasions the New Testament will act like a lawyer. It will cite a passage from the Old Testament, claim that it constitutes a legal document, and insist that its correct application to us depends on its terms being interpreted strictly according to sound legal practice. We will thus consider the New Testament's treatment of Case Law, Inference, Legal Paradigm, Intention and the Interpretation of Legal Covenants. For, as we shall see, the New Testament itself insists upon the legal basis of our Christian salvation.

Category Three—Literary Devices
Not surprisingly, the New Testament employs a range of devices that are explicitly literary in nature. One of its obvious and most frequently used devices is its quotation of Messianic prophecies. At other times it will cite a verse or passage from the Old Testament and claim that it provides authority for the theological doctrine that the New Testament is enunciating.

Less obviously it will sometimes use an apparently simple simile or metaphor which is actually based on some Old Testament incident or practice. But often enough the full enjoyment of the significance of the apparently simple simile or metaphor will require in its reader a detailed knowledge of its Old Testament background; otherwise the force of the simile or metaphor will be lost. Likewise its use of formal comparisons and allusions, both explicit and implicit, may well require on our part some detailed Old Testament research. When we add to these the New Testament's use of what some have disparagingly called allegorical interpretation (whether they have accurately done so we will have to consider), we begin to appreciate the range of the literary devices that it uses.

Category Four—Implied Features

The New Testament also recognizes certain implications of the way in which the Old Testament has been written. It will recognize, for instance, that a lesson, person or event in the Old Testament can have significance on more than one level without contradicting itself. It will also recognize the logical thought-flow of a passage and the intentional silences within particular narratives. At other times it will take the implied internal coherence of the Old Testament as the basis of its exposition. In other words, it will behave like a preacher. It will first quote an Old Testament passage in full. Then it will go over it again step by step, and not only expound each word and each clause carefully, but urge their practical implications on its readers with fervent exhortation. In each case the New Testament recognizes the significance of these implied features and uses them as it expounds the Old Testament's meaning.

Category Five—Typological Shadows

We will conclude our study of these categories of thought by investigating the New Testament's interpretation of the tabernacle as a type. First, we will consider its interpretation of the tabernacle as a shadow of what the epistle to the Hebrews calls 'the heavenly things', that is, of God's revelation through the tabernacle of great eternal realities. And, secondly, we shall consider the New Testament's interpretation of the tabernacle as a shadow of the glorious benefits brought to us by our Lord Jesus Christ, as 'a shadow of the good things to come', as Hebrews 10:1 puts it. Then we shall turn to a special case of the

New Testament's interpretation of the tabernacle and consider the Revelation's use of tabernacle symbolism.

Part Three—Guidelines

At the end of this book, we shall suggest some practical steps that we may take when the New Testament does not give us any immediate guidance as to how an Old Testament narrative is to be interpreted. Having studied the principles of Old Testament interpretation found in the New Testament's exposition and taking them as our basis, we shall be better prepared to attempt to formulate guidelines for our further study. But there is one final introductory matter to consider.

The example

By now it should be clear that this book proceeds on the assumption that both Old and New Testaments are the inspired and authoritative Word of God. In this it follows the example of our Lord Jesus. Therefore, to prepare ourselves for the study that lies ahead, let us worshipfully recall our Lord's personal attitude to the Old Testament as it is shown us in the New Testament. For in this regard he is our supreme example.

Christ's personal attitude to the Old Testament

The four gospels make it clear beyond all doubt what our Lord's attitude was toward what we now call the Old Testament Scriptures: he revered them, read them, knew them in detail, obeyed them, quoted them, expounded them, preached them—in a word, he loved them.

The general term which Christ used to refer to the Bible of his day was either 'the Scripture' (especially when he was quoting a particular verse or passage), or the plural noun, 'the Scriptures' (indicating a number of passages, or the whole of the Old Testament). These terms show by their very meaning that he regarded the Old Testament as God's *written* Word, and therefore as possessing divine authority. It is instructive to observe that though he was the Son of God, enjoying unbroken communion with the Father, and constantly full of the Holy Spirit and led by the Spirit, yet he did not rely simply on direct spiritual communications from God, but was also guided throughout his life and ministry by the written Word of God.

At the temptation, before he began his public ministry, he countered the devil's allurements by citing three verses from the Scriptures, introducing each one by the authoritative formula, 'It stands written' (Matt 4:4, 7, 10).[2]

Then at the beginning of his public ministry he chose to announce the programme for his life's mission by entering the synagogue at his hometown, Nazareth, and standing up in front of the whole congregation to read. Thereupon, he was handed a scroll of the prophet Isaiah, he took the scroll, unrolled it, and found the passage:

> The Spirit of the LORD is upon me, because he has anointed me to preach the good tidings to the poor . . . to proclaim the acceptable year of the Lord. (Isa 61:1–2)

He then publicly read this passage from the scroll. That finished, he closed the scroll, handed it back to the attendant, and sat down. Then with every eye in the place fastened on him he began to say to them: 'Today this Scripture has been fulfilled in your ears' (Luke 4:16–21). He could not possibly have made it plainer that his life's work was laid out for him in God's written Word.[3]

Similarly, at the end of his life on earth in the garden of Gethsemane, a few hours before his death, he rebuked Peter for drawing his sword in an attempt to prevent his arrest. He himself, he said, even at that late hour, could easily have avoided arrest and crucifixion, had he chosen to. Why then did he choose not to? He explained the reason:

> Do you think that I cannot appeal to my Father, and he will at once send me more than twelve legions of angels? *But how then should the Scriptures be fulfilled,* that it must be so? (Matt 26:53–54)

---

2 The Greek perfect tense, γέγραπται (*gegraptai*), used in these verses, means 'it has been written and still stands written'. Compare the use of the same tense in John 19:22.
3 He was also claiming to be the Messiah predicted by Isaiah.

His statement shows that his choice was completely free: he could have chosen one way or the other. But as throughout all his life and ministry, so now in face of arrest and crucifixion, he freely chose to be governed by God's written Word.

Christ's attitude toward those who neglected or transgressed the written word

Given, then, Christ's personal conviction that the Old Testament was God's written Word, and given also his personal devotion and obedience to it, we cannot be surprised when we read that at times he sharply chided his religious opponents. He did so particularly when their criticisms of himself exposed the fact that they had not even read the relevant statements of Scripture, or, if they had read them, they had not troubled to ponder their meaning and practical implications:

> Have you never read what David did when he was in need . . .? (Mark 2:25, citing 1 Sam 21:1–6)

> Have you never read in the Scriptures: 'The stone that the builders rejected has become the head of the corner. . .'? (Matt 21:42, citing Ps 118:22)

> Go and learn what this means, 'I desire mercy and not sacrifice.' (Matt 9:13, citing Hosea 6:6)

> Is this not the reason you are wrong, because you know neither the Scriptures nor the power of God . . . have you not read in the book of Moses . . . how God spoke to him . . .? (Mark 12:24–26, citing Exod 3:2–6)

To Christ the Scriptures were his Father's written Word, and the temple at Jerusalem was his Father's house. He was therefore moved to holy indignation when on one occasion he observed that the Pharisees had invented a religious law that contradicted an explicit command of God in the law of Moses:

things that were so fulfilled. It was that he himself deliberately and intentionally set out to fulfil the Old Testament.

For instance, at the beginning of his public ministry he announced that the purpose of his coming was to fulfil the Law and the Prophets:

> Do not think that I have come to abolish the Law or the Prophets; I have not come to abolish them but to fulfil them. For truly I say to you, until heaven and earth pass away not an iota, not a jot, will pass from the Law until all is accomplished. (Matt 5:17–18)

Similarly, on his last visit to Jerusalem he deliberately set himself to fulfil a prophecy by Zechariah. Zechariah had prophesied the coming of the King–Messiah to Jerusalem:

> Rejoice greatly, O daughter of Zion! Shout aloud, O daughter of Jerusalem! Behold, your King is coming to you; righteous and having salvation is he, humble and mounted on a donkey, on a colt, the foal of a donkey. (Zech 9:9)

And so, when on his final visit Christ reached the outskirts of Jerusalem, he deliberately sent two of his disciples to a neighbouring village to borrow a donkey. And when they brought it to him, he mounted it and rode into the city. He was thus claiming to be their King–Messiah officially coming to his earthly capital city, Jerusalem; and the crowds of ordinary citizens, sensing what was happening, responded joyfully:

> Hosanna to the Son of David! Blessed is he who comes in the name of the Lord! Hosanna in the highest! . . . This is the prophet Jesus from Nazareth of Galilee. (Matt 21:1–11)

The crowd was eventually urged on by its leaders to shout for his crucifixion. But after his resurrection he pointed out to his disciples that his suffering and death did not prove that his claim to be the Messiah was not true; it was proof that it was:

> O foolish ones, and slow of heart to believe all that the prophets have spoken! Was it not necessary that the Christ should suffer these things and enter into his glory? And beginning at Moses and all the Prophets he interpreted to them in all the Scriptures the things concerning himself. (Luke 24:25–27)

Christ: the one to establish the new covenant

Christ, then, claimed that the purpose of his coming was to fulfil the Law and the Prophets. But through one of those prophets, namely Jeremiah, God had promised that he would one day make a new covenant with the house of Israel and the house of Judah (31:31–34); and at the last supper, on the eve of his crucifixion, Christ announced to his apostles that by his death he was about to establish that new covenant: 'This cup is the new covenant in my blood, which is poured out for you' (Luke 22:20).

Now in detailing the terms of this new covenant God had explicitly said through Jeremiah that this new covenant would in many respects be different from the old covenant. It would be:

> . . . not according to the covenant that I made with their fathers in the day that I took them by the hand to bring them out of Egypt, which covenant they broke . . . (Jer 31:32)

That old covenant, however, had been made by God with Israel on the basis of the law given by God through Moses at Sinai. And this fact leads us back to the very questions which this book proposes to discuss: if the old covenant was based on the law, and Christ came to fulfil the law, how can the new covenant be significantly different from the old without, in effect, abolishing the law? What exactly is the New Testament's attitude to the Law, the Prophets, and the Psalms, and how does it go about interpreting the Old Testament in general? What principles and methods of interpretation does it use? And how does it justify the differences between itself and the Old Testament?

These are not questions which Christians can avoid, for they concern the very foundations of the gospel. Christians all down the centuries have discussed them, and still do. Some of the answers are easy to grasp. Some require a good deal of rigorous thinking. In consequence we might sometimes be tempted to prefer a more direct route to spirituality rather than rigorous study of Scripture. But if so, let us remind ourselves of what our Lord himself says to us:

> The words that I have spoken to you are spirit and are life. (John 6:63)

And it is these words that have been written down for us in the New Testament. Devotion to Christ will thus involve, as he himself told his disciples, keeping, that is, treasuring and understanding and obeying, his word. Indeed, that is one of the ways in which he manifests himself to us (John 14:21–24).

Moreover the Apostle Peter points out that it was the Spirit of Christ who through the Old Testament prophets testified in advance of the sufferings of Christ, the glories that should follow, and the benefits that would thereby flow to us (1 Pet 1:10–12). And it is the Spirit of God who 'takes of Christ's things and declares them to us' (John 16:14).

The Holy Spirit, therefore, calls on us to be grown-up adults in intellect, and not babies (1 Cor 14:20). We are to love the Lord our God with all our mind as well as with our heart, soul and strength (Matt 22:37). We must be ready to use to the full the intellect God has given us to understand his word. But above all let us pray that Christ will do for us what he did for his disciples after his resurrection:

> Then he opened their mind that they might understand the Scriptures. (Luke 24:45)

Without that, our unaided intellect would think in vain.

PART ONE

The General Relation of the New Testament to the Old Testament

have heard the voice of their Creator, and have put their faith in his Son, Jesus Christ. On that basis they have travelled through life at peace with God (Rom 5:1), happy in the possession of eternal life, and confident of being at last forever with Christ in the Father's house above (John 14:1–3).

That said, however, the New Testament itself will tell us (see, for instance, Heb 5:7–14), that for a mature understanding of the gospel, we must come to know ever more fully and exactly who Jesus Christ is, and what exactly he has done, is doing, and will yet do, for our salvation; for these things *are* the gospel. And we shall not come to understand these things as fully as we might and should, without considerable acquaintance with the Old Testament's record of history. The reason for this, when we grasp it, will bring us in its turn to a matter of fundamental importance.

A matter of fact

The Christian gospel is not a collection of timeless abstract truths, like the laws of mathematics. Though, of course, it is the case that at the heart of the gospel stands one who claims to be the truth (John 14:6). Nor is it a philosophy constructed by rational reflection on the universe around us and on our human experience within it. The validity of such a philosophy would depend, not on certain historical events, but on the soundness of its axioms and on its coherence as a system of thought. Still less is the Christian gospel a form of mysticism based on non-historical, theosophical speculation and attained to by psychological self-manipulation.

The Christian gospel is inextricably tied in with history. At its centre is the historical figure, Jesus of Nazareth, who was born of a virgin at a particular time in history—when Caesar Augustus was emperor at Rome, and Herod the Great was king of Judaea—and at a particular place, Bethlehem of Judaea; who lived and taught in a particular country, Palestine; who was crucified and buried at a particular time—when Pontius Pilate was the Roman Prefect in Judaea, and Tiberius Caesar the emperor in Rome; who three days later rose from the dead, and forty days later ascended into heaven.

But there is more to the historical dimension of the Faith than that. The gospel did not first take root in history when Christ entered our world. The gospel was rooted in history centuries before he was born. For it is an integral part of the Christian gospel that God spent centuries preparing the way for the coming of Christ, by repeatedly giving advance notices of his coming through a succession of prophets, specifying the method and place of his birth, the message he would proclaim, and the atonement he would make for human sin—and by having these notices, promises and descriptions actually written down in what Christians now call books of the Old Testament. Thereafter they were copied out and made available for reading and study during the long centuries right up until Christ was born (see, for instance, Jer 36:1–32; Dan 9:2).

It is therefore understandable that the Apostle Paul, in his major exposition of the gospel, should introduce our Lord Jesus Christ by pointing to three historical facts, each of huge, basic significance:

1. The fact that the gospel was promised by God before Christ's coming, through the prophets in the holy Scriptures (i.e. the Old Testament)—(Rom 1:1–2).

2. The fact that Christ was born of the seed of David, according to the flesh (Rom 1:3), David having been king of Judah c. 1000 BC.

3. The fact of Christ's resurrection, which declared him to be the Son of God with power (Rom 1:4).

Fully to appreciate the force and significance of the first two of these three facts, one would have to read quite extensively in the Old Testament. But not only so, for in Paul's other summary of the gospel (1 Cor 15:1–4) he asserts that both Christ's death and his resurrection also happened according to the Old Testament. His words are:

1. 'Christ died for our sins according to the Scriptures';

2. 'He was buried';

3. 'He has been raised on the third day according to the Scriptures'.

For the first Christians the fact that Christ's death, as well as his resurrection, was foretold in the Old Testament proved in practice to be the very sheet-anchor of their personal faith. Take, for instance, the two disciples in Luke's famous story (Luke 24:13–35). Three days after Christ's crucifixion they were on their way home to their village, Emmaus, when a stranger joined them. They opened their hearts to him and explained their profound disillusionment. They had felt convinced that Jesus of Nazareth was the Messiah, sent by God to liberate Israel from the oppressive rule of the imperialist Romans. But three days earlier things had come to a crisis in Jerusalem; and instead of rising up and leading the forces of Israel in triumph over their enemies, Jesus without any attempt at resistance had allowed himself to be arrested, condemned, tortured, and crucified.

The disciples were still in shock. True, some of the Christian women, so they said, had reported seeing a vision of angels who said that Christ was alive (24:23); but the story had done nothing to relieve their own bitter disappointment—and that for a very good reason. According to their reading of the Old Testament Scriptures Israel's promised Saviour and Liberator was destined to be a triumphant Messiah–King after the pattern of King David. Therefore, a messiah who allowed himself to be killed by his enemies was a contradiction in terms. By definition he could not truly be the Messiah. There was little use listening to women's talk of a resurrection. The true Messiah would not have needed a resurrection: he would not have been killed in the first place.

Their basic mistake, of course, was not that they had not read the Old Testament. They had; but they had read it selectively, seeing what they wanted to see, and not seeing what they did not like to see. They had concentrated on passages indicating that Israel's Redeemer would be a triumphant Messiah–King, like David; they had overlooked the passages that said, with equal clarity, that as the Servant of the Lord he would have to suffer as a sacrifice for the sins of Israel and of the world (cf. Isa 53).

The stranger gently but firmly chided them: 'How foolish you are and how slow of heart to believe after *all* that the prophets have spoken'; then taking them on a survey of the whole Old Testament he pointed out that to fulfil *all* that the prophets had spoken, the Messiah would have to suffer first, and then, and only then, enter his glory (Luke 24:13–27).

At that, returning faith rose in their hearts like the incoming of a mighty tide. If Jesus' suffering and death were according to the Scriptures, then the fact that he had suffered was powerful evidence, not that he wasn't the Messiah, but that he was![1] And if the Scriptures indicated that the Messiah would not only die, but rise again, perhaps they ought to listen to the Christian women, and to investigate the evidence that Jesus was alive.

At their evening meal that same day they discovered that the stranger was he.

God, then, prepared for the coming of his Son, by issuing advance notices in the prophets of his birthplace, birth, life, atoning death, resurrection, ascension, high-priestly ministry, and second coming. But there was more to it than that: for there is a sense in which, not just these advance notices, but the whole history of the nation of Israel was a preparation for the coming of Christ.

Three great epochs in the nation's spiritual development

This we see from Matthew's Gospel. Its introduction identifies Jesus Christ as the son of David, the son of Abraham. Obviously, Matthew is not suggesting that we just notice in passing that there happened to be two men, among others, in Christ's ancestry, one called David and the other Abraham, but that we need not concern ourselves further with either of them. These men were mighty figures in their day: one was the founder of a nation unique in the annals of world history; and the other was famous as the founder of its royal dynasty. In telling us that Jesus Christ is the son of Abraham and the son of David, Matthew is not merely saying that he is physically descended from these two men: he is claiming that Jesus Christ is heir to what they were and stood for, and to the covenants that God made with them

1 For a similar argument see Acts 13:27–30.

(see Genesis 15; 2 Samuel 7). And we shall scarcely comprehend all that without studying lengthy passages of the Old Testament.

Moreover, in prefacing his Gospel with Christ's detailed genealogy, as he does, Matthew is obviously not content simply to list the individual links in the chain of Christ's biological descent from Abraham;[2] for Matthew divides the generations that led from Abraham to Christ into three roughly equal groups (Matt 1:17):

1. From Abraham to David, the king (1:1–6);
2. From David to the exile to Babylon (1:6–11);
3. From the exile to the birth of Christ (1:12–17).

This at once tells us that God's preparation of Israel for the coming of Christ was not achieved through a mere succession of monotonous, undifferentiated sequences of births. Within the centuries that led from Abraham to Christ there were three great, easily distinguished, epochs in the experience and spiritual education of the nation. The Old Testament's record shows that each period began with God setting before his people a great and glorious hope, designed to motivate and energise them to move forward into the future with confident expectation of greater and better things to come. Each period, of course, had its darker side. Just as a child has little idea of the endless ramifications of sin, and discovers them only by experience as it progresses through life, so the nation of Israel, and so, of course, all nations, have had to learn the extent of the seemingly ineradicable poison of sin in individuals, families, nations, national and international institutions, that blights human progress and frustrates our best hopes and endeavours.

But learning this sad lesson was in its way progress towards the coming of Christ; for how else would Israel come to realise that the only solution would be the coming of a more than human, divine Saviour?

At the same time God kept alive, strengthened, and progressively enlarged Israel's hope, not only by issuing advance notices,

2 Contrast Luke's genealogy of Christ (3:23–38), which simply lists the biological links between Christ and Adam, because its special purpose is to assert that Christ is truly — though not solely — human.

predictions and prophecies of the coming Redeemer, but by shaping history so as to give them from time to time provisional examples, foreshadowings, types, prototypes, illustrations, thought-models of what the Redeemer and his redemption would be like. Thus did God educate people, expand and refine their concepts, and provide criteria by means of which they might eventually evaluate the claims of Jesus Christ to be the son of Abraham, the son of David, the Son of God, the Son of Man, the Lamb of God who takes away the sin of the world, the priest for ever after the order of Melchizedek.

With this in mind let us briefly review the three periods in Israel's history to which Matthew's arrangement of Christ's genealogy points. As we do, we will see that each period had a different trajectory; none simply replicated what had gone before.

The trajectory of the first period:
From Abraham to David (Matt 1:2–6)

The first period began with God's call of Abraham out from his native pagan culture, in order to found a new, distinct nation as a witness to the one true God, and as a protest against the idolatrous interpretations of the universe that were endemic everywhere else (see Josh 24:2–3; Isa 41:8–10; 43:1, 10–12). Thus began Israel's famous stand for monotheism. True, Abraham's descendants often subsequently compromised in practice with polytheism, so much so that to cure them of it, God eventually had the nation exiled to Babylon, and the temple at Jerusalem destroyed. But monotheism was never completely abandoned: a long succession of Israelite prophets saw to that. And when the nation was eventually restored to the land of Palestine, it had been virtually cured of idolatry; and by the time Jesus Christ entered the temple at Jerusalem there was no idol to be found anywhere within its courts or walls. Orthodox Judaism has never again lapsed into polytheism.

It took God centuries, then, to establish monotheism in Israel; but it was an indispensable preparation for the coming of Christ. What use would it have been to proclaim Jesus as the Son of God, if no one knew who God was, and still thought in terms of scores

of gods and goddesses, major and minor, and of supposedly dei-
fied human beings, all with their imagined sons and daughters, and
guilty of the same immoralities as the humans who had fashioned
them after their own image?

Having revealed himself to Abraham, called him out of his
homeland, and brought him into Canaan, God then outlined his
centuries-long purpose for Abraham and his descendants by making him a fourfold promise:

1. A promised land for himself and his seed to inherit (Gen
   12:1; 13:14–18; 15:7–9, 18–21).
2. Descendants as numerous as the sand on the seashore and as
   the stars (Gen 12:2; 13:16; 15:5; 22:17).
3. Blessing on him and his seed, so that eventually through his
   seed all the nations of the earth would be blessed (Gen 12:3;
   22:18).
4. Kings should come from him (Gen 17:16).

Observe, then, the trajectory of the fulfilment of these promises.

Abraham's progeny had not yet had time to develop into much
more than an extended family of about seventy members (Gen 46:8–
27), when they were given to witness an early fulfilment of Promise
Three: by God's providence Jacob's son Joseph was brought through
a period of innocent, non-retaliatory suffering to become the eco-
nomic saviour both of Egypt and of all the surrounding little tribes
and nations (Gen 41).

It was a genuine, if only a partial, fulfilment of the promise.
But it was more: it was a prototype of the grand final fulfilment,
when Abraham's seed, the man, Jesus Christ should as a result of
his innocent suffering (1 Pet 2:21–25; Heb 2:9–10) be crowned with
glory and honour, and be proclaimed morally worthy to receive
the power, riches, wisdom, might, honour, glory and blessing and
to administer the universe both for the glory of God and for the
blessing of mankind.

Prototypes, by definition, do not last; but after Joseph's death
his fellow tribesmen, now living in Egypt, developed into a rec-
ognisable nation. Promise Two was beginning to be fulfilled; but

for most of four hundred years they were reduced to slavery—as God had forewarned Abraham they would be (Gen 15:13–16). But then God's purpose moved on, and he sent Moses to the enslaving Pharaoh with the peremptory demand, 'Let my people go that they may worship me' (Exod 8:1).

That clarion call has resounded all down the centuries and inspired the oppressed to struggle for freedom. But there was more to it than that. For it was not merely a question of liberation from social and political slavery. At that time Israel herself had to be delivered from the angel of God's judgment—and was so delivered through the blood of their Passover lambs (Exod 12).

It was, then, for Israel a genuine, historical experience of God's redemption. But it also served as another prototype of the greater redemption from a greater slavery that would be provided by the blood of Christ, our Passover Lamb (see 1 Cor 5:7; 1 Pet 1:18–20).

Moses then led the Israelites out of Egypt, and Joshua brought them at length into their promised inheritance right on schedule according to Promise One (see Gen 15:13–16). Round about another four hundred years later the first period's trajectory realised its triumphant goal: David, son of Jesse, the Lord's Anointed, was crowned king, first over two tribes and seven years later over all Israel (2 Sam 5:1–5). Promise Four had begun to be fulfilled.

Israel, then, had come a long way since God first made his promises to Abraham; and, historically, this was genuinely a time of realised hope, of advance, of attainment and achievement, and of fulfilment. Israel under David had been freed from all its enemies and was now self-consciously a unified nation in its own right in its own land, with its own king, able to hold up its head as a free nation among all the other nations. David, their courageous warrior hero, much loved king, and poetic genius, had earned the respect of the surrounding monarchs; and, whether he knew it or not, he had stamped his name indelibly on history. Millions still sing his psalms to this day.

Moreover, in David, God had given Israel—and the surrounding nations—a real, but faint, foreshadowing, a prototype, an inkling, the beginnings of an idea, of what the Christ, the Son of David, would be and do, when he finally came. But then, of course, David was not the Christ himself. In many respects the Christ would have to be—and would be—very different from David; for a Christ that was merely a copy of David, or even a much enlarged version of David, would never have been the final solution to mankind's problems.

David's empire was tiny compared with the contemporary world powers; he certainly had not established world peace. David had built his empire, such as it was, by the sword and spear, by bloodshed and sometimes by sheer cruelty (cf. e.g. 2 Sam 12:31). Long centuries of experience have shown us that a ruler who tries to achieve world dominion by spear and sword, or by atomic bombs and intercontinental missiles, could never be the saviour of the world, still less establish the kingdom of God on earth.

Moreover, relatively powerful as David was, his own character, like that of many another merely human ruler, was blemished by lust, self-indulgence, and murder (see 2 Sam 11). David realised it and confessed it (Ps 51); and in his prophetic Psalm 110 he sang by contrast of a future son of his, who, though his son, would be his Lord. For that Son would be found morally worthy to be invited by God to sit at God's right hand, and to be appointed by God to be a priest forever after the order of Melchizedek (Ps 110:1, 4).

Thus Israel's concept of the coming King began to be enlarged.

The trajectory of the second period:
From David to the Exile to Babylon (Matt 1:6–11)

Early in his reign David captured the Jebusite city, Jerusalem, and set it up as his royal city and the capital of the now united twelve tribes (2 Sam 5:4–10).

He did more than he knew. Some thousand years later Jesus Christ, son of Abraham, son of David, the man who was God, would ride into that city as Zion's long-promised King (Zech 9:9; Matt 21:1–11). A week after that, just outside the city's walls he would offer himself to God as the Lamb of God to take away the sin of the world (John 1:29). Since then, beginning from Jerusalem, a message of repentance and forgiveness in his name has gone out to all the world (Luke 24:47). Millions have believed it; and though millions do not, yet Jerusalem continues to this day to be the heart's centre not only for the Israelis but for worldwide Jewry as well, a holy city for Islam's millions, and a centre of political concern for the nations of the world.

But to return to the beginning of the second period. Like the first period it began with a magnificent promise from God: David would have a son who would be allowed to build a house for God's name; and God undertook to establish David's throne and royal dynasty for ever. The promise was, of course, in part, conditional. If David's son misbehaved, God would chastise him; but severe as the chastisement might be, God would never bring David's dynasty to a complete and permanent end (2 Sam 7:12–16).

With that, this second period blossomed forth into an age of splendour, peace and plenty. David's son, Solomon, had an international reputation for wisdom (1 Kgs 4:29–34; 10:1–25). Under him religion reached a new height: he built a permanent temple which God deigned to grace with the cloud of his glory, and set up as a centre of recourse to maintain Israel throughout the centuries and to restore them if ever they went astray (1 Kgs 8:22–53). Politically, there was neither adversary nor evil occurrent (1 Kgs 5:4). Economically, there was unprecedented prosperity (1 Kgs 4:20, 25; 10:27). It must have seemed a veritable golden age, as indeed it was.

It was more: for it served as an early prototype, a foreshadowing, of the messianic age-to-come, when, under the reign of a 'greater than Solomon' (Matt 12:42), Isaiah's vision of world peace would be fulfilled:

> And it shall come to pass in the latter days, that the mountain of the LORD's house shall be established in the top of the mountains . . . and all nations shall flow unto it . . . and they shall beat their swords into ploughshares and their spears into pruning hooks: nation shall not lift up sword against nation, neither shall they learn war any more (Isa 2:1–4). And in this mountain shall the LORD of hosts make unto all peoples a feast. . . . He has

swallowed up death for ever; and the LORD God will wipe away
tears from off all faces. . . . (25:6–8)

It goes without saying, that Solomon's golden age fell far
short of the messianic-age-to-come; and, of course, it did not last.
Towards the end of his reign Solomon himself descended into outrageous folly, compromised extensively with the idolatrous reli-
gions of his many foreign wives (1 Kgs 11:1–13), and made excessive demands on the nation's workforce (1 Kgs 12:1–4). As a result,
immediately after his death ten of the tribes seceded from the
house of David, and set themselves up as an independent nation
under their own king. That king forthwith abandoned the Lord's
temple at Jerusalem and led the ten tribes into idolatrous and, in
the end, utterly pagan, worship (1 Kgs 12:25–33). None of the kings
that followed him repented of this idolatry (see 2 Kgs 15:9, 18, 24,
28); and in the end God allowed the Assyrians to deport most of
the populace to Assyria (2 Kgs 17).

Several of the kings of David's line that ruled over the remaining
two tribes were better men; and some of them, like Asa, Jehoshaphat,
Joash, Hezekiah and Josiah, promoted notable revivals of true religion. But eventually the Judaean kings too led the people into virtual
apostasy from the true and living God. In the end God could not tolerate it any longer (2 Chr 36:11–21). He did what for many Jews was
unthinkable (Jer 7:1–34): He allowed the armies of Nebuchadnezzar,
king of Babylon, to destroy the famous temple of God in Jerusalem,
to sack Jerusalem the city of David, and to bring the long succession
of the Davidic kings to an abrupt end.

It was an enormous shock to many Judahites (see Ps 89); but
it was a very necessary part of the nation's ongoing education and
preparation for the coming of the Messiah, Son of David. Israel and
Judah had to be taught that being God's chosen people to witness
to the one true God was not a form of favouritism that gave them
licence to sin with impunity (cf. Amos 3:1–2). They had to learn
that nominal religion, hypocritical prayers and rituals debased to
the point of superstition, sacred buildings and venerable institutions, cannot bribe God to overlook public and private immorality,

commercial and political corruption, and oppression of the poor (see Isa 1:1–31). God's discipline was drastic; but they had to be made to face the seriousness of sin. If not, what need would the nation ever feel for a saviour from their sins when God eventually sent him?

So now at this point in the nation's education another lesson had to be taught. The depth of sinfulness into which the nation had sunk made it all too clear that they could not be restored simply by the force of arms of some military conqueror like King David. Adequate atonement for the nation's sin would have to be made. And it would one day be made, said Isaiah (ch. 53), by a figure whom he portrayed as God's Suffering Servant. How this figure would be related to the promised, victorious, Messiah–King of David's line, Isaiah did not spell out in detail. History would make that clear.

But meanwhile the prophet Jeremiah, who also denounced the sins of the kings and people, and warned of the coming, inevitable exile, nevertheless proclaimed in God's name that God would eventually restore the nation to their land, restore their temple and Jerusalem city, and send them a Son of David to sit on David's throne (Jer 30:1–22; 33:1–26). Thus was the nation's hope maintained. In spite of their low state, they were now nearer the coming of Christ than ever before.

The trajectory of the third period:
From the Exile to the birth of Christ (Matt 1:12–16)

It was with Jeremiah's words of hope ringing in his ears that a young Judaean prince by the name of Daniel was taken off by Nebuchadnezzar's troops into exile in Babylon (Dan 1:1–7). Jeremiah had said that his nation's exile in Babylon would last for seventy years and then God would restore the nation to its land (Jer 25:11–12; 29:10–14). Daniel never let go of this promise (Dan 9), which was eventually fulfilled in the reign of Cyrus, king of Persia (2 Chr 36:22–23; Ezra 1:1–11). Under Zerubbabel and Jeshua's leadership the temple in Jerusalem was rebuilt (see Ezra 3:1–6:22); and under the governorship of Nehemiah the walls of the city of Jerusalem were restored (see Neh 1:1–13:31).

But no king of David's royal line was restored at that time; the nation, back in the land, remained under the control of the kings of Persia, and then of the Greek Alexander and his Ptolemaic and Seleucid successors.

That would not have surprised Daniel. A long career in high office in the imperial civil service first of Babylon and then of Persia had convinced him that God's Messiah could never be restricted to solving the problems of little Israel, and to being the king of a pocket-handkerchief-size state in the Middle East. To be worthy of God, the Creator and sovereign Lord of the universe, the Messiah would have to solve the problems of the whole world, including those of the dominant super-states.

He saw, moreover, that the world's problems would not ultimately be solved by an international arms race in which one world-wide super-state was eventually able to control all other states (Dan 2:25–45; 7:1–12). The Messiah, the King of kings, the ruler of the princes of the earth, as Daniel foresaw him in his vision, would certainly be human: not only the Son of David, but the Son of Man (Dan 7:9–14). But when he came to take over world dominion, he would, like God himself, come with the clouds of heaven (7:13–14; cf. Luke 21:27; 22:69–70; Rev 1:5–7); for he would, in fact, be God incarnate.

True, when later on in the third period, in 167 BC, the Seleucid Emperor, Antiochus IV Epiphanes, instituted a brutal religious persecution of the Jews, the Maccabees, loyal, as they saw it, to their God-given faith, took to arms, and by guerrilla warfare and brilliant battle tactics eventually achieved freedom and political independence for Israel. Thus began the so-called Hasmonaean dynasty, which lasted till 37 BC, and at one stage even restored Israel's borders to near what they had been in King David's time. But their kingdom, based on military prowess and sometimes on brute force, itself degenerated into cruelty, intrigue and corruption; and eventually it succumbed to the might of imperial Rome.

Once more, Daniel would not have been surprised. This attempt, he had said (Dan 11:34), to found God's kingdom by force of arms, would be of little strength and would in the end be corrupted by false adherents. But this very failure ought to have alerted Israel to the futility of supposing that they could establish God Almighty's kingdom on earth by force of arms, and to have driven them to the unavoidable conclusion that Daniel had been right: only the Messiah, by his supernatural power, could save Israel and the world (Dan 2; 7). Israel must wait for his coming.

But now the trajectory of the third period was drawing to its end. Centuries of preparation were complete. The fullness of the time had come for Abraham's seed, Moses' Passover Lamb, David's Son, the greater than Solomon, Isaiah's Suffering Servant, Daniel's Son of Man, to enter our world.

And God sent forth his Son.

2

Continuity and Discontinuity

The New Testament is Not Just a Continuation of the Old Testament

THE INTRODUCTION TO Matthew's Gospel showed us quite clearly that the New Testament's gospel of our Lord Jesus Christ was the goal to which the Old Testament was designed to lead. That being so, we might expect that the New Testament would show very obvious and important continuities with the Old. And so it does. Let us consider some of them before turning to consider several other important distinctions and the way in which the New Testament justifies them.

Continuities between Old and New

The God who speaks is the same
The God who speaks in the New Testament is the very same God as the One who spoke in the Old. This the New Testament itself states explicitly:

> God, having of old time spoken unto the fathers in the prophets by various portions and in various manners, has at the end of these days spoken unto us in his Son. (Heb 1:1–2)

Jews brought up as they have been in their magnificent monotheism, and having had to strive for their faith against polytheism at great cost and with great courage, have not always understood Christian belief. They have imagined that in declaring Jesus to be the Son of God, the New Testament has lapsed into a form of polytheism. That is not so, of course. The New Testament insists as strongly as the Old does, that 'there is one God' (1 Tim 2:5); and with this all the great creeds of the Christian Church agree.

Other people from time to time have felt that the God of the New Testament is somehow more loving and kind than the severe God of the Old. The impression rests on a misapprehension. Let the Old Testament speak first, and describe the love of God, as it knows it:

> The LORD is full of compassion and gracious, slow to anger, and plenteous in mercy. He will not always chide; neither will he keep his anger for ever. He has not dealt with us after our sins, nor rewarded us after our iniquities. For as the heaven is high above the earth, so great is his mercy toward them that fear him. As far as the east is from the west, so far has he removed our transgressions from us. Like as a father pities his children, so the LORD pities them that fear him. For he knows our frame; he remembers that we are dust. . . . But the mercy of the LORD is from everlasting to everlasting upon them that fear him. . . . (Ps 103:8–17)

The New Testament says the same:

> God is love. . . . Herein is love, not that we loved God, but that he loved us, and sent his Son to be the propitiation for our sins. (1 John 4:8, 10) If we confess our sins he is faithful and just to forgive our sins. . . . (1 John 1:9) I will be merciful to their iniquities, and their sins will I remember no more. (Heb 8:12)

On the other hand, the Old Testament uses unashamedly severe language to describe God's holy and persistent wrath against sin: 'God is a righteous judge, yea a God who expresses his wrath every day' (Ps 7:11).

But the New Testament is equally severe on this score:

> For the wrath of God is revealed from heaven against all ungodliness and unrighteousness of men who hold down the truth

'when I will make a *new* covenant with the house of Israel and with the house of Judah: *not* according to the covenant that I made with their fathers . . .' (Jer 31:31–32). And the New Testament comments: 'By calling this covenant "new", he has made the first one obsolete.' And then it adds: 'what is obsolete and ageing will soon disappear' (Heb 8:13 NIV; see also 2 Cor 3). So the old covenant does not live on in the new, in a somewhat improved form: it has gone for ever.

Christ's sacrifice is different

Christ's sacrifice, on which the new covenant is based, is not just one more sacrifice added to the thousands that were offered in Old Testament times. It was not even the last and best sacrifice in that series of sacrifices: it was not part of that series at all. 'Those sacrifices were but shadows of the good things to come' (Heb 10:1); his sacrifice was the great reality. And between shadows of a thing and the thing itself there is a whole category-difference. His sacrifice was certainly not the best of all the shadows!

The Old Testament sacrifices were of animals; his of himself. Their blood never took away sins (Heb 10:4); his does (Heb 9:14). Those sacrifices could not 'as touching the conscience, make the worshippers perfect' (Heb 9:9) and so they had to be constantly and repetitively offered (Heb 10:1–3). By contrast his sacrifice 'perfects for ever those who are sanctified' (Heb 10:14); and, in consequence, he has sat down, and the process of offering a sacrifice in order to obtain forgiveness has altogether ceased (Heb 9:15–26; 10:17–18).

Christ's priesthood is different

Christ is a priest, but not just another priest in the line of succession from Aaron. He was not even the best and greatest priest in that Old Testament order of priests. He was not in that order at all. The Old Testament itself would have forbidden him to act as a priest in the temple at Jerusalem. By God's own ordinance that priesthood was restricted to the tribe of Levi, whereas our Lord was of the tribe of Judah (Heb 7:13–14).

Christ is a priest after a different order, that of Melchizedek.

His priesthood is after the *pattern* of Melchizedek's (Ps 110:4; Heb 6:20–7:28); but he did not gain his priesthood by being physically descended from Melchizedek, in the way that Aaronic priests gained theirs by physical descent from Aaron. Christ entered his priesthood by direct, personal appointment by God, accompanied by the divine oath, on the grounds of his being the Son of God as well as being human (Heb 5:5–6; Ps 110:4; Heb 7:20–22). And seeing he lives by the power of an endless life, none shall ever succeed him in his priestly office (Heb 7:23–24).

Christ's role as a prophet is different

Christ was not just one more prophet in the honourable succession of the Old Testament prophets. Christ is, of course, occasionally referred to in the New Testament as a prophet. The Acts, for instance, claims that Christ is 'the prophet like Moses' whom Moses predicted that God would raise up for Israel (Acts 3:22; 7:37; cf Deut 18:15). At the same time the New Testament is careful to distinguish Christ from the prophets of the Old Testament. They were a recognised group: *the prophets*; Christ belongs to a different category, of which he is the sole member. Hebrews 1:1–2 uses precise language to distinguish between *the prophets* on the one hand, and the Son of God on the other: 'God having of old time spoken . . . in [or, by] *the* prophets . . . has at the end of these days spoken . . . in his Son'. And the description of the Son which immediately follows shows how utterly distinct he is from the prophets:

> . . . his Son whom he appointed heir of all things, through whom also he made the worlds; who being the effulgence of his glory, and the very image of his substance and upholding all things by the word of his power, when he had made purification of sins, sat down on the right hand of the majesty on high. (Heb 1:2–3 RV)

The working of the Holy Spirit is different

The coming of the Holy Spirit at Pentecost and the baptism of believers into the Body of Christ (John 1:33; Acts 1:4–5; 2:1–4; 1 Cor 12:13) was not a repetition on a larger scale of what had constantly been happening all down the centuries. Pentecost was historically unique. It was prophesied in the Old Testament (Joel 2:28–29; Acts 2:1–18); but it could not, and did not, happen until Christ was glorified (John 7:39) and had gone away (John 16:7)—until, in fact, ten days after Christ ascended (Acts 1:4–5, 8; 2:1). Nowhere in the whole of the Old Testament is mention made of any such entity as the Body of Christ.

Moreover, the union of Jew and Greek in the Body of Christ has not been achieved simply by adding rather a lot of Gentile believers to an already existent Jewish body. What Christ has done, according to Eph 2:14–15, is to take Jew and Gentile and of the two to create in himself *one new* man. And this, according to Paul (Eph 3:1–13), was a mystery not made known in previous generations, but revealed for the first time to Paul and the Christian apostles and prophets.

The House of God is different

The Christian temple of God is not a copy, nor an enlarged, or enriched, version of the tabernacle of Moses (Exod 25–31), nor an adaptation of the temples of Solomon, Ezra, and Herod the Great. It is a different kind of temple, a spiritual house, built of living stones, based on Christ who is its foundation stone (1 Pet 2:4–7; 1 Cor 3:11, 16–17; cf. John 2:19–22). In Old Testament times ordinary believers, not being priests, were not allowed inside the temple; nor in his day would Christ have been. Now, in Christ, believers *form* the temple of God, and themselves constitute a holy priesthood, to offer up spiritual sacrifices, acceptable to God through Jesus Christ (1 Pet 2:5).

The inheritance is different

The inheritance which God gives us through Christ is incorruptible, undefiled, and fadeless, and is reserved in heaven for us (1 Pet 1:3–4). It is not, therefore, simply an enlarged version of the inheritance which God gave Israel through Joshua (Josh 1:1–4; Heb 4:8–9). It differs in both location and nature.

The Christian's weapons are different

The weapons of our Christian warfare are not carnal (2 Cor 10:4). Christ strictly forbade his followers to fight with swords to defend him or to establish his kingdom (John 18:36; Matt 26:51–52). This prohibits Christians from reverting to Old Testament-style warfare, such as Joshua and David conducted, in order to defend or promote the kingdom of God and the Christian gospel.

The New Testament's own justification of these discontinuities

An important question now arises. If the New Testament accepts the Old Testament Scriptures as the inspired and authoritative Word of God, as in fact it does (see, for instance, 2 Tim 3:15–17); and if it likewise regards ancient Israel's religious institutions as ordained by God; how can it possibly justify these—or any—basic discontinuities between itself and the Old Testament?

The New Testament's answers to this question are manifold.

The Old Testament had announced that these changes would come about

The new covenant
It was, as we saw earlier, the prophet Jeremiah who first declared that the days would come when God would put aside the old covenant, and institute the new covenant in its place (Jer 31:31–34; Heb 8:6–13).

Christ's sacrifice of himself
It was the voice of Messiah through David, the psalmist, which first announced that the sacrifice of animals as commanded by the Old Testament law could not satisfy God, and that their place would eventually be taken by Messiah's coming into the world to do God's will (Ps 40:6–8; Heb 10:5–10).[1]

1 The Hebrew of Ps 40:6 says '. . . mine ears have you pierced'. To translate the force

Christ's Melchizedek-priesthood

It was certainly God who instituted the Levitical line of priests in the time of Moses; and God certainly executed summary judgment on Korah, Dathan and Abiram when they disputed the high priest Aaron's God-given office; and likewise God struck King Uzziah with leprosy for usurping the priests' office and entering the temple to burn incense (Exodus 28–29; Leviticus 8–9; Numbers 16–18; 2 Chr 26:16–21). But it was likewise God himself who in the Old Testament (Ps 110:4), spoke of appointing David's lord to a different priesthood, after the order, not of Aaron, but of Melchizedek. And in doing that, the New Testament points out, God himself changed the law regarding the Levitical priesthood which he himself had originally laid down (Heb 7:12).

The heavenly tabernacle versus the earthly one

The New Testament's argument here is this: the Old Testament itself admits that the Tabernacle which Moses made (and on which all the subsequent temples in Jerusalem were basically modelled) was only a copy and shadow of the heavenly things, constructed according to the pattern that was shown to Moses on Mount Sinai (Exod 25:40; Heb 8:5). Now, as we have already noticed, according to the Old Testament law Christ could not have ministered as a priest in the temple at Jerusalem (Heb 8:4). But in any case, it was never the divine intention that he should. When his sacrifice was complete and he was risen from the dead, he did not enter into the innermost room of the temple-building in Jerusalem. He was summoned by God himself to sit at God's right hand, as Psalm 110:1 had prophesied he would be. The temple at Jerusalem, being at best only a copy and shadow of the real thing, would have been an utterly inadequate place for him to minister in. 'For Christ entered not into a holy place made with hands, like in pattern to the true, but into heaven itself, now to appear in the presence of God for us' (Heb 9:24). And again,

---

of this metaphor into Greek, the Septuagint renders it dynamically: '. . . a body you have prepared for me'. The Holy Spirit has chosen to use this rendering in Heb 10:5, as being easier for New Testament readers to understand.

> Now in the things which we are saying the chief point is this: we
> have such a high priest who sat down on the right hand of the
> throne of the majesty in the heavens, a minister of the sanctu-
> ary, and of the true tabernacle, which the Lord pitched, not man.
> (Heb 8:1–2 RV)

The Old Testament had been preparatory

To explain the difference between the way God treated his people
in Old Testament times and the way he treats them now that the
Son of God has come, the New Testament uses an analogy (Gal
4:1–7). A child born to a wealthy Roman father would legally be
his father's son simply by being begotten and publicly recognised
by his father. But as long as the child was a minor, he would be
treated practically the same as a slave. For the sake of his education
and behaviour the father would put the child under the control of
guardians and trustees, who themselves might well be slaves. The
child had no freedom; he had to obey them. They would have the
responsibility of seeing to it that he attended school, learned his
lessons, and generally behaved properly. And they had authority
from the father to chastise the child if he misbehaved.

But all that changed when the child attained his majority, ceased
to be a child, and became an adult. Now he was no longer kept under guardians and trustees; he was his father's fully grown up son,
expected of his own volition to show in his behaviour the spirit and
character of his father.

This analogy Paul then applies to himself and to his fellow
Christians to explain the difference that the Redeemer's cross and
the coming of the Holy Spirit have made to the power and motivation of a Christian's behaviour: a believer is no longer driven like
a slave by fear of the law's penalties; he is led by the Spirit (Rom
8:14–17).

> So we also, when we were children, were held in slavery under
> the basic principles of the world. But when the time had fully
> come, God sent his Son, born of a woman, born under the law,
> that he might redeem those who were under the law, that we
> might receive the adoption of sons. And because you are sons,
> God sent forth the Spirit of his Son into our hearts, crying, Abba,

Father. So that thou art no longer a slave, but a son; and if a son, then an heir through God. (Gal 4:3–7)

One could ask, of course, about the appropriateness of applying the analogy of childhood/manhood to the spiritual experience of the nation of Israel, or to the religious experience of the Gentiles, for that matter. But the analogy is one that God himself uses in the Old Testament: 'When Israel was a child, then I loved him, and called my son out of Egypt. . . . I taught Ephraim to walk, taking them by the arms' (Hos 11:1–3). Though Israel's exodus from Egypt was some four hundred years later than Abraham's time, God still refers to the nation as in its spiritual childhood. The New Testament's point is that, compared with the new epoch inaugurated by the coming of the Holy Spirit, the experience of all the previous epochs was but childhood and teenage. And that brings us to the New Testament's next answer to the question of how it can justify its basic discontinuities with the Old Testament.

The coming of the Son of God inaugurated a new epoch

The New Testament holds that with the coming of the Son of God into the world, and more so with his resurrection and ascension and the coming of the Holy Spirit, a new epoch has dawned in the ways of God with men.

According to Hebrews 1:2 (literally translated) Christ was born 'at the end of these days', meaning, at the end of the period when Israel was the centre of God's developing plans for the world. Similarly, Hebrews 9:26 (again, literally translated) remarks that Christ appeared in our world to put away sin by the sacrifice of himself 'at the consummation of the ages'. In other words: Christ's atoning death was the goal, and therefore the end, of all the preceding ages. First Peter 1:19–20 says the same: Christ, the Lamb of God, by whose blood we are redeemed, was 'foreknown indeed before the foundation of the world, but was manifested at the end of the times for your sake . . .' (RV).

With the resurrection and ascension of Christ and the coming of the Holy Spirit a new epoch began. Its commencement was marked by the special manifestations of the Holy Spirit on the day of Pentecost, described by Peter as 'this is that which has been spoken by the prophet Joel, "And it shall be in the last days", says God, "I will pour forth of my Spirit on all flesh . . ." ' (Acts 2:16–17). The epoch, thus begun, will be brought to its end by the great and glorious Day of the Lord (Acts 2:20), when, following cosmic disturbances, the Lord Jesus shall come 'in a cloud with power and great glory' (Luke 21:27) to execute the judgment of God on the great harvest of God-defying evil (2 Thess 2:3–12).

The purposes of God

The New Testament provides an account of the changes in strategies and tactics necessitated by God's purposes for the Christian epoch and does not simply take them for granted.

The going out of the gospel to the Gentile nations

Before the cross, when Christ sent out his apostles on their evangelistic mission, he instructed them: 'Go not into the way of the Gentiles, and enter not into any city of the Samaritans; but go rather to the lost sheep of the house of Israel' (Matt 10:5–6). Again, on another occasion, he remarked of his own mission: 'I was not sent but unto the lost sheep of the house of Israel' (Matt 15:24 RV). In vivid contrast, after his resurrection, his former commissioning was reversed. Now he commanded his apostles: 'All authority has been given unto me in heaven and on earth. Go, therefore, and make disciples of all the [Gentile] nations . . . and lo, I am with you always, even unto the end of the age' (Matt 28:18–20).

Isaiah in his age had prophesied that one day the Messiah, sprung from the rod of Jesse (King David's father), would become the centre of attraction for Gentiles. Their hope would be set on him, and he would rule over them (see Isa 11:10; 49:6; Acts 13:47; Rom 15:12). The plain fact of history is that in this age since Pentecost multi-millions of Gentiles have been attracted to Jesus Christ, and have put their faith in this Jewish Son of David. It was, as we have just seen, prophesied in the Old Testament by Isaiah seven hundred years before Christ was born. But nothing remotely like it happened in any previous age before Pentecost.

The abolition of the Old Testament regulations relating to food laws and ceremonial cleanings

For centuries these laws had served as an external barrier to prevent excessive social contact between Jews and Gentiles, and so to preserve Israel, as best as might be, from the corruptions in Gentile society. But as Christ pointed out, these external practices did not touch the source of pollution, which is the human heart. He cancelled them (Mark 7:1–23).

With the coming of the Holy Spirit a new power was available to cleanse people's hearts, and to protect them, whatever society they mixed in. And if the early Christians were going to break out of their narrow Jewish circles and take the gospel to Gentiles, they would have to mix socially with Gentiles. With a dramatic object lesson God set them free to do so (Acts 10).

The change in attitude to circumcision

Circumcision had never, even for Jews, been necessary for salvation. It was for Abraham a seal of the righteousness which he had by faith (Rom 4:9–11); and for his descendants it was an outward token of physical descent from Abraham (Gen 17), and of their commitment to keep God's law (Rom 2:23–29). Under the old covenant, therefore, any Gentile male that wished to become a member of the people of God, had to be circumcised.

All that changed under the new covenant. It was still regarded as utterly false doctrine to say that circumcision was necessary for salvation either for Gentile or for Jew (Acts 15:1–11). But now circumcision was not obligatory either for Gentiles or for Jews even after salvation (Gal 5:1–6); and certainly not necessary for becoming a member of the people of God.

The change in the mode of worship

In Old Testament days the Israelites were allowed only one temple; and that was the temple in Jerusalem. They had, of course, many synagogues throughout Palestine and the Diaspora; and in them they read Scripture and sang God's praises. But no priesthood operated in the synagogues nor were sacrifices offered there. If Jews wished to offer a sacrifice to God, they had to go to the temple at Jerusalem;[2] and the Samaritans who rejected the temple at Jerusalem, and built one for themselves on Mount Gerizim, were held, not only by Jews, but by Christ himself, to have acted in ignorant disobedience (John 4:22).

Christ changed this; and it is important to notice in what direction he changed it. He did not relax the Old Testament rule, and allow people thereafter to build temples and offer sacrifices in any place they pleased. He did away with the very idea of a physical temple and the offering of sacrifices on physical altars in specially sacred places, and instituted a higher form of worship. When a Samaritan woman remarked to him (John 4:20):

> Our fathers worshipped in this mountain; and you [Jews] say that in Jerusalem is the place where people ought to worship.

> [Christ replied:] Woman, believe me, the hour comes, when neither in this mountain, nor in Jerusalem, shall ye worship the Father ... the hour comes and now is, when the true worshippers shall worship the Father in spirit and truth: for such does the Father seek to be his worshippers. God is spirit; and those who worship him must worship in spirit and truth. (John 4:21, 23–24)

In the Christian age the true temple is the body of the Lord Jesus (John 2:19–21), the body of each individual believer (1 Cor 6:19), each local congregation of believers (1 Cor 3:16–17), and the aggregate of all believers from Pentecost to the second coming of Christ (Eph 2:21–22; 1 Pet 2:4–5).

---

2 In this the God of Israel stood in vivid contrast to the pagan gods. Zeus, or, as the Romans called him, Jupiter, had hundreds of temples all over the Roman world, and so did the other gods and goddesses worshipped in Christ's day.

Stephen's account of God's strategies and tactics

Now the New Testament itself tells us that when the Jews first heard the early Christians say that with the resurrection and ascension of Christ, and the coming of the Holy Spirit, God had introduced a new epoch, in which many of the religious customs of the previous epochs would be discontinued, they considered the very idea to be not only revolutionary but blasphemous (see Acts 6:8–7:60). Indeed, so strong was their revulsion at this idea, that they executed Stephen, the first Christian martyr, for daring to preach it.

In his defence Stephen pointed out that every Jew familiar with the Old Testament must surely realise that there had likewise been different epochs in God's dealings with Israel in Old Testament times, each with its own strategies and tactics.

To initiate the whole process, said Stephen, God called Abraham out from among the Gentiles, brought him to Canaan and commanded him to live in the land of Canaan as a nomad (Acts 7:2–8). He told him that his descendants would at a subsequent period be strangers in a foreign land for four hundred years (7:6–7); but for the present they were to stay as nomads in Canaan (see Gen 26:2–3). This was *the first epoch*.

The second epoch began when God sent Abraham's grandchildren and their families, in precisely the opposite direction, back among the Gentiles, to live in Egypt, not as nomads but in houses (Acts 7:9–16).

Then after some centuries there came *a third epoch*, which once more reversed the situation. Through Moses God liberated the Israelites from Egypt and directed them to live in tents and to make a portable tabernacle for God, as they made their way across the desert to the land of Canaan (7:17–44).

The fourth epoch began when they entered Canaan with Joshua, conquered the land, and settled down as permanent residents in their own country. Yet for some hundreds of years God would not let them build him a permanent, stationary temple (7:45–46).

It was not until *the fifth epoch* dawned with the accession of Solomon to the throne of David that God allowed a stationary temple to be built (7:47–50).

Stephen ended his survey of Israel's history at this point. But he could have proceeded, had he wished, to mention the two other distinct epochs: *the sixth*, after the destruction of Jerusalem and the temple by Nebuchadnezzar, when by God's own overruling the Jews had to live in exile without any temple at all; and *the seventh* when a minority of the nation, encouraged by the emperor, Cyrus, returned to Palestine and rebuilt the temple and the walls of Jerusalem city.

Now with the coming of Jesus the Messiah, his death, resurrection and ascension, and the coming of the Holy Spirit, God, so Stephen argued, had instituted *another new epoch*. Their ancestors, he added, whenever God sent them a leader, like Joseph or Moses, to lead them into the next epoch, had invariably at first rejected that leader. Let them not, said Stephen, repeat the pattern and reject Jesus. For to refuse to move on, when God moves on into another epoch, is to depart from the living God.

Conclusion: A question of relevance

Upon inspection, the New Testament exhibits clear continuities with the Old Testament. However, it is clearly not just a continuation of the Old, for it shows a number of discontinuities as well. As we have seen, the New Testament carefully explains how these discontinuities arise from the ongoing strategies and tactics of God as he works out his purposes. That leads to one last very important question: does the existence of these discontinuities mean that large parts of the Old Testament are no longer relevant for us and that they have no message for us?

Christ has forbidden us to engage in physical warfare in order to further, or to protect, his kingdom. Does that mean that the accounts of Israel's warfare in the books of Joshua, Judges, 1 and 2 Samuel, 1 and 2 Kings, and 1 and 2 Chronicles, have nothing to teach us, and that we can neglect them without loss?

Again, the new covenant has made Israel's tabernacle, offerings, and priesthood obsolete. Does that mean that the long chapters in

Exodus, Leviticus, and Numbers that describe these ancient institutions hold no interest for us, except the historical and antiquarian?

The answer in both cases is no. It certainly does not mean that. Quite the reverse. The New Testament explicitly affirms

> *All* scripture [*scil.* Old Testament Scripture] is given by inspiration of God, *and is profitable* for teaching, for reproof, for correction, for instruction in righteousness, that the man of God may be complete, furnished completely unto every good work. (2 Tim 3:16–17)

But how that can be so, if what we have said about the discontinuities between the Old and New Testaments is true, is a topic for the next chapter—and indeed for the rest of the book.

3
All of it Profitable

The New Testament's Attitude to the Old Testament

IN THIS CHAPTER we do not set out to investigate whether or not Christ and his apostles believed in the divine inspiration and authority of the Old Testament. We take it for granted that they did; for in two notable passages in the New Testament this belief is explicitly stated, and it is everywhere else implied. Accepting this basic fact, we set out rather to investigate how the New Testament's belief in the divine inspiration and authority of the Old Testament affects its interpretation and application of the Old Testament.

Old Testament Scripture is profitable for a variety of spiritual purposes

The first of the two notable passages mentioned above is 2 Timothy 3:14–17. Referring to the Old Testament Scriptures it states: 'All scripture is inspired by God'; and from that fact it draws the obvious, logical conclusion that the Old Testament is all of it profitable.

The second notable passage is 2 Peter 1:20–21. It states that the source and initiator of all biblical prophecy is not the prophet who spoke it, but God; and on that basis it asserts that the fulfilment of Old Testament prophecy is absolutely certain.

For Christian evangelism

So now let us concentrate, to start with, on the first of these two passages. The passage which states explicitly that all Old Testament Scripture is profitable forms part of Paul's second letter to his younger fellow-worker, Timothy:

> But continue thou in the things that thou hast learned and hast been assured of, knowing of whom thou hast learned them; and that from a babe thou hast known the sacred writings which are able to make thee wise unto salvation through faith which is in Christ Jesus. All scripture is inspired of God, and profitable for teaching, for reproof, for correction, for instruction in right-eousness, that the man of God may be complete, thoroughly equipped unto every good work. (2 Tim 3:14–17)

From this we see at once that the Old Testament is profitable for Christian evangelism.

The persons from whom young Timothy had learned Old Testament Scripture were his mother and his maternal grand-mother (2 Tim 1:5); and this reminds us of a very important fact. In ancient Jewry, the teaching of Holy Scripture to children was not left to the formal, public reading of the Old Testament in the synagogues and to the sermons preached there every Sabbath (cf. Acts 13:14–16, 27; Luke 4:16–30). Prime responsibility for teaching the Bible to children rested with their parents. Timothy's father was a Greek; but his mother (and therefore, according to the reckoning of Jewish religious law, his maternal grandmother) were Jewesses; and they had obviously done for Timothy what the Old Testament had said they should:

> And these words, which I command thee this day, shall be upon thine heart; and thou shalt teach them diligently unto thy chil-dren, and shall talk of them when thou sittest in thy house, and when thou walkest by the way, and when thou liest down, and when thou risest up . . . (Deut 6:6–7)

The result for Timothy was that the Old Testament proved to be of immeasurable and eternal profit: it made him wise, as Paul puts it, unto salvation. It alerted him to the fact that he needed salvation, and that God had promised to send a Saviour who would die as a sin offering for mankind; and thus it prepared him to recognise the Lord Jesus as this Saviour and to put his faith in him.

A similar thing happened to the Gentile Chancellor of Ethiopia (Acts 8). Having bought a scroll of the prophecy of Isaiah at Jerusalem, he had reached its fifty-third chapter and was considering who this sin-bearer was whom the prophet described so graphically, when Philip the evangelist accosted him and led him to faith in Christ.

Indeed, the Acts of the Apostles shows us how all the early Christian preachers used the Old Testament to great effect in their evangelisation of both Jews and Greeks.

But then we see from the use that the New Testament makes of it that the Old Testament is profitable in another significant way.

For establishing doctrine

The doctrine of creation (Gen 1:1–2:3)
The distinctiveness of the biblical doctrine of creation has long since been seen to rest on its insistence on the complete 'otherness' of the Creator, or, to use the biblical term, the holiness of the Creator. He is not, as in many pagan cosmologies, part of the stuff of the universe; nor is he subject to some ultimate principle, or power, called Fate. He is self-existent and almighty.

But it has taken the modern understanding of information theory to alert us to the eloquent truth of the Old Testament's account of creation. We now know that the biochemical system, DNA, for instance, is a code that carries information; and that it is that information, and not the individual chemicals which at any one time carry it, that persists from one generation to another. Even from a scientific viewpoint it begins to look as if the basic 'stuff' of the universe is not matter, but information.

Genesis 1, with its repeated 'and God said', has all down the centuries insisted that God created the universe by his word, commanding it to exist, and stamping on matter the information necessary for its development.

itself eternal. As Christ put it: 'God is not the God of the dead but of the living' (Matt 22:32 RV).

For guidance and help

According to the New Testament, the Old Testament is also profitable for the guidance of truly Christian conduct and for resisting the temptations of the devil.

The example of Christ

The supreme example is that of Christ himself. He answered all three of Satan's temptations by quoting the Old Testament as the unquestionable, authoritative word of God (Matt 4:4, 7, 10):

It stands written:	Man shall not live by bread alone, but by every word that proceeds out of the mouth of God. (Deut 8:3)
It stands written:	Thou shalt not tempt the Lord thy God. (Deut 6:16)
It stands written:	Thou shalt worship the Lord thy God and him only shalt thou serve. (Deut 6:13)

The warning of the Israelites

The Apostle Paul also corrects the Corinthians by citing from the Old Testament instances of misbehaviour on the part of the Israelites when they were in the desert, and by using them as warnings to Christians not to behave in the same way (1 Cor 10:1–13).

Love guiding Christian behaviour

According to Christ and some, at least, of his Jewish contemporaries, the manifold, detailed commandments of the Old Testament law could be epitomised in two of the Old Testament's general injunctions (see Luke 10:25–28; Matt 22:34–40):

> Thou shalt love the Lord thy God with all thy heart, and with all thy soul, and with all thy strength, and with all thy mind (Deut 6:5) [and] Thou shalt love thy neighbour as thyself. (Lev 19:18)

In this same spirit the Apostle Paul urges his fellow Christians to love one another and so to fulfil the law:

> For he who loves his neighbour has fulfilled the law. For this, . . . Thou shalt not kill, Thou shalt not steal, Thou shalt not covet, and if there be any other commandment, it is summed up in this word, namely, Thou shalt love thy neighbour as thyself. Love works no ill to his neighbour: love therefore is the fulfilment of the law. (Rom 13:8–10)

Mercy towards others
Moreover, Christ urged his contemporaries to observe the fine moral balance inculcated by the Old Testament. Some of them were sticklers for Old Testament ritual, but mercilessly censorious toward others. Christ corrected their grotesque imbalance by quoting God's own preference expressed in the Old Testament: 'But go and learn what this means: I desire mercy and not sacrifice [Hos 6:6]; for I came not to call the righteous, but sinners' (Matt 9:13).

And again: 'If you had known what this means: I desire mercy and not sacrifice, you would not have condemned the guiltless' (Matt 12:7 ESV).

For strengthening our Christian hope
According to the New Testament, moreover, the Old Testament is also profitable for maintaining and informing our Christian hope. Speaking generally of the Old Testament Scriptures Paul says:

> For everything that was written in the past was written to teach us, so that through endurance and the encouragement of the scriptures we might have hope. (Rom 15:4 NIV)

In his famous vision, recorded in chapter 7 of his memoirs, the prophet Daniel was given to see God's final solution to the seemingly endless violence and destruction brought about by the savage rivalries between the political power-blocs of this world:

> I saw in the night visions, and, behold, there came with the clouds of heaven one like unto a son of man. He came even to the Ancient of Days and they brought him near before him. And

there was given him dominion, and glory, and a kingdom, that
all peoples, nations, and languages should serve him; his dominion is an everlasting dominion, which shall not pass away, and
his kingdom that which shall not be destroyed. (Dan 7:13–14 RV)

Now in the Gospels our Lord more than once identified himself
with this Son of Man whom Daniel saw coming with the clouds of
heaven. In doing so he indicated both to his friends (Matt 24:30)
and to his hostile judges (Matt 26:64) that this is how the world will
see him when at his return he comes with power and great glory to
put an end to evil and to set up the kingdom of God on earth. And
thus, by our Lord's interpretation of this Old Testament prophecy,
our Christian hope is both informed and maintained.

The historical record of the now obsolete institutions and rituals of the Old Testament is still profitable for us

So far, then, it has been easy to demonstrate that the New Testament
puts certain parts of the Old Testament to profitable use. But what
can be said about those institutions and rituals, such as the Aaronic
priesthood and its system of animal sacrifices, which the New
Testament declares to be now obsolete? The Old Testament books
Exodus, Leviticus and Numbers, which describe these institutions
and rituals in great detail, and record their ordination by God, are
undeniably part of the Scripture of which Paul says 'All Scripture is
inspired of God.' In fact to Jews, these books are contained in the
Torah, which for them is the most important and sacred part of the
Old Testament.

Can the New Testament, then, seriously maintain that the record
of these now obsolete institutions and rituals is profitable for us in
this present age? It can indeed—and does; only now we must be prepared to discover that they have meaning and significance at various,
distinct levels.

Level 1 – Their significance for the people who lived in Old Testament times

The book in the Old Testament that most concerns itself with sacrifices, priesthood, laws of ceremonial and moral cleanness, and religious feasts, is, of course, Leviticus. There is no doubt what the dominant theme is that runs through all its diverse topics. In the course of its twenty-seven chapters the word 'holy' occurs some ninety times. This is the record of God's system for educating ancient Israel in the understanding of what holiness is, and how it is achieved; and what lies at the heart of this historical lesson in holiness, we shall very soon find is profitable still for us.

Some people, it is true, have regarded Leviticus as a repellent book, with its concentration on the inner parts of animals, on distressing diseases and discharges, and its legalistic minutiae in regard to human sexual behaviour. To them it smacks too much of excessive religious scrupulosity; and they profess to prefer what they see as the broader, more warm-hearted, general principle of love expressed in the New Testament. They overlook the fact that it is this very book of Leviticus that enunciates the basic principle: 'Thou shalt love thy neighbour as thyself' (Lev 19:18). The fact is that love without holiness is not true love; and conversely, holiness without love is not true holiness.

At the heart of Leviticus' programme for education in holiness lies the character of God himself. Attached to some forty commandments is the phrase 'I am the LORD', reminding the people who it is that is setting the standard of behaviour. Time and again Israel are warned not to profane God's holy name or God's holy things. Five times over in the course of the book the reason for the requirement that Israel be holy is spelled out: 'You shall be holy, for I am holy' (Lev 11:44, 45; 19:2; 20:7, 26); and six times (20:8; 21:8, 15, 23; 22:9, 16) Israel is reminded who the instigator of their holiness is: 'I am the LORD your God who sanctifies you'.

Quite apart, then, from what we shall discover in a moment or two about the significance of the sacrifices, it is already clear that the main message of Leviticus still speaks to us Christians today: for the

New Testament repeats its central exhortation with undiminished power:

> As obedient children, not fashioning yourselves according to your former lusts in the time of your ignorance, but like as he who called you is holy, be ye yourselves also holy in all manner of living; because it is written, You shall be holy, for I am holy. (1 Pet 1:14–16)

But we look now to see what the function of the sacrifices was in relation to the central theme and objective of Leviticus.

Leviticus 1:1–6:7 is addressed to the people, informing them of the different kinds of sacrifice they must offer as they approach God. Leviticus 6:8–7:38 is addressed to the priests, and lays down the detailed regulations they must follow to maintain this complicated system of sacrifices. Not surprisingly, the words 'holy' or 'most holy' are used some dozen times in these seven chapters: for these sacrifices also are concerned with developing the people's holiness.

And it is easy to see how. If the Israelites—or any one else for that matter—were ever to attain to holiness, their first need would be to be made aware of the holiness of God and simultaneously of their own individual and national sinfulness. And so it was ingrained in them by habitual practice that such was their sinfulness, that they could not approach the presence of God without a sin-atoning sacrifice and the shedding of blood.

On the night of their deliverance from Egypt each Israelite family had been saved from the judgment of God by the blood of their Passover lamb (Exod 12:21–23). But now God had graciously caused the cloud of his presence to dwell in the tabernacle; and therefore they would need to develop a deeper and more detailed awareness of sin. This, then, was achieved by teaching them that for different aspects of sin they needed different sacrifices.

First in order stood a sacrifice called in Hebrew עֹלָה ('ōlāh, the ascending offering), but in Greek ὁλοκαύτωμα (holokautōma), because the distinguishing feature of this sacrifice was that the whole of it (except the skin) had to be burned on the altar for God (Lev 1:9). With other offerings a sizeable portion would be given to the officiating priest (see Lev 6:26; 7:1–10); and in others, the major part of the animal would be given back to the offerer and form the basis of a fellowship meal between God, the worshipper, his family and friends (Lev 7:15–20).

But not so the *holokautōma*, or burnt offering: *all* (except the skin, see Lev 7:8) had to be offered to God. In this respect this first and foremost of the offerings resembled the first and greatest commandment: 'Thou shalt love the LORD thy God with *all* thine heart, and with *all* thy soul, and with *all* thy might' (Deut 6:5). At first sight we might, without thinking, suppose that the Israelites were encouraged to offer this particular offering simply to show the extent of their genuine devotion to God. But that is not a sufficient explanation of its significance. Each Israelite was instructed to offer it, so that it shall be accepted for him 'to make atonement for him' (Lev 1:4).

The fact is that no Israelite (except Christ) ever perfectly carried out the requirement of God's law, to love God with *all* his heart, mind, soul and strength; and what this first of the offerings was saying was this: that not to love the Lord with the whole of one's heart, mind, soul and strength, is sin that requires to be atoned for.

Now today we live in an age when these Old Testament sacrifices are obsolete. But we still need the lesson which this first of the offerings taught. Most of us have a very inadequate idea of what sin is. We imagine that as long as we do not engage in bad, negative things such as lying, cheating, adultery, murder and so forth, our behaviour must be acceptable to God. But when it comes to positively loving God, we are what Christ described as lukewarm (Rev 3:15–16). We are not cold—we are not against God; we are, however, not hot—we do not positively love the Lord our God with *all* our heart, mind, soul and strength—and we remain blissfully unaware that not to love God so, is to break the first and greatest of the commandments. It is the very root of every other sin, which is why, of course, we need the sacrifice, not of animals, but of Christ to make atonement for us.

There were, of course, many other sacrifices in the Old Testament, each with its own diagnosis of human need before God.

Let us content ourselves here with briefly noticing two others: the 'sin offering' (Lev 4:1–35) and the 'guilt offering' (Lev 5:1–6:7).

The regulations for the sin offering do not mention specific sins; but they grade the size of the required offering according to who the person was who committed the sin. If an ordinary, private citizen sinned, he or she had to bring a female goat or lamb (Lev 4:27–28, 32). If a ruler sinned, he had to bring a male goat (Lev 4:22–23). Male animals were more valuable than females for the purpose of increasing the flocks. If the whole congregation sinned, they had to offer a young bullock (Lev 4:13–14); and if an individual priest sinned in his duties as the representative of the people, he had to offer a young bullock, as much as the whole congregation did for its sin (Lev 4:2–3).

The principle behind these gradations is clear. Take any sin: its seriousness is aggravated according to the status of the person who commits it. If a private citizen steals somebody's purse, that is bad; if a judge, who condemns other people for stealing, or a government minister who passes the laws against stealing, steals somebody's purse, it is a far greater sin and scandal.

Granted that Old Testament sacrifices are now obsolete, this principle that lies behind the regulations for the sin offering is still valid for our modern assessment of the gravity of sin. The New Testament recognises and applies it: 'Be not many teachers, my brethren', says James (3:1), 'knowing that we shall receive heavier judgment'; heavier—because by teaching others we profess to be experts on morality, and we exhort other people not to sin; if, then, we ourselves do what we tell others not to do, the gravity of our sin is compounded.

The regulations for the guilt offering (Lev 5:1–6:7), on the other hand, grade the required sacrifices and the compensation that has to be paid according to the damage that the offence has caused (though Lev 5:7 makes allowance for the inadequacy of some people's means). Again, the principle behind the regulations is clear. When it comes to the damage sin does, the damage is the same, whoever commits the sin. If a careless driver causes an accident in which three people are killed, the damage done is the same, no matter who the driver is.

Once more this assessment of the gravity of sin is of permanent validity. It is one of the most heart-chilling aspects of sin: its potential to inflict irreversible physical, psychological, and spiritual damage on other people.

The lessons, then, taught by the Old Testament sacrifices at what we have called Level 1, were certainly part of God-inspired Scripture, and are still profitable for us.

But now we must move on to the lessons taught at the next level.

Level 2 – The very inadequacies of the Old Testament sacrifices help us by contrast to grasp more clearly the perfection of the sacrifice of Christ

We have already dealt with this matter in Chapter 2, and we need not repeat here what was said there. But we should notice that the very existence of the second veil in the Old Testament tabernacle and in subsequent temples was deliberately designed by the Holy Spirit to call attention to the inadequacies of the Old Testament sacrifices and rituals, and thus eventually to help us perceive, both intellectually and in our personal experience, the glorious superiority of the sacrifice of Christ (Heb 9:8–12; 10:19–22).

Entrance into even the first division of the tabernacle, the Holy Place, was barred to the ordinary Israelite in spite of his own, and the nation's, sacrifices; entrance there was reserved for the priests. But even they were not allowed into the Holy-Place-within-the Veil, the so-called Holy of Holies, or, Most Holy Place. Only the high priest had access there; and even he was warned not to enter at any other time except on the once-yearly Day of Atonement (Lev 16).

The trouble was that the gifts and sacrifices which the people offered were not able to clear the conscience completely (Heb 9:9). Each time they brought the prescribed sacrifices in true repentance and faith, they were forgiven (Lev 6:7) for that particular sin. But every year on the Day of Atonement the matter of the sins of the people was brought to remembrance again. There was never any finality; never did people receive such a complete cleansing of the conscience that they were able to enter the Most Holy Place in the tabernacle on earth, let alone the Most Holy Place in heaven (Heb 9:9–10).

To be reminded of that is very profitable; for it helps us to comprehend the exceeding glory of what Christ has done for us. As our high priest he has 'through His own blood entered once for all into the holy place, having obtained eternal redemption' (Heb 9:12). Moreover, lest there should be any doubt, the holy place in question is further defined: 'Christ entered not into a holy place made with hands ... but into heaven itself, now to appear in the presence of God for us' (Heb 9:24). And in consequence we too, so we are told (Heb 10:19–22), have boldness to enter the holy place by the blood of Jesus, and are exhorted to use our God-given boldness to draw near with a true heart, by the new and living way which he has dedicated for us (Heb 10:20, 22).

At this level of interpretation, then, the glory of the work of Christ lies altogether in the difference between his sacrifice and the Old Testament sacrifices, both in respect of his sacrifice itself and in respect of the results it has achieved for us. Hence the New Testament's insistence that his sacrifice is not a continuation, or even a development, of the Old Testament system, but the end of it. There is now no longer any valid process of offering a sacrifice, not even the sacrifice of Christ, in order to obtain forgiveness of sins (Heb 10:18). The completion of his sacrifice at the cross neither needs nor allows any further such sacrificing.

But once we have grasped this all-important difference, we are ready to move on to the next level of interpretation of the Old Testament sacrifices.

Level 3 – The significance of the Old Testament sacrifices as shadows of the coming good things

According to the New Testament the ancient tabernacle, its associated priesthood and sacrificial systems, had a dual function. In the first place they served as 'copies' of heavenly things (Heb 8:5; 9:23); and as such by means of symbols and symbolic rituals they brought eternal truths and principles down to the level of understanding of the people in those far off centuries. People still use that kind of thing with children. They bring the abstract truths of mathematics within the grasp of a child by the use of different coloured beads, or wooden bricks of various sizes.

But in addition to being copies of the heavenly things the tabernacle, its priesthood and sacrifices served another function, whether many ancient Israelites at the time were aware of it or not: they served as 'shadows of the coming good things' (Heb 10:1), that is, as foreshadowings of the person and the redemptive work of Christ.

As such these shadows fulfilled their function when Christ eventually came: they helped people to identify Christ. People had simply to match him with the divinely given shadows to discover and be sure that he was the great reality of which they were the foreshadowings. These shadows can still perform that function for us. For we too can study the ancient tabernacle and its sacrificial system, compare them with the person and work of Christ, and, perceiving the remarkable similarities, be assured that among all the religious leaders of the world, Christ stands out as the Lamb of God foreknown from before the foundation of the world.

But the Old Testament shadows can do more for us than identify the Saviour. Let's use an analogy. If I know that later in the year I shall be visiting a world famous art gallery, I should do well to buy an illustrated guide and study it in detail before I go to the gallery. Of course, I shall realise that the colour reproductions in the guide are nowhere near as splendid as the masterpieces themselves will prove to be when I get there. The printed reproductions are but 'shadows' of the great 'realities' that I shall eventually see. On the other hand, the great masterpieces when I eventually see them will be so full of significant detail, that at my first viewing I might well fail to notice all the detail, unless I had first studied the 'shadows' and been alerted by them as to what to look for in the masterpieces.

So it is with the Old Testament shadows. Detailed study of them can alert us to see significance in the person and work of Christ that otherwise we might miss. Let's take one example of how the New Testament uses an Old Testament shadow to help us perceive some delightful details in the work of Christ.

The three appearances of Israel's high priest

At Hebrews 9:23–28 the writer is discussing the cleansing of the 'copies of the things in the heavens', that is the cleansing of the ancient tabernacle, which took place annually on the Day of Atonement (Lev 16:16–19); and he compares and contrasts that cleansing of the copies with Christ's cleansing of the heavenly things themselves. As one might expect, he contrasts the annually repeated cleansing of the copies by Israel's high priest, with the once-and-for-all-time cleansing of the heavenly things themselves by Christ. And he also contrasts the tabernacle-made-with-hands into which Israel's high priest entered on the Day of Atonement, with heaven itself into which our Lord entered after his death, resurrection and ascension. But then he makes a vivid and very instructive comparison between three 'appearances' of Israel's high priests and three appearances made by Christ. Let's set them out formally.

On the Day of Atonement Israel's high priest had first to make atonement for himself (Lev 16:6, 11–14); there was, of course, no counterpart to that in the sacrifice that Christ made on the cross. The three ritual appearances of Israel's high priest in which we are interested are those he made in connection with the two goats which formed the sin offering for the people (Lev 16:5, 7–10).

Appearance 1 (Lev 16:15): the high priest came out of the tabernacle, and appeared in full view of the people at the big altar in the court. There he killed the first goat and collected the blood.

Appearance 2 (Lev 16:15–16): he then disappeared from the view of the people as he took the blood into the Most Holy Place within the veil. He thus 'appeared in the presence of God' for and on behalf of the people as their representative, and sprinkled the blood upon and before the mercy seat on the ark, the symbolic throne of God.

Appearance 3 (Lev 16:18–22): now he came out of the tabernacle again, and appeared for the second time before the people to deal with the second goat for the people's sin offering. He confessed over its head the sins of the nation; and then it was taken by a man, appointed for the task, into a solitary part of the wilderness and there let go.

Three ritual appearances, then, by Israel's high priest. But alongside them the writer puts three appearances of our Lord.

The three appearances of Christ

Appearance 1: 'once at the consummation of the ages he has been manifested [*scil.* in our world, at the cross] to put away sin by the sacrifice of himself' (Heb 9:26 NASB), in full view of heaven, earth and hell.

Appearance 2: 'Christ entered . . . into heaven itself, now to appear in the presence of God for us' (Heb 9:24)—and God, who knows that he is appearing as our representative has, in accepting him, accepted all whom he represents.

Appearance 3: 'So Christ also . . . shall appear a second time, apart from sin, to those who wait for him, unto salvation' (Heb 9:28). That is, Christ who after his sacrifice for our sins, left this world, and now appears in the presence of God for us, will at his second coming leave heaven (1 Thess 4:16) and appear to his people who are waiting for him. Unlike Israel's high priest at his second appearance before the people, Christ at his glorious appearance (Titus 2:13) will 'appear without sin', that is, without having to offer another sin offering, since his offering was completed at Calvary. He will appear 'unto salvation', that is, for the redemption of our bodies (Rom 8:23), and gather all his redeemed into the Father's house above (John 14:1–3).

So does the Old Testament shadow point us not merely to the fact that Christ is our redeemer; it calls on us to notice the three major phases of that redemption: his incarnation and sacrifice in our world; his present ministry in the presence of God for us; and his second coming, for which we wait, to complete our salvation and the redemption of our bodies. Of these three appearances perhaps the second is the most comforting. It is no small thing to know that our representative who at this moment appears for us in the presence of God, has been accepted by God, and along with him, all whom he represents.

4

Whose Intention?

*The New Testament's Attitude to Authorial
Intention in the Old Testament*

R<small>EADERS OF THE</small> New Testament have often remarked on the profound change that suddenly comes over the disciples of Christ in the opening chapters of the Acts of the Apostles. A few weeks earlier they had been cowering behind locked doors in an upper room in Jerusalem, afraid that the authorities, who had just crucified their Master on a charge of blasphemy and sedition, might hunt them down too and consign them to a similar fate. But all of a sudden they were out on the streets of Jerusalem and in the temple—openly preaching to the crowds that Jesus was the Messiah and boldly accusing the authorities of his judicial murder. Their own explanation of this startling transformation—and it obviously requires some explanation—was that Christ had risen from the dead and that they had met with him over a period of forty days. They had then witnessed his ascension, and had received the Holy Spirit sent forth in his name.

But another profound change is equally visible in the apostles in the early chapters of Acts, and that is their sudden understanding of the Old Testament. It is, perhaps, not unfair to the apostles to say that, according to the Gospels, before the cross they had been slow in their understanding of what Christ told them. When he forewarned them of his crucifixion at Jerusalem, Peter had even rebuked him for entertaining any such idea; and the other apostles likewise could not understand what he meant (Matt 16:21–23; Luke 9:45; 18:31–34). When he died, they were devastated.

But immediately after the ascension, Peter is found quoting Scripture after Scripture. He quotes Psalms 69:25 and 109:8 as prophecies about Judas Iscariot, the traitor, and about what should be done with his now vacant apostleship (Acts 1:20–26). He quotes the prophecy of Joel 2:28–32 to identify the phenomena of Pentecost; and he quotes Psalms 16:8–11 and 110:1 as prophecies of Christ's resurrection and ascension (Acts 2:17–36). Brought for investigation before the Supreme Council (Acts 4:1–21), Peter and John astonish the members of the bench. The two of them were obviously uneducated, fishermen by trade, without any formal training whatsoever in the rabbinic seminaries (Acts 4:13); yet here they were quoting Old Testament Scripture with uncanny (and, to the priests, disconcerting) appositeness against the religious experts themselves. Jesus, they claimed, was the stone which, according to Psalm 118:22, was rejected by the builders, but made by God the head of the corner; and the high priest, the chief priests, and their council, they asserted, were the builders who rejected him.

The Council banned them from preaching or teaching any further in the name of Jesus, and threatened them with punishment if they broke the ban. But they ignored it. Psalm 2, they observed among themselves, was a prophecy of the concerted effort of the Gentiles, Pilate and Herod, along with leading Israelites, to do away with Jesus; but it also prophesied God's reaction to this opposition: God would set his king on his holy hill of Zion. The apostles declared they had seen it fulfilled before their very eyes in the crucifixion, resurrection and ascension of Christ; and, assured by this psalm that God would continue to vindicate his Son, they went on preaching (Acts 4:18–31).

The Council, at a loss otherwise to understand how these biblically uneducated fishermen could have developed such knowledge and interpretation of Scripture, observed among themselves that they had been with Jesus (Acts 4:13). In this they were on target; for Luke tells us that the risen Lord spent much of the forty days after his resurrection opening the apostles' minds that they might understand the Scriptures, and interpreting to them in all the Scriptures from the Pentateuch onwards the things concerning himself (Luke 24:27, 44–47; Acts 1:3).

This christological interpretation of the Old Testament, then, stems from Christ himself. It is ubiquitous throughout the Acts and the rest of the New Testament. But it also pervades the four Gospels; for as the Evangelists after the resurrection and ascension looked back over the life and ministry of Christ before his cross, they now saw with enlightened eyes how much of it was a fulfilment of the Old Testament.

Some, however, find difficulty with this christological interpretation.

An apparent hermeneutical problem and three questions arising

It is undeniable that there are places in the New Testament where a writer will quote a verse from the Old Testament and apply it to Christ, when, at first sight, it might appear that, according to the normal principles of exegesis, the verse had nothing to do with Christ at all. And sometimes a New Testament writer will appeal to an Old Testament prophecy to corroborate, say, the Christian doctrine of the deity of the Lord Jesus, when it cannot be supposed that the Old Testament prophet himself intended to express or support any such doctrine, or even that he would have understood it.

An example of this is the prophecy spoken by the prophet Nathan to King David, and recorded by the author of 2 Samuel (whoever he was; the prophet Samuel was dead by this time). The prophecy concerned the future of David's royal dynasty:

> When thy days be fulfilled, and thou shalt sleep with thy fathers, I will set up thy seed after thee ... and I will establish

his kingdom. He shall build an house for my name, and I will establish the throne of his kingdom for ever. I will be to him a father and he shall be to me a son: if he commit iniquity, I will chastise him with the rod of men and with the stripes of the children of men. But my mercy shall not depart from him as I took it from Saul, whom I put away before thee. And thine house and thy kingdom shall be made sure for ever before thee: thy throne shall be established for ever. (2 Sam 7:12–16)

Now the Old Testament itself records (1 Kgs 5:5; 8:17–20; 1 Chr 22:9–10; 28:5–7; 2 Chr 6:8–10) that David's immediate successor, Solomon, was the one who built the house of the Lord in Jerusalem; and both David and Solomon believed that God's promise 'I will be to him a father and he shall be to me a son' was fulfilled in Solomon. Said David 'He [the Lord] said to me, Solomon . . . shall build my house . . . for I have chosen him to be my son, and I will be his father' (1 Chr 28:6 rv).

In the New Testament, however, the writer to the Hebrews (1:5) quotes this same statement 'I will be his father and he shall be my son', and applies it, not to Solomon, but to Christ. What is more, he cites it, among a number of other statements drawn from the Old Testament, to corroborate his claim that the Old Testament indicated that the Messiah would be the Son of the Father in the tri-unitarian sense (Heb 1:5–13).

The hermeneutical problem is at once apparent. The prophet, Nathan, could not possibly have intended this statement in the tri-unitarian sense, when he originally spoke the prophecy to David. At the same time, the writer to the Hebrews presumably would not have denied that the statement, as originally delivered by Nathan, did refer to Solomon. Certainly he would not have wished to claim that the rest of the sentence, 'If he commit iniquity, I will chastise him . . .' referred to Christ; obviously it referred to Solomon, and to others of David's descendants, but not to the Messiah. That being so, it must be that the writer to the Hebrews considered that one and the same statement, 'I will be to him a father and he shall be to me a son', carried two meanings: one, a lesser meaning, referring to Solomon, and the other, a fuller meaning, referring to Christ.

that the permanent house should be built, He intended to command a son of David's, not David himself, to build it.

The contrast, then, between Nathan's first message to David and his second is instructive. The first was brought to David by the will of Nathan; by definition it was not a true, God-inspired, prophecy— though God inspired the author of 2 Samuel to record it in order to teach us a lesson. Nathan's second message, by contrast, came from God, at God's initiative; Nathan was simply God's mouthpiece.

And this is now the point which the second half of the New Testament's notable statement on the 'mechanics' of Old Testament prophecy will make.

The positive statement

> . . . but borne along by the Holy Spirit human beings spoke from God. (2 Pet 1:21)

This declares that all true Old Testament prophecy originated with, and came from, God. Human beings spoke it; but they spoke simply what they first heard God speak. And to ensure that they correctly conveyed to their audiences what God spoke, they were carried along in their speaking by the Holy Spirit.

That does not mean that to achieve this, God had to suppress the mind or personality of the prophet. A close acquaintance with the writings of the Major Prophets, for example, Isaiah, Jeremiah and Ezekiel, will show that each has his own, individual, distinctive style; but God, not they, was the author of the prophecies which they delivered.

A master musician, wishing to play a tune which he has composed, may choose to play it on a piano, or violin, or clarinet. Whichever instrument he chooses, the basic tune will be the same. On the other hand, he will not need, nor try, to suppress the distinctive characteristics of the instrument he chooses, but will exploit them to the full. The fact remains, however, that the chosen instrument neither composes, nor chooses the tune, nor takes the initiative in playing it: it is the musician who does all that.

Strictly speaking, then, Nathan was not the author of the prophecy that he conveyed to David: God was; and that fact is doubly emphasised in the text:

> *Now, therefore,* thus shalt thou say unto my servant David, *Thus says the* LORD *of hosts* . . . (2 Sam 7:8 RV)

> Moreover *the Lord tells thee* that the LORD will make *thee* an house . . . (2 Sam 7:11)

That being so, when we come to assess the full meaning of the various statements in the prophecy, it would be a category mistake to demand that their meaning must be limited to what Nathan understood them to mean. Nathan's understanding was doubtless true as far as it went: but it was confined to his immediate context and to what general, though true, impressions of the future he had derived from other prophecies and from this present one. Not so God! When he spoke to David through Nathan, the whole of future world history lay open before him in all its detail (cf. Isa 42:9; 46:9–10), and certainly all the detail of the future of David's royal dynasty. What he said, therefore, to David, he said in the light of that foreknowledge. It would not be surprising, then, if the implications of what God said were later seen to go beyond what Nathan understood or intended.

The future of David's dynasty as prophesied and the question of context

We now have the beginnings of an answer to the first question that we felt should be put to the writer to the Hebrews. But there was a second: how could he justify taking this one statement—'I will be his father and he shall be my son'—out of its context and referring it to Christ? We can now begin to answer this second question, too, by examining the whole context in which God made this statement. We can then decide whether the writer to the Hebrews has in fact taken the statement out of its context, or not.

The first thing that must strike us, if we read the whole of the prophecy, is that it concerned not just David, nor just his immediate successor, Solomon, but the entire, indeed the eternal, future of David's royal dynasty.

> And thine house and thy kingdom shall be made sure for ever before thee: thy throne shall be established for ever. (2 Sam 7:16 RV)

David himself understood this; for in his prayer of response he exclaimed:

> Thou hast spoken also of thy servant's house for a great while to come. (2 Sam 7:19 RV)

We, of course, who live in this advanced period of history know with hindsight what Nathan who delivered this promise to David on God's behalf could not possibly have known, namely that some four hundred years after God made this promise, the Babylonian emperor would sack Jerusalem, demolish the temple, and put a long but temporary halt to the Davidic dynasty. The urgent question now becomes not, Did Nathan know this? but, Did God know this at the time when he was making the promise to David about the perpetuity of David's dynasty?

Of course God knew it; indeed in this very prophecy, spoken through Nathan, he warned David's 'seed' that if he committed iniquity, he would chasten him with the rod of men, and with floggings inflicted by men (2 Sam 7:14), which was precisely the language God repeated later through the prophet Isaiah, when he announced the imminence of the Assyrian attacks on Israel and then on Judah (cf. Isa 10:5–15).

That being so, the next, inevitable question is: Did God know when he was making his promise to David, what in the end he would have to do to ensure the fulfilment of his promise of perpetuity to David's dynasty?

Again the answer is, Of course, God knew: he foresaw the persistent sinfulness and the degeneration of David's successors; but he also foresaw that the only way to secure the fulfilment of the promise of permanence to David's dynasty would be the birth into

David's line of the Son of God. And so it was, when Gabriel eventually announced to Mary:

> Behold, thou shalt conceive in thy womb, and bring forth a son, and shalt call his name Jesus. He shall be great, and shall be called the Son of the Most High; and the Lord God shall give him the throne of his father David; and he shall reign over the house of Jacob for ever; and of his kingdom there shall be no end ... wherefore that which is to be born shall be called holy, the Son of God. (Luke 1:31–33, 35)

Gabriel was not announcing an emergency scheme that God had only recently thought up when he discovered to his surprise the inadequacy of mere mortal kings!

Indeed, centuries before the Annunciation, God had already published this solution to the problem:

> For unto us a child is born, unto us a son is given; and the government shall be upon his shoulder: and his name shall be called Wonderful Counsellor, Mighty God, Everlasting Father, Prince of Peace. Of the increase of his government and of peace there shall be no end, upon the throne of David, and upon his kingdom, to establish it, and to uphold it with judgment and with righteousness from henceforth and for ever. The zeal of the LORD of hosts shall perform this. (Isa 9:6–7)

To imagine, therefore, that when God made his promise of perpetuity to David's house, he did not yet have all this in mind about the eventual sending of his Son, would be to imagine the incredible. As far as God was concerned, his promise to David through Nathan required, and therefore implied, the eventual sending of his Son. And that means that the writer to the Hebrews, in citing one statement from this prophecy and applying it to the Son of God is, at least, not dragging it altogether out of its original, divinely intended context, however little Nathan may have understood the full implications of the prophecy.

But now we must consider another dimension to the New Testament's interpretation of the Old as we begin to answer our third question.

Advantage, conviction, original prophecy and the question of double-meaning

The advantage of hindsight

The writers of the New Testament had a distinct advantage over Nathan, and over all other Old Testament prophets: they lived after the resurrection and ascension of the Lord Jesus. Even during his life on earth his disciples had confessed him to be the Messiah, the Son of the living God (Matt 16:16) and therefore also the Son of David (Matt 20:30). But it was his resurrection that clinched the matter for them and made them increasingly aware of the full significance of the term 'Son of God' as applied to the Lord Jesus (see Rom 1:3–4). They now looked back on the prophecies and histories of the Old Testament from the vantage point of having witnessed the great fulfilment of those prophecies and histories. In that light it was inevitable that they should perceive that the intended meaning and scope of God's Old Testament prophecies were often far greater than many people realised at the time.

Already on the day of Pentecost Peter, for instance, was arguing that David's words 'Thou wilt not allow thy holy one to see corruption' (see Ps 16:8–11) could not have been intended to refer to David himself, since his dead body and sepulchre were still in Jerusalem in Peter's day ten centuries after David's death. Indisputably, David himself had seen corruption. But David, Peter argued, was a prophet. He was aware, moreover, that the Lord had sworn with an oath to him that of the fruit of his loins he would set one upon his throne (Ps 132:11). It must be, Peter concluded, that when David spoke the words 'Thou wilt not allow thy holy one to see corruption', he was speaking with prophetic foresight of the resurrection of his son, the Messiah (Acts 2:25–31).

Similarly James, at the conference of the apostles and elders in Jerusalem (Acts 15:13–18), when he heard of the unprecedented number of Gentiles that were being converted to faith in the Messiah, the Son of David, saw in that phenomenon the fulfilment of God's promise through the prophet Amos: 'In that day I will raise up the tabernacle of David [that is, David's royal house] that is fallen down . . .' (Amos 9:11–12).

With similar hindsight the writer to the Hebrews would have studied God's promise to David through Nathan regarding the maintenance of his royal dynasty.

But now we must consider yet another dimension to the New Testament's understanding of the Old.

The conviction that the Old Testament is the living word of God

This is how the New Testament writers regard the Old Testament. The writer to the Hebrews, for instance, having cited Psalm 95:7–11 and commented on it at length, observes 'the word of God is living, and active and sharper than any two-edged sword . . .' (Heb 4:12 RV). To him, and to all the other New Testament writers, the Old Testament was not simply a record of things past and gone, of divine statements made centuries ago and now to us dead and irrelevant. When they read the written record, they believed that it was the living God speaking livingly to them and wanting them to know what he did and said to others in times past. And incidentally, that is how all true Christians should read the Old Testament still, in the conviction that if God opened the heavens and spoke to us direct, he would still say to us now what he says in the Old and New Testaments.

It means, then, that as the writer to the Hebrews read Nathan's prophecy, he would have read it as the voice of the living God speaking to him (the writer to the Hebrews) and asking him to listen in to what he was saying to David about the maintenance of David's dynasty and the means he would adopt to that end.

Consider, then, the dynamics of this situation. It was God rehearsing what he had earlier said to David about maintaining his dynasty through David's son, Solomon, and had said in full knowledge of what he himself would eventually do through David's son, Jesus Christ, and rehearsing this for the benefit of the writer to the Hebrews who already knew what God had recently done through David's son who was also God's Son.

A similar situation is to be found at Galatians 3:8: 'And the scripture, foreseeing that God would justify the Gentiles by faith, preached the gospel beforehand to Abraham, saying, In thee shall all the nations be blessed.' The quotation is of God's own words to Abraham (Gen 12:3). At the time Abraham would not necessarily have realised that this blessing would involve the Gentiles being justified by faith as Abraham was. But when Paul read Genesis 12:3, it was obvious to him that even when God was speaking to Abraham about the blessing of the Gentiles through him, God had already foreseen that the Gentiles would be justified by faith as Abraham was; and therefore this particular blessing was included in, and implied by, God's promise.[1] A simple (though not perfect) analogy may help us to understand the dynamics of situations like this. A little girl of four enters her daddy's study and announces in her childish way, 'Mummy says that Aunt Matilda is coming tomorrow and staying with us for a month.' The little girl is old enough to understand every word in the sentence, and uses all her mental powers to deliver this message to daddy exactly as mummy gave it to her. But mummy knew that daddy would see more in the simple message than her little daughter did. For both mummy and daddy knew Aunt Matilda's character and how adept she would be at disrupting family harmony by her eccentric ways and unreasonable demands.

So God knew that when through Scripture he rehearsed for the benefit of the writer to the Hebrews what he originally prophesied to David through Nathan, the writer to the Hebrews would see more meaning in that prophecy than Nathan or even David did.

The three salient and crucial points
in the original prophecy

As the writer to the Hebrews, then, listened to Nathan's prophecy, he would certainly have noticed its three salient points.

[1] The phrase 'scripture foreseeing' is another way of saying 'God foreseeing'.

God's promise to maintain David's dynasty for ever

He would have had no difficulty in understanding or believing this; nor would he have had to resort to fanciful typology or allegory in order to interpret it. Jesus Christ was literally and physically 'of the house and seed of David' (Luke 1:27; Rom 1:3; 2 Tim 2:8). Now God had made him both Lord and Christ. He was risen from the dead, and was alive 'after the power of an endless life' (Heb 7:16; Rev 1:18). God's promise made to David was thus eternally secured.

God's programme for the building of a house for his name

David's suggestion that he be allowed to build it was disallowed. God's own programme was:

1. The Lord would build David a house (i.e. dynasty).
2. But David's son, yet to be born, not David, would build the Lord's house.

The writer to the Hebrews probably smiled when he heard God declare that that was his purpose. David's son, Solomon, certainly built the house of the Lord at Jerusalem. But it was at best a material, physical house. By New Testament times it had long since been destroyed. Its successor, built under Ezra had been dismantled. And the contemporary house built by Herod was doomed to be destroyed very shortly (in AD 70, in fact). But David's son, Jesus Christ, was already discharging his God-given office of building God an eternal, spiritual house, formed of God's people both as God's household and as God's temple and dwelling place (Matt 16:18; Heb 3:1–6; 10:21; Eph 2:15–22).

One cannot think, then, that God's desire to have a house built for his name was so completely satisfied by Solomon's physical temple, that thereafter it was God's intention to allow his temple-building project to lapse. History has shown that the house that Solomon built for God was, in God's mind, only the first of an intended succession of houses, the last of which should be the house built by David's son, Jesus Christ. In commissioning Solomon to build a physical house, then, God was evidently creating a prototype of the eternal house to be built by Christ.

God's announcement of a special relationship with David's son

In order to have his house built by a son of David's, God would have to secure David's succession, both immediate and long term. And in order to secure that, at its most crucial point, God announced that he would adopt a special, Father–son, relationship with Solomon.

The first weak point in that succession would come immediately upon David's death, as God pointed out to David (2 Sam 7:15). Saul, David's predecessor on the throne, had been chosen and anointed by God (1 Sam 9:1 – 10:1); but because of his serious insubordination and downright disobedience he was eventually told that his dynasty would not continue (1 Sam 13:13–14; 15:26–29). Upon his death he was succeeded on the throne by his son Ishbosheth; but after a few years Ishbosheth was assassinated (2 Sam 4); and Saul's dynasty was brought to an end, never to be revived.

The like of this would never happen, said God, to David's dynasty. If Solomon—or any other king in the succession—misbehaved, God would chasten them; but the special father–son relationship which he would adopt with David's seed (2 Sam 7:12–15; note the multivalent term, 'seed') would secure that David's royal succession, however severely disciplined, would never be fully and finally abolished.

So now at last we come back to where we started, God's promise originally regarding Solomon: 'I will be his father, and he shall be my son'; and we ask again our final question. How could the writer to the Hebrews justify taking this Father–son relationship between God and Solomon and the rest of David's successors, and apply it to the infinitely higher Father–Son relationship between God and the Son of God?

Two answers are obvious.

1. At the lowly level at which Solomon and all the rest of David's royal seed enjoyed a father–son relationship with God, Mary's son, being a royal son of David, had a right to claim that relationship too.

2. But just as the house which David's son, Solomon, built for God was a prototype, pointing forward to the infinitely

superior house that David's son, Jesus, would build for God, so the father–son relationship which God adopted with Solomon, was a divinely given and intended pointer to the unique relationship between the Father and the Son which David's son, Jesus Christ our Lord, eternally sustains. It is this unique relationship which has in fact secured, and will forever secure, the promise of permanence made to David through Nathan.

Looking ahead

Now the New Testament claims that there are many such divinely-arranged prototypes in the Old Testament; and we shall eventually have to ask what the point and purpose of the existence of these prototypes is. But then, there are many other interpretative devices which the New Testament uses in order to apply the wealth of the Old Testament to our spiritual benefit. It is time, therefore, that we gather our conclusions and consider the further questions that they have brought to our attention as we leave our introductory studies and begin to examine these devices in detail.

5
Conclusions and Questions Arising

As we expected, two things now stand out clearly. On the New Testament's own authority:

1. *The Old Testament is valid in its own right.* It was originally inspired by God. Not some of it merely, but all of it. It still is. It has not ceased to be inspired since the advent of the New Testament. The God who originally spoke it to the fathers by the prophets speaks it still to those who will listen.

2. *The Old Testament is profitable*, not some of it merely, but all of it. 'Whatever was written in former days,' insists the New Testament (Rom 15:4 esv), 'was written for our instruction, that through endurance and through the encouragement of the Scriptures we might have hope.'

History justifies the claim

The claim of ongoing profitability is justified by the experience of God's people. All down the centuries Christians have received endless encouragement from the Old Testament. The detailed messianic prophecies have confirmed their faith that Jesus is the Christ, the Saviour of the world. The Levitical sacrifices have served as types to aid their understanding of Christ's atoning death. And in spite of life's normal pains, and in face of persecution, Christians' endurance has been mightily strengthened by the Old Testament's descriptions of the glories that shall be at 'the restoration of all things, of which God spoke by the mouth of his holy prophets' (Acts 3:21).

Christians have also felt (though perhaps not as often as they should) the force of the prophets' denunciation of religious, commercial, social and political corruption. Moreover in the practicalities of daily living they have been guided by the pithy maxims of Proverbs, taught the sanctity and joy of married love by the Song of Songs, and have been sobered by Ecclesiastes' exposure of the emptiness of life under the sun without God.

By contrast, the exploits of the Old Testament's heroes of faith have fired their own courage. And when sometimes inordinate suffering, illness and bereavement, or inconsolable tragedy have forced into their minds dark queries about the love and fairness of God, Job's story has brought relief. They were not the only ones to have entertained dark thoughts about God: Job did too; and in the end God justified him rather than the pseudo-piety of his so-called friends, and dispelled his doubts.

Difficulties remain

That said, it remains true that there are difficult areas in the Old Testament, not least in its apparently straightforward historical narratives. Particularly is that so in passages on which the New Testament itself makes no specific comment. Take, for example, David's behaviour as king. First Samuel records God's rejection of King Saul for twice disobeying God's orders. Then it declares David to be 'a man after God's own heart' (1 Sam 13:14), relates his exemplary treatment of Saul, and his refusal to avenge himself. Second Samuel follows with his eventual acceptance as king by all twelve tribes, the consolidation of his power, and God's eternal covenant with him and his royal house (2 Sam 7).

With this impressive build-up, and with the New Testament's confirmation that King David was 'a man after God's heart' (Acts 13:22), we might have expected the record of his actual reign to be studded with political acts of God-given wisdom. Instead, a cursory reading suggests that throughout his reign David was helplessly dependent on the brutal commander-in-chief of his army, and powerless either to control or correct him.[1] How, then, are we meant to interpret 2 Samuel's narrative of David's reign?

Moreover, it is not only in Old Testament narratives on which the New Testament makes no comment that difficulties of understanding arise; sometimes they do so too in passages on which the New Testament does comment. Abraham's sacrifice of Isaac is a famous example (Gen 22).

At its outset there lies a moral problem: why does God command Abraham to do something that God himself later on strictly forbids and declares to be an abomination to him?[2] Hostile critics have sought to make capital out of this problem. What answer should be given them? The New Testament makes no comment.

The Danish philosopher Søren Kierkegaard suggested that devoted obedience to God demands that we leave behind the moral and ethical law 'Thou shalt not kill', since the divine lawgiver himself transcends rational, and even ethical, principles.[3] But this suggestion can hardly be right: if adopted, it would lead into a subjective quagmire. People have often justified heinous crimes simply on the ground that they believed God told them to commit them.

Would it be right, then, to say that God never really intended Abraham to sacrifice Isaac: he only pretended he wanted him to? But pretence? What would that imply about God's character?

The New Testament's comment on this incident is that in offering up his son, Isaac, on the altar, Abraham was justified by his

---

1 Joab murdered Abner; David publicly disapproved, but confessed himself powerless to do anything about it (2 Sam 3:26–29). Joab induced David to bring back the fratricidal Absalom and pardon him. The result was disastrous (2 Sam 14ff). Against David's explicit instructions, Joab killed Absalom (2 Sam 18:5–17). David then demoted Joab, and appointed Amasa in his place. Joab assassinated Amasa, and in spite of David carried on as before as commander-in-chief (2 Sam 19:11–13; 20:4–12). The only time (in the record) that David insisted on having his own way against Joab was when, in spite of Joab's protest, he numbered the people — with ruinous results (2 Sam 24:1–17).

2 Cf. Deut 18:10; 2 Kgs 16:3; 2 Chr 28:3; Mic 6:7.

3 *Fear and Trembling*.

works, and thereby becomes an example to us all. For God demands that all believers must justify their profession of faith by their works (Jas 2:20–22).

On the other hand, a long Christian tradition holds that Abraham's offering up of his son to God on the altar is somehow a type of God's offering up of his Son for us on the cross.[4] But what, we may ask, has that got to do with justification by works?

All this raises important questions that will direct us in Part 2 of our study.

Three questions arise

How are we to set about interpreting difficult narratives like that of David's reign? Is it enough to determine linguistically as accurately as we can what it says, and then leave each reader to decide for himself or herself what it means? And when we have decided what the event meant to its contemporaries, and what it means to those who first read the record of it, are we right to expect it has a message for us who read it now? Or should it be regarded as simply a historical fact, a museum piece, so to speak, and any attempt to extract a meaning for ourselves as simply an expression of our own subjective reaction, our own likes and dislikes, determined by our own set of moral values?

Can a single narrative have valid meaning on multiple levels? Given a variety of interpretations of a passage like Abraham's sacrifice of Isaac, are we to think that only one of the proffered interpretations can be the right one intended by the Holy Spirit? Or may we think—without falling into post-modernistic relativism—that one and the same narrative can sometimes have meaning at more than one level?

What hermeneutical principles are available to control our interpretations? We want to be sure that we do not create our own meaning from the narratives of the Old Testament. On the other

4 For a highly nuanced and well-argued advocacy of this view see Wenham, *Genesis.*, 2:117.

hand, we want to know all that the Old Testament itself intends us to know. What principles are there to guide us in this dilemma? Where shall we find guidelines?

Discovering guidelines from the New Testament's practice

Honesty demands that we admit that there can sometimes be difficulties, as well as delights, in interpreting the long stretches of Old Testament narrative on which the New Testament does not comment, or does so only in part. But there is no need to despair. The New Testament can still give us helpful guidelines if we study its detailed practice in what it does comment on.

Hitherto, in Part One, we have surveyed its general relation to the Old Testament; and that has proved to be a comparatively simple matter. It could be summed up in Augustine's neat phrase: 'The New lies in the Old concealed, the Old lies in the New revealed.' Or we could quite reasonably say: the Old Testament was promise, the New is its fulfilment; the Old was seed-bed, the New is full flowering.

But the New Testament's general relation to the Old is one thing: its detailed exposition of the Old is another; and that is what we are going to study in Part Two. We shall find that its interpretational practice is far too varied to be summed up in one or two short phrases. The wisdom of God, says Paul, is multi-faceted (Eph 3:10). We should not be surprised if the New Testament's interpretation of the Old turns out likewise to be multifaceted. This surely is no reason to be disheartened. The more multifaceted it is found to be, the more we shall rejoice in the wealth of the Old Testament that it thereby uncovers.

We shall study the New Testament's interpretational categories in the first place for their own sake, since they are an integral part of God's Word. But in so doing, we shall find guidelines which we may subsequently follow in our own interpretation of the Old Testament.

PART TWO

New Testament Thought Categories
for Old Testament Interpretation

CATEGORY ONE

Prophetic Insights

6

Christ's Interpretation of Old Testament Prophecy

D URING HIS EARTHLY ministry our Lord frequently quoted the Old Testament, and several of his scriptural references will occupy us in due course. But to begin with we choose to concentrate on his assertion that the Old Testament predicted two comings of the Messiah and not just one. We do so because this interpretation is fundamental to his claim to be the God-promised Messiah of the Old Testament; and secondly because it is fundamental to our faith in the Christian gospel (see 1 Cor 15:3–4, 20–23; Rev 1:7) and therefore likewise fundamental to our proper understanding of Old Testament prophecy and to our witness to the world, whether Jew or Gentile.

Christ's own assertion

The Old Testament had said that the Messiah would come to Jerusalem as Zion's King, lowly and riding on an ass (Zech 9:9). It had also predicted that the Son of Man would come with the clouds of heaven (Dan 7:11–14). Now common sense might have concluded that 'coming lowly on a donkey' and 'coming with the clouds of heaven' could hardly be descriptions of one and the same coming. But nowhere did the Old Testament explicitly say that there would be two comings of the Messiah. It was Christ himself who interpreted the Old Testament to this effect.

On his last public visit to Jerusalem (Matt 21:1–11) he deliberately provided himself with a donkey and entered the city riding
on its back, to the acclaim of the crowds as Zion's King. He thus
interpreted Zechariah's prophecy of the coming King as referring
to his first coming.

A week later he stood on trial for his life before the Sanhedrin.
The high priest put him on oath and demanded that he tell the
court whether he was the Christ, the Son of God (Matt 26:63–64).
Now it must have been obvious to everyone in the court, as it was
to him, that if he said he was, he would be sentenced to death. In
reply, therefore, he alluded to two Old Testament Scriptures that
foretold what would happen to him after they had put him to
death. The one, Ps 110:1, foretold his enthronement at the right
hand of God; the other, Dan 7:11–14, his second coming.

Whose Son? Christ's allusion to Psalm 110:1

This was not the first time our Lord had referred to Psalm 110:1. Only
a day or two before his trial he had cited the whole verse in a public
discussion with the Pharisees (Matt 22:41–46), and had pointed out
that it implied the more-than-human sonship of the Messiah. 'What',
he had asked, 'did they think about the Messiah (whoever he turned
out to be): whose son would he be?' 'The son of David,' they replied;
and in part that was true. But it couldn't be the whole truth, Christ
countered; for David, speaking under the inspiration of the Spirit,
called the Messiah Lord. And with that Christ quoted the whole
verse: 'The LORD [Yahweh] said to my [David's] Lord [Sovereign]
"Sit at my right hand until I put your enemies under your feet".'

If David called Him 'Lord', how could he be merely David's
son? David would never, while he was still king, call a mere son
of his 'my Lord'. If, then, the Messiah was not a mere son of David,
whose Son was he as well, if not the Son of God?[1]

Indirectly, therefore, he had already anticipated the high priest's

---

1 It is worth noting here for the sake of future reference that, strictly speaking, our
Lord was interpreting, not merely what the psalm explicitly said, but the implication
of what it said.

demand that he tell the court whether he was 'the Christ, the Son of God'. The only thing that could possibly be in doubt at this late stage was whether he would now go further and openly in court, at the cost of his life, claim that he was himself the Christ, the Son of God. His reply put the matter beyond doubt: 'Yes, it is as you say' (Matt 26:64 NIV).[2] Some have thought that this phrase is somewhat less than affirmative, and should be taken to mean: 'Those are your words; I would not put it that way.' But Mark's equivalent passage has the unequivocal 'I am' (Mark 14:62). And in Matthew itself, in the near context (Matt 26:25), Christ uses the same Greek phrase in answer to Judas' question: 'Surely it's not I, Lord, is it?' The NIV correctly paraphrases Christ's reply: 'Yes, it is you.'

Since the court's sentence of death was a foregone conclusion, Christ went on to cite what the Old Testament predicted would happen to him after they had put him to death, namely his enthronement at the right hand of God. What is more, he informed the Sanhedrin that they would hereafter 'see'—presumably in the sense of 'become aware of', 'perceive it to be so', perhaps one day 'literally see'—the Son of Man seated at the right hand of God, and so demonstrably the Christ, the Son of God.

Our Lord was alluding to Psalm 110:1 and God's invitation to the Christ, the Son of God, to sit at God's right hand. But since in Christ's earlier conversation with the Pharisees he had interpreted not merely what the psalm explicitly said, but the implication of what it said (see note 1), we may be allowed to point out another implication. The very invitation to come and sit at God's right hand implied that there would first be a period when the one who was the Son of God, yet also the Son of David, was not seated there. In other words it implied his incarnation, life and ministry on earth, death, resurrection and then the glorious event that would terminate his first coming, namely his ascension and enthronement.

Moreover Psalm 110:1 also foretold—and this time explicitly—that the day would come when God would put all Christ's enemies under his feet. And that is precisely the event depicted in Daniel's

2 The Greek says simply: 'You have said [it]'.

prophetic vision of the coming of the Son of Man with the clouds of heaven, to which also Christ alluded at his trial.

Which Son of Man? Christ's allusion to Daniel 7:11–14

Let us quote the appropriate part of the vision itself *in extenso*:

> Then I continued to watch because of the boastful words the horn was speaking. I kept looking until the beast was slain and its body destroyed and thrown into the blazing fire. (The other beasts had been stripped of their authority, but were allowed to live for a period of time.) In my vision at night I looked, and there before me was one like a son of man, coming with the clouds of heaven. He approached the Ancient of Days and was led into his presence. He was given authority, glory and sovereign power; all peoples, nations and men of every language worshipped him. His dominion is an everlasting dominion that will not pass away, and his kingdom is one that will never be destroyed. (Dan 7:11–14 NIV)

And then from the interpretation of the vision:

> As I watched, this horn was waging war against the saints and defeating them, until the Ancient of Days came and pronounced judgment in favour of the saints of the Most High, and the time came when they possessed the kingdom. (Dan 8:21–22 NIV)

It is evident, then, that Christ was interpreting this vision as a prophetic depiction of his personal second coming. Some scholars, however, deny that the Son of Man figure represents the Messiah personally. They point out that in the description of the vision (7:1–14) universal dominion is given to 'one resembling a son of man'; but in the explanation of the vision, subsequently given to Daniel (7:16–28), no further mention is made of this son of man. Instead, universal and everlasting dominion is repeatedly said to be given to 'the saints of the Most High' (7:18, 21, 22, 25, 27). According to these scholars, then, the 'one like a son of man' in the vision is a collective symbol of what in the sober reality of the explanation turns out to be the long line of merely human martyrs. It cannot, therefore, they argue, be taken to represent the Messiah personally, nor yet his personal second coming.

The observation of the text of Daniel 7 on which this view rests is accurate enough; but the deduction drawn from it is wide of the mark. In the vision it is repeatedly noticed that the beast severely persecuted the saints (7:21–22, 25–27). It is only just, therefore, that when the beast is destroyed, God should give dominion to the saints. Our Lord said the same to his disciples: 'Don't fear, little flock, it is your Father's good pleasure to give you the kingdom' (Luke 12:32). But not, of course, to them apart from him, as our Lord made clear on other occasions. 'In the new world', said he, 'when the Son of Man shall sit on the throne of his glory, you also who have followed me shall sit on twelve thrones, judging the twelve tribes of Israel' (Matt 19:28). And if we ask to what time or period he was referring when he talked of the Son of Man sitting on the throne of his glory, then once again he put the matter beyond doubt: 'But when the Son of Man shall *come* in his glory, and all the angels with him, *then* shall he sit on the throne of his glory; and before him shall be gathered all nations . . .' (Matt 25:31–32). Without any doubt, Christ is talking of his second coming: the Son of Man coming with the clouds of heaven, as depicted in Daniel 7.

Moreover, just as in Daniel's vision the saints who have endured persecution by the beast are given universal dominion at the coming of the Son of Man, so in Matthew 25:31ff (see above), and in the similar passage in Luke 22:28–30, Christ stresses the fact that those who have suffered for his sake will reign with him at his second coming.[3]

One further objection should perhaps be dealt with here before we move on to weightier matters. Some scholars protest that in Daniel's vision the Son of Man comes to the Ancient of Days in heaven—and that observation is true. But on that basis they argue that Daniel's vision cannot rightly be taken to refer to Christ's second coming to earth at his Parousia. Their logic is deficient. The Son of Man comes to the Ancient of Days to receive universal dominion

3 This is given classic expression by Paul's description of what shall happen when Christ comes from heaven with the angels of his power, to give relief to his persecuted people, to be glorified in his saints, and to execute judgment on their persecutors (2 Thess 1:4–10).

over all nations; but reception of that universal dominion implies and involves the coming of the Son of Man to earth to take possession of it. So in 2 Thessalonians 1:5–10 it is God who gives rest from persecution to the saints and affliction to their persecutors; but he does so, says the context, by the coming of the Lord Jesus from heaven to earth. Similarly in 1 Timothy 6:13–16 it is God, the blessed and only Potentate who stages the appearing of our Lord Jesus Christ. But that appearing by definition implies his coming from heaven to earth.[4]

The two comings of Christ and the problem of evil

Christ's interpretation of the Old Testament as predicting two comings of Christ, and not just one, is of more than academic interest. It bears directly on a problem that eventually haunts every sensitive person, the problem of evil.

Long years ago a fellow-student of mine who was a Jew, and whose parents had recently perished under Hitler, accosted me after a lecture, and said: 'David, your Jesus cannot be the Messiah.'

'Why not?' I asked.

'Because', he replied, 'the Old Testament said that when the Messiah came, he would put down all evil throughout the world. And your Jesus just hasn't done that. And don't try to get round it', he added, 'by claiming that he has set up a spiritual, as distinct from a literal, kingdom. The Old Testament knows nothing of any such kingdom. Your Jesus just is not the Messiah.'

It is not only Jews that feel this problem. Non-Jews will express it in their own terms: 'If there's a God who cares for justice', they say, 'and if Jesus Christ is his Son, why doesn't Jesus intervene in the world and put down evil? He's supposed to be risen from the dead, isn't he, and seated on the throne of the universe. Then why

4 Cf. D. A. Carson: 'Unless one thinks of the location of the Ancient of Days in some physical and spatial sense, it is hard to imagine why Christ's approaching God the Father to receive the kingdom might not be combined with his returning to earth to set up the consummated kingdom' (*Matthew*, EBC 8:506).

has he not long since suppressed all evil?'

Now this is not the place to attempt a full-scale answer to the problem of evil. It is enough here if we point out the relevance of this doctrine of the two comings to God's strategy, revealed in the Old Testament, for the final putting down of evil.

The Old Testament certainly prophesied that when the Messiah came he would execute the wrath of God on an evil world and deliver the godly in Israel from their persecutors. Take, as an example, Isaiah's prediction with its awesomely vivid metaphors:

> Who is this coming from Edom, from Bozrah,
>   with his garments stained crimson?
> Who is this, robed in splendour, striding forward
>   in the greatness of his strength?
> 'It is I, speaking in righteousness,
>   mighty to save.'
>
> Why are your garments red,
>   like those of one treading the winepress?
>
> 'I have trodden the winepress alone;
>   from the nations no one was with me.
> I trampled them in my anger
>   and trod them down in my wrath;
> their blood spattered my garments,
>   and I stained all my clothing.
> For the day of vengeance was in my heart,
>   and the year of my redemption has come . . .
> I trampled the nations in my anger;
>   in my wrath I made them drunk
> And poured their blood on the ground.'
> (Isa 63:1–6 NIV)[5]

The problem for many a godly Israelite was that in the face of the extreme suffering of Israel God remained silent for such long periods of history, and appeared to do nothing to fulfil such messianic prophecies of deliverance. Hence the anguish of the psalmist's cry:

> O LORD, God of vengeance,
>   O God of vengeance, shine forth!

5 Cf. the similar language description of Christ at his second coming, Rev 19:11–21.

> Rise up, O judge of the earth;
>> repay to the proud what they deserve!
> O LORD, how long shall the wicked,
>> how long shall the wicked exult?
> They pour out their arrogant words;
>> all the evildoers boast.
> They crush your people, O LORD,
>> and afflict your heritage.
> They kill the widow and the sojourner,
>> and murder the fatherless;
> and they say, "The LORD *does not see;*
>> *the God of Jacob does* not perceive."
> (Ps 94:1–7 ESV)

Yet two psalms later the psalmist has found the beginning of an answer to his problem. It is the coming of the Lord to judge the world:

> Let the heavens be glad and let the earth rejoice ... before the LORD, for he comes; he comes to judge the earth. He will judge the world in righteousness and the peoples in his truth. (Ps 96:11, 13; repeated in Ps 98:7–9)[6]

But in what form would Yahweh come? And when would that coming take place? Actually, a little further on in the Psalter came a psalm that contained answers to these questions; but its meaning would not become clear until the Messiah came and by his incarnation and ministry interpreted it. That psalm was Psalm 110.

The psalmist predicts a pause between Christ's enthronement and God's judgment of evil

When Christ rose from the dead and appeared bodily to his disciples, one might have expected, as the apostles apparently did (Acts 1:6–8), that he would proceed immediately to put down all evil and fulfil the Old Testament's promises of Israel's deliverance. They soon learned otherwise; and within a short time Peter is found stating publicly of Christ: 'the heavens must receive [*scil.* and retain] him until the times of the restoration of all things, of which God spoke through his holy prophets . . .' (Acts 3:21). Psalm 110:1 was one of those prophecies. It

6 This is part of the gospel that Paul preached to the Athenians (Acts 17:31).

said that between Christ's ascension and enthronement and the time when God would put all his enemies under his feet, there would be a period of unspecified duration: 'Sit at my right hand *until* I put your enemies under your feet.'

This *until* period, then, is not an idea invented by the early Christians to cover their disappointment that Christ did not at once proceed by force to put down all evil throughout the world. It was a deliberate, and long foretold, part of God's strategy for dealing with the problem of evil. Christ himself made the same point in his parable of the Wheat and Tares in which he announced his plans for the putting down of evil. When, in the parable, the farm labourers ask the master if he wants them to root out the tares, he says No; for in rooting out the tares, they might, with their fallible judgment, root out the wheat as well. Let both grow together, he told them, until harvest. And the harvest, according to Christ's own interpretation of his parable, will take place at the end of the age (Matt 13:30, 39–43).

Justice will eventually be done. Evil shall be put down. This is part of the gospel both of the Old Testament and of the New. That there is going to be a final judgment is magnificent, good news. In view of it the psalmist called on the whole of creation to rejoice (Pss 96 and 98). And why not? Who would want earth's evil and injustice to go on for ever?

Why, then, the long delay? No better answer can be given than Peter's reply to his critics. When they objected: 'Where is the promise of His coming?', Peter replied, 'The Lord is not slow to fulfil his promise as some count slowness, but is longsuffering towards you, not wishing that any should perish, but that all should come to repentance. But the Day of the Lord will come . . .' (2 Pet 3:9–10).

The many prophesied activities of the Messiah and the necessity of his two comings

It is important to remember that the Old Testament prophets at times listed the whole range of the Messiah's predicted activities without indicating which he would perform at his first coming and which at his second. A famous example is the detailed description in Isaiah 61:1–4, which our Lord quoted in his programmatic sermon in Nazareth (Luke 4:16ff). When he had been handed the scroll of Isaiah, he opened it at 61:1 and read from it the delightful things that it predicted Messiah would do, down to and including 'to proclaim the acceptable year of the Lord' (v. 2). Then abruptly he closed the scroll and announced 'Today this Scripture has been fulfilled in your hearing.' Since then commentators and preachers galore have explained how good it was that Christ stopped reading where he did. For the very next clause was 'the day of vengeance of our God'. It was of the mercy of God, they say, that he did not quote that clause and add 'Today this Scripture is fulfilled in your hearing.'

The preachers are right; but it is doubtful whether the people in the synagogue would have agreed with them. For in that same context of Isaiah 'the day of vengeance' is coupled with 'my year of redemption' (63:4 ESV) or 'the year of my redeemed'. And the congregation in the synagogue may well have understood it to mean that God would, by pouring out his vengeance on the enemies of Israel (as long ago in Egypt), thereby deliver, or redeem, the Israelites from the oppression and persecution of their enemies. In that case they would have been disappointed that Christ was not proposing there and then to execute God's vengeance on Israel's enemies and so liberate Israel.

Like many others their idea of God's solution to the problem of evil was only partially developed, if not downright simplistic. The solution could never be simply putting the good people in one group, the bad in another, eliminating the bad group and being left with only the good; for in varying degrees all are sinful and guilty, both the oppressors and the oppressed.

Christ did not deny that God would one day 'avenge his elect who cry to him day and night'; but that would take place, he explained, at the coming of the Son of Man, when he shall be like the lightning 'that flashes and lights up the sky from one side to the other' (Luke 17:24; 18:7–8). In that day he will be simultaneously visible to all the earth, and utterly irresistible (Rev 1:7). 'But first',

Christ added, 'he [the Son of Man] must suffer many things and be rejected by this generation' (Luke 17:25).

Why must? Because Scripture declared it, and man's guilt required it. In the Upper Room just before his death he repeated this 'must': 'For I tell you that this Scripture must be fulfilled in me: "And he was numbered with the transgressors." For what is written about me has its fulfilment' (Luke 22:37). This was an explicit reference to Isaiah 53:12, that famous chapter that predicted the atoning, substitutionary death of God's Suffering Servant by means of which forgiveness and justification are made possible for all who repent and believe.

Christ, then, interpreted the Old Testament as predicting two roles for him: certainly that of the victorious Messiah–King; but first that of God's Suffering Servant, who would come not to be served, but to give his life a ransom for many (Mark 10:45) to save people from the coming judgment. Hence the necessity for two comings: both roles could not be fulfilled in one coming.

7
The Concept of Fulfilment

It is commonly claimed that in the New Testament the Old Testament finds fulfilment; and the claim is profoundly true. Indeed, it is true to a greater extent than we might at first realise. For when the New Testament speaks of some part of the Old Testament as having been fulfilled it can, and often does, mean simply that some Old Testament prediction or prophecy has now come true. But often enough it means something rather different, as we shall now see as we investigate four different senses in which the verb 'fulfil' is used in the New Testament:

1. Fulfilment as the fulfilling of predictions
2. Fulfilment as the final, higher expression of basic principles
3. Christ's fulfilment of the Law
4. The Christian's fulfilment of the Law

Fulfilment as the fulfilling of predictions

On many occasions the New Testament observes that some Old Testament prediction has been fulfilled in the life and work of the Lord Jesus, in the spread of the gospel, or in the formation of the church. Typical examples would be:

(*a*) The birth of the Lord in Bethlehem (Matt 2:4–6) fulfilling the prediction made by the prophet Micah (5:2).

(*b*) His riding into Jerusalem on an ass (John 12:13–16) fulfilling the prediction made by the prophet Zechariah (9:9).

(*c*) The coming of the Holy Spirit on the Day of Pentecost fulfilling the prediction made by the prophet Joel (2:28–29).

On other occasions it affirms, as we have already seen, that other Old Testament prophecies will yet be fulfilled in the future. Notable examples would be:

(*a*) Daniel's prophetic vision of the Son of Man coming with the clouds of heaven will be fulfilled at the second coming of the Lord Jesus (Mark 14:62; Luke 21:27).

(*b*) The prophetic programme foretold in Psalm 110:1 'sit at my right hand until I make thine enemies thy footstool', shall be brought to its conclusion at our Lord's return (Heb 10:13).

The occasions are so numerous, and the principle—prediction > fulfilment—is so self-evident, that no explanation is necessary.

But there is another class of fulfilment claimed by the New Testament that does perhaps, for us moderns at least, require some explanation.

Fulfilment as final expression

In this class, what is meant by the concept is fulfilment as the final expression at the highest possible level, of basic principles that were first expressed at a lowlier level in the course of Old Testament history. This type of fulfilment comes sharply to our attention when the New Testament claims that something in the Old Testament has been fulfilled, and upon investigation that something turns out not to have been a prediction in the first place, but simply, say, a record of some past historical event, or even an Old Testament institution. How then, the question goes, can the record of a past historical event, that was never intended to be a prediction, be rightly said to be fulfilled by some New Testament event or situation? Here are some typical examples.

'Until it be fulfilled': The fulfilment of the Passover

According to Luke, as Christ sat down with his disciples in the Upper Room on the eve of his crucifixion, he said to them:

> I have eagerly desired to eat this Passover with you before I suffer; for I say unto you, I will not eat it, until it be fulfilled in the kingdom of God. (Luke 22:14–16)

The problem stated

Passover fulfilled? Was Passover, then, a prediction? Hardly. At least, not in the normal sense of that word. The original Passover was an historic event that lay at the foundation of Israel's existence as a free, independent nation; and the subsequent annual celebration of the Feast of Passover was a means of recalling that past event to the memories and minds of later generations. It was originally, then, a looking back to the past, rather than a prediction of the future. So, what did the Lord Jesus mean by saying that the Passover was now going to be fulfilled in the kingdom of God?

The answer to the problem

To answer that question we must consider not only what was achieved at the first Passover, but the detail of how it was achieved, and therefore what it was that all subsequent Passovers vividly recalled. The first Passover effected Israel's deliverance from the destroying angel of God's wrath, by means of the blood of a sacrificial lamb (Exod 12:23). That same wrath of God broke Pharaoh's stubborn resistance so that he let Israel go free, while God's power at the Red Sea made them an escape route as they fled his attempt to get them back. It was Israel's initial experience of God as redeemer and liberator, their first national enjoyment of the benefits of physical and political redemption.

Passover as a model of hope for Israel's future

But in the nature of things it was only a first experience. Its benefits were to be gratefully accepted and dutifully remembered each year.

But they did not last. In later centuries Israel came under Gentile subjugation again and lost its political independence and freedom. Yet when that happened, we gather from Old Testament prophets like Isaiah that Israel's annual celebration of Passover eventually took on an added dimension. Remembrance of the first Passover began to foster hope in their hearts that what God had done long ago in the past, he would do again in the future, if anything, on an even greater scale. Once more he would break the Gentile oppression, once more he would stage an exodus and set the nation politically free and bring them home. (For vivid descriptions of Israel's hope couched in Passover language, see Isa 51:9–11; 63:11–19.) That hope survives still: inquisitions, pogroms and holocausts have not quenched it, and never will.

Passover for all mankind

Nonetheless, human history has shown that there is a bigger slavery than political subjugation; and Satan is a more sinister and powerful tyrant than ancient Pharaohs or modern Hitlers. All mankind needs deliverance from his power, and protection from the wrath of God by a more effective shield than the blood of an innocent lamb. So what Christ was saying when he talked about Passover being fulfilled was this: through his death as the Lamb of God, God's redemption, first exemplified at the comparatively lowly level of Israel's physical and political liberation from Egypt, was now about to be put into effect, on the same basic principle of redemption by blood, but at the highest possible level and to the widest possible extent (see John 12:31; 16:11; Col 1:13). Christ, our Passover, was about to be sacrificed for us (cf. 1 Cor 5:7).

Passover: a divinely designed prototype

Now God's purpose to redeem mankind by the death of his Son was formed long before ancient Israel came into Egypt (1 Pet 1:19–20). It was not, therefore, that when Christ came to die, God suddenly realised that the Passover which he had earlier organised to effect

Israel's liberation from Egypt, could now, by a stroke of good fortune, be used as an illustration of the redeeming death of his Son. It was the other way round. When God came to redeem ancient Israel from Egypt, he already had in view the ultimate redemption of mankind through his Son's death. He therefore arranged the Passover so that it should be not only the means of redeeming Israel at the time, but also a kind of prototype[1] of that ultimate redemption.

In that sense it was that Christ's death eventually 'fulfilled' Passover. It hardly needs to be mentioned that interpreting the original Old Testament Passover as a prototype of Christ's death does not in any way detract from the original significance and effectiveness of the first Passover as an historical event in its own right.

'Out of Egypt': The fulfilment of Hosea 11:1

We see another example of this type of fulfilment, this time originating in the Prophets. Matthew records how Joseph was supernaturally commanded by an angel of the Lord to take the child, Jesus, and his mother to Egypt in order to escape the murderous intentions of Herod the Great (Matt 2:13–15, 19–23). Joseph was further informed that he was to stay in Egypt until the angel instructed him to return. Matthew then adds that all this—the flight to Egypt and especially the staying there until instructed by the Lord's angel to return to the land of Israel—was ordained by God in order that what the Lord had spoken by Hosea, the prophet, might be fulfilled: 'Out of Egypt did I call my son' (Hos 11:1).

Matthew's supposed blunder

Matthew's unfriendly critics have clapped their hands at this: Matthew, they say, has made an egregious mistake. Hosea 11:1, they point out, was never intended as a prediction. How then could it be fulfilled, as Matthew says it was?

The critics, of course, are right in this, at least: Hosea 11:1 was not originally intended as a prediction: it was simply a reference

1 For the meaning of 'prototype' see p. 116.

to a past historical event, namely the exodus at the time of Israel's infancy as a nation. This is undeniably clear when one reads the whole verse: 'When Israel was a child [*scil.* in the infancy of the nation], I loved him and out of Egypt I called my son.' That being so, how can Matthew say that this past historical event was fulfilled centuries later by Christ's being taken to, and then brought back from, Egypt into the land of Israel? It is a sheer blunder on Matthew's part, say his unfriendly critics; and they put forward a suggestion as to how he managed to make such a glaring mistake.

Matthew, they explain, was convinced that, as Messiah, Jesus must, *ex hypothesi*, have fulfilled every Old Testament prophecy relating to Messiah. So Matthew went looking for such prophecies in the Old Testament. When he found one, he would select some event in the life of Jesus which bore some resemblance to the prophecy, and would announce it as a fulfilment. When he could find no actual event in Jesus' life to match a given prophecy, his piety led him to invent an imaginary story which represented Jesus as fulfilling the prophecy, as Matthew was sure Jesus must have done.

At Hosea 11:1, however, he blundered. He remembered the verse, but inexactly. He thought it was a prediction, and accordingly he invented the story of the Flight to Egypt and the return, in order to have Jesus fulfil this prediction. Unfortunately for him, it was not a prediction, and therefore could not have been 'fulfilled' by any event in the life of Christ. Matthew is thus caught out. The story of the flight to, and return from, Egypt is thus exposed as sheer invention on Matthew's part, based on a misunderstanding of this Old Testament verse, as if it were a prediction.

The meaning of the term 'fulfil' in Matthew 2:15

In actual fact, however, it is not Matthew, it is his critics who have blundered. Their criticism rests on the assumption that whenever the New Testament uses the word *fulfil* in connection with some Old Testament passage, it means the fulfilling of a prediction. They have overlooked the other meaning of the term *fulfil*, which we have just noticed in connection with the Passover: the final expression, at the highest possible level, of basic principles or strategies, that were first expressed at a lowlier level in the course of Old Testament history.

To see that this is how the term *fulfil* is being used in Matthew 2:15, we must now do two things, which sound interpretation would demand of us in any case. We must first investigate the whole context of the phrase 'Out of Egypt did I call My son' in Hosea 11:1. That done, we must then examine the whole context in which Matthew cites this phrase from Hosea.

The context of 'Out of Egypt did I call my son' in Hosea 11:1

In Genesis 15 God promised to give the land of Canaan to Abraham's seed for an inheritance, but not at once: only after an interval of four hundred years in a foreign land, spent mostly in slavery (Gen 15:13, 16). Accordingly, some years after this promise, famine compelled Abraham's descendants—still no more than an extended family of some seventy persons—to leave Canaan for Egypt. But they went with God's promise ringing in their ears: 'I will surely bring you back again' (Gen 46:14). So when at last they had become a young nation, God, true to his promise, brought them out of Egypt back into the land of Canaan. Recalling this strategic move God later says through Hosea:

> When Israel was a child, I loved him and out of Egypt I called my son. . . . It was I who taught them to walk, taking them by the arms. . . . I led Ephraim with cords of human kindness, with ties of love; I lifted the yoke from their neck and bent down to feed them. (Hos 11:1, 3, 4 NIV)

But then at once God begins to denounce and lament Israel's apostasy from him (Hos 11:2) and threatens them with exile:

> Will they not return to Egypt, and will not Assyria rule over them because they refuse to repent? Swords will flash in their cities, and will destroy the bars of their gates and put an end to their plans. (Hos 11:5–6 NIV)[2]

2 It is better to read the whole of verse 5 as a question, and not to translate the first clause as a statement—*they will not return* . . . It is true that the 10 tribes of Israel were exiled to Assyria, not to Egypt. But see Hos 8:13 and 9:3. Assyria became Israel's metaphorical Egypt.

Almost immediately, however, God exclaims that he cannot, and will not, give up Ephraim (the ten tribes) permanently (Hos 11:8–9). He will roar like a lion, and Israel will return:

> They will come trembling like birds from Egypt, like doves from Assyria. I will settle them in their homes, declares the Lord. (Hos 11:10–11 NIV)

So God's original calling out of his son, Israel, from Egypt in order to give him possession of the land of Palestine, was not a one-off exercise. Though it was reversed through Israel's apostasy, it would be repeated. God would once more call Israel, his son, out of Egypt. Isaiah said similarly about the return of the two tribes from their exile in Babylon (Isa 51:9–11 — 'Rahab' in v. 9 is another name for Egypt. See also 52:3–12 with its reference to both Egypt and Assyria).

The context of 'Out of Egypt did I call My Son' in Matthew 2

Matthew introduces the Lord Jesus as the son of David, the son of Abraham (Matt 1:1): heir, therefore, to the land covenanted to Abraham and to his seed (Gen 15), and heir also to the throne covenanted to David and his seed (2 Sam 7). Appropriately, according to the prediction of Micah 5:2, he was born in Bethlehem, David's original hometown (Matt 2:4–6). But by this time the nation had fallen once more under another Gentile imperial power, Rome, which ruled Judaea by a foreign vassal king, Herod the Great, an Edomite. His buildings were magnificent; some of them survive to this day. But he himself was a monstrous tyrant and psychopath, as cruel and murderous as any of the Assyrian or Egyptian emperors. He knew, of course, of Israel's hope in a coming Messiah. But when he heard of the birth of Jesus, 'the King of the Jews' (2:2–3), he determined to stamp out this rival to his power before he had time to grow and capture popularity with the people.

At this point in his narrative, however, Matthew records that it was not left to Joseph's initiative to decide whether and whither to take the child to safety; nor was he left to decide when it was time to return. The angel who told him to take the child to Egypt, likewise distinctly instructed him to stay there until he received further orders (2:13). In other words, Joseph was to wait until once more God called his son out of Egypt.

The flight to Egypt and the return were thus not emergency measures suddenly thought up by Joseph to meet an unforeseen difficulty. This was God deliberately adopting the same strategies that he had used before. For just as God had given to Abraham the beginnings of the promised seed while he was in Canaan; and just as he had then preserved them by sending Jacob and his family to Egypt with the express promise that he would bring them, when grown to a nation, back to Canaan (Gen 46:1–4); and just as, finally, he had eventually called his son Israel, in its political infancy, out of Egypt and had given them the land of promise and the Davidic royal dynasty; so God was now about to use the same strategies and tactics again. The promised seed of Abraham and David was born in the land, in David's town. Then, to preserve him as a baby, God was sending him down to Egypt, so that, when the time was ripe, he might call him out of Egypt and send him back to the land of Israel, to begin the great campaign to re-take the promised land and to rebuild the royal house of David.

The same strategy then, but this time at an infinitely higher level. The first time he called his son out of Egypt: this time he would call his Son. The first time it was the nation: this time it would be the individual, Christ.

The nation as God's son had, as God lamented through Hosea, miserably failed, and seemingly wrecked God's purposes in calling it out of Egypt. Now all the hopes of Israel, all the purposes of God for Israel and the world, were vested in this individual, Christ, the true Israel, *the* Son of God. This time when God called his Son out of Egypt, he would not be frustrated by subsequent failure. Final victory was assured.

The fulfilment, then, of Hosea 11:1 was the fulfilment, not of a prediction, but of a prototype. But before we leave this incident, we might do well to consider the other three fulfilments recorded in Matthew's immediate context, and to notice their differing characteristics.[3]

'Rachel weeping for her children': The fulfilment of Jeremiah 31:15

At the dramatic moment in Matthew's narrative when the child Jesus has been taken to Egypt (2:14–15), and the order for his return (2:19–20) has not yet been given, Matthew records Herod's slaughter of all the male children, of two years old and under, in David's city, Bethlehem.[4] Matthew then adds:

> Then was fulfilled that which was spoken by Jeremiah the prophet, saying: A voice was heard in Ramah, weeping and great mourning, Rachel weeping for her children; and she would not be comforted, because they are not. (2:17–18)

Doubtless Herod's massacre of the children in Bethlehem provoked bitter weeping and wailing among their mothers and fathers. But our question must be, In what sense did this weeping fulfil what was spoken of by Jeremiah the prophet? Once more, we go back to Jeremiah 31:15 and the context from which this quotation comes.

First we notice that *Rachel*, originally the name of the patriarch Jacob's favourite wife, here denotes, not so much a group of individual mothers, but a personification of the nation, Mother Israel, so to speak. The general context of this, as of so many of Jeremiah's prophecies, is the impending invasion by the emperor Nebuchadnezzar and the Babylonian armies. This particular prophecy is forecasting the weeping and wailing of Mother Israel, as in a short while her children, that is her citizens, will be either slaughtered in the land or carried off into exile. It is, therefore, in the first instance, a prophecy of the near future.

The remarkable thing, however, about this prophecy in Jeremiah is that it is surrounded on all sides, before and after, by call upon

3 In what follows I am much indebted to the treatment by R. T. France, *Matthew*, 85–9.
4 Historians and population experts suggest that this would have involved about twenty children—a small item in the long list of Herod's atrocities!

Christ's fulfilment of the Law

Much has been written about our Lord's insistence that he had not come to abolish the Law, but, on the contrary, to fulfil it (Matt 5:17). A frequently heard explanation is that he fulfilled the Law by insisting that mere abstention from outwardly committing a crime is not enough to fulfil the law against murder. Anger fostered in the heart, for instance, is murderous, even if it does not express itself in actually killing one's brother. Certainly it is true that our Lord emphasised that the Law is spiritual, and is not fulfilled by mere external conformity.

But this common explanation needs supplementing. Christ did not say, 'Don't think I came to destroy the Law.' He said, 'Don't think I came to destroy the Law or the Prophets, I came not to destroy but to fulfil.' And that shows us at once that in mentioning the Law, he was not thinking simply of the Ten Commandments. 'The Law', when twinned with 'the Prophets', stands for the five Books of Moses, the Torah; and the Law and the Prophets together refer to the first two divisions of the Hebrew canon. The phrase is repeated elsewhere in Matthew in this sense (see 7:12; 11:13; 22:40).

This then means that the Law which Christ came to fulfil included the demands for animal sacrifices in the temple, the laws of ceremonial cleansing and the food laws. Christ did not dismiss them as pointless. He fulfilled their demands, by offering himself as the great sacrifice for sin. Yet in so doing, he made these animal sacrifices obsolete. A candle, necessary when it is dark, is no longer needed when the sun floods the world with light. At the same time the sun fulfils the purpose for which the candle was invented.

The Old Testament's food laws had limited Israel's social contact with Gentiles, and so had tended to guard them from the uncleannesses—physical, moral and spiritual—of Gentile society. But Christ's baptising of his people in the Spirit on the day of Pentecost and thereafter, made the food laws no longer necessary; and God himself cancelled them (Acts 10). For now Christians had a far superior power to keep them holy even while they mixed freely with

Gentiles in their homes and at their tables in order to preach them the gospel.

The Ten Commandments themselves were not dismissed by Christ but upheld; and so they are in the New Testament epistles.[5] Christ agreed with the rabbis of his day, and they with him, that the two greatest commandments are first, 'You shall love the Lord your God with all your heart, and with all your soul, and with all your mind'; and second, 'You shall love your neighbour as yourself.' On these two commandments, Christ said, hang the whole law and the prophets (Matt 22:37–40).

Yet even here he went beyond his contemporaries. He exhorted his followers to love, not merely their neighbours, but their enemies too, and to pray for those who persecuted them. In so doing they would show themselves to be not merely moral children, but fully mature and grown up sons of their Father, rightly representing his perfection (Matt 5:43–48). Fulfilling the law can in some circumstances be a matter of degree. Behaviour acceptable in a school boy, as it was for centuries in Israel's spiritual childhood (see Gal 4:1–4), would no longer be acceptable in an adult. Christ's behaviour and teaching were the exact imprint of the nature of God. He certainly fulfilled the Law and the Prophets—and much more besides.

Our fulfilment of the Law

'Love', says Paul, 'is the fulfilment of the law' (Rom 13:10); and in this context 'fulfil' means simply doing what the Law commands and not doing what it prohibits. It is used here in its common or garden sense. Nonetheless Paul's phrase 'love is the fulfilment of the law' has sometimes been misunderstood to mean that so long as we love our neighbour, and act in love, we need not be directed, still less controlled, by the Ten Commandments or any other rules and regulations.

---

5 Sabbath is nowhere imposed on Gentile believers. It is not a 'moral' commandment. Of the Sabbath Christ could say that in the temple on the Sabbath the priests profane the Sabbath and are guiltless (Matt 12:5). This could not be said of any of the other nine commandments.

But the flow of Paul's argument in this passage shows that this view is false. Paul lists the Law's prohibition of acts and attitudes that would harm one's neighbour; and then sums up these prohibitions in the words of the Law's positive command: 'Thou shalt love thy neighbour as thyself.' In other words, true love towards one's neighbour means doing him no harm; and that in turn means obeying the Law's detailed prohibition of things that God declares would harm him.

So then, the New Testament's use of the verb 'fulfil' has significance for our day-to-day lives and is not limited to its formal and primary meaning as the fulfilling of predictions. It likewise encompasses Christ's fulfilment of the Law with all that implies. And, as we have considered at some length, the New Testament speaks of fulfilment as the final expression, at the highest possible level, of basic principles that had been expressed at a lowlier level in the course of Old Testament history. And in regard to this sense of fulfilment, one final point needs to be made for the sake of clarity in the following chapters.

The meaning of the term 'prototype'

In the course of this chapter I have begun to use the term *prototype*. Before I use it again, let me explain what I mean by it, indeed, why I use it at all. Why not be content with the word that is normally used in these contexts, namely *type*?

My reason is first that the Greek word τύπος (*typos*, from which we get the English *type*) is used in several different senses in the New Testament. Here are those which might have a bearing on our subject:

1. *An example*: either of good behaviour, like that, say of Paul, to be followed (Phil 3:17), or of evil behaviour, like that of the Israelites in the desert, to be avoided (1 Cor 10:6, 11).

2. *A model, or pattern*, following which a full-scale building is to be constructed, as was the tabernacle from plans shown by God to Moses on Sinai (Heb 8:5).

3. *A type* (in the popular, theological sense), a person, thing or institution that in some way foreshadows the future. So Adam is said to be 'a type of the one to come' (Rom 5:14).

It will be seen at once that meanings 1 and 3 are very different. The evil behaviour of the Israelites in the desert is not held up to us as a foreshadowing of our behaviour, but as an example to be avoided. Their behaviour should not foreshadow ours, nor ours reflect theirs. There should be no parallels between their evil lifestyle and ours; though if there are, their example warns us that we could suffer the same discipline as they suffered (cf. 1 Cor 11:27–32).

Adam, on the other hand, who, because he was the head of the race, damaged by his one act of disobedience all who descended from him, is a type in a different sense: he is a foreshadowing of Christ who, because he is the head of the new race of redeemed men and women, saves by his one act of obedience all those who are incorporated in him (Rom 5:19). In this respect (though not in others) the parallel between Adam and Christ is clear and obvious. To call attention to it as Paul does, emphasises the fact that God's ways are fair: if we were born sinners through no fault of our own but through what someone else (Adam) did, we can be constituted righteous before God, not by our own effort, but by what someone else (Christ) did.

The word *type*, then, is used in different senses even within Scripture itself. But in addition, in popular parlance the word 'type' does not always run on all fours with the scriptural usage. People often say, for instance, that the Mosaic tabernacle, its priesthood and rituals, were a type of Christ, his sacrifice and ministry. In the sense they mean it, that is perfectly true. Similarly, they say that Christ, his sacrifice and ministry are the *antitypes*, that is, the realities of which the tabernacle was merely a type. Again, in the sense they mean it that is true. But that is not how the New Testament itself uses these terms in this connection: in its parlance the tabernacle itself is not the type but an antitype. At Hebrews 8:5 'type' (KJV and NIV, 'pattern') is the word used to refer to the set of plans for the tabernacle which God showed Moses on Mount Sinai. The tabernacle itself, built according to this set of plans, is then referred to as an *antitype* (KJV 'figures'; NIV 'only a copy') of the true, that is, of the heavenly tabernacle (Heb 9:24).

So for the moment, and for some chapters to come, in order to reduce the risk of confusion, I shall not use the word 'type', though I firmly believe in typology as a valid way of expounding the Old Testament. Instead, to describe a particular way in which the New Testament treats certain events and persons in the Old Testament I shall be using the term *prototype*, but not in the sense of a perfect original, or archetype, from which all subsequent examples are derived. I shall use it in the sense we mean when we say that the very early aeroplanes were prototypes of our modern, sophisticated airliners. Those early aeroplanes were primitive contraptions and often broke down. They certainly were not the same in every respect as the modern jumbo jet. And yet, for all their primitiveness, they embodied certain basic principles of aerodynamics which are still followed today, though now expressed with far greater sophistication, at the much higher level of the jumbo jet. In the same way when we read the lives of Old Testament men like Abraham, Moses, David, we can see all too clearly their faults and failures which Scripture records with vivid honesty. And yet we can also see working in their lives principles that are later to be seen worked out more fully at the higher level of the gospel revealed by Christ, and indeed at the highest level of all in the person, life and work of the Lord himself. We therefore call those earlier historical events and characters not *types*, but *prototypes*.

CATEGORY TWO

Legal Concepts

8

Case Law: Legal Precedent and Analogy

Examples in Romans 3–4

THE MATERIAL OF the Old Testament is very varied. Some is verse, some is prose. Some is history, some is prophecy. Some contains narrative, some proverbial wisdom. Some resounds with psalms of praise, some sobs with bitter lamentations. One book is basically a love story. Yet other passages, by contrast, are concerned with detailed law and sound legal practice. It is with this last category of material and its interpretation in the New Testament that we shall be concerned in this and the following two chapters.

Now to some people it may seem strange, or even off-putting, to stress, as we are about to, the legal side of our Christian salvation. They freely grant that the Old Testament is full of law; but here, they claim, is the difference between the Old Testament and the New. Law and legality ruled the Old;[1] the New, by contrast is marked by grace which God extends to all sinners indiscriminately. Take the father in the parable of the Prodigal Son. When the prodigal came home, the father ran to meet him, kissed him, clothed him, put a ring on his finger and shoes on his feet, and celebrated

---

1 They seem to overlook the Old Testament passages that speak of the compassion and mercy of God: e.g. Exod 34:6–7; Ps 103:8–18.

his homecoming with a sumptuous banquet. Nothing here about law and justice, or adequate penalties having to be paid. Nothing but overwhelming mercy and forgiveness. Therefore to use the language of the law-court to describe our relation to our Creator is, they suggest, to introduce a harsh Old Testament discord into the Christian music of God's unconditional grace.

Not to be outshone, however, a notable New Testament epistle similarly speaks with great enthusiasm about God's 'superabundant grace'. It describes believers as having been 'introduced into grace', and 'standing in grace', and 'being justified by grace', and of being not under law but under grace.[2] Yet it is this very same epistle of Paul to the Romans that insists on the legal basis of our Christian salvation. Indeed it maintains that it is the soundness of this legal basis that magnifies the grace of God.

Now, this comes about because the New Testament believes with all its heart that the law laid down in the Old Testament was given by God, and was the expression of his holy character. Understandably, therefore, it insists that our salvation, proceeding as it does from that same God, cannot disregard or flout that law: it must uphold it. In consequence, as it expounds in detail the principles upon which the Christian doctrine of salvation rests, the New Testament will throughout its exposition appeal to the Old Testament as its legal authority.

Our main purpose, therefore, in these chapters is to examine the legal categories under which the New Testament cites the authority of the Old Testament in support of its New Testament principles of salvation. In order to understand more accurately these legal categories, we will begin by reminding ourselves of how the New Testament expounds the justice of its gospel. We will give particular attention to the New Testament's citation of the case of Abraham as a legal precedent of the principle of justification by faith.

---

2 Rom 3:24; 5:2, 20; 6:14. Other epistles say the same: e.g. Eph 1:7; 2:7–8.

The New Testament's need to expound
the justice of its gospel

Consider what Paul writes in the Epistle to the Romans:

> Now we know that whatever the law says, it says to those who are under the law that every mouth may be stopped, and all the world may be brought under the judgment of God. Because by the works of the law shall no flesh be justified in his sight; for through the law comes the knowledge of sin; But now apart from the law a righteousness of God has been manifested, being witnessed by the law and the prophets; Even the righteousness of God through faith in Jesus Christ unto all those who believe; for there is no distinction; For all have sinned, and fall short of the glory of God; Being justified freely by his grace through the redemption that is in Christ Jesus: Whom God set forth to be a propitiation, through faith, by his blood, to show his righteousness, because of the passing over of the sins done in previous times, in the forbearance of God; For the showing of his righteousness at this present season: that he might himself be just, and the justifier of him who has faith in Jesus. (Rom 3:19–26 ESV)

The first thing to notice in this passage is the term that is used to describe God's great salvific act towards the sinner: he is 'the justifier of the one who has faith in Jesus' (v. 26).

'To justify' is a legal term, as we see from the instructions issued to judges in the Old Testament:

> If there be a controversy between men, and they come to judgment, and the judges judge them, then they shall justify the righteous, and condemn the wicked. (Deut 25:1)

Isaiah, for his part, denounces judges who take bribes to pervert the course of justice. They 'justify the wicked for a reward, and take away the righteousness of the righteous from him' (Isa 5:23).

In passages like this, 'to justify' means, of course, not 'to *make* someone righteous', but 'to *declare* someone to be righteous'. When the judges 'justify the righteous', it is not a question of *making* the righteous man righteous. The man was righteous to start with; that is, he was the innocent party. He was not guilty. The duty of the judges was simply to *declare* him to be not guilty. Similarly, if a corrupt judge justified a wicked man, the judge's sentence did not turn this wicked man into a practically righteous, good-living, person. It simply declared, against all the evidence and against the truth, that the wicked man was 'innocent', 'not guilty', 'in the right'.[3]

That being so, it is understandable that when people met the Christian gospel for the first time, many of them were scandalised. Many still are! For the New Testament declares that God 'justifies the *ungodly*' (Rom 4:5)! In other words, it appears to represent God as doing what he strictly forbids all human judges to do. No wonder Paul's Jewish contemporaries—and some indeed of those who professed to believe that Jesus was the Messiah (see Acts 15:1–5)— were outraged. They felt that the Christian gospel was a perversion of justice and morality, a contempt of God's law, and that it turned upside down everything the Old Testament stood for. On what possible ground could God justify the one who has faith in Jesus? Paul obviously had some explaining to do.

What the ground of God's justification cannot be

Justification cannot be on the ground that the person concerned has been, and still is, doing his honest best to keep God's law. The reason for this stems from the basic purpose for which the law was given.

The purpose of the law

All would agree that the law was an excellent, God-given, guide for life. The more anyone kept it, the better life would be lived (Lev 18:5). But while that was so, the law was never given, says the New Testament, in order that by keeping it, or by endeavouring to keep it, we sinners might gain acceptance with God.

The difference here is exceedingly important. Let's use an analogy. It is true that the more a child studies, the more likely it is to get good marks in its examinations. Parents, therefore, will encourage

---

3 For another, very different, instance of 'to justify' in the sense 'to *declare* someone to be in the right', and not 'to *make* someone right', see Luke 7:29.

the child to study hard. But no parents—at least no reasonable parents—will drive the child to study, on the understanding that if it does not achieve one hundred per cent perfection in all its examinations, it will incur its parents' wrath and they will reject it.

God's law, by contrast, is a demand for perfection. Fail to continue in all it prescribes (Deut 27:26; Gal 3:10), break just one of its commandments, and the law, no longer a perfect whole, stands broken (Jas 2:10). In all realism, therefore, God never gave his law in order that by keeping it we sinners might eventually gain acceptance with God. Quite the reverse: 'what the law says, it says to those who are under the law that every mouth may be stopped, and all the world may be brought under the judgment of God' (Rom 3:19), that is, proved guilty and exposed to the wrath of God, without a word to say in self-defence. (That, incidentally, is what the New Testament means by repentance towards God, Acts 20:21.) And since this is the purpose of the law, there inevitably follows its intended effect.

The effect of the law

There dawns on those who take the law seriously that 'by the works of the law shall no flesh be justified in His sight'. Already the Old Testament psalmist had come to realise this was so: 'Enter not into judgment with thy servant,' he pleads, 'for in thy sight shall no man living be justified' (Ps 143:2 RV). This awareness arises because, as Paul explains (Rom 3:20), 'through the law comes the knowledge of sin'—and he speaks from his own experience which he details at length in Romans 7:7–24. The fact is that the more seriously we set ourselves to achieve its standard of perfection, the more we become aware of our sinfulness. The law, we may say, is like a thermometer: it can force us to face the fact that we are running a dangerously high temperature and are seriously ill; but it cannot cure us. It was never designed to. Its true use is to drive us to go to a doctor who can cure us. So, says the New Testament (Gal 3:24), the true purpose of the law is to alert us to our sinfulness and thus drive us to Christ for him to save us.

What the ground of God's justification is
Now let us consider the ground upon which God can remain just and yet justify the sinner. For Paul also sets out several positive truths about the righteousness of God (Rom 3:21–26).

It is 'apart from the law'
It is not partly on the ground of our keeping of God's law, and partly on the ground of Christ's sacrifice. Nor is it that Christ gives us the grace and strength to keep the law sufficiently to qualify us for acceptance with God. Our justification before God must be, and is, apart from the law altogether.

It is 'a righteousness of God'
That is to say, it is a righteous status conferred on us by God; not a righteousness 'of our own', that we have achieved through our works (cf. Phil 3:9).

It is received through faith in Jesus Christ
It is, 'the righteousness of God through faith in Jesus Christ for all who believe' (Rom 3:22 ESV).

It is conferred without discrimination on all who believe
All are alike in this that 'all have sinned in the past, and still do come short of the glory of God', whether much or little; and all are alike in this as well, that they can, if they wish, be justified by God's grace.

It is given as a free gift
We are justified freely (Greek: δωρεάν, dōrean), that is, without cause on our part, without our doing anything to deserve it. Compare Christ's use of this same term in John 15:25. Speaking of his contemporaries he says, 'They hated me *without a cause*' (Greek: dōrean), that is, without his having done anything to deserve it. So our justification by God is totally an act of his grace, independent of our merit, indeed in spite of our substantial demerit.

It is 'through the redemption that is in Christ Jesus'

God has himself provided the Lord Jesus as a propitiatory sacrifice for our sins. Far from implying that our sin does not really matter, far from ignoring the law and belittling its standards, Christ by his sacrifice has upheld the law, paid to the full the penalty which the law demanded for our sin, satisfied the righteous indignation of God against sin, and vindicated God's holiness. The law's penalty having thus been paid, there remains no further penalty to be paid; and that in turn makes it possible for God to acquit, to justify completely, all who have faith in Jesus, without lowering the standard of his justice one iota.

All down the long centuries before the cross of Christ, believers were taught to offer innocent animals as sacrifices for their sins. Clearly those sacrifices did not, and could not, pay the real penalty of sin. They were only token acknowledgements of sin, and pointers to the true payment. How then could God justify his forbearance in not exacting the real penalty for sin from these believers? The answer, according to the New Testament, is that his forbearance has now been justified by the sacrifice of Christ, which has actually paid the penalty which those animal sacrifices merely symbolised (Rom 3:25).

God, then, is not only loving and longsuffering, he is just. Not only is he just, he has been openly and publicly demonstrated to be just in justifying those who have faith in Jesus. Since Christ has paid the penalty of their sin, it is perfectly just of God to acquit them. It would in fact be unjust of God, if he first laid on Christ their iniquity, bruising him for it (Isa 53:6, 10), and then punished them as well for the same sins!

So far, then, the New Testament has argued that the sacrifice of Christ shows God to be just in justifying the believer. Now it turns to justify its claim that the believer receives this 'righteousness of God' through faith and not by the works of the law (Rom 3:28).

Justification by faith is a very healthy principle

Three reasons for the benefits of this principle are expounded in Romans 3:27–31.

By definition it excludes all boasting

If we could achieve justification before God by works of the law, then our confidence would rest ultimately on our works, and we could boast in our achievement. Moreover, if righteousness is through the law, then, the New Testament argues, Christ died needlessly: we could have been justified without his death, and God's grace would have been unnecessary (Gal 2:21). As it is, we are justified by faith; and this excludes boasting entirely, because in contexts like this, faith is the opposite of works. Works are what *we do*; faith is believing God and resting entirely on what *Christ has done*.

It puts everybody on the same level, whether Jew or Gentile

The Jews were certainly a privileged people, religiously speaking, chosen by God to witness to the one true God in a world largely given over to idolatry (for a list of their privileges see Rom 9:1–5). But their privileges could not save them, nor even contribute to their salvation. It would have been grossly unjust to the other nations, if they could have. In actual fact, in spite of their privileges the Jews, like everyone else, sinned, and were in need of salvation; and that put them on the same level as Gentiles. And the fact that justification is by faith, and not by the works of the law, makes salvation equally available to Gentiles as to Jews, and on exactly the same terms.

It is the only principle that establishes the law

Popular belief holds that the only way to maintain the authority of God's law is to insist that ultimately salvation will depend not solely on the sacrifice of Christ, but also substantially on our works. If, then, at the final judgment, our works are found to be good enough, we shall be saved; if not good enough, we shall be condemned.

The trouble with this theory is that no one can say what 'good enough' will turn out to be. The theory is therefore driven to fall back on the hope that if we have done our best, whatever that is, God will be merciful, overlook the inevitable, serious discrepancy between our achievement and the standards of his holy law, and admit us into his heaven.

But that would mean that in the end the demands of God's own law were not met, but overlooked; that our sinful shortcoming was excused, not dealt with justly. That would not be 'to establish the law', but rather to undermine it. Only justification solely through faith in the propitiatory sacrifice of Christ can establish the law according to the standards of God's justice.

So much, then, for Paul's statement of the principles on which, according to the Christian gospel, justification is offered to all mankind. But Paul knew from his preaching in Jewish synagogues and from the questionings that arose among Jewish members of the early Christian churches, how startling and how difficult to take in, his main contention was. It is ingrained in the natural religious mind that somehow and somewhere along the line justification and acceptance with God must depend, in part at least, on our works. So now to meet their objections Paul turns to the Old Testament, and cites the case of Abraham.

The case of Abraham — A legal precedent

Paul begins his citation (Rom 4:1–5) by asking what exactly Abraham's experience was: was he justified by works or by faith? If by works, Paul argues, he could have boasted of his attainments before his contemporaries and throughout all succeeding generations, much in the manner of Paul himself in his unconverted days (Phil 3:4–7). But such boasting on Abraham's part is impossible. Why? Because, Paul points out, God in his word has told the world exactly on what terms he justified Abraham: 'Abraham believed God, and it [i.e. his believing, his faith] was counted to him for righteousness' (Gen 15:6).

It is of the utmost importance, therefore, to perceive how Paul is treating the Old Testament here. He is not spiritualising an Old

Testament story, nor treating it as a type or an allegory. He is citing the case of one, actual, historical person, namely Abraham, and
quoting the inspired, authoritative statement of Scripture as to the
terms on which Abraham was justified. And Paul's argument is
that if righteousness before God was credited to one man, Abraham,
on the ground of faith, and not of works, then that has established
a permanent legal precedent. Anyone, thereafter, desiring to be declared righteous before God, can be, and must be, justified on the
same principle as Abraham was.

Moreover, because Abraham's case constitutes a legal precedent, Paul is careful at once to illustrate the essential difference, in
this context, between works and faith. And not without need; for
many people still suppose that faith and works are like conjoined
twins. If only one is mentioned, nevertheless the other is implied.
'Justified by faith' and 'justified by works', they think, are really one
and the same thing. And so they will explain themselves by saying
that they have great faith that the works they do will be sufficient
to gain them acceptance with God at the last.

But no, says Paul; in the context of God's justifying the sinner,
works and faith are opposites. If our justification had to be earned
from God by our works, then once we had done the works, God
would be in debt to us, and obliged to grant us justification. It would
no longer be a matter of grace on his part to grant us justification,
any more than it would be an act of grace on the part of an employer
to give an employee the wages he had earned by his work.

Justification by faith involves, by contrast, a very different attitude to God. It means accepting God's verdict that we are ungodly.
It means that because of what Christ has done, God can justify us,
ungodly though we are. And then it means putting our faith in God,
and depending entirely on him, to do precisely that for us by his
infinite grace.

Another test case arising in the course of Paul's argument

Two giant figures stand out in Israel's history: Abraham the father
of the nation, and David the founder of its royal house. Abraham's

story was foundational for the nation, and Paul has just argued that in his case it was a question of positive righteousness being credited to him. Utter faith in, and dependence on, God, such as Abraham evinced, is, after all, the only proper attitude for a creature to take towards his Creator.

But now Paul cites the case of that other foundational figure, David (Rom 4:6–8); and this time it is an instance of the negative aspect of justification: the wiping out of past sins, and the pronouncement of the verdict, 'No condemnation, justified, acquitted'. Paul cites David's own statement of the situation:

> Blessed are they whose iniquities are forgiven, and whose sins are covered. Blessed is the man to whom the LORD will not impute sin. (Ps 32:1–2)

David makes no mention of any work of the law that he was required to do in order to earn this forgiveness. All that he did was to stop covering up his sin, and openly confess his guilt:

> I acknowledged my sin unto Thee, and mine iniquity have I not hid. I said, I will confess my transgression unto the LORD; and thou forgavest the iniquity of my sin. (Ps 32:5)

Paul cites this case, therefore, not simply as the record of someone's interesting experience, but as a further legal precedent that establishes for all time the basis on which God grants forgiveness and justification by faith and not by works.

The timing of Abraham's circumcision in relation to his justification

So far, in discussing Abraham's case, Paul has cited just the one verse: 'And Abraham believed the LORD, and it was counted to him for righteousness' (Gen 15:6). His opponents, therefore, may well have felt that they had an easy case to answer. Both Abraham and David submitted to the law of circumcision. Therefore, to argue on the basis of Gen 15:6 alone that righteousness was credited to Abraham solely on the ground of faith was erroneous. Both

Abraham's case and David's showed, they claimed, that it was still true that 'unless you are circumcised after the custom of Moses you cannot be saved' (Acts 15:1).

Paul answers by pointing to the biblical record of the timing of Abraham's circumcision (Rom 4:9–12). 'We say, To Abraham his faith was reckoned for righteousness. How then was it reckoned? When he was in circumcision or in uncircumcision?' Paul's answer to his own question is swift, for it is indisputable: 'Not in circumcision but in uncircumcision' (Rom 4:9–10). According to Genesis, the sequence of events was:

1. Abraham believed God and it was credited to him for righteousness (Gen 15:6).
2. Sometime later, when Abraham was 86 years old, his son Ishmael was born (16:16).
3. When he was 99 years old, both he and Ishmael were, at God's command, circumcised (17:23–24).

The historical fact, therefore, is that righteousness was credited to Abraham on the ground of his faith over 13 years before he was circumcised, over 13 years, indeed, before circumcision was even mentioned. Arguing like a lawyer, and rightly so, Paul points out the legal implication of this timetable: if righteousness was credited to Abraham before he was circumcised, circumcision cannot have been a necessary pre-condition for righteousness being credited to him. And if not in his case, then—if God is consistent—not in David's case, and not in anybody's case. The circumcision which Abraham received as a sign over 13 years later, was, according to Paul a seal of the righteousness of the faith which he had while he was in uncircumcision—a token, a seal, but not a pre-condition (Rom 4:11).

Moreover, Abraham's case set the legal precedent for all Abraham's posterity. The males among them were circumcised eight days after birth. But when, like David, they were forgiven and justified, it was not on the ground that they had been circumcised—circumcision never at any time contributed to people's salvation—but on the ground that they walked in the steps of that faith of our father Abraham which he had 'in uncircumcision' (Rom 4:12).

The promise of world inheritance

But perhaps, even at this stage in the argument, there might remain in our minds a lingering doubt: is not Paul building a very large argument on one little verse, Genesis 15:6, taken out of its context?

The answer is, not so. For at Romans 4:13–16 he proceeds to point out that in the very context in which it is said that Abraham believed God and it was credited him for righteousness, God promised to give Abraham and his seed a vast inheritance, and guaranteed the fulfilment of that promise by means of a legally binding covenant. We shall be studying that covenant in Chapter 10, so that all we need to say about that promise and covenant now is what Paul says about it here in Romans 4:13: God made that covenant with Abraham and his seed *before* Abraham was circumcised; and the blessings it guaranteed were given to Abraham and his seed not on the pre-condition that they kept the law, but on the ground of faith and altogether on the basis of God's unmerited grace. On that ground alone could the fulfilment of the promise be guaranteed: 'That is why it depends on faith, in order that the promise may rest on grace and be guaranteed to all his offspring—not only to the adherent of the law but also to the one who shares the faith of Abraham . . .' (Rom 4:16 ESV).

The nature of Abraham's faith

It does not escape Paul's legal mind, however, that if he is going to deduce from Genesis 15:6 that righteousness was credited to Abraham solely on the basis of faith, he had better define what is meant in this context by faith. He does so, not by making up his own definition of faith, but by appealing to Genesis' subsequent record of what 'believing God' meant for Abraham (Rom 4:17–22).

Now the particular promise to which Abraham was responding when he believed the Lord and it was counted to him for righteousness, was that God would give him a son and heir, and through that son offspring as multitudinous as the stars (Gen 15:2–6). At the time, Abraham was childless for the simple reason that Sarah, his wife, was barren; but he himself was still able to father a child. And so it came about that Sarah and he between them got it into their heads that believing God's word and promise meant that they had to do their best and use their own resources in order to fulfil God's promise. So at Sarah's suggestion Abraham took Sarah's servant-girl, Hagar, and fathered a son, Ishmael, by her. But God would not agree that that was what he meant by his promise.

And thirteen years later God had still not fulfilled his promise; and now, not only was Sarah still barren, but Abraham's body was decrepit, and beyond fathering a son. Abraham suggested to God that perhaps now he would consider regarding Ishmael as the promised son. Still God refused, and simply reiterated the promise, assuring Abraham and Sarah that it would soon be fulfilled (Gen 17:15–19). At this point in the story it is worth quoting Paul's comment in full; it will put beyond doubt what Paul means by 'faith', when he says that Abraham was justified by faith.

> . . . God, in whom he believed, who gives life to the dead and calls into existence the things that do not exist. In hope he believed against hope, that he should become the father of many nations, as he had been told, 'So shall your offspring be'. He did not weaken in faith when he considered his own body, which was as good as dead (since he was about a hundred years old), or when he considered the barrenness of Sarah's womb. No distrust made him waver concerning the promise of God, but he grew strong in his faith as he gave the glory to God, fully convinced that God was able to do what he had promised. That is why his faith was counted to him as righteousness. (Rom 4:17–22 ESV)

Abraham's faith, then, was not a momentary profession of belief, soon made, and looked back upon over the years as something increasingly remote. It was a living faith, persistent, constantly renewed, and anchored in the character of the living God. Faith meant believing God who, when all human resource and effort was shown to be helpless and hopeless, could and would do what he originally promised to do, and bring life out of death.

The analogy between Abraham's faith and ours and its practical importance

One further step remains for Paul to take if he is to press home his contention that Abraham's justification by faith constitutes a legal precedent for our similarly being justified by faith (Rom 4:23–25). Abraham was called upon to believe that God was going to give him and Sarah a son (and then multitudes of descendants) even though he was old and his wife barren. But surely we ourselves are not required to believe that God is going miraculously to give us a child when we are old or barren or both? How then can there be any similarity between Abraham's faith and ours?

Paul's answer is that there is a strict analogy between Abraham's faith and ours. Abraham had to learn to believe in a God who could bring life out of death. We, too, in order to be justified must 'put our faith in God who raised our Lord Jesus from the dead, who was delivered up for our trespasses, and was raised for our justification' (4:24–25).

The analogy is very instructive and helpful. Many people lack complete peace with God because they misunderstand what is meant by 'faith' when Scripture says: 'being justified by faith we have peace with God' (5:1). They have read of faith in other connections in the New Testament where people are rebuked for their little faith; and they fall to thinking that the reason they have no peace with God is that their faith is not strong enough. They then imagine that faith is a kind of work that must be performed up to a certain standard before it qualifies for justification and peace; or that it is a force which, if only it can be geared up to measure sufficient strength on a spiritual pressure gauge, will effect justification, but otherwise not.

But that is not what 'faith' means when used in the context of justification, as the analogy between Abraham's faith and ours clearly shows. Abraham was justified when he put his faith in God who said he could and would bring life out of death. It was not Abraham's faith that produced the miracle: long years of believing and hoping left his body as good as dead. It was God who accomplished the miracle. Similarly, we are justified when we put our faith in God who raised the Lord Jesus from the dead. It was not our faith, strong or weak, that raised the Lord Jesus from the dead: it was God who did it.

Imagine the impossible for a moment. Imagine we were standing with the apostles round the grave of Christ before his body was raised from the dead. And imagine further that we realised the fact that Christ's body was in the grave because he died for our sins; and unless he was raised from the dead, there would be no justification for us: we would simply remain as we were, unforgiven and liable to God's wrath (1 Cor 15:17). Aware of the gravity of the situation, we say to one another: 'Look, let's stand round the grave, join hands and start believing as strongly as we can. For if only we can manage to believe with strong enough faith, our faith will cause the Lord's body to rise from the grave, and we can then be sure that we are justified and have peace with God.'

Would the strength of our faith bring Jesus out of the grave? Of course not. The very idea is grotesque. The resurrection of Christ was something that lay beyond any human power to effect. God alone could do it. In fact, if God had not done it, there would never have been any gospel for us to believe (1 Cor 15:14–17). Faith, for us, then means believing that God has done what we could never do, in raising Christ from the dead, and then resting entirely on that and on its significance: for the sake of our trespasses God delivered up his Son to the sanctions of the law; and so Christ died, and was buried. But then God raised him from the dead for our justification, thus declaring that God is satisfied with the sacrifice of his Son on our behalf; and all who put their faith in him are justified completely and for ever (Acts 13:38).

A Closing Note

As we have briefly considered the way in which the New Testament expounds the justice of its gospel, we will have noticed that Paul has laid great emphasis on Genesis 15:6—'Abraham believed the

Lord and it was counted unto him for righteousness'. And Paul has stressed the fact that what was counted to him for righteousness, was not any work that he had done, but his faith in the Lord.

But a similar phrase is used in Psalm 106:30–31 of Phinehas, the priest: 'Then stood up Phinehas, and executed judgment, and so the plague was stayed. And it was counted unto him for righteousness, unto all generations for ever more.' Here it is not Phinehas' faith in God, but his work in executing God's wrath and staying the plague that was counted to him for righteousness. The question arises: how are we to marry up those two statements in our minds, when one says it was faith and not works, and the other says it was work, that was counted for righteousness?

Perhaps the best way to go about it is to start with Phinehas, and ask what he did, why it was counted for righteousness, and what he got from God on the strength of it.

The situation was that the Israelites had committed sexual immorality and idolatry with Moabite women, as a result of which God sent a severe plague on Israel. In the midst of that distress an Israelite prince brought a Midianite woman into the camp, openly flaunting his idolatrous immorality in the face of the congregation of Moses and of God himself. Whereupon the priest, Phinehas, took a spear and ran both the man and the woman through.

It was undeniably a very severe action; but God declared it to be right and just. Phinehas had perfectly expressed God's jealousy, and had thereby made atonement for the people, turned away God's wrath, and brought the plague to an end. He was not merely a priest in name; by his action he had shown himself to be a true priest between God and the people. And the reward he got from God for his action, was not justification in the salvific sense, but a perpetual priesthood (see Num 25:1–15).

It is this, then, that Psalm 106:30–31 is referring to when it comments: 'and that was counted to him for righteousness unto all generations for evermore'. He had signally justified his claim to be a priest by his action. God approved that action, declared it to be right. It was a case of justification by works.

It remains true that in Abraham's case it was not any action of his, but his believing God that was counted to him for righteousness; and what he received as a result was not a priesthood, but a right relationship with God, justification in the salvific sense.

It likewise remains true that later on Abraham was justified by his works when he offered up his son Isaac on the altar (see Jas 2:21–24). We shall discuss his sacrifice of Isaac at length in Part Three, ch. 23. It is enough here to point out that what that sacrifice demonstrated was that Abraham's faith was utterly and completely in God, and not in any one else, not in himself, not even in Isaac. In other words Abraham's work demonstrated that his faith in God was genuine: Abraham was a true believer.

9
Inference, Legal Paradigm, Intention

In this chapter we are to study three more devices which the New Testament uses in its interpretation of the Old Testament: inference, legal paradigm, and intention.

Inference

The New Testament will sometimes argue that a law which, as it stands, explicitly applies to a smaller thing or situation, must, by inference, be allowed to apply all the more to a greater thing or situation not explicitly mentioned by the law. The argument is of the form *a minore ad maius* (from the less to the greater). So natural and so common is this type of reasoning that the Jewish rabbis formally labelled it *qal wahomer*, 'the light and the weighty'; and it was similarly recognised by the classical Greek and Roman jurists (from whom the rabbis probably took over this formal classification) as an acceptable, and indeed necessary, method of interpreting their law. Here are three examples.

Regarding the law of Sabbath and service (Matt 12:1–8)
The Lord used this type of argument to justify his disciples when they were criticised for plucking corn and rubbing it in their hands on the Sabbath day:

> Or have you not read in the Law that on the Sabbath the priests
> in the temple break the Sabbath and are innocent? I tell you that
> one greater than the temple is here. (Matt 12:5–6)

In other words, if the Law explicitly authorised—indeed commanded—the priests to work in the temple on the Sabbath although
it broke the Sabbath, because they were working in and for the temple, a fortiori it must be right for the disciples to break the Sabbath,
since they were working for one who was greater than the temple.

Regarding the law of Sabbath and healing (John 7:23–24)

> If a man receives circumcision on the Sabbath that the Law
> of Moses may not be broken, are you angry with me because
> I made an entire man completely well on the Sabbath? Do not
> judge according to appearance, but judge with righteous judg-
> ment. (John 7:23–24)

The rabbis held that submission to circumcision made a man ceremonially complete. Therefore it was right that the performance
of this small ceremonial operation on part of a man should over-
ride the Sabbath law. A fortiori, argued Christ, the making of a
whole man *actually*, and not just *ceremonially, completely* well on the
Sabbath must rightly be regarded as overriding the law of Sabbath.

Regarding Christ's claim to be the
Son of God (John 10:34–36)

> Is it not written in your law, 'I said, You are gods'? If he called
> them gods to whom the word of God came (and the scripture
> cannot be broken), do you say of him whom the Father sanctified
> and sent into the world 'You are blaspheming' because I said, 'I
> am the Son of God'? (John 10:34–36)

The quotation is from Psalm 82:6; and the argument is: if according
to Scripture certain mere human beings could rightly, without blasphemy, be called, in some sense, 'gods', a fortiori it is not blasphemy
for the one whom the Father has sanctified and sent into the world to
claim to be the Son of God in the fullest sense of that term.

Legal paradigm

As well as inference the New Testament, like the Jewish rabbis, also invokes another slightly different principle in interpreting the Old Testament: it argues that some of its laws were intended as legal paradigms. The idea here is that God, the lawgiver, did not set out to cover every conceivable instance of a given principle of behaviour by legislating separately for each one. Rather the lawgiver would lay down a specific commandment covering a particular situation, on the understanding and with the intention that the general principle embodied in this particular situation and in the law dealing with it, should apply with equal authority to all similar and analogous situations. We call a specific commandment of that kind a paradigm because it sets an example to be followed in all similar situations.

It would not be difficult to see the lawgiver's wisdom in guiding his people by means of such paradigms. In the first place, a code of laws that tried to cover every conceivable, particular situation by a specific, tailor-made law, would become impossibly detailed and unwieldy. Secondly, to give one concrete example as a practical expression of a general principle is often a better way of helping people to grasp the general principle and then to apply it in other cases. A long and necessarily complicated statement of the general principle couched in abstract legal terminology would be more difficult to understand and, therefore, to apply.

Paul's use of an Old Testament law as a legal paradigm

At Deuteronomy 25:4 God issues an explicit and particular command: 'You shall not muzzle the ox while it is treading out the corn'. Citing this command at 1 Corinthians 9:8–10, Paul maintains that God intended it to apply not solely, or even predominantly, to oxen and their owners, but to Christian apostles, evangelists, pastors, teachers and their converts: 'Surely he says this for us, doesn't he?' (1 Cor 9:10).

The reasoning behind Paul's claim is clear enough. In the first place, oxen ploughed, helped in reaping the harvest, and in threshing the corn; Christian workers ploughed, sowed and produced a harvest; the oxen literally, the others metaphorically; but otherwise the work was the same (1 Cor 3:6–8; cf. John 4:35–38; Matt 13:3–30).

Secondly, the thrust and direction of the original command and of Paul's application of it are the same. The law 'You shall not muzzle the ox while it is treading out the corn' (Deut 25:4) was not imposed as a duty on the ox: it was imposed as a duty on the people who enjoyed the benefits of the ox's work. They were not to make it impossible for the ox to lower its head from time to time and eat some of the corn it was threshing, so sharing in the benefits produced by its work. Similarly, when Paul sums up and applies the basic principle and purpose involved in the original command, he puts it this way: 'that the plougher ought to plough in hope and the thresher to thresh in hope of sharing' (i.e. in the harvest).[1] The 'ought' in this statement, as Bengel long ago pointed out, puts the responsibility not on the plougher and the thresher, but on the persons for whom they worked.[2] Paul is not saying that the Christian worker has an obligation to hope for remuneration as he works. He is saying that those for whom he works have an obligation to see to it that he has a genuine prospect of reaping some material benefits from the results of his work. They are not to withhold such reaping from him any more than the owners were from the ox.

The two cases, then, are on all fours. It is perfectly reasonable, therefore, for Paul to declare that the lawgiver himself, right from the very start, intended the principle enunciated in the case of the ox to apply to all other similar cases, including especially that of the Christian worker and the churches. At least no classical Greek or Roman jurist would have thought this interpretation to be unreasonable or fantastic.[3]

1 Translations which put 'ploughman' here rather than 'plougher' obscure the fact that Paul's statement of the basic principle applies equally to the ox as to the Christian worker.
2 Bengel, Gnomon, 3:261.
3 For a very helpful discussion of the attitudes of Roman jurists to the XII tables compared with the rabbis' attitudes to the Mosaic law, see D. Daube, 'Rabbinic Methods', 239–64.

Objections to Paul's usage

Some scholars have tended to make heavy weather of this passage. First they insist on treating Paul's rhetorical question 'It is not for oxen that God is concerned, is it?' (1 Cor 9:9) as an absolute statement: 'God doesn't care for oxen at all'. Yet other similarly worded statements elsewhere can be shown not to be intended as absolute statements. Romans 14:17, for example, ('the kingdom of God is not eating and drinking, but righteousness and peace and joy in the Holy Spirit') was surely not intended to say that the kingdom of God is not at all concerned with gluttony or drunkenness, but only with righteousness, joy and peace. It was intended to say that the kingdom of God is not concerned so much with eating and drinking as it is with righteousness and peace and joy in the Holy Spirit.

Then they insist on translating Paul's next phrase as 'Or does he say it altogether for our sake'. Actually the crucial Greek word πάντως (*pantōs*) does not necessarily mean 'altogether', but can mean 'surely' or 'certainly' (cf. Luke 4:23 πάντως ἐρεῖτέ, *pantōs ereite*: 'you will surely say'). The two phrases can rightly be taken as 'Is it (merely) for oxen that God cares? Surely he says this for us, doesn't he? Yes, for us . . .'.

But having insisted on reading Paul as saying that God doesn't care for oxen at all, they then charge Paul with denying the straightforward and obviously intended meaning of the original command and of foisting on it a meaning it was never meant to have.

Accepting this 'absolutist' translation, other scholars have tried to avoid its unwelcome implications, by suggesting that in Deuteronomy 25:4 the command was from the very start intended in a metaphorical, and not in a literal, sense. But that won't do. The whole force of an injunction against muzzling a metaphorical ox, would depend on the prior fact that the muzzling of a literal ox was generally regarded as an inhumane and unlawful thing to do; and in that case the law would naturally have been understood as applying first at the literal level, and then at the metaphorical.

Nearer the mark have been the suggestions that the original command was from the first concerned to require that any who employed workers, whether animal or human, and benefited from their labours, should recognise the workers' rights to their just share in the produce of their work. In which case Paul is simply urging on the Christians at Corinth this same concern for those who worked for them. Which in turn comes very near to regarding the original command as a deliberately intended legal paradigm.[4]

Intention

Besides inference and legal paradigm, the New Testament also raises this third legal principle. Consider the implications of our Lord's words:

> And he said to them, 'The Sabbath was made for man, not man for the Sabbath.' (Mark 2:27 NIV)

Here Christ raised the question of what the intended purpose of the Sabbath law was. Man was not created for the purpose of having some rational creature around who could be prevailed upon to keep the already existent Sabbath. It was the other way round. Man was first created and then the Sabbath rest was ordained for man's benefit. It would be contrary to the intention of the Sabbath, if enforcing it would damage a human being. A speed limit is imposed in cities with the intention of preventing accidents and saving lives. But if paramedics are driving a critically injured patient to hospital as fast as they can, it would be against the intention of the speed limit law to demand they slow down. Less speed and the patient might lose his life before they reached hospital.

On a Sabbath day a woman whom Satan had bound for eighteen years entered a synagogue. Christ set her free. The ruler of the synagogue criticised him for breaking the Sabbath. But to enforce the Sabbath law if it meant leaving the woman in the grip of Satan for even one more day was a perversion of the law's intention. And Christ rebuked the ruler publicly (Luke 13:10–17).

4 See the helpful summary by Moo, 'Sensus Plenior', 189.

10

Interpreting Legal Covenants

A̲ᴛ Gᴀʟᴀᴛɪᴀɴs 3:29 the Apostle Paul declares it to be true of all believers in Christ, whether Jew or Gentile, slave or free, male or female: 'If you are Christ's, then you are Abraham's seed, heirs according to promise.' Anyone who believes this—and all Christians should—may well find herself or himself asking questions:

1. How can Gentile Christians possibly be regarded as Abraham's seed? And what does it matter whether they are Abraham's seed or not?

2. And what does the term 'seed' mean anyway?

3. And what inheritance is it that they are supposed to be heirs of?

4. They are said to be 'heirs according to promise'. What promise? And, more importantly, what kind of promise? Promises come in two kinds: conditional or unconditional. Which is it here?

The answer to this fourth question is: it is the promise of an inheritance, which God made to Abraham, guaranteeing its fulfilment by an unbreakable covenant. The details both of the promise and of the covenant are given in Genesis 15:1–21.[1]

Our task now, therefore, is to examine how the New Testament interprets this covenant. To do this adequately, however, we must

---

1 These details are given in the very same chapter and in the very same context that proclaim for all time the principle of justification by faith.

first spend time considering the significance of this covenant against the immediate background of its Old Testament context. Then we must study the exact nature and legal status of the covenant. That done, we shall have a sound basis for examining Paul's interpretation of the precise meaning of the terminology which the covenant uses to specify both the beneficiaries under the covenant and the benefits accruing to them. As we do we will find it necessary to address questions that arise concerning the covenant made at Sinai. We can then consider the force and function which, according to Paul, this covenant was intended to exercise in relation to the subsequent history of Abram's descendants, and indeed of the world. And finally we will conclude by considering the significance of these points as they are seen in the new covenant of which Christ is the mediator and guarantor.

The Old Testament background and immediate context of the covenant

God's initial call and commissioning of Abram is related in these terms:

> Now the LORD had said to Abram: 'Get thee out of thy country and from thy kindred, and from thy father's house, *unto the land that I will show thee*. And I will make of thee a great nation, and I will bless thee, and make thy name great; and be thou a blessing. And I will bless those who bless thee, and him who curses thee will I curse; and in thee shall all the families of the earth be blessed.' (Gen 12:1–3)

It is to be noted in passing that God's long-term purpose in choosing Abram to be the founder of a new nation and in promising to give him and his descendants a land of their own was the eventual blessing of all the nations of the earth. That has often become obscured; Israel herself has often forgotten it. But Paul in his interpretation of the covenant will appeal to this intended connection between Israel's promised inheritance and the blessing of all the nations (Gal 3:8–14).

When subsequently Abram first set foot in Canaan (Gen 12:5), we are told that the Lord appeared to him and said: 'Unto thy seed *will I give this land*' (Gen 12:7).

Later on God once more repeated his promise:

> Lift up now thine eyes, and look from the place where thou art, northward and southward and eastward and westward: for *all the land which thou seest, to thee and to thy seed will I give it for ever.* And I will make thy seed as the dust of the earth, so that if a man can number the dust of the earth, then shall thy seed also be numbered. Arise, *walk through the land* in the length of it and in the breadth of it, for unto thee will I give it. (Gen 13:14–17)

We can scarce miss the repeated emphasis that what God promised to give to Abram and to his seed was the land of Canaan.

The years, however, went by and still Abram did not possess the land. Worse still, he remained childless. If he continued childless to the end of his life, how could God's promise to give the land to his seed be fulfilled? There never would be any seed to give it to! Naturally, Abram raised his perplexity with the Lord:

> O Lord God, what wilt thou give me, for I continue childless, and the heir of my house is Eliezer of Damascus? And Abram said, Behold you have given me no seed, and a member of my household[2] will be my heir. (Gen 15:2–3)

In reply God not only assured Abram that he would have a son of his own who would be his heir (15:4–5), but reiterated his promise regarding the land:

> I am the Lord who brought you out from Ur of the Chaldeans to give you this land to possess it. (15:7)

But this time Abram was not content simply to have the promise repeated: he wanted some guarantee that the promise would be fulfilled, so that he could be absolutely sure of the fulfilment:

> But he [Abram] said, O Lord God, how am I to know that I shall possess it? (Gen 15:8)

---

2 i.e. one of my household servants.

It was, then, in answer to Abram's request for guaranteed certainty that God made the covenant with Abram to which Paul appeals in Galatians 3:15ff. But if it was guaranteed certainty of fulfilment that Abram was looking for, then we must ask how, and to what extent, the covenant could provide such certainty; and that will depend on the kind of covenant it was, and on the terms and conditions it laid down.

The nature of the covenant

Suppose in our modern world a builder undertakes to build a house of such and such specifications for a client, and the client agrees to pay the builder a fixed sum on the condition that the finished house meets all the required specifications. On these terms they draw up a written contract and then they both sign it, because both parties to the covenant, the builder and his client, are required by the terms of the covenant to fulfil certain promises. If either of them defaults, the covenant is broken, and in addition the defaulting party can be sued for damages. We could call this form of contract a two-party covenant, because each of the two parties has conditions and promises to fulfil.

On the other hand, if in the modern world a man is unable at the moment to pay his creditor the money he owes, his creditor may allow him to write a promissory note, stating that he owes the creditor such and such an amount, and will pay it by a certain date. In this case, only the debtor signs the promissory note, for only he is making any promise. The promissory note does not commit the creditor to do anything. We could call this kind of covenant a one-party covenant. The ancient biblical world knew of both of these covenants, though its ways of signing up to them differed considerably from our modern practices.

In ancient times covenants of various kinds were commonly solemnized by shedding the blood of sacrificial animals or birds; but the practices connected with such ceremonies differed significantly according to the nature of each particular covenant. One form of covenant sacrifice was as follows: animals and birds were killed, and the animals cut in pieces. The pieces and the birds were then placed in two parallel rows with space enough between them for people to walk ceremonially between the two rows. But who walked between the rows depended on the nature of the particular covenant.

Both one-party and two-party covenants were solemnized in this way. To illustrate the distinctions involved let us take another example of a one-party covenant before turning back to the covenant recorded in Genesis 15. Our special interest will be to notice on each occasion who walked between the pieces.

A covenant made by the Judaeans regarding slavery (Jer 34:8–22)

In this covenant, the Judaeans promised to let their Hebrew slaves go free. The background was as follows. The law, given by God to Israel after the Exodus, prescribed that at the end of every seven years the Israelites would let any Hebrew slave they had acquired go free (Jer 34:13–14). In Jeremiah's day, however, the people in general had for a long while flouted this law. But then, at a certain stage, they professed to repent, and made a covenant before God in the temple, guaranteeing that they would let their Hebrew slaves go free (34:8–10). Nevertheless soon afterwards they reneged on this covenant, re-enslaved their fellow-Hebrews, and brought on themselves the judgment of God.

Our interest in this story at this moment is to notice the form which the making of this covenant took: 'they cut the calf in two and passed between the pieces' (34:18). Notice especially who it was that walked between the pieces: it was all the princes and all the people (34:10). Naturally so; for it was these men (34:18) that were making the covenant and solemnly binding themselves by this means to fulfil their promise to God to let their Hebrew slaves go free. Nothing is said about God, or a symbol of his presence, walking between the pieces. Of course not. God was not here making any promise: he had no conditions to fulfil. Only the men who had conditions to fulfil walked between the pieces. It was a one-party covenant.

The covenant made by God with Abram
and his seed (Gen 15:8–21)

The making of the covenant which Paul expounds in Galatians 3 followed the same practice as the one we have just considered. Animals and birds were killed, and the animals divided in pieces. Then the pieces of the animals and the birds were laid in two parallel rows with a space between, ready for the covenant party, or parties, to make the covenant by solemnly walking between the pieces.[3] Abram prepared all this and then waited; waited so long, in fact, that the birds of prey came down on the carcasses, and Abram had to drive them away (Gen 15:11). Why did he have to wait? Why did he not proceed forthwith to walk between the pieces? The answer is, because he had not been told the terms of the covenant; had not been informed what, if any, conditions he had to fulfil in order to secure this great inheritance that God was covenanting to give him. If he was to be given conditions to fulfil, he would have to walk between the pieces, in order to bind himself to fulfil those conditions. On the other hand, if he had no conditions to fulfil, he would not be required to walk between the pieces. Given the far-reaching legal implications of whether, in the event, Abram had to walk between the pieces or not, we shall look to the text with eyes wide-open to see what actually happened. And there we shall find two highly significant facts.

Abram did not walk between the pieces

In the event he couldn't, for he fell fast asleep before the covenant ceremony began (Gen 15:12). God certainly spoke to him while he was asleep, and Abram certainly heard God speaking and was aware of what God was saying. But it will not do to argue from that that since this was a dream or vision, we may assume that

3 The fact that Abram provided and prepared these animals and birds would not have been regarded as a ground for claiming the benefits of the covenant. A solicitor who provides his client with the paper, pen and ink to write out his will, cannot on that account claim to be a beneficiary under the will.

Abram was regarded as having walked between the pieces, even though no mention is made of it in the text. In dreams and visions in the Bible people having the dream or vision see themselves doing various things (see e.g. Joseph's dream, Gen 37:5–7). If in the vision Abram had walked between the pieces, he would have seen himself doing so, and he would have been described in the narrative as having done so.

The reason why Abram did not walk between the pieces was that he had no conditions to fulfil. Neither in the prophetic preamble (Gen 15:13–16), nor in the actual terms of the covenant (15:17–20) is Abram set any conditions, or asked to make any promises. In fact he says nothing.

God did walk between the pieces
It was the presence of God symbolised by a smoking furnace and a flaming torch that is explicitly said to have passed between the pieces (Gen 15:17–18). This, of course, was legally appropriate, for, as we now see, God alone was making all the promises, and therefore God alone was binding himself to fulfil those promises.[4] This is borne out by the formal statement of the terms of the covenant:

> In that day the LORD made a covenant with Abram, saying: Unto thy seed have I given this land, from the river of Egypt unto the great river, the river Euphrates: the Kenite and the Kenizzite, and the Kadmonite, and the Hittite, and the Perizzite, and the Rephaim, and the Amorite, and the Canaanite, and the Girgashite and the Jebusite. (Gen 15:18–20 RV)

Abram himself promised nothing. It was a one-party covenant. And the fact that we are understanding Paul's interpretation of this covenant correctly, is confirmed when we pay close attention to the meaning of the term *promise* which Paul repeatedly uses in this connection (see Gal 3:14, 16, 17, 18, 21, 24; 4:28; Rom 4:13, 14, 16, 20, 21).

---

4 For the phenomena connected with the divine presence on this occasion, compare the phenomena at the Burning Bush, Exod 3:2–4.

Paul's interpretation of 'promise' in connection with the inheritance

For if the inheritance is of the law, it is no longer of promise; but
God has granted it to Abram by promise. (Gal. 3:18)

Conditional and unconditional promises

In our ordinary everyday language promises can be of two kinds:
either conditional, or unconditional.

A conditional promise can be illustrated by a father saying to
his teenage son: 'If you work hard, and pass all your examinations
well, I promise I will give you £1,000.' This is certainly a genuine
promise; but whether the son receives the promised money or not,
will depend on whether he works well and passes his examinations.
If he does not fulfil the conditions laid down by his father, his father
will not fulfil the promise, and he will not receive the money.

An unconditional promise can be illustrated by the father saying
to his teenage son: 'Because you are my son and simply because I
love you, I solemnly promise that, when you are twenty-one years
old, I will give you £10,000.' In this particular promise the father
lays down no demands that his son must perform in order to deserve and to receive the promised money. Simply out of sheer love
for his son the father promises to give him the money as an unmerited, free gift. It is an unconditional promise; and if the father is true
to his promise, it will be fulfilled.

When, therefore, Paul says that God has granted the inheritance
to Abram by promise (Gal 3:18), does he mean by a conditional, or
by an unconditional, promise? The answer is beyond dispute: he
means 'by an unconditional promise'. For look at his argument:
'if the inheritance is of the law', he says—i.e. if the fulfilment of
the promise depends on Abram's keeping of the law—'then it is
no longer of promise'; and that argument makes no sense, unless
Paul regarded the promise as having been originally unconditional.
Let's work through the implied steps in his argument.

Suppose the original promise had been conditional, i.e. that it had contained, explicitly or implicitly, a condition that possession of the promised inheritance would depend on Abram's keeping of the law. This would not have meant that God was not making Abram a genuine promise. It still would have been a genuine promise: only in this case it would have been a conditional promise.

But suppose that the original promise of the inheritance was originally an unconditional promise. Then, in that case, if God, or anyone else, had subsequently added to it the condition that its fulfilment depended on Abram's keeping of the law, the addition of this condition would have fundamentally changed the nature, intention and legal status of the original promise. For now it would no longer be an unconditional promise, for a promise cannot be both unconditional and conditional simultaneously. The two kinds of covenant are incompatible. Moreover, add this condition of law-keeping to the original unconditional promise and the consequences would have been disastrous for Abram and his seed. As long as their eventual possession of the inheritance depended on the unconditional promise of a God who never breaks his promises, they could be utterly sure of its fulfilment. But had the fulfilment of the promise depended on the condition that they kept the law, then their eventual possession of the inheritance would have been not merely uncertain, but downright impossible. For, as Paul observes a little earlier in his argument, no one can keep all God's law as it should be kept, and all, therefore, are in consequence under its curse (Gal 3:10–12).

This, then, is what Paul implies by his statement (quoted above):

> For if the inheritance is of the law, *it is no longer of promise; but God has granted* it to Abram by promise. (Gal 3:18)

And he backs up his interpretation by appealing next to sound legal practice.

Sound legal practice

First, he appeals to what was generally regarded in the world of his day as sound legal principles in the interpretation of covenants:

> Brothers, I speak after the manner of men: though it be but a man's covenant, yet when it has been confirmed, no one [subsequently] either makes it void, or adds to it [*scil.* conditions not stated in the original covenant]. (Gal 3:15)

He then observes that the unconditional, one-party covenant that God made with Abram and his seed, was confirmed 430 years *before* the Law of Moses was promulgated at Mount Sinai.[5]

On that ground he then insists that in giving Israel the law on Mount Sinai, God cannot have intended to add it to his original covenant with Abram as a condition that must be fulfilled before the promised inheritance could be granted to him. For if God had intended it so, Paul argues, God would have rendered the original unconditional promise null and void, and thus have disannulled the first covenant. Paul's words are:

> Now this I say: A covenant confirmed beforehand by God, the law, which came four hundred and thirty years after, does not disannul so as to make the promise of none effect. (Gal 3:17)

Questions arising

But Paul's insistence that God's original unconditional promise stands unaffected and unmodified by the law issued at Sinai raises a number of questions that can be summed up by Paul's own phrase: 'What then is the law?' (Gal 3:19). For it is indisputable:

1. that God himself imposed the law on Israel, at Sinai, and did so before they entered the promised land;
2. that the covenant between God and Israel which was based on that law was a two-party covenant, and that the benefits promised under that covenant were conditional upon the keeping of the law;
3. that Moses explicitly made Israel's entry into their promised

---

5 And, we may add, not less than 13 years before God instituted the covenant of circumcision for Abram and his descendants (see Gen 17:10). Ishmael's birth followed some time after God's first covenant (Gen 15), and is recorded in Gen 16. It was 13 years later that this second covenant was subsequently made (see Gen 17:25). The two covenants, then, were not the same. See Paul's argument at Rom 4:9–16; and notice that it applies both to Abram's justification and to the promised inheritance.

land dependent on their keeping all the requirements of the
law;

4. and that Moses further warned Israel that if they broke the
   terms of the covenant and failed to keep its laws, God would
   throw them out of the promised land and scatter them
   among the nations.

Does not this begin to look as if Israel's inheritance of the
promised land was, after all, conditional, contrary to Paul's interpretation? But before we decide so, we ought at least to establish
the full facts in greater detail and with more precision.

The relationship with the covenant made at Sinai

This covenant is commonly called the Mosaic covenant, because
Moses acted as the mediator between God and the Israelites at its
making. Alternatively, in the New Testament it is referred to as the
old covenant to distinguish it from the new covenant (Heb 8:6–13).
It was enacted at Horeb, a range of mountains among which was
Sinai, the particular mountain from which the law was given. Here
is the account of the enactment:

> And he [the LORD] said . . . Moses alone shall come near unto
> the LORD. . . . And Moses came and told the people all the words
> of the Lord, and all the judgments; and all the people answered
> with one voice, and said, All the words which the LORD has spo-
> ken will we do.

> And Moses wrote all the words of the LORD, and rose up early in
> the morning, and built an altar under the mountain, and twelve
> pillars, according to the twelve tribes of Israel. And he sent
> young men of the children of Israel, who offered burnt offerings,
> and sacrificed peace offerings of oxen unto the LORD.

> And Moses took half of the blood, and put it in basins; and half of
> the blood he sprinkled on the altar. And he took the Book of the
> Covenant, and read in the hearing of the people; and they said:
> All that the LORD has spoken will we do and be obedient. And
> Moses took the blood and sprinkled it on the people, and said,

Behold the blood of the covenant which the LORD has made with you in accordance with all these words. (Exod 24:1–8)

Differences

The legally significant differences between this Mosaic covenant and the covenant which God made with Abram and his seed are at once obvious and very striking.

First, in the covenant with Abram, God spoke to Abram direct; in this Mosaic covenant, a mediator was appointed between the two parties, between God on the one hand and the people on the other (see Paul's comment in Gal 3:19–20).

Secondly, in this Mosaic covenant, the mediator was given God's demands and relayed them to the people. First he recited them orally, and the people responded: 'All the words which the LORD has spoken will we do' (Exod 24:3). Then the mediator wrote all God's demands in a book, and read them from the book in the hearing of the people (Exod 24:4, 7). There was to be no uncertainty in the minds of the people about what they were now undertaking and promising to do, and the conditions they were binding themselves to fulfil. And once more the people responded: 'All that the LORD has spoken will we do and be obedient' (Exod 24:7). God had already stated what he for his part would do if they kept his covenant:

> Now therefore, if you will obey my voice indeed, and keep my covenant, then shall you be a peculiar treasure unto me from among all peoples: for all the earth is mine. And you shall be unto me a kingdom of priests, and a holy nation. These are the words which thou shalt speak unto the children of Israel. (Exod 19:5–6)

Now, at the enactment of the covenant, the people were being told the conditions which they for their part must fulfil. Beyond all doubt it was a two-party covenant.

Finally, to indicate that they were an active contracting party in the making of this covenant, the people as well as God's altar were ceremonially sprinkled with the blood of the covenant sacrifices. In other words, this Mosaic covenant was not a one-party, unconditional promise on God's part, as his covenant with Abram was. It was a two-party conditional contract according to which enjoyment of its benefits explicitly depended on Israel's carrying out all the conditions to which they solemnly bound themselves first by their promises and then by being sprinkled with the blood of the covenant sacrifices.

Lasting conditions and consequences

Forty years later when, under Joshua, the Israelites were on the brink of entering the promised land for the first time, Moses explicitly reminded them that their entry depended on their keeping the commands of the Horeb–Sinai covenant:

> All the commandments which I command thee this day shall you observe to do, that you may live, and multiply, and go in and possess the land which the LORD promised on oath to your ancestors. (Deut 8:1)

Similarly he warned them that, after they entered the promised land, their continuing to possess and enjoy it would likewise depend on their full and faithful obedience to God's laws. Persistent disobedience would forfeit possession of the land.

> But it shall come to pass, if thou wilt not hearken unto the voice of the LORD thy God, to observe to do all his commandments and his statutes which I command thee this day, that all these curses shall come upon thee and overtake thee . . . . and thou shalt be plucked from off the land whither thou goest in to possess it. And the LORD shall scatter thee among all peoples, from the one end of the earth even unto the other end of the earth. . . . These are the words of the covenant which the LORD commanded Moses to make with the children of Israel in the land of Moab, beside the covenant which he made with them in Horeb. (Deut 28:15, 63–64; 29:1)

Certainly, then, under the Sinai–Horeb–Moab covenant Israel's possession of the promised land depended on their meeting and fulfilling certain conditions; and Israel's subsequent history has shown that these were no idle conditions.

An incomplete fulfilment

But now we encounter a very significant thing about Israel's entry into the promised land under the terms of the Sinai covenant: neither God nor Moses supposed, expected, or stated that it would prove to be the complete and final fulfilment of the unconditional promise made by God in his covenant with Abram. Far from it. Listen to Moses addressing the Israelites even before they entered the land:

> When . . . you shall have been long in the land, and shall corrupt yourselves, and make a graven image in the form of anything, and shall do that which is evil in the sight of the LORD thy God, to provoke him to anger: I call heaven and earth to witness against you this day, that you shall soon utterly perish from off the land whereunto you go over Jordan to possess it; you shall not prolong your days upon it, but shall utterly be destroyed. And the LORD shall scatter you among the peoples, and you shall be left few in number among the nations, whither the LORD shall lead you away. (Deut 4:25–27)

And there was no doubt that Israel would break the covenant and thus forfeit possession of the land:

> And the LORD said to Moses, Behold, thou shalt sleep with thy fathers; and this people will rise up and go a whoring after the strange gods of the land . . . and will forsake me and break my covenant . . . then my anger shall be kindled against them in that day. . . . (Deut 31:16–17)

And Moses added:

> *For I know that after my death you* will utterly corrupt yourselves, and turn aside from the way which I have commanded you; and evil will befall you in the latter days. . . . (Deut 31:29)

The historical books of the Old Testament tell us how literally and painfully these prophecies came true. In spite of the warnings of their prophets, the ten tribes of Israel persisted in idolatry and evil; and God allowed, indeed sent, the Assyrians to remove them from the land.

Subsequently, for similar reasons, God allowed Nebuchadnezzar to deport the remaining two tribes to Babylon. So much then for

Israel's possession of the promised land under the terms and conditions of the Sinai covenant.

But perhaps we are in danger of overlooking another significant feature of Israel's experience of being under the old covenant of the law. Simultaneously with his prophecies of their future apostasy and their consequent banishment from the land, Moses indicated that if they repented God would restore them to the promised land.

> And it shall come to pass, when all these things are come upon thee, the blessing and the curse, which I have set before thee, and thou shalt call them to mind among all the nations, whither the Lord thy God has driven thee, and thou shalt return unto the Lord thy God, and shalt obey his voice according to all that I command thee this day, thou and thy children, with all thine heart, and with all thy soul; that then the Lord thy God will turn thy captivity, and have compassion on thee, and will return and gather thee from all the peoples, whither the Lord thy God has scattered thee. If any of thine outcasts be in the uttermost parts of heaven, from thence will the Lord thy God gather thee, and from thence will he fetch thee; and the Lord thy God will bring thee into the land which thy fathers possessed, and thou shalt possess it. . . . (Deut 30:1–5)

Such a restoration actually happened when some Jews, at least, encouraged by prophets like Jeremiah and Daniel, and with the permission of the emperor, Cyrus, returned from exile in Babylon, and rebuilt the temple and the walls of Jerusalem. We have no need to belittle their spiritual achievements during the following centuries; but the fact remains that they were still under the terms of the old covenant, and their possession of the land proved not to be either complete or permanent. Eventually, the nation officially rejected their Messiah, and, as a consequence, God allowed them to be led captive once more into all the nations, and Jerusalem to be 'trodden down by the Gentiles until the times of the Gentiles be fulfilled' (see Luke 21:24).

After nearly two thousand years a minority of worldwide Jewry has returned and now occupies a part of the promised land. Jerusalem again is their capital city; but their hold on it is precarious indeed (see Zech 14:1–2).

What we conclude

In all the centuries from Abram until now, only a minority of Israelites has ever fully possessed the promised land; and certainly their possession, such as it has been, has never proved permanent. We may well ask what real hope is there that the original promise will ever be fully and permanently fulfilled? Paul, we imagine, would reply: None . . . so long as Israel lives under the law of Sinai, and less still if they live in disregard of it.

But it is time we went back to Paul to see on what ground he assures us that God's original, unconditional promise to Abram and his seed still stands, and shall most certainly be finally and completely fulfilled.

Paul's interpretation of the term 'seed' in God's covenant with Abram

Possible meanings of the word 'seed'

The Hebrew word for *seed*, like the English words *offspring* and *progeny*, when used to signify someone's descendants, can function in several ways.

It can refer to one particular individual. So Isaac was Abram's seed. An only child can be described as the offspring of its parents. So any one descendant of Abram's at any time in history could be called Abram's seed.

It can act as a collective noun. So Abram's seed, said God, would be as numerous as the stars (Gen 15:5).

It can refer to a subgroup. This could be any subgroup within the vast total of Abram's seed, whether large or small, at any time in history.

It can be used with moral and spiritual connotations. In this case 'Abram's seed' would mean not necessarily all those physically descended from Abram, but those who show the same attitude of faith in God as Abram did. So Isaiah describes some of Abram's physical descendants as being 'the seed of the adulterer and the whore' and a 'seed of falsehood' (Isa 57:3–4). Similarly, Christ told some of his fellow-Jews that he knew they were Abram's seed physically, but that if they were really Abram's children, they would do the works of Abram. Their deeds, however, showed them to be children of the devil (John 8:37–44).

A particular primary meaning

Paul's interpretation of the term *seed* is that it refers to Christ personally:

> Now to Abram were the promises spoken, and to his seed. He says not, And to seeds, as of many; but as of one, And to thy seed, which is Christ. (Gal 3:16)

Paul insists, then, that in the first instance the term should be interpreted as referring to one particular historical individual, namely Christ. Now Paul had not available to him modern, precise, grammatical and linguistic terminology such as we use nowadays. He therefore expresses himself in a way that to us may seem quaint:

> He [God] says not 'to his seeds as of many, but to his seed as of one'. (3:16, literal translation)

Now in fact the Hebrew word for seed is not normally used in the plural (seeds) in any case. What Paul actually means, however, by saying 'not to his seeds as of many', is that the word 'seed' at this point is not intended as a collective noun referring to a plurality of individual people. It is being used as a singular referring to one particular individual, that is, the historical person, Christ. And Paul further makes this clear when he remarks 'it (the law) was added because of transgressions until the seed should come to whom the promise has been made' (3:19), that is, until the man Christ Jesus should enter our world at his first coming. God's promise, then, to give the land to Abram's seed, meant that he would one day give it to Christ. That being so, there would never be any possibility that the promise would be cancelled or unfulfilled.

A particular secondary meaning

Paul's interpretation of the term *seed* is that it refers in the second place to a unity composed of Christ and his believing people:

> For as many of you as were baptised into Christ did put on Christ. There is neither Jew nor Greek, there is neither slave nor free, there is neither male nor female; for you are all one in Christ Jesus. And if you are Christ's [or, of Christ], then you are Abram's seed, heirs according to promise. (Gal 3:27–29)

In other words, all who have put their faith in Christ are viewed by God as being 'in Christ'. This is their legal position. They have been incorporated into Christ. To use another figure of speech they have 'put on Christ', as a person might put on a robe that covers him completely and hides all other distinctions, such as differences in race, social position or sex. Since Christ, then, is Abram's seed as denoted by God's covenant with Abram, all who are 'in Christ' are thereby likewise Abram's seed, and heirs with Christ of the promise of that covenant.

To put it yet another way: God's covenant with Abram was one of the 'covenants of promise' that God had made with Abram's descendants. In Old Testament times Gentiles were 'strangers from these covenants of promise'. But now Gentiles who put their faith in Christ are no longer strangers but 'fellow heirs . . . of the promise in Christ Jesus through the gospel' (Eph 2:11–12; 3:6).

Not an arbitrary meaning

Paul's assertion that the seed is Christ is neither far-fetched nor arbitrary. There is no denying that the man, Christ Jesus, was personally the seed of Abram. Simply as a man and a Jew, he was 'an heir of the promise' every bit as much as Isaac and Jacob (Heb 11:9) or any other Jew.

But Christ was more than merely a man and a Jew. He was the Son of God, the Son of Man, the seed of the woman (Gen 3:15), the Son of Abraham, of the seed of David. In a parable, spoken to the religious authorities who were about to engineer his execution, he likened Israel to a vineyard. God was its planter and owner. Christ himself was the owner's beloved Son, and therefore heir to the inheritance of the vineyard (Luke 20:13–15). 'God has appointed him heir of all things', says Heb 1:2. Certainly he, then, if anyone, had the title-deeds to the inheritance promised to Abram and his seed.

But when he came to earth, he was not given possession of the land of promise. 'The Son of Man had not where to lay his head' (Matt 8:20). 'He was in the world, and the world was made by him, and the world did not recognise him. He came to what were his own things, but those who were his own people [i.e. nationally and physically] did not receive him' (John 1:10–11); and as a young man of thirty-three, he was violently removed from the land by crucifixion, death and burial.

But God raised him from the dead, and he now sits at the right hand of God. One day God, the Father, will invite him to:

> Ask of me and I will give thee the nations for thine inheritance, and the uttermost parts of the earth for thy possession. Thou shalt break them with a rod of iron; thou shalt dash them in pieces like a potter's vessel. (Ps 2:8–9 RV; cf. the quotation at Acts 4:25–27; Rev 19:15)

And when shall that be? According to the New Testament, at Christ's second coming. He shall then come with power and great glory to execute the judgments of God, not simply on corrupt Amorite society (as Joshua did when Abram's seed returned from Egypt to Canaan; see the preamble, Gen 15:16, and the book of Joshua), but on the whole world (see Luke 21:25–28; 2 Thess 1:6–12). He shall take possession of the whole planet; not simply the land of Canaan by itself without the rest of the earth; nor yet, of course, the whole earth without the land of Canaan.

Moreover, we are told that at Christ's second coming those who are Christ's—and therefore Abram's seed—will be raised from the dead, and those still alive physically shall be changed (1 Cor 15:23, 51–52). Together they shall share with Christ in the promised inheritance (cf. Rom 8:17).

The plain statements of the New Testament, then, about Christ's identity, his first coming, and what he will do at his second coming, indicate that Christ will in fact inherit what God covenanted to give to Abram and his seed. Christ is that seed.

A meaning with great significance

The interpretation that the seed is Christ is the only interpretation that gives Abram, Isaac, Jacob and Joseph (and thousands of their believing descendants) any hope whatever of actually possessing the inheritance that God promised to them. Genesis 15:7, 18 explicitly says that God promised to give the land to Abram and his seed. Immediately the covenant was enacted, therefore, they held the title deeds, so to speak, to the land. They were 'heirs of the promise', as the New Testament puts it (Heb 11:9). The land legally belonged to them; but they never gained actual possession of it. Abram lived 'as an alien in the land of promise *as if the land did not belong to him*; and so did Isaac and Jacob' (11:9).

But this should not surprise us. The preamble to the very covenant by which God guaranteed to give the land to Abram and his seed informed Abram that none of his descendants for the next four hundred years would gain actual possession of it (Gen 15:13). Eminent men and women of faith, like Joseph, and Moses' mother, and even Moses himself, died even before Joshua initiated Israel's partial, and often suspended, possession of the land. If Christ was not the seed intended by the covenant, if there is no resurrection and thus no hope of sharing the inheritance with him, then they will never see the fulfilment of the covenant promise, never possess the land to which the covenant gave them the title deeds. If that were so — and thank God it isn't — as far as they personally were concerned, the covenant promise was no better than Marxism, which persuaded millions of people to struggle, suffer and die in hope of a utopia which they were told was sure to come, but which by definition they themselves would never live to see. The only way that Abram himself will experience the fulfilment of the promise is if the seed is, as the New Testament says it is, Christ. Seeing, however, it is Christ, the promise is sure to him and to all the seed (Rom 4:16).

The historical purpose and function of the Law in relation to the promised inheritance

Paul's interpretation of God's unconditional one-party covenant with Abram and his seed, as being different from, and unaffected by, the law from Sinai, inevitably raises two questions. He himself raises both of them in his Letter to the Galatians, and proceeds to answer them.

'Is the law then against the promises of God?'

A careless reader of Paul's interpretation might suppose that Paul disparaged the law and implied that God's imposition of the law on Israel for many long centuries was an unfortunate episode in Israel's history in which God was acting inconsistently with the promises he had earlier given to Abram. But Paul implies nothing of the kind. Far from it. He insists that the law had a positive strategic purpose to fulfil in Israel's history. It was the only way God knew of bringing Israel—and the world—to that state of heart in which they would be prepared to accept the promised inheritance on those terms on which alone he could give it to them.

Entitlement to the inheritance, and eventual enjoyment of the fulfilment of the promises was in God's mind always to be dependent on people's faith in Christ. Hence Paul describes the promise as 'the promise by faith in Christ Jesus' (Gal 3:22). Entitlement and enjoyment, therefore, could be given only 'to those who believe' (3:22).

But what do 'faith in Christ Jesus' and 'believing' mean in this context? For Paul they mean abandoning faith in oneself and in human meritorious achievement, and putting one's faith solely in Christ. But to bring people to the position where they are willing to do that, is, curiously enough, nowhere near so easy as might first appear. Hence God's imposition of the law on Israel throughout the long centuries was in order to prepare them to adopt the right attitude to the promised seed when he came. The law was designed to have particular effects.

First, according to Galatians 3:19, it made people more clearly aware of what was right and what was wrong by explicitly declaring God's standards. One cannot transgress a law which has never been laid down. A man may drive at too great a speed through a built-up area; but if the authorities have not explicitly passed a law setting the speed limit, the man cannot be accused of breaking that law. The existence of law, on the other hand, makes him aware that what hitherto he thought was an acceptable speed, is in fact dangerous and illegal.

Moreover, the law of God made people aware of the gravity of sin by the penalties it demanded. It certainly taught them that sin would destroy the enjoyment of the inheritance; and thus the law tended to restrain transgression.

More seriously still, it exposed the fact that some Israelites—all too many at times—were not, like Abram, true believers in God, but rebels and apostates, who committed, or connived at, grievous social injustice, abandoned allegiance to the one true God and went over to the practice of idolatry (see the Old Testament historical books and the Prophets).

On the other hand, there are some things the Law was not designed to do. According to Galatians 3:20–21, the law was not, and is not, against the promises of God. Its aim has never been to cancel the promises made by God to his believing people who followed in the steps of Abram's faith (see Rom 4:12). But it deliberately made them increasingly aware that however sincerely and strenuously they strove to keep God's law, they invariably fell short, and deserved its penalties. To use Paul's vivid phraseology: it 'imprisoned everything under sin' so that they might come to see that their only hope of being justified was not through their effort to keep the law, but through faith in Christ, as Redeemer and Saviour. Until Christ came, therefore, and the gospel of justification by faith, on the basis of his atoning sacrifice, was fully proclaimed, the law acted like the slave in a Roman household who was responsible to see to it that the boys behaved, and to discipline and punish them if they didn't.[6]

---

6 In Paul's Greek the word for this slave is παιδαγωγός (paidagōgos); but it did not mean, as its equivalent, 'pedagogue', means nowadays, a teacher, but simply a child-minder.

Furthermore, according to Galatians 3:21 and 4:1–7, the law was not designed to give life. Paul is careful to stress that he is not disparaging the law; he is simply pointing out its essential inability: it could not give life. 'If', says he, 'a law had been given that could give life, then righteousness would indeed be by the law' (Gal 3:21). But 'giving life' is something that the law cannot do, and never was intended to do. It can tell us how we ought to live; it cannot impart to us spiritual life that possesses the nature and power to live as we should. Only the gift of the Spirit of God through faith in Christ Jesus can do that.

'What then is the law?'

The law, Paul answers, had a very positive and important, though temporary, role to play during the period of Israel's spiritual childhood and teenage years: 'It was added to warn against and to restrain transgressions *until* the seed should come to whom the promise had been made' (Gal 3:19), that is, until the incarnation of the Son of God.

Paul is not disparaging Israelites: he was one himself (Rom 11:1). Still less is he saying that no Israelite was ever forgiven, or justified, before Jesus was born, or that no Jew acted as an inspired prophet of God until the New Testament was written. That would be nonsense. But he is saying that until Christ came, died as the Lamb of God—the one perfect sacrifice for sins—rose again, ascended, received the promise of the Father and baptised his people in the Holy Spirit, Israel had not, and could not, become fully grown up sons of God. They were still spiritually children or teenagers. And for that reason God kept them temporally under the law as being the most appropriate form of spiritual education for the time being.

To illustrate what he means Paul uses an analogy (Gal 4:1–7). In his day a child in a large patrician Roman family would, as son of his father, be heir to his father's estate. But so long as he was not an adult, he would scarcely be allowed to touch, and certainly not to administer, the estate. The father would place him under guardians and tutors, who would treat him little differently from a slave—all to prepare him for the time when he was grown up enough to share the running of the estate with his father.

So, argues Paul, even believing Israelites were placed by God under the law during the centuries of their spiritual childhood, until the time came in history when God sent forth his Son, born of a woman, and born under the law himself, so that as their representative he might redeem those who were under the law, and pay the penalty for their transgressions of that law. With that the way was open for God to put within their hearts the very Spirit of his Son and so to give them the life and status of full-grown sons of God, destined to share with God's Son the inheritance which God covenanted to give to Abram and his seed, and infinitely more beside.

Christ the mediator and guarantor of the new covenant

We cannot conclude this study of the New Testament's interpretation of Old Testament covenants without considering the new covenant of which Christ himself is the mediator (Heb 8:6; 9:15; 12:24) and guarantor (Heb 7:22).

The enactment of a new covenant

The idea that God would one day make a new covenant with the house of Israel and with the house of Judah was not an invention of the early Christians. Sometime between the seventh and sixth centuries bc God had already announced through Jeremiah that he would one day establish such a new covenant, and had spelled out what its terms would be (Jer 31:31–34). It was the establishment of this new covenant that our Lord announced when in the Upper Room he took a cup of wine, and handing it to his disciples said: 'This cup is the new covenant in my blood, which is poured out for you' (Luke 22:20).

The covenants we have so far studied in the Old Testament—the covenant with Abram and his seed (Gen 15), the covenant with Israel at Sinai (Exod 24), and the covenant made by the princes and people (Jer 34)—were all signed, sealed and settled, so to speak, and thus established by law, when the covenant sacrifices were offered and the associated ceremonies were carried out. So the new covenant: it was established when Christ offered himself as the covenant-sacrifice on the cross.

The new covenant *'has been* enacted' (Heb 8:6, written about AD 64), it has already been legally established. When 'all Israel', that is, Israel as a whole, turns to the Lord and is saved (Rom 11:25–27), then Israel and Judah will certainly come into the benefit of the new covenant. But the new covenant itself has long since been in force: it was enacted at Calvary. The Jewish believers to whom the Letter to the Hebrews was written were assured on the grounds of the new covenant that their sins had been blotted out from God's record and would never be brought up against them any more (Heb 10:14–18). And it was because the new covenant was now in place, that the old covenant, with its tabernacle, priesthood and sacrifices, was obsolete and ready to vanish away (Heb 8:13). Gentile believers had never been under the old covenant, and before their conversion to Christ were 'strangers to the covenants of promise'—the new covenant included. But now in Christ, they were told (Eph 2:12–22), they were no longer strangers and aliens. And from the very beginning of the Christian era both Jewish and Gentile believers were taught that every time they drank of the cup at the Lord's Supper, they were to remember that it was the new covenant in Christ's blood (1 Cor 11:25).

The superiority of the new covenant

The basic weakness of the old covenant was that it was a two-party covenant as we earlier saw. God set his laws before the people, and they for their part promised to keep them all. But they didn't keep them: 'they continued not in my covenant', says God (Heb 8:9; '. . . my covenant they broke', Jer 31:32). Their trouble was 'weakness through the flesh', as Paul puts it (Rom 8:3); they did not fulfil their promises, because they did not have the moral and spiritual power to do so.

The new covenant 'has been enacted upon better promises' (Heb 8:6). That is true for two reasons. In the first place the clauses of the new covenant, without exception, are all about what God promises to do. Nothing is said about what the people have to do, or promise to do. From first to last the new covenant's clauses specify what God himself undertakes to do (Jer 31:33–34; Heb 8:10–12).

God promises to implant his laws on the mind and to write them on the heart. And the New Testament elsewhere explains that God does this by imparting his life-giving, regenerating Spirit, who writes God's laws, not on tablets of stone, as at Sinai, but on tablets of human hearts (2 Cor 3:3), thus making it possible for believers to do what the law rightly requires (Rom 8:3–4).

The result will be, not merely a general awareness that there is a God, but a deep relationship with God, and a direct personal knowledge of God:

> And I will be to them a God, and they shall be my people. And they shall not teach everyone his fellow-citizen, and every person his brother, saying Know the Lord; for all shall know me from the least to the greatest of them. (Heb 8:10–11)

But then, what about their shortcomings and sins? God's promise is:

> I will be merciful to their iniquities, and their sins will I remember no more. (Heb 8:12)

Not only so. The fact that the new covenant has been enacted on better promises than Israel made at Sinai, is true for another reason also: the Lord Jesus is both the mediator and the guarantor of the new covenant.

Christ and the new covenant
He is its mediator (Heb 8:6; 9:15; 12:24) and is uniquely qualified to act as mediator. As both God and man, he can represent God to us human beings, and us human beings to God. He did that supremely at Calvary when he offered himself as the covenant sacrifice, thus making it possible for God justly to fulfil the third clause of the covenant: 'I will be merciful to their iniquities and their sins will I remember no more.'

He it is, also, that has 'declared the Father's name' to us, and has promised to continue doing so (John 17:6, 26) so that we can know the Father and see the light of the knowledge of God in the face of Jesus Christ. That makes, both for God and for us, a deep reality of personal relationship promised in the second clause of the new covenant: 'I will be to them a God, and they shall be my people.'

But Christ is not only the mediator of the new covenant: he is its guarantor. It is not left to us and to our puny efforts to achieve the fulfilment of the terms of the covenant. Christ has pledged himself, on our behalf, as guarantor that all the terms of the covenant shall be fulfilled. And because he is the guarantor, the Epistle to the Hebrews draws the conclusion: 'He is able to save to the uttermost those who draw near to God through him' (Heb 7:22, 25).

The New Testament insists that the old covenant, given at Sinai, and written on tablets of stone, was magnificently glorious. But it adds: 'What was glorious [then], has no glory now in comparison with the surpassing glory [of the new covenant]' (2 Cor 3:7–11).

CATEGORY THREE

Literary Devices

11

Quotations and Citations

In this and the following four chapters we shall consider seven key literary devices that the New Testament writers have used to appropriate the lessons of the Old Testament. The first and simplest of these devices is the quotation, or citation, of some law, principle, exhortation, promise, character or event. It will be enough for our purpose to list a few examples; for the matter is straightforward and requires little or no comment.

Laws

1. 'Honour your father and your mother', says Deuteronomy 5:16. 'Honour your father and your mother', says Ephesians 6:2, and points out that this is the first commandment in the Decalogue to have a promise attached to it; which it then proceeds to quote: 'that it may be well with you and that you may live long on the earth.'

2. 'You shall not tempt the Lord your God', says the Old Testament (Deut 6:16). 'You shall not tempt the Lord your God', said Christ, as he applied the law to himself in answer to the devil's temptation (Matt 4:7).

Principles

1. Habakkuk 2:4 lays down the principle 'The righteous shall live by his faith'; and this principle is quoted in the New Testament as being basic to salvation (e.g. Rom 1:17; Gal 3:11).

2. 'Was not Abraham our father justified by works, in that he offered up Isaac his son upon the altar? ... And ... was not also Rahab the harlot justified by works, in that she received the messengers, and sent them out another way?' So argues James in the New Testament (2:21–25) as he applies this same principle to his readers and demands that those who have been justified by faith, as Abraham was (2:23), should demonstrate the reality of their faith by their works.

Exhortations

1. 'My son, despise not the chastening of the LORD, neither be weary of his reproof; for whom the LORD loves he reproves, even as a father the son in whom he delights.' So said the ancient proverb (Prov 3:11–12); and the writer to the Hebrews gently chides his fellow Christians for seeming to have forgotten this Old Testament exhortation (Heb 12:5–6).

2. The psalmist's recipe for a long and good life (Ps 34:12–16) is repeated by the Apostle Peter verbatim:

> He that would love life, and see good days, let him refrain his tongue from evil, and his lips that they speak no guile; and let him turn away from evil and do good; let him seek peace and pursue it. For the eyes of the Lord are upon the righteous, and his ears unto their supplication; but the face of the Lord is upon them that do evil. (1 Pet 3:10–12)

Promises

1. 'I will not fail you, nor forsake you', said God to Joshua on the eve of Israel's entry into the promised land (Josh 1:5). Hebrews 13:5

repeats the promise; and millions of believers in all ages have found in it, as Joshua found, the necessary stimulus and strength for courageous achievement.

2. 'For, behold, I create new heavens and a new earth' (Isa 65:17). So ran God's promise in the Old Testament; and Peter, relying upon it, says, 'According to his promise we look for new heavens and a new earth' (2 Pet 3:13).

Characters

1. 'You have heard of the endurance of Job, and have seen the end of the Lord, how that the Lord is full of pity, and merciful', says James (5:11), as he refers not only to the whole book of Job, but in particular to its conclusion.

2. 'Remember Lot's wife', warned Christ, and expected his hearers to know how her story was relevant to the future situation which he was predicting (Luke 17:32).

3. 'The time will fail me if I tell of Gideon, Barak, Samson, Jephthah; of David and Samuel . . .' (Heb 11:32). All of them, according to the writer to the Hebrews, achieved great exploits by faith — though he leaves us to fill in the precise details from our knowledge of the Old Testament.

Events

1. 'No prophet is acceptable in his own country', remarked Christ. 'But of a truth I say unto you, There were many widows in Israel in the days of Elijah, when the heaven was shut up three years and six months, when there came a great famine over all the land; and unto none of them was Elijah sent, but only to Zarephath, in the land of Sidon, unto a woman that was a widow. And there were many lepers in Israel in the time of Elisha the prophet; and none of them was cleansed, but only Naaman the Syrian' (Luke 4:24–27).

2. Particularly solemn and instructive are the two historical cases that Christ cites:

The men of Nineveh shall stand up in the judgment with this generation, and shall condemn it: for they repented at the preaching
of Jonah; and, behold, a greater than Jonah is here. The queen of
the South shall rise up in the judgment with this generation, and
shall condemn it: for she came from the ends of the earth to hear
the wisdom of Solomon; and behold, a greater than Solomon is
here. (Matt 12:41–42)

Christ is here describing what shall happen at the final judgment
(at which, of course, he will be the judge: see John 5:22–23), when
the case of his contemporaries is called. The point at issue will be
whether there was enough evidence available to his contemporaries
to convince them beyond all reasonable doubt that Jesus was the
Christ, the Son of God and Saviour of the world, and to lead them to
repent and to put their faith in him. To prove that the evidence available to them was more than enough—if only they had been willing
to consider it seriously—the 'prosecution' will call two witnesses.

First, the men of Nineveh. The only evidence they had, that
God was summoning them to repent, was the sign and the preaching of the prophet Jonah; yet they repented. Christ's contemporaries, by contrast, heard the preaching—and would eventually hear
of the resurrection—of one infinitely greater than Jonah. But so
determined were they not to believe him, that when they could
not deny the supernatural power of his miracles, they attributed it
to Satan, thus calling black what in every other circumstance they
would have called white (Matt 12:22–37).

The second witness called by the 'prosecution' will be the
queen of the South. The only evidence she had in her home country was the report that in a distant land there was a king endowed
with exceptional, God-given wisdom. But such was her determination to find true wisdom, that she travelled all the long distance to
hear the wisdom of Solomon. Christ's contemporaries, by contrast,
with the wisdom of God incarnate in their very midst, professed to
believe it was folly, and in the end could not be bothered to cross
the street in order to hear it.

At the final judgment, then, the witness of the men of Nineveh
and of the Queen of Sheba will remove from Christ's contemporaries

the only valid excuse they could have had for not believing, namely, that they did not have sufficient evidence (see John 15:22–25).[1]

A representative sample

This short list of straightforward quotations and citations from the Old Testament could be almost endlessly extended. But enough has been said to illustrate this simple device for appropriating the lessons of the Old Testament. We must now turn to other devices.

1 It goes without saying that Christ regarded both these Old Testament stories as historical. The book of Jonah, then, is not a religious novel. Fictitious characters out of novels cannot be called on to stand up in the court of the final judgment as witnesses for the prosecution!

12

Formal Comparisons, Similes and Metaphors

L ET'S START ONCE more with the obvious.

Formal comparisons

The New Testament often formally compares, or contrasts, situations, events and people with situations, events and people described in the Old. Consider the following examples:

> He [Jesus] was faithful to the one who appointed him, *just as* Moses was faithful in all God's house. (Heb 3:2, citing God's explicit commendation of Moses' faithfulness from Num 12:7)

> *As it was* in the days of Noah, *so also* will it be in the days of the Son of Man. (Luke 17:26)

> We should love one another, *not as* Cain was of the evil one and murdered his brother. (1 John 3:11–12)

Such comparisons are so obvious and so numerous that we need not stay longer over the matter, except to notice that the details of the comparison, especially on the Old Testament side, are not always spelled out. It is assumed that the reader (or hearer) will know the Old Testament story well enough to see the detailed parallels for himself.

In the conversation with Nicodemus

It is so, for instance, with the famous comparison between our Lord's being lifted up on the cross, and Moses' lifting up of the serpent in the desert:

> As Moses lifted up the serpent in the desert, so the Son of Man must be lifted up, that everyone who believes in him may have eternal life. (John 3:14–15)

Of course, if we wanted to be pedantic, we could insist that the only point of comparison that is explicitly made, is between the bare fact that Moses lifted up a serpent and the fact that the Son of Man had to be lifted up. And we could further argue that since neither the purpose for which Moses lifted up the serpent, nor the result of his lifting it up, is mentioned in John's text, we are not entitled to go searching around in the details of the Mosaic story in the Old Testament to find these other points of comparison.

To argue like that would be not only pedantic but misguided. It would reduce the comparison to a mere formal similarity (two liftings up) of no help whatever either to Nicodemus or to us in understanding why it was necessary for the Son of Man to be lifted up in order for the believer in him to have eternal life. In other words, the comparison would be interpretationally valueless; and a hermeneutic that drove us to this conclusion would be absurdly reductionist.

If, on the other hand, we are allowed to compare the unmentioned (i.e. in John's text) detail of the serpent story with the detail of our Lord's conversation with Nicodemus, the similarities listed in Table 2 appear.

A minimum of thought will then show that the points illustrated by this comparison were the very points that Nicodemus, in his conversation with Christ, needed to have explained and confirmed.

A well-chosen picture

Nicodemus had begun by being amazed at our Lord's insistence that people must be born from above, born of water and of the

	NUMBERS 21:4–9	JOHN 3:14–16
1.	In consequence of sin against God the Israelites were bitten by serpents and were perishing.	Men and women need to be saved from perishing.
2.	To save the people from perishing Moses, at God's command, lifted up a bronze serpent on a pole.	To save people from perishing the Son of Man must be lifted up.
3.	People who wished to be saved were told to look to the serpent.	People who wish to be saved are told to believe on the Son of Man.
4.	Those who so looked 'lived'.	Those who believe receive eternal life.

Table 2. Comparison of serpent story in Numbers 21 and John 3

Spirit, in order to see and enter the kingdom of God. He should not have been amazed; as the leading teacher in Israel (John 3:10) he should have remembered that Israel's rebirth, promised through Ezekiel, was to be brought about by water (Ezek 36:25) and the Spirit (37:14). When presently he moved on to ask, 'How can these things come about?' (John 3:9), the answer could have been 'through faith in the crucified Son of Man'. Such bold and direct terms, however, might well have both mystified him and provoked his scepticism: what strange ideas were these? who was this Son of Man? and why had he to be crucified? and what had his being crucified got to do with people's receiving eternal life, if only they believed on him?

Christ mercifully and wisely forestalled his difficulties by referring to an Old Testament (and, for Nicodemus, an inspired and authoritative) passage that told of Moses' lifting up the serpent in the desert; and to facilitate the comparison Christ deliberately referred to his coming death not as a crucifixion, but as a lifting up. For though Moses' serpent had not been crucified, it had been lifted up; and so would the Son of Man be. Already Nicodemus might have begun to perceive that it was not such a strange idea after all that eternal life should be given to those who believed on the Son of Man lifted up; for according to the story in Numbers 21:4–9 the purpose of Moses' lifting up of a bronze serpent on a pole was that everyone who had been bitten by a serpent and was in danger of perishing, might live, that is, recover, be cured, receive new life, by looking to the bronze serpent on its pole.

That might then have whetted Nicodemus' curiosity: why were the people in Moses' day in danger of perishing in the first place? But as an Old Testament scholar he would have known the story off by heart and have had only to recall it. The Israelites were bitten by serpents and were perishing as a punishment from God because of their sin (Num 21:6). But the very fact that Christ had cited this incident to Nicodemus carried the implication that Nicodemus, in spite of his biblical and theological learning, and his status as senior rabbi (John 3:10), was equally a sinner as his ancestors, standing under the wrath of God, and needing to be saved by the Son of Man from perishing eternally.

In John's record of the conversation this implication remains unspoken; and in that we see Christ's grace, wisdom and tact. Nicodemus, as a theologian, would have freely admitted that he, along with all other men, was a sinner. But to tell an eminently respected rabbi point-blank to his face that he was a helpless sinner in dire danger of perishing unless he believed in a crucified Saviour, might not have been the best way of getting that true but shocking fact home to his heart. It would be kinder, and more effective, to let this implication gradually sink in, as he went away and privately pondered the meaning of the Old Testament story.

If he did that, the story would also illustrate another vital point. 'The Son of man must be lifted up', said Christ, 'that whoever *believes* may in him have eternal life' (John 3:15). Then, what did it mean to believe? And why was believing in this Son of Man necessary?

When our Lord had talked of the necessity of being born of the Spirit, Nicodemus had professed not to understand: 'How can these things come about?' he had asked (3:9). But failure to understand was not his only problem. More fundamental was his and his contemporaries' failure to believe. 'If I have told you earthly things and you do not believe', said Christ, 'how will you believe, if I tell you heavenly things?' (3:12). And belief in him and his testimony was, in this context, absolutely indispensable, as Christ went on to explain, and that for the following reason: he had sole and exclusive knowledge of these heavenly things. No mere man had ever ascended into heaven, and then come down again to tell mankind of these heavenly realities. By contrast Christ, the Son of Man, who was, and never ceased to be, in perfect intimacy with the Father, had come down to earth for that very purpose. If Nicodemus was ever to know these things, he would know them through believing Christ's testimony. If he never came to believe him, he would never know them.

So what did it mean to believe? And what did you have to believe? And how did you get the necessary faith? In the serpent on the pole story, the counterpart to *believing* is *looking*: 'and it came to pass that if a serpent had bitten any man, when he looked unto the serpent, he lived' (Num 21:9). The analogy is both psychologically and spiritually helpful. It was no casual, disinterested or merely academic look that the dying men and women in the desert took in the direction of the serpent. At God's command they looked to the bronze serpent that God had had set up; and with his assurance that if they looked they would live (21:8), they looked to it, away from all else, as their only hope of salvation. By analogy, then, Nicodemus would perceive what was meant by 'believing on the Son of Man lifted up': it meant recognising that the Son of Man lifted up was God's provision for his salvation; and then, turning away from all other means of salvation, and putting his faith for eternal life solely in the Son of Man (cf. the later explanations, 1 Cor 1:23–25; Gal 6:14).

Even so, when the conversation ended that night, Nicodemus may well have been left wondering what exactly this 'lifting up of the Son of Man' would entail, and why it was necessary for his salvation. Certainly, right at the end of our Lord's public ministry the Jerusalem populace still found the term perplexing: 'We have heard out of the law', they said, 'that the Christ abides for ever. How sayest thou, The Son of Man must be lifted up? Who is this

Son of Man?' (John 12:34). But Nicodemus eventually witnessed the crucifixion, and boldly took his stand for Christ, and against the Sanhedrin, by helping to bury Christ. Doubtless he came, like all the other disciples, to understand the significance of the cross: 'Him who knew no sin, God made to be sin on our behalf, that we might become the righteousness of God in Him' (2 Cor 5:21). And he doubtless came to understand Christ's being lifted up in its further sense of Christ's resurrection and exaltation to God's right hand.

The meaning in the detail

Now for us to spend all this time and effort, proving what millions of Christians down the centuries have regarded as self-evident, may well seem perverse, and certainly tedious. But we are contending for the principle that when the New Testament refers to an Old Testament story, psalm, or prophecy, full understanding of the point and purpose of the reference may sometimes require us to recall much more detail from the Old Testament passage than the New Testament actually mentions. Seeing this principle at work in this simple and well-known instance will later help us to see it at work in more complicated contexts.

Similes

Unlike formal comparisons, similes need not employ the full 'as a.b.c., even so x.y.z.' construction; they can be introduced by a simple 'as' or 'like'.

Such a simile is used by Peter: '. . . you were redeemed, not with corruptible things, with silver or gold . . . but with the precious blood of Christ' (1 Pet 1:18–19). And there he could easily have ended his statement. It makes excellent sense as it stands, and adequately stresses the cost of our redemption by contrasting the *blood* of Christ with *silver* and *gold*, and the *precious* blood of Christ, with *corruptible* silver and gold. But he does not end his statement there: he adds a simile, '. . . the precious blood of Christ *as of a lamb without blemish and without spot*' (1:19).

Why, then, the simile? It is not simply emphasizing the character of Christ—he was as innocent, guileless and harmless as a lamb—though that is perfectly true, and is the point which Isa 53:7 and 1 Pet 2:21–23 make. It is talking of redemption by blood as of a lamb; and that means surely that it is a reference to some part of the Old Testament's sacrificial system. All lambs offered in sacrifice under that system had to be without blemish, whatever type of sacrifice it was. But if it was a question of redemption, then in that connection the sacrifice par excellence was the Passover lamb, by the blood of which the Israelites were redeemed from the judgment of God, and set free from slavery in Egypt (see Exod 12).

That this was Peter's intended allusion is further indicated by the other evocations of the Passover story which he introduces into this first chapter of his epistle.

The promised inheritance
God's purpose in redeeming Israel out of Egypt was, we remember, so that he could eventually bring them into the inheritance, flowing with milk and honey, which he had sworn to their fathers to give them for their possession (Deut 1:8 et passim). 'And God', says Peter, 'has begotten us [Christians] again unto a living hope . . . unto an inheritance incorruptible, and undefiled, and that fades not away, reserved in heaven for you' (1 Pet 1:3–4).

The covenant at Sinai
Delivered from Egypt, Israel, on their way to their inheritance, arrived at Sinai. There God made a covenant with them, and they solemnly promised to obey its terms:

> And he [Moses] took the book of the covenant, and read it in the audience of the people: and they said, All that the LORD has spoken will we do, and be obedient. And Moses took the blood, and sprinkled it on the people, and said, Behold the blood of the covenant, which the LORD has made with you concerning all these words. (Exod 24:7–8)

Evoking this very scene and using its symbolic terms, Peter

addresses his fellow-Christians:

> Peter . . . to the elect . . . according to the foreknowledge of God
> the Father, in sanctification of the Spirit unto obedience and
> sprinkling of the blood of Jesus Christ. . . . (1 Pet 1:1–2)

Peter, then, we conclude, is in this chapter deliberately evoking Israel's redemption by blood, the inheritance that was the goal of their desert journey, and the obedience to which they pledged themselves en route. Why? Well, not so that he can show off his detailed knowledge of the Old Testament, but because he believes that the whole story of Israel's redemption was a divinely arranged foreshadowing of our redemption through Christ. He uses that foreshadowing, therefore, as a vivid, God-given illustration to help us grasp with our imagination the doctrine of redemption and its consequences which the New Testament presents to our intellect. We are redeemed by the blood of Christ; we are journeying towards our eternal inheritance; and we have been set free, not to please ourselves, but to live a life of obedience to our Redeemer, by whose blood we have been sprinkled.

But he does more than that; for at 1 Peter 1:13 he uses another detail from the Passover story to press home upon his readers their need to engage in rigorous thinking in order to work out the logical implications of their Christian hope.

But this time, he appropriates the Passover detail by means, not of a simile, but of a metaphor. So let us first remind ourselves of the difference between similes and metaphors.

Metaphors

Simile is when one thing, experience, or activity, is explicitly compared with another: 'fear held him like a chain'. Metaphor is when one thing, experience or activity, instead of being compared to another, is described directly in terms of another: 'the government has a *stranglehold* on the opposition'. The term stranglehold is taken from the game of wrestling, in which one player can seize his opponent's body in such a way that the opponent cannot move without strangling himself. Used to describe a bout of wrestling, the term implies a physical contest, with literal arms laid round literal throats. But when we say 'the government has a stranglehold on the opposition', we are not talking of a physical contest, in which literal hands are laid on literal bodies. We are talking of a contest of a different kind, where no physical contact takes place. And yet we can describe it in terms taken from physical wrestling, because this contest also is in its way a kind of wrestling. And because government tactics have placed the opposition in a position where it cannot move without damaging itself, this too can be spoken of as a kind of stranglehold.

Metaphor, then, is a very vivid way of conjuring up a picture in the mind. It uses a process in a realm already known to the reader, to help him or her to understand an analogous process going on in another realm. Nor is the use of metaphor confined to the literary and sophisticated. People of limited experience and vocabulary are inclined, if anything, to use more frequent and more vigorous metaphors than others do. When a countryman says of someone who has angered him, 'I will put the harrows over him', he may not know that he is using a metaphor; but he knows a lot about harrowing fields. And the only satisfactory way he can think of to describe the rough time he is going to give his enemy, is to speak of it as if it were the harrowing of a field.[1]

Peter's metaphor and its source

> Wherefore, *girding up the loins* of your mind, be sober and set your hope perfectly on the grace that is to be brought unto you at the revelation of Jesus Christ. (1 Pet 1:13)

Minds do not have loins! 'Girding up the loins of your mind', therefore, is obviously a metaphor, but its source may not be as obvious to us today as it was to Peter. Its general source arose from a practical necessity. It was customary in the ancient world, as it still is in

---

1 When the rest of us, who knowing little of agriculture, talk of a 'harrowing' experience, we are probably no longer aware that the word was originally a metaphor. To us 'harrowing' simply means 'distressing'. The metaphor, as they say, is dead.

many countries, for men to wear a strong belt round their loins, to help the lower part of the body to take the strain of heavy work or lifting. In the Middle East men customarily wore a long, robe-like outer garment. But when they engaged in rigorous work, or strode out on a serious journey, they would tuck up the bottom of their flowing garments into a belt so as not to impede their stride (for an example, see 1 Kgs 18:46). 'To gird up your loins', then, meant 'to prepare oneself for rigorous work or travel'.

The metaphor's particular source was a specific event when this practical necessity arose. On the night of the Exodus the members of each Israelite household had to roast their Passover lamb and eat it. But they were not allowed to eat it any way they pleased, for eating the roast Passover lamb was a highly significant part of their experience of redemption. The directive was:

> And thus shall you eat it: with your loins girded, your shoes on your feet, and your staff in your hand; and you shall eat it in haste: it is the LORD's Passover. (Exod 12:11)

Girded loins, shoes, and staff all proclaimed readiness to start at once on the journey out of Egypt, and to keep on journeying until they arrived at the promised land. And the directive insisted that you could not partake of the Passover lamb unless you were prepared and willing to journey. An Israelite who imagined that he could be protected from the destroying angel by the redeeming blood of the lamb, but then stay on in Egypt and not take the trouble to journey to the promised land, had seriously misunderstood the nature of God's redemptive plan. There were certainly three logically distinguishable parts to this plan: deliverance from Egypt, journey through the desert, and entry into the promised land. But none of these parts was optional. The three parts formed an indivisible whole. You willingly and deliberately took all three—or else none.

Peter's application of the metaphor

'Gird up the loins of your mind', says he; in other words, prepare to do some rigorous thinking. About what? About your Christian

hope and its detailed implications for your present attitudes and behaviour. 'Set your hope perfectly on the grace that is to be brought
unto you at the revelation of Jesus Christ' (1 Pet 1:13).

True Christian hope is not a vague, shallow, irresponsible thing:
it carries far-reaching practical implications; and we must think hard
and long in order to work out what these implications are, and then
rigorously apply them to our conduct.

If we have been redeemed by the precious blood of Christ, it is in
order that God may bring us at last into our heavenly inheritance, incorruptible, undefiled and fadeless. Meanwhile, life becomes a journey of moral and spiritual progress, in the course of which our faith
is tried and refined like gold so that it 'might be found unto praise
and glory and honour at the revelation of Jesus Christ' (1 Pet 1:5–7).

According to the Old Testament (Num 11:4–35), the Israelites
had not gone far on their journey towards their promised land,
when they allowed their lusts to divert them from their professed
goal and draw their hearts back to Egypt. Their record gives further
force to Peter's exhortation:

> . . . hope perfectly . . . as obedient children, not fashioning your-
> selves according to your former lusts in the time of your igno-
> rance, but like as he who called you is holy, be you yourselves
> also holy in all manner of living. (1 Pet 1:13–15)

The Apostle John says the same. In 1 John 3:2–3 he first reminds his fellow-believers that they are already children of God
and assures them that at Christ's second coming they shall be like
him. But then he states categorically as a fact: 'Every one who has
this hope set on him [Christ], purifies himself even as he [Christ]
is pure'. Any one who makes no effort to purify himself, and has
no intention of doing so now, just does not have the hope of being
like Christ hereafter.

Only think. Suppose you could enter a time machine, go back
in history, and arrive in ancient Egypt ten years after the depar-
ture of Moses and the Israelites for the promised land. Presently
you meet an Israelite still living in Egypt. Upon your inquiry, he
claims to have been redeemed by the blood of the Passover lamb,

and says that he really does hope to be in the promised land one day somehow. But for the present he has no intention of girding up his loins and journeying across the desert. He prefers to stay in Egypt. And suppose, in answer to your question, 'How, then, and by what means do you think you will eventually arrive at the promised land?' he replied: 'I don't know. I just don't think of such things'. What would you say?

13

Explicit Allusions

Yᴇᴛ ᴀɴᴏᴛʜᴇʀ ᴅᴇᴠɪᴄᴇ by which the New Testament draws on the riches of the Old Testament in order to illustrate its message is the use of explicit allusions. In their effect these allusions resemble formal comparisons and similes: they invite us to compare some person, or some situation, in the New Testament with a similar person or situation in the Old. But their literary form is different. A formal comparison will follow the scheme: 'as a.b.c. so x.y.z.'. A simile will use an 'as' or 'like': 'he swam like a fish', 'she was as sharp as a tack'. An allusion dispenses with these formal indicators, and speaks more directly.

So, for instance, in a letter addressed to the church at Thyatira, the risen Lord complains:

> Nevertheless, I have this against you: you tolerate that woman Jezebel, who calls herself a prophetess; and she teaches and seduces my servants to commit fornication, and to eat things sacrificed to idols. (Rev 2:20)

Allusions of this kind are easily understood, for we employ the same mode of expression in many modern languages. If we say of a man 'He's a modern Hitler' we mean that the man in question is a monstrous tyrant like Hitler was. If we say of someone else 'He's a quisling', we mean that he behaves like the Norwegian Vidkun Quisling, who collaborated with the Germans, and was rewarded by them by being placed as the puppet prime minister of Norway.

So when our Lord refers to some teacher or other in the church in Thyatira as 'that woman Jezebel', he is castigating that teacher for corrupting his, or her, fellow Christians in the same way as Jezebel, the wife of Ahab, king of Israel, corrupted her husband and the Israelites in general. She induced them to abandon the one true God, and to engage in the idolatrous worship of Baal (1 Kgs 18:13 – 19:2; 21:25–26).

Now the New Testament's explicit allusions to the Old Testament are easy to trace, for the simple reason that they explicitly refer to some person or situation; and even if that person or situation is one of the less well known persons or situations in the Old Testament, a good concordance can easily track it down.

On the other hand, when we have tracked down the person or situation in question, we may find that we still have considerable work to do in order to be sure that we are focussing in on precisely that feature to which the New Testament is alluding. In order to illustrate this device and the care needed when interpreting particular instances of it, let us consider Jude's triple allusion in verse eleven of his epistle.

> Woe unto them! They have gone in the way of Cain, and they have rushed unrestrainedly in the error of Balaam for hire, and they have perished in the rebellion of Korah. (Jude 11)

The first interpretative stage

Step one

We must first notice the kind of men to whom Jude is here referring and whom he characterises by these allusions to the Old Testament. These men, says Jude, have 'secretly slipped in' among the believers (v. 4). They pretend, then, to be genuine believers, but they are in fact bogus Christians; for no true believer 'secretly slips in' among the other believers, sailing in, to change the metaphor, under false colours.

Moreover, they advocate, both by their behaviour and their powerfully stated views, a complete perversion of the Christian gospel:

'they are godless men who change the grace of God into licence for immorality' (v. 4).

Worst of all, while professing to be Christians, they 'deny our only Master and Lord, Jesus Christ' (v. 4). It is little wonder, then, that, pretending to be shepherds of the Lord's people, they undermine their integrity and seek only their own personal pleasure and gain (vv. 12–13).

In sum they profess to be religious, indeed to be Christians; but their religion is utterly false.

Step two

Our next step might well be to notice the general appropriateness of Jude's allusions. Cain, Balaam and Korah were all three of them false *religious* men. We meet Cain (Gen 4) in the context of his offering God a sacrifice. We encounter Balaam (Num 22–24) in the course of his conducting a whole succession of sacrifices; and we watch Korah and his supporters perish in the very act of burning incense before God (Num 16).

Step three

We should now observe the features which differentiate these three men; for while they were all religious, and all were false, they were not all exactly the same.

They differed in the degree of their wickedness

Cain was bad enough. In the context of offering sacrifice to God, he murdered his brother. Grievous perversion of religion as that was, it must be said that, unlike the next two, Cain was only a layman.

Balaam was worse, for he was a professional prophet, who knowing God's truth, was prepared to go counter to God's will, and prostitute his prophetic office for the sake of monetary gain and social advancement.

Korah was worse still: for Balaam, when all was said and done, was only a pagan prophet. Korah was an ordained Levite—a kind of lesser priest—in the service of the tabernacle of the true God of Israel.

Jude's depiction of each man's sin is different
With Cain, it is the way which Cain took that Jude particularly and precisely mentions. He does not accuse the false teachers in the church of murdering their brothers like Cain murdered Abel. Their fault is: 'they have gone *in the way of Cain'* —and what that way was, Genesis 4 will presently tell us.

With Balaam, it is his inordinate and perverse determination to make money out of religion that Jude particularly denounces.

With Korah it was a matter of spiritual rebellion against God's apostle and high priest.

The second interpretative stage

Our preliminary investigations completed, we must now move on to the second interpretative stage. In the Old Testament the stories of Cain, Balaam and Korah are all three very detailed; and so, if we were not careful, we could content ourselves with gathering a number of general impressions from each one. There would, of course, be no harm in that; but in our present context our task is rather to make sure, if we can, that we concentrate, in each story, on the precise point to which Jude calls our attention. Let's start with Cain.

Jude's allusion to Cain
Cain is mentioned three times in the New Testament, once by John (1 John 3:12), once in Hebrews (11:4), and once by Jude (v. 11). Each writer has a different point to make; and if we first consider the points made in 1 John and Hebrews, we shall be the better able to see the difference between them and the point Jude is making.

John points out the reality of Cain's condition
First, John observes that Cain was 'of the evil one' (1 John 3:12). He certainly made a show of being religious by offering a sacrifice to God. But he was not a regenerate man, not a child of God. He was 'of the evil one'; and, as evidence of that, instead of showing love to another child of God, he murdered him.

Second, John observes the reason for the murder: 'his works were evil and his brother's righteous' (1 John 3:12). The difference between Abel's lifestyle and Cain's was all too evident. It exposed as a sham the religious veneer with which Cain tried to cover up his unrepentantly evil way of life; and in so doing it provoked his murderous resentment.

The writer to the Hebrews points out the grounds of Abel's acceptance

First, the writer observes how, and on what grounds, Abel managed to offer to God a better sacrifice than Cain did:

> By faith Abel offered to God a better sacrifice than Cain. By faith he had witness borne to him that he was righteous, God bearing witness concerning his gifts. (Heb 11:4)

It was, then, by faith that Abel offered a better sacrifice than Cain. Now *faith* in Scripture does not refer to a man's self-confidence that what he is doing is right. *Faith* is always a response to God and his word (see Rom 10:17). Cain, for all we know, may have felt very confident that by offering God a sacrifice, he could cover his unrepentantly evil life with an air of respectability. But his confidence was baseless. God rejected his sacrifice for the hypocrisy that it was. Abel, by contrast, offered by faith. That is, he was responding to God's word, in true repentance, acknowledging his need of a sacrifice on the basis of which he could approach God: and then in bringing such a sacrifice as God had taught his parents to bring, when he first forgave them and clothed them with an innocent animal's skin (Gen 3:21).

Second, the writer observes on what grounds God declared Abel to be righteous. God, says the writer to the Hebrews (11:4), bore witness to the fact that Abel was righteous. Abel was not sinlessly perfect, of course. But God declared him to be 'right with God', and did so 'in respect of his gifts', that is, by accepting his sacrifice. In other words, God pronounced him righteous not because his works were better than Cain's, but because his sacrifice was better than Cain's: 'By faith he offered a better sacrifice than did Cain', offered it in genuine repentance and faith, and was on that basis declared to be righteous.

Jude points to the way of Cain

> Woe unto them! for they have gone in the way of Cain. (Jude 11)

In drawing attention to Cain's way (i.e. the path, or road he took) Jude is not simply re-telling the Genesis story in his own words. He is referring to an actual statement in the text of Genesis: 'And Cain *went out from the presence of the* LORD and dwelt in the land of Nod . . .' (Gen 4:16).

This, then, was Cain's way, and to see its significance we should consider one of the dominant themes in Genesis 2, 3 and 4, namely, man's relation to the ground.

The earth before man:

> . . . there was no man to till *the ground*. . . . (2:5)

Man's basic substance:

> And the LORD God formed man of the dust of *the ground*. . . . (2:7)

Man's raison d'être:

> And the LORD God took the man and put him in the garden of Eden to dress it and to keep it (2:15) . . . to till *the ground* from whence he was taken. (3:23)

God's response to Adam's sin:

> . . . cursed is *the ground* for thy sake; in toil shalt thou eat of it all the days of thy life; thorns also and thistles shall it bring forth to thee . . . in the sweat of thy face shalt thou eat bread, till thou return unto *the ground*, for out of it wast thou taken: for dust thou art, and unto dust shalt thou return. (3:17–19)

God's response to Cain's sin:

> And now cursed art thou *from the ground* . . . when thou tillest *the ground*, it shall not henceforth yield unto thee her strength; a fugitive and a wanderer shalt thou be in the earth. . . . And Cain

said . . . Behold thou has driven me out this day *from the face of the ground,* and from thy face I shall be hid; and I shall be a fugitive and a wanderer in the earth. (4:11–14)

It is immediately obvious that the punishment imposed on Cain was far more severe than that imposed on Adam. According to Genesis 2, one of the purposes for which man was made was to till the ground, to dress and guard the garden of Eden. In that garden tilling the ground would doubtless have been nothing but a pleasure. When Adam disobeyed God, he was ejected from the garden, lost physical immortality, and had rigorous disciplines imposed on him. But he was not deprived of the purpose for which he was originally made: he could still till the ground, even though now it would be hard, and often frustrating, work (3:17–19). Moreover he knew that he and Eve were forgiven by the gracious act of God who killed an innocent animal and used its skin to cover their guilty shame (3:21). And not only forgiven! God promised Eve that the seed of the woman should bruise the serpent's head. That carried the clear indication that the human race had not been damaged beyond redemption. Far from it! There was a triumphant future in store for mankind. Adam saw this implication; and responding in faith, he called his wife's name, Eve—because she was the mother of all *living* (Gen 3:20), not the mother of the doomed.

Cain, by contrast, not only disobeyed God, he defied him. When God declined his hypocritical sacrifice, he was angry. When God graciously counselled him and pleaded with him to take the way that would lead to acceptance with God, Cain point-blank rejected God's way (Gen 4:6–7). He not only would not bring God what God required, he murdered the man who would. According to Cain, if God would not have what Cain brought him, God would not have what Abel brought him either. God would get nothing.

God's response to this defiance was to drive Cain out from the face of the ground. With him it would not be, as it was with Adam, that when he tilled the ground, it would bring forth thorns and thistles and turn his work into hard labour. It was that now when Cain tilled the ground, it would no longer yield to him its strength at all. If, therefore, the purpose for man's creation was to till the ground, then Cain had now lost the purpose for which God had made him. And with that he was banished from the face of God. He must get out. Whatever occupation he subsequently took up, he would never have the satisfaction of realising that he was doing what God made him to do, and doing it in fellowship with God. He would lose all sense of ultimate purpose, and become a fugitive and a wanderer in the earth.

Cain, we are told, immediately realised the horror of his punishment (4:13). He was also afraid that anyone who found him would slay him. God therefore put a mark on him to protect him from death by execution. But there is something worse than death, and that is to live and work hidden from the face of God and therefore without any sense of ultimate purpose and meaning. So 'Cain went out from the presence of the LORD' (Gen 4:16).

That, then, was Cain's way. He not only lived a sinful life, and tried to conceal his sin by a hypocritical religious sacrifice; but when God pointed out to him the way of redemption and acceptance with God, he irrevocably rejected it and God as well.

His resultant way was awesome beyond words: 'he went out from the presence of the LORD' (4:16).

According to Jude, the false teachers in the church had gone down the same road as Cain. They pretended to be religious and members of the church. They put themselves forward as leaders and teachers. In spite of that they lived sinful lives. They abused the grace of God, and encouraged immorality. But worse than all that: they denied our only Master and Lord, Jesus Christ and rejected his way of salvation. The road they were treading was Cain's way. It would lead them where it led him.

Jude's allusion to Balaam

> They have rushed unrestrainedly in the error of Balaam for hire. (Jude 11)

Jude's allusion to Balaam points to three things about Balaam, and therefore to three features evident in the false teachers in Jude's day.

His error

Balaam's error (Greek: πλάνη, *planē*) was his 'wandering' from the truth. Pagan prophet though he was, he knew a great deal of truth, and indeed was compelled by God on seven occasions to speak it (Num 22:35; 23:5, 16, 20, 26; 24:4, 13). But aware of God's truth, and of God's purpose for his people, Balaam wandered from it, indeed criminally deserted it. He it was who, having no option but to announce God's determination to bless Israel, subsequently advised the Moabites how to corrupt the Israelites' loyalty to God by entrapping them into sexual immorality and idolatry (Num 25:1–2; 31:15–16).

His motivation

Worldly gain, money, wealth, social status, influence in royal circles drove him (22:7, 15–18, 37; 24:10–13).

His determination

He was determined, if possible, to break through all divine restraint. When the king of Moab's glittering invitation first came to Balaam to go and curse Israel, Balaam consulted God, and God forbade him to accept it (22:8–12). Balak, the king, then significantly increased the promised reward (22:15–17). Balaam, very much aware that God had strictly forbidden him to go and curse Israel, told Balak's emissaries to stay the night while he enquired of the Lord once more (22:18–19). Why the need to pray about it again? He already had God's word. Yes, but God's word stood in the way of his getting Balak's glittering reward; and he hoped either to get God to change his word, or to find a way round it.

This time, seeing his determination to go, God allowed him to go, but on the strict condition that he should do and speak nothing but what God told him (22:20). Then God put another restraint in his way: an angel with a drawn sword (22:23–35). At first Balaam had no eyes to see the angel, though his donkey did. Each time the donkey tried to turn aside, so as to avoid running straight into the angel, Balaam in his blind, headlong determination drove the donkey straight forward. At length, he entered a narrow lane where the donkey could no longer swerve aside; and at that moment Balaam's eyes were opened to see the angel with his drawn sword, threatening Balaam with summary execution if he perversely persisted in trying to get Balak's rewards by cursing Israel (22:35).

In spite of it, he then went twice with Balak to the high places, and along with Balak built altars, offered a bullock on each altar, and engaged in black magic in an endeavour to get God to change his word, and curse Israel (23:1–3). Though a prophet, Balaam, like Balak, was a complete pagan. He imagined that if he offered God a richer sacrifice than Israel did, he could manage to bribe God to be disloyal to Israel and curse them; and then Balaam would get his large reward from Balak.

He failed, of course, and was obliged to report to Balak God's immovable and unchangeable determination to bless Israel. With that, one might have supposed that Balaam would have desisted and submitted to God's word. But no! Balaam still had his eye on worldly reward. God would not be disloyal to Israel; but Balaam worked out a method of getting Israel to be disloyal to God and his word. And he advised the Moabites how to do it, by first tempting them to sexual licence, and from that to participating in Moabite idolatry (25:1–9; 31:15–16).

So much, then, for Balaam's persistent determination to win worldly reward, even if it meant as a prophet subverting God's word and corrupting God's people.

An appropriate allusion
In the light of Balaam's behaviour, as described here in the Old Testament, Jude's depiction of the false teachers in his day is very apt: 'They have rushed unrestrainedly in the error of Balaam for reward' (Jude 11).

The verb he uses, ἐξεχύθησαν (*exechythēsan*, here translated 'rushed unrestrainedly'), is a very colourful word, though difficult to translate. In its literal sense it is used of liquids being poured out, or pouring out, of a container. Escaping from a container, water will pour out unrestrainedly; if dammed up, it will try to get round the dam. In its metaphorical sense it is used of people who 'give themselves up to', or 'abandon themselves to' some activity or passion. It is well used in connection with the prophet Balaam, whose unrestrained desire for worldly reward drove him to persist in circumventing God's word.

It is aptly used by Jude to categorise the false teachers of his day—and of ours—who professing to be Christians, outdo each other in denying the word of God, the authority of our Master and Lord Jesus Christ, and in the name of God's grace advocate permissive sexual morality, and compromise with idolatry. Like Balaam, they get the reward they seek—but at the same ultimate cost (Num 31:8; Rev 2:14–16).

Jude's allusion to Korah

> They have perished in the rebellion of Korah. (Jude 11)

Jude's allusion to Korah specifies his sin as rebellion (Greek: ἀντιλογία, antilogia, 'speaking against', in the sense of hostile opposition, or rebellion). Jude thus is laying a similar charge of rebellion against the false teachers. What we need to know therefore is the nature of Korah's rebellion: against what or whom he was rebelling.

His story is told in the book of Numbers (chs. 16–17). But upon inspection the second half of Numbers, from ch. 11 to the end of the book, relates no less than four rebellions that occurred (plus one event that seemed to Moses to be a rebellion, but actually was not) during Israel's years in the desert. (See (1) chs. 11, 13–14; (2) chs. 16–17; (3) 20:1–13, 23–29; (4) ch. 25; (5) ch. 32.) Obviously, rebellion in those days was a frequent and many-coloured thing. We need, therefore, to distinguish the particular issues at stake in these different rebellions.

The first rebellion recorded in Numbers
The New Testament comes to our aid here, for it cites three of the rebellions (nos. 1, 2 and 4), and it expounds and applies two of them in considerable detail.

The first of them it deals with in Hebrews 3–4, and it applies it as a warning not simply against a lack of thoroughness in devotion on the part of believers, but against the danger of outright apostasy on the part of people who, while outwardly Christians, have never actually believed the gospel. (See Heb 3:19; 4:2; and our discussion of this passage in Chapter 18.) At Hebrews 3:18 these people are described as disobedient; and certainly true believers can on times be disobedient. But the Greek verb used for 'disobedient' here is ἀπειθέω (*apeitheō*). This verb and its related noun and adjective occur twenty-nine times in the New Testament. They are never used to describe the disobedience of a true believer. They invariably denote those who reject God, reject his law, reject his gospel and refuse to believe either him or it. Compare God's verdict given at Numbers 14:11; 22:23, and in Psalm 106.[1]

The fourth rebellion recorded in Numbers
The fourth rebellion is cited at 1 Corinthians 10:8 where Paul refers to the immorality in which Israel indulged in the course of their participation in the worship of Baal (Num 25:1, 6–8), and to the plague that fell on them in consequence. In Numbers, God explains that the plague came as a result of his jealousy that Israel, like an unfaithful wife, should 'join themselves' to Baal-peor; and he further commends Phinehas who 'turned back my wrath from the people of Israel, in that he was jealous with my jealousy among them, so that I did not consume the people of Israel in my jealousy' (Num 25:11 ESV). Paul likewise in the Corinthian passage, warns his fellow-Christians of the evil of compromise with pagan idolatry and demon worship. He reminds them that such compromise on their part would again provoke God's jealousy: 'You cannot drink the cup of the Lord and the cup of demons; you cannot partake of the table of the Lord and the table of demons. Or do we provoke the Lord to jealousy? We are not stronger than he is, are we?' (1 Cor 10:21–22; cf 11:30–32; 2 Cor 11:2–3). Jealousy in this context, of course, is a good thing. A man

1 For a full discussion see the present writer's *An Unshakeable Kingdom*, 109–24.

who was not jealous if some rival tampered with his wife's loyalty, could not be said really to love his wife.

Korah's rebellion (Num 16–17)

But when it comes to Korah's rebellion, the New Testament alludes to it, but does not indicate what its special features were. We shall therefore have to make up our own mind from a reading of the Old Testament story itself. Clearly it was not another case of compromise with pagan religion. Nor was it a question of refusing to enter the promised land. Korah had of course joined in that refusal along with the great majority at the time of the first rebellion; but now he engineered another, and a different, rebellion of his own. His rebellion was primarily an attack on Moses and Aaron (Num 16:3). Not on them as private individuals, but on the special, and, in Korah's estimation, preposterous, claims that they made for the offices to which God had appointed them.

Now Moses was in fact—and this was God's own pronouncement—unique in his day as the mouthpiece of God's self-revelation to Israel:

> And he said 'Hear now my words; if there is a prophet among you, I shall speak with him in a dream. Not so with my servant Moses, he is faithful in all my household; with him I speak mouth to mouth, even openly, and not in dark sayings, and he beholds the form of the LORD.' (Num 12:6–8)

Moses was the apostle of Israel's faith, the bringer to Israel of God's directly inspired word, his uniquely authoritative revelation.

It was this that Korah attacked and denied. It was not that he intended to abandon (his version of) Israel's faith. He was a Levite, that is a minor cleric in Israel's priestly establishment; and he had no intention of giving up his incumbency, nor the dues that went with it. No, his claim was, 'all the congregation are holy, every one of them, and the LORD is in their midst; so why do you exalt yourselves above the assembly of the LORD?' (16:3). In other words he denied Moses' special office and his authority over the rest of Israel. It was true, in a sense, that all the congregation was holy;

but the deduction Korah made from it was false. To Korah there was no need or room for Moses' special and overriding authority as God's inspired apostle. No need for everyone in Israel to accept, and to bow down to, what Moses said because he was God's special mouthpiece. Everybody had as much right to his own views as Moses did to his. The authoritative claims Moses made for his teaching were, according to some of Korah's followers, a form of obscurantist intellectual tyranny that would put people's very eyes out (16:14).

Korah and his associates also rejected the special claims that were made for Aaron. Aaron was the high priest of Israel's faith. According to God's own pronouncement Aaron, and Aaron alone, had the right on the Day of Atonement to enter the Holiest of All as the nation's representative and mediator before God (Lev 16:17). Korah would have none of that: all the people were holy, all of them equally fit to enter God's presence without any mediator or high priest.

Korah's associates also held that the direction in which Moses and Aaron had hitherto led the people was perverse. Egypt was in fact the land flowing with milk and honey (Num 16:13)! All talk of a land flowing with milk and honey out ahead somewhere in the future was a con trick deliberately perpetrated on the people to get them out of Egypt into the desert where Moses could establish his religious tyranny over them. Egypt was the promised land: there was none other.

We need go no further with the details of Korah's rebellion, interesting though they are, to perceive the kind of false teacher that Jude had in mind when he dubbed them Korahs. For there are still plenty of them around in Christendom in our own day: churchmen who not only deny the inspiration and divine authority of Moses' writings, but also do not hesitate to deny our Lord's deity and his unique authority as the revealer of God to men. They would freely hold that in various matters Christ was mistaken, and that we need not necessarily accept everything he said, still less acknowledge the divine inspiration and authority of his apostles' writings.

Moreover, they would equally deny that Christ's death was an atoning sacrifice for sin; they would in fact dispute the need for any such sacrifice anyway. God forgives everybody is their theory, without the need for any atoning sacrifice, or for our Lord's mediation as our high priest.

To see how serious this false teaching is, which has so widely infected Christendom in some quarters, we ought to go back to an intermediate stage on the road between the Old Testament's Korah and our apostate modernists. We need to go back to the cross of our Lord Jesus Christ. Describing what happened there, the writer to the Hebrews uses the same word 'rebellion' (Greek: *antilogia*) as Jude uses in reference to Korah:

> looking unto Jesus, the author and perfecter of our faith, who for the joy that was set before him endured the cross, despising the shame, and has sat down at the right hand of the throne of God. For consider him that has endured such rebellion [*antilogia*] of sinners against himself . . . (Heb 12:2–3)

In other words, what Korah and his associates did to Moses and Aaron, official Judaism did to Christ. They repudiated his claim to be the prophet like Moses (Acts 3:22), to be one 'greater than the temple' (Matt 12:6), and therefore one greater than Aaron. They denied 'the apostle and high priest' of God's final revelation to man (see Heb 1:1–2; 3:1; 7:11–28). That is unspeakably sad. But it is infinitely sadder when theologians who profess to be Christians join in the same revolt, along with the false teachers of Jude's day who denied our only Master and Lord, Jesus Christ.

When Korah and his co-rebels perished, consumed in the fire of God's judgment, God ordered Moses to have their bronze censers taken up out of the blaze, hammered out flat, and attached as plating to the altar (Num 16:36–40). Thereafter, no knowledgeable Israelite could approach and contemplate that altar without being reminded of Korah's rebellion.

And still today whenever we contemplate the cross of Christ, we too are reminded of what religious but unregenerate and rebellious intellects and hearts did to Christ at Calvary, and do in effect to him still.

Numbers records how God finally vindicated Aaron's claim to be high priest. God commanded each one of the leaders of the twelve tribes to deposit his ceremonial staff of office in the tabernacle overnight. In the morning they found that eleven of those staffs were unchanged; but Aaron's staff had put forth buds, blossomed, and borne ripe almonds (Num 17:1–11).

We need not stay to contemplate this detail. It is enough to recall that God has vindicated Christ's claim to be high priest and has demonstrated his superiority over Aaron, by raising him from the dead and seating him at his right hand, where he now lives by the power of an endless life (Heb 7:16).

Conclusion

So far then the New Testament's use of the literary device of explicit allusions. The work necessary to ensure that we are focussing in on the precise feature of the Old Testament's narrative that the New Testament is alluding to can be demanding. Yet it is, for all that, rewarding. And so we will find with the next, related, device that we now come to consider.

14

Implicit Allusions

In our last chapter we examined some examples of the New Testament's habit of alluding explicitly to characters, situations or events in the Old Testament. Such explicit allusions, we noticed, are easily recognised, for the simple reason that they are explicit.

But some New Testament passages allude to characters, situations or events in the Old Testament without explicitly indicating that they are doing so. We call these allusions implicit. Once recognised for what they are, these implicit allusions will cast a flood of light on the New Testament passage in which they occur. On the other hand, unless one knows one's Old Testament well, and is alert to the possible occurrence of implicit allusions to it in the New Testament, it is easy to miss them. In that case the New Testament passage will remain perfectly intelligible and profitable; but the reader will miss the further illumination which the implicit allusion, had it been noticed, would have cast on the passage. Let us take a relatively easy example as we begin and then consider the Gospel of John as a case study of a more complex use of this device.

The paradise of God

At Revelation 2:7 the risen Lord says to the church at Ephesus: 'To the one who overcomes I will grant to eat of the tree of life, which is in the paradise of God'. Now this statement is perfectly intelligible as it stands; and in the light of further references to the tree of life later on in the book (Rev 22:2, 14), it is obviously a promise of eternal life and blessing.

But precisely because it is intelligible as it stands, a reader unfamiliar with the contents of Genesis 2 and 3, might easily miss the implicit allusion. *Paradise* was originally a Persian word, used to denote an enclosed pleasure-park which Persian kings planned and planted for their enjoyment. The ancient Greeks took the word over from Persian, and with them it became παράδεισος (*paradeisos*). When, therefore, the Jews of Alexandria translated the original Hebrew Bible into Greek, around 280 BC, they used this word *paradeisos* for the garden which the Lord God planted in Eden (Gen 2:8–9). It was in that *paradise* that the tree of life stood; and it was out of that *paradise* that God drove our guilty first-parents, when they sinned, so that they should no longer be able to eat of the tree of life and live for ever (Gen 3:22–24).

Of course, when our Lord said to the repentant, dying criminal, 'Today you will be with me in paradise' (Luke 23:43), he was not any longer talking of the earthly garden of Eden, but of God's eternal heaven. And it is the same, when he says 'To the one who overcomes I will give to eat of the tree of life which is in the paradise of God'. But the allusion to the Genesis story which this promise contains, reminds us in the first place of man's fall, his removal from the garden, his loss of access to the tree of life, and his eventual return to the dust from which he was taken. It then underlines the warning to the church: 'Remember . . . from whence thou hast fallen and repent . . . or else I will remove thy lampstand out of its place' (Rev 2:5). But at the same time it triumphantly proclaims that Christ will restore—and more than restore—to his redeemed people the life and blessing lost to the race through Adam's sin.

	EXODUS	GOSPEL OF JOHN
1.	The Prince of Egypt, the tyrant Pharaoh	The Prince of this world, the devil, the Evil One (12:31; 14:30; 16:11; 17:15)
2.	Egypt, Israel's house of bondage (20:2)	'The world' in its evil sense (15:18–19; 16:8–11; 17:14–16)
3.	Moses sent by God into Egypt (3:10, 13–15; 4:13)	Christ sent by the Father into the world (3:17; 5:38; 8:16, 18; 9:4; 10:36)
4.	Moses is to tell the Israelites the Name of God (3:13–14)	Christ: 'I have made known to them your Name and will make it known.' (17:6, 26)
5.	I AM WHO I AM (3:14)	Christ: I AM (8:24, 28)
6.	Moses is given signs to do, so that Israel will believe that God has appeared to him (4:1–9, 28–31)	'The works which my Father has given me to do . . . bear witness of me.' (5:36) 'Many other signs did Jesus that are not written in this book; but these are written that you may believe that Jesus is the Christ, the Son of God . . .' (20:30–31)
7.	The Passover lambs (ch. 12)	The Lamb of God (1:29)
8.	The Passover directive: 'you shall not break a bone of it.' (12:46)	'They did not break his legs . . . for these things happened that the scripture might be fulfilled, A bone of him shall not be broken.' (19:33, 36)
9.	The manna (ch. 16)	The manna contrasted with the Bread of Life from heaven (6:31–33, 48–51, 58)
10.	Moses and the Law (chs. 19–24; 31:18–34:28)	'The Law was given through Moses; grace and truth came through Jesus Christ.' (1:17)
11.	'Let them make me a sanctuary that I may dwell among them.' (25:8)	'If any one love me . . . my Father will love him, and we will come unto him, and make our abode with him.' (14:23)

Table 3. Allusions to Exodus in the Gospel of John

The book of Exodus as a thought model for understanding the Gospel of John

Throughout the Gospel of John there is a long line of allusions to the book of Exodus; some are explicit, but most of them implicit. Consider the list in Table 3.

In this list items 8, 9 and 10 are explicit allusions. The other eight John leaves for his readers to detect for themselves; they are implicit allusions.

Of course, a Gentile reading this gospel for the first time could not be expected to pick up these allusions—and would not need to. The gospel's basic message is clear and direct; it makes sense as it stands. Millions have read it without any prior knowledge of the Old Testament, have understood its main argument, and have thereby been brought to faith in Christ and to the personal possession of eternal life.

But John did not suppose that those who read his book would never read it more than once. He anticipated converts who would go on to read it over and over again. So doing, they would eventually learn to place the final revelation of God which it contains against the background of all those partial self-revelations of God given in the older testament.

Serious students of world-ranking literature spend endless time and energy tracking down every possible allusion in their chosen authors to previous literature. How would one fully understand an author like Virgil without tracing the similarities between his *Aeneid* and Homer's *Iliad* and *Odyssey*? It would be a strange comment on Christians' estimate of the profundity of John's Gospel, if they were not equally enthusiastic to trace the parallels between that gospel and the Old Testament in general and the book of Exodus in particular.

Moreover, this would not be a merely academic, literary exercise. The parallels between Exodus and the gospel turn the detailed story of Exodus into a thought-model by the help of which we can analyse some of the more difficult concepts in the gospel.

This world and its prince

A mere glance at the list of parallels between Exodus and the Gospel of John is sufficient to show that Egypt and Egypt's Pharaoh in Exodus are the counterparts to 'the world' and 'the prince of this world' in the gospel. This at once suggests that Egypt and Pharaoh will provide a vivid illustration of what this gospel means by its terms 'the world' and 'the prince of this world'.

If so, that will be very helpful; for when it comes to the term 'the world', two things can at once be said. The first is that the term occurs frequently in the writings of the Apostle John, sometimes in a good sense (e.g. 'the world' which God made), and frequently in a bad sense (e.g. 'the world' over which Satan rules as prince). The second thing is that when the term is being used in a bad sense, it has proved notoriously difficult to define precisely.

Difficulties in understanding the term 'world'

What, then, does the Bible mean by the term *world* in its bad sense? How would one define the term? And what is more difficult, how would one explain it to someone who had never met this usage of the term before? It is easy enough (and, of course, perfectly proper) simply to repeat the biblical injunction 'Love not the world, neither the things that are in the world'; but failure to explain what the *world* means has frequently led, in the course of the centuries, to mistaken behaviour.

At the one extreme, pietistic interpretations of the 'world' have led people to think that apart from Bible reading, prayer and spiritual exercises, anything beyond what is strictly necessary for making a living — music, art, literature, the pursuit of scientific knowledge for its own sake, games and recreation — is by definition worldly and to be avoided. In extreme cases this interpretation of worldliness has led people like the Amish to reject all modern inventions, such as cars, electric light and up-to-date clothes.

At the other extreme are people who take the 'world' to mean solely things, attitudes and activities that are sinful in themselves. Faced with John's list of the things that are in the world, namely 'the desire of the flesh, the desire of the eyes, and the pride of life' (1 John 2:16), they take it to be referring simply to sexual immorality, greed and pride. Provided, then, that they avoid these sinful attitudes and activities, they feel safe, even if the beautiful, interesting, and in themselves healthy, things of life so preoccupy their thoughts, hearts, ambitions, time and energy that they have little or no time for God, and, as a result 'the love of the Father', as John would put it, 'is not in them'.

Towards a definition of the term 'world'

We need, therefore, to come to a biblical understanding of what the *world* is and stands for. To do that, let us first consider the three different aspects of the world that John presents in his first epistle; then, we shall be in a better position to see more distinctly that other aspect of the *world* which he describes and illustrates in his gospel.

The 'world' and its attractiveness (1 John 2:15–17)

There is nothing wrong, or even surprising, in the world's being attractive. It came from the mind and hand of the Creator 'who gives us richly all things to enjoy' (1 Tim 6:17). The danger is that Satan will do with us what he did with Eve: he will take the good and beautiful things of life, and instead of allowing them to lead our hearts into gratitude, love and obedience to God, will use them to lure our hearts away from him.

Satan pointed out to Eve that the tree of the knowledge of good and evil in the garden of Eden was 'good for food' (that is, physical satisfaction), 'a delight to the eyes' (that is, aesthetic satisfaction) and 'desirable to make one wise' (that is, intellectual satisfaction). Of course it was, for God himself had created it and put it in the garden. But Satan suggested to Eve that it was out of jealousy and spite that God had forbidden her and Adam, for the time being, to enjoy its fruit, because if they ate it they would be 'as God, knowing good and evil' (Gen 3:5). So Satan assured Eve that they could enjoy these beautiful and attractive things independently of God, and in total disregard of his word.

Eve and Adam yielded to Satan's urging; but they discovered that to try to enjoy the beautiful things of life independently of God, out of fellowship with him, and in defiance of his word, leads at length not to the enrichment of life but to the dust of death.

The Apostle John says likewise. If we allow life's lovely things to draw our hearts away from the Father, instead of leading us to him, then life's lovely things become themselves perverted. They become idols, ends in themselves, to be pursued for their own sake. Healthy desire for things good in themselves becomes lust; and humble gratitude for gifts received from God gets displaced by 'the pride of life', a false set of values and goals that depends on having more and better things, and particularly more than other people. Says John, that 'world', being 'not of the Father', has no permanent significance: 'it passes away' (1 John 2:16–17).

The 'world' and its hostility (1 John 3:13–15)
The world is not always attractive: it can be deadly hostile to a true believer. It was so towards Christ in the end; and he forewarned his disciples not to be surprised if it was so towards them as well (John 15:18–25).

Christ explained the basic cause of this hostility: 'If you were of the world, the world would love its own: but because you are not of the world, but I chose you out of the world, therefore the world hates you' (John 15:19; cf 17:14).

There is no ground here for believers to develop a persecution mania; nor is our Lord denying the basic human kindness that normal people exhibit. But the world of unregenerate men and women is alienated from God; and their ignorance of God, coupled with their guilty conscience, makes them feel instinctively that God is against them. Genuine believers in consequence can seem to them to be 'traitors' that have gone over 'to the other side'.

Nor is it alone the starkly atheistic world that hates genuine believers. The religious world also, sometimes more bitterly than the atheistic world, will seek to persecute true believers. Cain, so

John reminds us (1 John 3:12), fresh from his unworthy religious sacrifice, murdered his brother Abel whose sacrifice was acceptable to God. So it was, too, in Christ's day: it was Judaism's chief priests and religious leaders that were chiefly responsible for getting Christ crucified. Religion that persecutes people is most certainly 'worldly'.

The 'world' as a dead weight to be overcome (1 John 5:3–4)

True love for God, says John (1 John 5:3), means keeping his commandments. But the plain fact is that the world often makes it difficult for a believer to keep God's commandments. It is not necessarily because the world is hostile to believers. It is simply the way that the world is organised and the principles on which it conducts its affairs. The director of a factory, trying to evade his creditors, may well instruct his secretary to tell any callers that the director is away travelling—when all the while he is in fact in his office on the premises. If the secretary is a believer, and for conscience sake refuses to tell this lie, she may well lose her job.

A friend of mine, in a country that shall be nameless, complained to his local income tax inspector about the excessive amount of tax which the government demanded of him. The inspector explained that most people he knew cheated the government by not declaring large parts of their income. The government, therefore, tried to compensate for this loss of taxes by raising the rate of tax on the amount that people did declare. Said the inspector to my friend: 'If for the sake of your Christian principles you refuse to cheat, and honestly declare all your income, there is nothing we can do about it: we shall have to charge you this enormous amount of tax.'

Obviously, one could cite many other, different kinds of situations where the way the world runs makes it difficult for a believer to keep God's commandments. But then, says John (1 John 5:3–4), for a believer God's commandments are not burdensome, 'for whatsoever is born of God, overcomes the world'.

A. Israel's liberation from Egypt and its prince

The elements in God's strategies for Israel's liberation:

1. *God's self-revelation to Moses at the Burning Bush* (Exod 3:1–10) as:
   (a) the God of Israel's past (3:6).
   (b) the God of Israel's future (3:8).
   (c) the God of Israel's present: come down to earth to deliver them (3:8).

2. *The 'sending' of Moses* to Israel and to Pharaoh to convey this revelation to them and thus to deliver Israel out of Egypt (3:10, 14).

3. *The evidence by means of which Moses was to convince the Israelites* that God had sent him, and to bring them to believe in him and thus in God (3:13 – 4:9).
   (a) the declaration of God's Name: *the I AM THAT I AM.*
   (b) *miraculous signs given to Moses* to perform (4:1–8, 27–31).

4. *The Passover* was simultaneously:
   (a) *God's judgment on the prince of Egypt* and the breaking of his power over Israel. The first nine plagues were indisputable evidence to Pharaoh that the Lord was God in the midst of the earth (8:22; cf. 8:19; 9:11, 27). But when he obstinately rejected God's demand, judgment fell on him, and broke his power.
   (b) *Israel's deliverance* from the destroying angel of God's judgment (12:23) and from the power of Pharaoh (12:29–36).

5. *The manna* (Exod 16) sent daily to maintain Israel on the journey from Egypt to their promised inheritance.

6. *The tabernacle* (26–31; 35–40) built so that God might dwell among his people on their journey, and that now their life and daily work might be centred round, and geared to, the worship and service of God.

Table 4. Liberation of Israel and the world

B. The liberation of men and women from the world and its prince

1. *Christ is the final and full self-revelation of God*
   (a) In the beginning he already was; he was with God and he was God (John 1:1–2).
   (b) He came down from heaven to earth to make God known (1:14; 6:38). He has fully told God out (1:18).
   (c) He is the God of the future (14:3; 17:24).

2. *Christ was 'The sent one of God'* sent into the world that the world might be saved through him (3:17; 4:34; 5:36–37; 6:39, 57; 7:18, 28, 29; 8:16, 18, 26; 10:36).

3. (a) *Christ declared, and still declares, the Father's Name* in order to bring his disciples to faith in himself and thus in God (17:6–8), and to enjoyment of the Father's love (17:26). Christ is himself the I AM (8:24; and 6:48; 8:12; 11:25; 14:6; 15:1).
   (b) *Christ was given signs, i.e. miraculous works, to do*, so that we might believe that he is the sent one, the Christ, the Son of God (5:36; 10:32, 37–38; 20:30–31).

4. *Christ was the Passover Lamb of God* (1:29; 19:31–36).
   (a) by Christ's death, and subsequent resurrection, the prince of this world has been judged (16:11) and shall be cast out and his grip on mankind broken (12:31–32).
   (b) by Christ's blood we are saved from the wrath of God against our sin (1:29).

5. *Christ is the manna, the living bread from heaven* to maintain believers on their journey from earth to heaven (John 6:48–58).

6. *Christ and his Father make their dwelling place in the heart of believers* (John 14:23).

Pharaoh's Egypt as an aspect of the 'world'

The Pharaohs made Egypt a 'house of slavery'
(Exod 20:2) and a prison for Israel

It was not merely that they made the Israelites' work torturously hard, though they did that, of course, as part of their deliberate policy for subjugating them (Exod 1:8–14).

It was not merely that they tried a form of population control, bordering on genocide, though they tried that as well (Exod 1:15–22).

It was that when in the name of God Moses called on Pharaoh to allow the Israelites to go three days' journey into the wilderness to hold a religious feast to God, Pharaoh downright refused permission. Indeed, he then made their work ten times harder so that they should have neither time nor energy left even to think of going on such a religious festival. Life for the Israelites was to be nothing but working, eating and sleeping; for them there was to be no spiritual dimension to life (Exod 5:1–19).

Worse still was the ground on which Pharaoh refused: 'Who is the LORD', said Pharaoh, 'that I should hearken to his voice to let Israel go? I know not the Lord, and moreover I will not let Israel go' (Exod 5:2).

Pharaoh himself, of course, recognised and worshipped many gods; but they were merely deifications of the forces of nature. The one true God, he neither knew nor was prepared to recognise.

The implication of Pharaoh's denial of God for Israel's worldview

Long before Israel had entered Egypt, God had appeared to their patriarchal ancestor, Abraham, and had communicated to him his purpose and plan for the nation (Gen 15). Their stay in Egypt, while the extended family developed first into twelve tribes and then into a nation, was to be long—but not permanent (Gen 15:13–16). There was to be an 'afterwards', a future, when Israel would leave Egypt and enter on their God-promised inheritance.

In refusing to recognise the Lord, Pharaoh was automatically denying that there had ever been any divine purpose or plan before and behind Israel's entry into Egypt; and simultaneously he was denying that there was a divinely planned future for them beyond and outside Egypt. Egypt, for them, was all there was, and all there was ever going to be: nothing but building store cities for the pharaohs (Exod 1:11).

Pharaoh's Egypt on a greater scale: atheistic materialism

Atheistic materialism is not concerned merely to deny God's intervention in past history on behalf of the little nation of Israel. Atheistic materialism denies that there was ever any purpose, divine or otherwise, behind the appearance of the human race itself upon earth, let alone behind the birth of any individual person.

It likewise denies that there is any future for the individual beyond his or her life on this planet, or any divinely planned future for the planet itself.

Thirdly, it denies that there is any genuine non-materialistic, spiritual dimension to human life even during the short time each individual lives on the planet.

In holding this view atheistic materialism turns our planet into a prison; and the more truly intellectual a person is, the more intellectually cruel the prison will appear. For materialism insists that human rationality is the unplanned, unpurposed, product of mindless forces, which eventually proceed systematically to annihilate every individual's intelligence, love, hope, and very existence. In the end these same mindless forces will destroy planet Earth and every vestige of intelligence upon it, and—ultimate irony—when they have done it, they won't even know they have done it. Human intelligence, therefore, is the ultimately helpless prisoner of mindless matter.

The fact that this philosophical materialism is often urged upon us and taught to our children as the acme of intellectual thought, shows what its ultimate, anti-intellectual source is. It comes from the 'prince of this world' of whom Christ says in the Gospel of John: 'He was a murderer from the beginning, and stood not in the truth, because there is no truth in him. When he speaks a lie, he speaks of his own; for he is a liar, and the father thereof' (John 8:44).

Strategies for emancipation

We think first of God's strategies for setting ancient Israel free from bondage to the prince of Egypt, as told us in Exodus; and then secondly of God's strategies for setting men and women free from the intellectual, moral and spiritual grip of the prince of this world, as told us in the Gospel of John.

The point of these similarities

The similarities are obvious; their relevance to the deliverance of men and women from the world and its prince are worthy of long and detailed thought. Perhaps it is enough here to highlight four truths that emerge from this comparison. As we ponder them we will do well to remember that unless we are alive to the possibility of implicit allusions to the Old Testament we are not likely to appreciate all that the New Testament is saying.

God answers the lie

The incarnation of the Son of God, his death, resurrection and ascension are God's answer to Satan's attempt to banish God from the world, and to persuade mankind that this world is all there is. Summing up his mission Christ said to his disciples: 'I came out from the Father, and have come into the world; again I leave the world, and go unto the Father' (John 16:28). There is another world, then; this world is not all there is.

Christ refutes the slander

Christ's declaration of the Father's name and character is the answer to Satan's slander of God, originally perpetrated in the garden of Eden, and repeated ever since. Discovering what the Father is really like, breaks the hold of the world and its prince.

Christ breaks the chains

Christ's death as the Passover Lamb of God breaks the chain of guilt and removes the fear of death and of God's wrath by which Satan keeps people in alienation from God.

Christ resets the context

Christ thus delivers people from the prison of mere temporal life and gives them here and now a new dimension to life: the knowledge of God and personal relationship with God which is eternal life, to be enjoyed here in this life and for ever hereafter (John 3:16; 17:1–3). It thus places our life in this world in its true context: God's eternal purpose in the past (1:1–4; 17:5), fellowship with God in the present (14:23), and God's eternal purpose in the future (14:1–3; 17:24).

15

Allegorical Interpretation, or is it?

AT GALATIANS 4:21–31 Paul appears to commit what for some scholars is an unforgivable exegetical offence: he appears to indulge in an allegorical interpretation of a passage in the Old Testament — and what is worse, he appears openly to admit it. Appears, I say, for there is some uncertainty, linguistically speaking, about the meaning he intended by the crucial Greek phrase at 4:24: ἅτινά ἐστιν ἀλληγορούμενα (hatina estin allēgoroumena).

The Greek noun ἀλληγορία (allēgoria) means 'the description of one thing under the image of another'. It can, therefore, be used, and is frequently so used, of 'allegory' in its strict literary sense, and also of allegorical interpretations of mythical legends. But it can be used in a somewhat different sense to describe the metaphorical and figurative language used by an orator (cf. Cicero's use of the term in his Orator 27.94). What Paul actually means by estin allēgoroumena (perfect tense, passive of the verb ἀλληγορέω, allēgoreō) we can finally decide when we have examined in detail his interpretation of the Genesis story which he is citing at Galatians 4:21–31. But for the moment let the charge stand undiminished: Paul, it is alleged, has indulged in allegorical interpretation.

The chief charge against allegorical interpretation

Now it goes without saying that even the most unsympathetic of Paul's critics would not object to a writer who deliberately composed an allegory. Allegory is a perfectly respectable method of communicating truth. What the critics object to—and rightly so—is when someone takes a work that was intended by its author as history, or as straightforward narrative, and interprets it as if the author had intended it as allegory, when all the while the original author intended no such thing.

The method

Such allegorical interpretation has had a long and none too reputable history. Some expressions and stories in Homer's epics, for instance, seemed unacceptably shocking to the refined taste of later Alexandrian scholars. They therefore removed their unacceptability by arguing that Homer never really meant these expressions literally, but only allegorically; and they interpreted the text accordingly. They were wrong, of course, and their interpretations absurd. Anyone today can see that Homer meant literally what he said.

Later the Alexandrian Jewish philosopher, Philo, interpreted the whole of the Pentateuch allegorically.[1] He did not altogether reject the plain straight grammatical and historical sense of the original text. But he claimed that many details within the text were either naïve or downright false if interpreted literally; and this showed, he argued, that the real meaning of the whole of the Pentateuch was not its literal sense, but the 'higher' hidden meaning which his allegorising exegesis discovered in it. The system of doctrine which he built up by this method may have been an intellectual tour de force worthy of a genius. But a method that turned the ancient Hebrew Moses into a teacher of Platonic, Aristotelian and Stoic

---

1 Philo was born about 20 BC. His lifetime covered the lifetimes of John the Baptist and Christ, and much of that of Paul, though he appears to have known nothing about them. For an example of his allegorical interpretation see the Endnote that follows this chapter.

philosophy centuries before those philosophies were ever thought up, and then claimed that Moses was the originator of these philosophies, stands self-condemned as an exegetical system.

Later, in the Christian centuries, Origen and his followers turned to allegorical interpretation of both Old and New Testaments for all sorts of reasons (among others to get rid of ideas like a literal millennium which they found unacceptable). Saint Augustine's interpretation of the parable of the Good Samaritan (Luke 10:30–37) as if it were an allegory is notorious.[2]

The charge

The basic grievance, then, which modern scholars have against this kind of allegorical exegesis is that it foists onto the text a meaning that the original author never intended. It is, therefore, illegitimate. And also arbitrary; for if the method were permissible, it would allow the interpreter to make the text mean anything he cared to make it mean; and the reader would have no means of judging whether the interpretation was true or not.

In addition, allegorical exegesis falls foul of the grammatical-historical method which modern (along with many ancient) scholars feel to be the bedrock foundation of true exegesis. They insist, for instance, that if in Genesis Moses talked of Hagar, he meant Hagar, not the Sinai covenant, which Paul says she represents (Gal 4:24). If Moses had meant the Sinai covenant, he would have said the Sinai covenant. If he had wanted to say that Hagar somehow represented the Sinai covenant, he would have said so. If he didn't say it, he didn't mean it. This is the only sure foundation of responsible interpretation; and if the foundation be removed, what shall the righteous do? They therefore dismiss Paul's 'allegorical' interpretation of Genesis in Galatians out of hand, as false and unworthy.

Conservative scholars, believing Paul's letter to be the inspired word of God, naturally rally to his defence. But sometimes the excuse they offer for him turns out to be worse than the original

2 He suggested that the good Samaritan represented Christ, the inn was the Church, and the two pence were the two sacraments.

charge. The rabbis, they say, were in the habit of using this fanciful allegorical method of interpretation; so Paul decided to turn their own weapon against them. It was, they hasten to add, only an ad hominem argument, quite unsuitable for us to use with our contemporaries. Even Paul himself, they suggest, were he alive today, would not attempt to use it on us moderns.

But why not? Because, they say, modern people would immediately see that the argument is not actually valid. But why is it not? Because the Genesis passage does not mean what Paul says it means? Then it never meant what he says it meant! His exposition was false from the start. Granted that contemporary rabbis may have been convinced by his argument, that makes things worse not better. The God of truth would never use a false argument provided only that he could get away with it because his opponents could not see it was false. If Paul used such an argument, he was not inspired by God. If God inspired Paul, he did not use such an argument.

The issue

One thing at least can be said here in defence of Paul. He uses his allegedly allegorical interpretation of the Hagar story to illustrate and reinforce the argument he has already built up in his epistle so far. And that argument is based not on anything remotely allegorical, but on a succession of citations of plain, straightforward statements from doctrinal and legal contexts in the Old Testament (Gal 3:6, 8, 10, 11, 12, 13, 16–17). Fact though that is, it will not save his reputation, if he has then proceeded unjustifiably to allegorize what in Genesis is a plain historical narrative. The question is what has he done? Has he in fact allegorized the story in the technical sense of the term?

The Hagar–Ishmael–Sarah–Isaac story in Genesis

What then did Paul mean when he said that certain elements in the Hagar–Sarah story carry an 'allegorical' meaning? The only reliable way to find out is to look and see what he has in fact done with the details which he took from Genesis; and to examine not just the few verses in his own writing in which he uses these 'allegorical' elements, but the whole sweep of his surrounding argument. And similarly, to consider not just the passages and verses that he actually quotes from Genesis, but also the function those passages and verses perform in the narrative flow of their larger context in Genesis itself.

The last reference Paul makes in Galatians to the Hagar–Ishmael story is as follows:

> But what does the Scripture say? 'Cast out the slave woman and her son, for the son of the slave woman shall not be an heir with the son of the free woman.' (Gal 4:30)

These are Sarah's words taken from Genesis 21:10, with one slight difference: what Sarah actually said was '. . . shall not be an heir with my son Isaac'.

'There you are,' says someone, 'Paul is caught out changing the wording of the Genesis story to make it fit his allegorical interpretation.'

Well, certainly Paul adapts the wording in order to continue the point he has been making throughout his discussion, namely, that Sarah's son was the son of a free woman, while Hagar's was the son of a slave girl. But is Paul being less true to the historical reality when he does so? Was not Sarah's son Isaac the son of the free woman?

So let's leave that minor detail and come straight to the substantive point of Sarah's remark. It is concerned with the question: Who shall be Abraham's heir? Shall Ishmael? Or Ishmael and Isaac together? Or simply Isaac? Sarah's demand is that it shall be Isaac only; and it brings to a climax the major topic that has occupied the narrative since the beginning of Genesis 15.

The flow of the historical narrative from Genesis 15

It is a matter of simple observation that the leading theme running throughout these chapters is: who shall be Abraham's heir? (even Philo recognised that). The theme is developed through seven major incidents:

1. At Genesis 15:2, Abraham complains to God that he has no son of his own to be his heir: if he dies, his steward, Eliezer, will inherit all his wealth. God assures Abraham that he will have a child of his own to be his heir. Abraham believes God (15:6). By a solemn covenant God then guarantees eventual possession of the inheritance to Abraham's seed-to-be.

2. Genesis 16 raises the question: how shall the promised seed be produced? Sarah, being barren, despairs of ever producing a child. At her suggestion Abraham takes Hagar; and she, now pregnant, absconds; but God sends her back into Abraham's home. Ishmael is born.

3. In Genesis 17 Ishmael is circumcised along with Abraham himself and all his home-born servants (17:23). But when Abraham pleads with God to recognise Ishmael as the promised seed and heir, God refuses. The heir must, and will be, a son of Abraham by Sarah; his name shall be Isaac, and it is with him and with his seed after him that God's covenant will be established (17:18–21).

4. In Genesis 18:1–15 God visits Abraham and, in spite of Sarah's incredulity, announces that within the next nine months Sarah will give birth to a child.

5. Meanwhile Genesis 18:16–19:38 tells, by contrast, the sorry story of how Lot's seed was perpetuated after the destruction of Sodom and Gomorrah.

6. Genesis 20 then relates how, as a result of Abraham's less than truthfulness, a Philistine king took Sarah, and how the paternity of Sarah's child-to-be would have been placed in doubt, had God not intervened.

7. Genesis 21 then brings the theme to its climax: Isaac is born, and at Sarah's insistence the slave girl and her son are cast out, to make it certain that Isaac shall be Abraham's sole heir (21:12).

So much, then, for the storyline in Genesis.

Paul's attitude towards, and use of, this story as a whole
At Galatians 4:30, as we have seen, Paul cites Sarah's words from the climax of the story. But now we must ask: at what point in the

flow of his argument does he cite them? And how much else of the Genesis storyline does he cite?

The answer is that as far as the theme 'Who shall be Abraham's heir?' is concerned, he cites the whole of it from the covenant promise of Genesis 15 (Gal 3:15–29), through the birth of Ishmael from the slave-girl Hagar in Genesis 16 (Gal 4:22) and the explicit promise to Sarah that she should bear the promised seed in Genesis 17:15–21 (Gal 4:23), to Ishmael's mocking of Isaac and Sarah's climactic pronouncement in Genesis 21 (Gal 4:29–31). Paul not only refers to it all, he cites its details in the same order; he cites it for the same purpose, namely to prove who Abraham's seed and heir is; and uses Sarah's climactic statement as the climax of his own argument.

Leave aside, then, for the moment his supposed 'allegorising' of certain details. How does he treat the narrative as a whole? Altogether allegorically from start to finish? Or partly as history and partly as allegory? Or how?

Beyond any doubt he treats it altogether as history. Paul makes the point himself explicitly. The whole force of his legal argument (Gal 3:17), based on God's covenant with Abraham and his seed, depends on its historicity and dating. The law, he argues (as we saw in Chapter 10), was given 430 years after God's covenant with Abraham, and therefore cannot be used to cancel or invalidate it. Nor can the conditions and stipulations of the later law be added to the terms of the earlier covenant without perverting the nature of its unconditional promises (Gal 3:15–18). This, at least, is not allegorising exegesis: here speaks a strict historian and lawyer.

But he does go on to claim that the seed to whom the inheritance was promised was Christ (Gal 3:16). Is not this a bit of unhistorical allegorising? No, of course not. For Paul, Christ was not an allegorical descendant of Abraham's (whatever that might be), nor merely a spiritual descendant of his; he was literally and physically descended from him. He was Abraham's physical seed as much as Isaac was. And for that to be so, even God's statement to Abraham 'in Isaac shall your seed be called' (Gen 21:12), had for Paul to mean in the first instance, as it does in the Genesis passage, that Isaac was literally and physically descended from Abraham.

It is true that Paul later remarks that there was more involved in Isaac's birth than the normal unaided process of human generation: Ishmael was born after the flesh, Isaac was born 'through promise' and 'after the Spirit' (Gal 4:23, 29). But Paul does not even here mean that Isaac's birth 'after the Spirit' was only an allegorical, and not a physical birth. The birth was a miracle of God's grace and power performed in accordance with God's original promise; but in Paul's thinking it was no less a literal, physical, historical event for all that. Only consider his observation in Romans 4:19 that Abraham considered his own body, now as good as dead, and the deadness of Sarah's womb, without weakening in his faith. This was the historical and physical background to an historical and physical miracle.

It follows that Paul regarded Ishmael's birth as a literal, physical, historical event as well. Hagar was a real woman. And even in his treatment of Ishmael's mocking of Isaac, in the passage where Paul is supposedly at his most 'allegorical' (Gal 4:24–31), he incidentally indicates that he regards the story as historical: 'But *as at that time* he who was born according to the flesh persecuted him who was born according to the Spirit, *so it is now also*'. Not 'as in the story (still less, 'as in the allegory') so now in reality'; but 'as at that time in history, so now in the present day'.

The significance of Ishmael's birth 'after the flesh'

What then does Paul mean by claiming that Ishmael's birth was 'after the flesh', whereas Isaac's birth was 'through promise'? If both births were literal, physical births, what was the difference between them?

To answer that question in a way that is true to the historical development of Paul's thought we must first start with the revelation of the gospel which Paul received from the risen Lord (Gal 1:11–12; Acts 26:12–18). Before his conversion Paul (or Saul, as he was then) had endeavoured in all sincerity and earnestness to obtain eternal life and final acceptance with God on the ground of his keeping of the law given at Sinai (see his description of his religious life before conversion, at Phil 3:5–6). Conversion to Christ radically changed his attitude (Phil 3:7–12). He now saw with irresistible clarity that justification and eternal life could not be achieved through his meritorious effort to keep the law; but only as a gift of God's grace through Christ's propitiatory death and resurrection.

Moreover, when he came to describe the difference between the basic principle and motivation of his life before and after conversion, the phrase he used to describe his pre-conversion attitude was 'confidence in the flesh' (Phil 3:3–7). By that he meant trust in his own effort and religious discipline to develop a character that in the end would earn him acceptance with God. At conversion this confidence in the flesh and in his own righteousness were both entirely and for ever renounced. In their place came faith in God, and in the power of the Spirit of God, and in a righteousness that God imparted to him as an unearned gift, simply through faith in Christ (Phil 3:3–9).

When therefore he says Abraham acquired two sons, one by the slave woman and one by the free woman, but the son by the slave woman was born after the flesh . . . , he is using the term 'flesh' in the same sense as he used it to describe his own attitude in his pre-conversion days. He is not criticising Hagar for giving physical birth to a child. He is criticising Abraham for relying on his own resources, powers and exertions to achieve the fulfilment of God's promise; in other words, for having confidence in the flesh.

The nature of Abraham's mistake
According to Genesis 15 God had made Abraham an unconditional promise that he would give him a son and heir; and Abraham had genuinely believed God and it was counted to him for righteousness (15:6). The only question was: how and by what means was God's promise to be fulfilled?

At the time Sarah was barren (Gen 16). Left to her own powers and exertions, conception would be impossible. She need not have worried: God had known about her barrenness when he made his promise, and he intended to perform a life-giving miracle in Sarah's body so that she could conceive. She and Abraham were required simply to believe that God's promise meant what it said, and to put their faith solely in God, in his truthfulness, and in his regenerating power.

Instead of that, Sarah got it into her head that God's promise was actually not an absolute unconditional promise at all, but rather an exhortation or incentive to rely upon themselves and their own resources in order by their own effort to effect the fulfilment of the promise. So, being barren herself, she persuaded Abraham to take their slave woman Hagar, and father a child by her.

And that is what Paul means when he says that Abraham's son by the slave woman was born 'after the flesh'. He is not, of course, blaming Hagar: he is criticising Abraham and Sarah; but criticising them with sympathy born out of his own experience. Their attitude towards God's promise was precisely the same as his own pre-conversion attitude had been to God's promises of justification and eternal life. He too had mistakenly thought that these blessings, held out to mankind by God, had to be earned and achieved 'after the flesh'; that is by his own effort and works.

Paul, then, is not interpreting Abraham and Sarah's experience as an allegory. For him they were and remained historical people who at one point in their career adopted exactly the same wrong attitude as he did at one period in his career. But then, of course, God eventually taught Paul the same lesson as he subsequently taught Abraham and Sarah.

Isaac's birth through promise

When God first made his promise to Abraham, Sarah was barren; but Abraham was still vigorous and able to follow Sarah's suggestion to father a child by Hagar. As the years went by he came to dote on Hagar's son, and pleaded with God to accept Ishmael as the fulfilment of the original promise. God refused (Gen 17:15–22), and then left Abraham until now his body was, as far as fathering a child was concerned, as good as dead; until indeed he accepted the fact that he could not, and was not meant to, achieve the fulfilment of God's promise by his own effort and resources. The new life he sought was to be given him and Sarah as a free gift by an act of God's creative power according to the intention of the original unconditional promise.

The point is worth making again, therefore, that when at Romans 4:18–25 Paul cites Abraham's faith in God's promise and uses it, by analogy, to explain what 'faith' must mean in our case too, when we are said to be justified by faith, he is not interpreting Abraham's story as an allegory. He is quoting one historical instance of what it means for a human being to believe God's word, and he then applies it in our day to us who must learn what God means by 'faith', when he says that justification is by faith.

What Paul means by 'allegory' in Galatians 4:24

But with this we come to the verses which contain the Greek phrase that lies at the heart of our investigation: '*hatina estin allēgoroumena*'.

Our first task is to decide how this phrase should be translated. There are two possibilities:

1. '. . . which things have been interpreted allegorically';

or

2. '. . . which things have been spoken as an allegory'.

The first translation would take Paul to be saying that in his time the story of Hagar and Sarah had generally been interpreted by various expositors as an allegory. This would, of course, be true. Philo's exposition of this story is the outstanding example in the ancient world of such an allegorising interpretation. But Philo's interpretation is vastly different from Paul's (to see how different, consult the epitome of Philo's interpretation of Hagar and Sarah given in the Endnote); and certainly any contemporary rabbinic allegorisation of the story would again have been different from Paul's interpretation. It is hardly likely, therefore, that Paul would be appealing to contemporary allegorising interpretations as though they justified his allegorisation of the story.

It is much more likely that the second of the two translations given above is the right one: 'now all these things have been spoken [i.e. by the Old Testament writer] as an "allegory"'. In other words, whatever Paul intends by 'allegory' here, he is claiming that this allegory is part and parcel of the meaning intended by the Old Testament itself.

And this is confirmed by the way in which Paul introduces these verses (Gal 4:21–22): 'Tell me, you that desire to be under the law, do you not hear the law? For *it stands written* that Abraham acquired two sons'. 'Stands written' represents the Greek word γέ-γραπται (*gegraptai*), the perfect passive of the verb 'to write' (γράφω, *graphō*). It is the formula used in the New Testament in quoting an Old Testament passage as the authoritative, unalterable, and un-questionable word of God (see, for instance, Matt 4:4, 7, 10).

If this is so, it raises all the more urgently the question: what does Paul mean by 'allegory'? But now we can at once confidently assert that whatever else he means, he does not mean that the story of Abraham, Sarah and Hagar and their sons was intended by its author as a non-historical allegory. True, this is the sense in which pagan Greek literary critics would have used the term; but it is im-possible to think that Paul is using the term in their sense. In the light of what we have seen so far of Paul's attitude to the story, it is overwhelmingly evident that he regarded it as historical. Rather, what he means is that the story, *as well as* being a record of historical people, their attitudes and actions, carries an additional significance. Like many other Old Testament stories it is, as we shall soon see, a prototype. But first we should consider what Paul is arguing regard-ing law and slavery.

Let us set out the details:

> For these woman are [i.e. represent] two covenants, one [cove-nant, which was given] from mount Sinai, bearing children unto slavery, [and] which as such [Greek: ἥτις, *hētis*, not the simple relative pronoun, ἥ, *hē*] is [i.e. corresponds to] Hagar. (Gal 4:24)

Let us pause here to take in what Paul is saying. The core of the analogy between Hagar and the covenant from Sinai is the actual fact, according to Paul, that the covenant from Sinai brings forth children unto slavery. And since that is so, the Sinai covenant corresponds well to Hagar: for she was a slave herself, and when

Abraham used her to produce a son, that son was, and always retained the status of, a slave.

Of course, Paul's statement that the Sinai covenant 'brings forth children unto slavery' is couched in highly metaphorical, though typically Semitic, language. Hagar's son was a literal child; the Sinai covenant's 'children' were metaphorical children, that is, people whose attitudes, characters, and quality of life are formed by their attempt to live according to that covenant's principles. But the point that Paul is making about the Sinai covenant is no less real and historical because it is expressed in metaphorical language.[3] Even genuine Jewish believers, says Paul, who all down the centuries until the Son of God came, lived under the terms and conditions of the Sinai covenant, were like children in a wealthy family: heirs of their father, but during their childhood nothing different from slaves. 'We were held in bondage', he says, 'to the elementary rules of the world' (Gal 4:1–7).

Moreover, many—indeed most—of Paul's Jewish contemporaries lived in a kind of religious slavery (as multitudes of Gentiles as well as Jews still do) because of their mistaken attitude to the law. Just as Abraham misused Hagar in an attempt to achieve the fulfilment of God's promise of new life, so Paul's contemporaries were misusing the law. They imagined that God gave them the law from Sinai so that by their efforts to keep it they might gain justification and eternal life. And that was not the purpose of the Sinai covenant—and could never have been so. Let Paul explain why.

The basic principle of the law, he points out (3:12), was 'You shall therefore keep my statutes and my judgments, which if a man do, he shall live in them' (Lev 18:5). Now it is perfectly true that in the practical affairs of daily life, keeping God's law as best we can will tend to health and happiness and life. But not to eternal life and final acceptance with God! At that level the law of Sinai

3 Many modern languages use almost the same metaphor as Paul uses. We can say, for instance, that the French educational system produces students of a particular quality and outlook, whereas the products of the American educational system evince a somewhat different quality and outlook. No one would classify such language as allegorical.

can only convict us all of sin, and pronounce sentence of curse and death upon us for our failure to keep the law fully (Gal 3:9–10). Which is precisely why Christ had to die and be made a curse for us, so that he might redeem us from the curse of the broken law (3:13), and so set us free to receive and enjoy 'the blessing of Abraham in Christ Jesus; that we might receive the promise of the Spirit through faith' (3:14).

There was nothing wrong with the law, of course; and in giving Israel the law God was not cancelling the promises that he had originally given to Abraham's seed (3:21). Indeed, says Paul, 'if there had been a law given which could make alive, truly righteousness would have been of the law' (3:21). But that is what the law, by definition, could not do. The laws of hygiene are good; but they cannot create new life, cannot regenerate a dead body. Ask Abraham! So it is with the law. Eternal life has to be received, not by keeping the law but as a free gift through faith in Christ (3:11).

But that is what Jerusalem and the majority of her children—that is, her citizens—would not accept. Instead they worked hard to keep the law in the vain hope of gaining eternal life thereby, when all the while there was never any possibility of gaining it by that means, and failure meant eternal death. That was slavery indeed (see Rom 9:30–10:4).

But it is time we returned to the remainder of Paul's exposition of the Old Testament prototype.

Mount Sinai and Jerusalem as metaphorical mothers

For the Mount Sinai is in Arabia[4] and is in line with [Greek: συστοιχεῖ, systoichei] the present Jerusalem, for she is in slavery along with her children. (Gal 4:25)

We can start once more with the obvious. The fact that Paul refers to the present Jerusalem and her 'children' is no sign that he is speaking allegorically. He is referring to the literal contemporary city of

4 This is the reading supported by the best textual witnesses, and is most likely to be the original reading.

Jerusalem, the religious capital of worldwide Jewry. When he refers to her as a mother and to her citizens as her children he is using a metaphor very common in the ancient world and still alive in many languages today.

So Christ addressed Jerusalem city as a mother, and her citizens as her children (Luke 13:34). So Russians speak of their country as Mother Russia, and use the term *metropolis* to denote the mother-state. So students in many countries will speak of their university as their *alma mater*. None of these examples would be thought of as allegorical.

And because expressions like these are simply metaphors, an ancient prophet, like Isaiah, can happily mix his metaphors. In one passage he speaks of Zion as a mother and of Zion's citizens as her children (Isa 49:14–21); but in another passage he speaks of Zion's sons marrying her (62:5)!

So here in Paul's exposition of the Old Testament prototype, he can first say that because the covenant given at Mount Sinai brings forth children unto slavery, it corresponds to a slave woman, Hagar, who brought forth a son by Abraham into slavery. And then he can add that Mount Sinai is in line with Jerusalem city that now is, for she too is in slavery along with her children.

Once more Paul is not deducing the idea that contemporary Jerusalem is in slavery along with her children from the details of the story of Abraham and Hagar in the Old Testament. He is stating it as a fact of contemporary history that he knew only too well—he had himself lived a part of his life in that self-same religious slavery, and for the same reason, namely a mistaken idea of the purpose of the law from Mount Sinai.

And that was sad, not only because of the inevitable result-ant slavery, but for another historical and geographical reason. When God made the original covenant with Abraham and his seed, Abraham was already in Canaan. Hence in the preamble to the covenant God said to Abraham, 'I am the LORD that brought you out of Ur of the Chaldeans, *to give thee this land* to inherit it' (Gen

15:7). And when Abraham enquired how he could be sure he would inherit it, God replied by making an unconditional covenant guaranteeing to give it to Abraham and his seed (Gen 15:8–21).

But Mount Sinai, Paul points out, was in Arabia. Now Arabia was the part of the world that Hagar's son, Ishmael, and his descendants eventually regarded as their home (see Gen 21:21; Ps 83:6). But much more significantly, at the level of its prototypical meaning, Mount Sinai was not in Canaan, and Arabia was not part of the promised inheritance. When Israel received the covenant from Mount Sinai they were not in the promised land, but only on their way toward it. That covenant certainly showed them the behaviour that God expected of them both while they were in the wilderness and after they entered Canaan. But the basis of Israel's legal entitlement to their inheritance was the unconditional covenant God made with Abraham and his seed, not the law from Sinai. And, as Paul has earlier pointed out (Gal 3:16), the seed mentioned in the Abrahamic covenant was primarily Christ (see our earlier discussion, Chapter 10). All who put their faith in him, and not in their own efforts to keep the Sinai law, will most certainly inherit the inheritance promised to Abraham and his seed (3:29).

Unfortunately the Jerusalem of Paul's day, the religious capital and mother city of worldwide Judaism, rejected Christ as the key to the eventual possession of the promised inheritance, and instead based her hope of inheritance on her own effort to keep the law from Sinai. Official Judaism—and much of Christendom—does so still.

Jerusalem that is above

> But the Jerusalem that is above is free, and she is our mother. (Gal 4:26)

At verse 24 Paul told us that these women (i.e. Hagar and Sarah) represented two covenants. He then explained that Hagar represented the covenant from Sinai but did not tell us which covenant Sarah represented. But now this detail becomes clear: Sarah represents the unconditional covenant which God made with Abraham (Gen 15). It was according to the God-given promise of that covenant that she, the free woman, gave birth to the free-born son Isaac.

But if Hagar = the Sinai covenant = the Jerusalem that is now, Sarah = the Abrahamic covenant = the Jerusalem that is above. That Jerusalem is composed of the vast community of Jews and Gentiles who are the spiritual children of Abraham and Sarah because like them (and like Paul) they have learned to base their hope of eternal life, not on their efforts to keep the law of Moses, but solely on God's unconditional promise given to those who put their faith in Christ.

Isaiah's use of the Hagar–Sarah story as a prototype

> Rejoice, thou barren one that bearest not; break forth and cry, thou that travailest not; for more are the children of the desolate than of her that has the husband. (Isa 54:1)

Paul was not the only one to see that the story of Genesis 15–21 was both historical and a prototype. Isaiah had too, centuries before. At Isaiah 51:1–2 he calls on his nation to 'Look unto Abraham your father, and unto Sarah that bare you; for when he was but one I called him, and I blessed him, and made him many'. Since then, however, as a result of the nation's trust in itself and in its idols instead of in the living God who was their maker and husband, Jerusalem had experienced alienation from God, desolation of the city, and the carrying away of her children into exile and slavery.

But now Isaiah, in God's name, promises Jerusalem restoration of her children, and cites Sarah's experience as a prototype. Sarah at first had been barren. Losing faith in God's promise, she had suggested, to her great eventual sorrow, that Abraham take Hagar. For now, while she herself was barren, Hagar had the husband, bore a child, despised Sarah, and flaunted her son in mockery of Sarah's infertility as a woman (Gen 16). Moreover Abraham came to dote on Hagar's son, if not on Hagar, and would have been content for

Sarah to continue barren, provided that he could count Ishmael as his heir (Gen 17). Sarah's desolation must have seemed complete.

But in God's good time the tables were turned. Sarah, the one-time barren woman, had a child. And though God blessed Hagar and her son and promised them numerous descendants (Gen 16:10; 21:18), God promised Abraham vastly more children, both physical and spiritual, through Sarah (Gen 17:16; Rom 4:16–18).

Since Pentecost, Isaiah's glowing prophecy has already been fulfilled to an extent far beyond, perhaps, what Abraham and Sarah could ever have imagined. And even greater fulfilments lie ahead (Rom 11:12–27). For just as we might say that Copernicus is the father of modern science, since he, by his example, showed to all subsequent scientists the principles which they should follow, so Abraham and Sarah, by their experience, have demonstrated to multi-millions since, what it means to believe God and to be justified by faith. In this sense these millions are their spiritual children.

Unhappily another detail of the prototype has been repeatedly fulfilled. 'As then he who was born after the flesh [namely Ishmael] kept on persecuting him who was born after the Spirit [namely Isaac: see Gen 21:9], even so it is now', says Paul (Gal 4:29). The persecution of those born after the Spirit by those born after the flesh has continued all down the centuries. But it does but show the need to understand what justification by faith really means and then to stand unflinchingly for it. And here a precise understanding of the New Testament's interpretation of the Old Testament will be important.

Endnote

An epitome of Philo's interpretation of Sarah and Hagar based on a number of his treatises and composed by J. B. Lightfoot.[5]

> Abraham—the human soul progressing towards the knowledge of God—unites himself first with Sarah and then with Hagar. These two alliances stand in direct opposition the one to the other. Sarah, the princess—for such is the interpretation of the word—is divine wisdom. To her therefore Abraham is bidden to listen in all that she says. On the other hand Hagar, whose name signifies 'sojourning' (παροίκησις), and points therefore to something transient and unsatisfying, is a preparatory or intermediate training—the instruction of the schools—secular learning, as it might be termed in modern phrase. Hence she is fitly described as an Egyptian, as Sarah's handmaid. Abraham's alliance with Sarah is at first premature. He is not sufficiently advanced in his moral and spiritual development to profit thereby. As yet he begets no son by her. She therefore directs him to go in to her handmaid, to apply himself to the learning of the schools. This inferior alliance proves fruitful at once. At a later date and after this preliminary training he again unites himself to Sarah; and this time his union with divine wisdom is fertile. Not only does Sarah bear him a son, but she is pointed out as the mother of a countless offspring. Thus is realised the strange paradox that 'the barren woman is most fruitful'. Thus in the progress of the human soul are verified the words of the prophet, spoken in an allegory, that 'the desolate hath many children'.

> But the allegory does not end here. The contrast between the mothers is reproduced in the contrast between the sons. Isaac represents the wisdom of the wise man, Ishmael the sophistry of the sophist. Sophistry must in the end give place to wisdom. The son of the bondwoman must be cast out and flee before the son of the princess.

5 *Galatians*, 198–9.

CATEGORY FOUR

Implied Features

16

Multiple Significance

We NOW COME to a fourth category of thought in the New Testament's interpretation of the Old. In this and the following two chapters we will consider some implications of the way in which the Old Testament has been written. For the New Testament recognizes the significance of these implications and utilizes these very features as it expounds the Old Testament to its readers.

The first of these implied features that we will consider takes us back to the question raised in Chapter 5 of whether and how it is possible for a single passage or concept in the Old Testament to have significance at more than one level. Once again let us consider a concise example before moving on to one that is more expansive and detailed.

The case of Adam and Eve

The New Testament's interpretation of Adam and Eve shows that it regards their story as having significance at more than one level.

It goes without saying, of course, that the New Testament believes in the historicity of the Genesis account of the creation and the fall of Adam and Eve. Many are the places where it refers to the purpose of their creation, their relationship with the Creator, their stewardship of the earth, and their privilege of bearing the image and likeness of God. More than once, also, Adam the first man is compared and contrasted with Christ, the second man and the last Adam (cf. Rom 5:12–19; 1 Cor 15:45–49; Heb 2:5–18).

But our special interest here is to notice how the New Testament takes one of the details of the creation story and interprets it, now at the literal and historical level, and now at the prototypical and spiritual level. The particular detail is the creation of Eve as wife and helpmeet for Adam:

> And the rib which the LORD God had taken from the man, made he a woman, and brought her unto the man. And the man said, 'This is now bone of my bones, and flesh of my flesh: she shall be called Woman because she was taken out of Man'. Therefore shall a man leave his father and mother, and shall cleave to his wife: and they shall be one flesh. (Gen 2:22–24)

At Matthew 19:4–6, Christ cites this passage from Genesis and interprets it *at the literal and historical level*. Correcting the lax ideas of some of his contemporaries on the subject of divorce, he takes them back to God's ideal standard, set out at the creation of woman:

> Have you not read that he who made them from the beginning made them male and female, and said: For this cause shall a man leave his father and mother, and shall cleave to his wife; and the two shall become one flesh. What therefore God has joined together, let not man put asunder.

At 1 Corinthians 6:16 the Apostle Paul likewise cites this same detail from the creation record, and applies it at the same literal level to human sexual relationships. But he cites this same passage again, and this time he interprets it *at the prototypical and spiritual level*:

> . . . even as Christ also [loves and nourishes] the Church; because we are members of his body. For this cause shall a man leave his father and mother, and shall cleave to his wife; and the two shall become one flesh. This mystery is great: but I speak in regard of Christ and of the church. (Eph 5:29–32)

Obviously Paul did not regard God's revealed truth as being one-dimensional only. Nor would he agree that interpreting that truth at the prototypical and spiritual level destroyed its significance at the literal and historical level.

But now let us turn to a more detailed example of multiple significance.

The rite of circumcision

The New Testament's interpretation of the Old Testament's rite of circumcision is very instructive, for it shows that right from its very institution circumcision carried more than one significance. Then subsequently in the course of history it developed yet other significances, some good, and some bad. So it is not surprising that by the time one comes to the New Testament epistles, one finds that they comment now on one significance of circumcision, now on another; and thus they indicate that a full interpretation of Old Testament circumcision must allow that it carries significance at more than one level.

Abraham's personal circumcision (Gen 17)

In the case of Abraham, says Paul, circumcision was in the first place a sign and seal of the righteousness which he had by faith while he was still uncircumcised. In other words, Abraham was first justified, and then, and only then, circumcised (Rom 4:11). Circumcision did not effect his justification. It did not even accompany his justification: it was thirteen years and more after he was justified that he was circumcised (Gen 17:24–26). Circumcision was the outward sign pointing to the fact that he had been justified, and the divinely appointed seal that acknowledged and confirmed the righteousness that he had already received by faith.[1]

Moreover it would be false to say that the covenant of circumcision (Gen 17) was an integral part of the covenant which God made with Abraham and his seed in Genesis 15. The covenant of Genesis 15 was 'signed, sealed and settled', thirteen years before any

---

1 Some people have been tempted to equate Old Testament circumcision with Christian baptism. The equation is more than doubtful; but those who make it should be careful to note its implication; like circumcision, baptism does not effect justification. This is true anyway, quite apart from the question whether baptism is the counterpart of circumcision or not.

mention was made of the covenant of circumcision; and, according to the principles of sound legal practice enunciated in Scripture itself (Gal 3:15–18), once a covenant has been confirmed, no further conditions can be added to it by some subsequent covenant.

In the second place, however, Abraham's personal circumcision was a pledge on his part that, now he was justified by faith, he would 'walk before God and be blameless', that is, he would lead a consistent, godly life (Gen 17:1).

The circumcision of Abraham's clan (Gen 17:9–14)

In addition to his own personal circumcision Abraham was also required to circumcise all the males in his household and clan: not only his own children, but also his household servants, whether they were born in his house or bought with money (Gen 17:9–14). What then did circumcision signify for all these people? It was a sign that they were physically members of Abraham's clan. Any non-circumcised descendant of his would be 'cut off from his people' (Gen 17:14).

Circumcision, of course, did not make them spiritual sons of Abraham, let alone children of God. If any of them came to personal faith in God in the same way as Abraham had done *before* he was circumcised, then they became spiritual sons of Abraham (Rom 4:12); and in that case their circumcision was doubtless regarded as a seal of their righteousness-by-faith. But if not, not.

Indeed, circumcision did not in every case indicate God's recognition of the person concerned as one of the special nation for whom God had marked out a special role in history. Ishmael was physically a child of Abraham, and circumcised in addition (Gen 17:25); but he was not an heir according to the covenant of Genesis 15; he was not even allowed to continue as a member of Abraham's physical clan (Gen 21:9–14). And Paul takes up his case and extends it to many others in Israel: 'They are not all Israel, who are of Israel; neither, because they are Abraham's seed, are they all children; but in Isaac shall your seed be called' (Rom 9:6–7).

Circumcision as a token

As with Abraham himself, so with his descendants: circumcision was also a token of willingness to obey the Lord and his law. It was, of course, all too possible to carry the token, but not to exhibit the reality of which it was a token. Israel's own prophets complain of this:

> To whom shall I speak and testify, that they may hear? See, their ear is uncircumcised, and they cannot hearken: behold, the word of the Lord has become unto them a reproach; they have no delight in it. (Jer 6:10)

And Paul takes up the same point:

> Circumcision has value if you observe the law; but if you break the law, you have become as though you had not been circumcised. If those who are not circumcised keep the law's requirements, will they not be regarded as though they were circumcised? The one who is not circumcised physically and yet obeys the law will condemn you who even though you have the written code and circumcision are a law-breaker. (Rom 2:25–27)

In other words tokens are of no practical value without the reality to which they are meant to point. And it is not only ancient Jews who needed the reminder, but Christians too. Of what use is it to partake of the symbols of bread and wine at the Lord's Supper, if one does not possess the forgiveness which our Lord died to procure? Mere physical reception of the bread and wine will not *convey* the forgiveness. And what is more, it is positively dangerous to take the bread and the wine, if one is not prepared to observe the terms of the covenant of which the cup is the symbol. According to that covenant the Lord promises to write his laws on our hearts. For a believer to take the cup, but to have no intention of cooperating with the Lord in the ever deepening writing of those laws on his heart and in the fulfilment of them, is to invite severe divine discipline (1 Cor 11:27–32).

Of what use baptism, either, if the baptised person continues to live sinfully, and has no intention of doing otherwise? There is no magic in baptism. A woman can slip a wedding ring on her finger and wear it every day of her life: if she has no husband and never has had, wearing the ring will not turn her into a married woman. If we have not experienced faith-union with Christ, if we do not possess and live the new life it symbolises (Rom 6:1–4), to be baptised is an empty symbol, as meaningless as the unmarried woman's wedding ring.

A perversion of the rite of circumcision (Gal 5:2–4)

As the centuries proceeded, circumcision like the law itself, became perverted in people's minds, until it was no longer in their eyes simply a token of physical descent from Abraham and of physical membership of the nation of Israel; nor simply a symbol of their willingness to keep God's law; and least of all a seal of the righteousness which is by faith. It became the very opposite: they regarded it along with the keeping of the law, as a means of achieving salvation by their observance of this and all other rites and laws, and thus of meriting justification. And when that happened, it transformed circumcision from a wholesome, helpful, God-given seal, sign and symbol, into a perverted, dangerous ritual.

It is this perverted misuse of circumcision that Paul is protesting against:

> Mark my words! I, Paul, tell you that if you let yourselves be circumcised, Christ will be of no value to you at all. Again I declare to every man who lets himself be circumcised that he is obligated to obey the whole law. You who are trying to be justified by law have been alienated from Christ; you have fallen away from grace. . . . For in Christ Jesus neither circumcision nor uncircumcision has any value. (Gal 5:2–4, 6)

It goes without saying that the Christian symbols of baptism and the Lord's Supper can be perverted in the same way. Once let them be thought of as potent acts of merit that somehow earn, achieve, effect, procure acceptance with God, then works, albeit religious, have been substituted for faith, and law for grace, the way of salvation ruined, and Christ made of none effect.

The 'true' circumcision (Phil 3:2–9)

Not only is the above-mentioned misuse of circumcision wrong in itself; but it is a direct contradiction, so the New Testament points out, of the inner metaphorical meaning of circumcision. The outward removal of a piece of physical flesh was meant to symbolise the complete abandonment of all confidence in 'the flesh' in its moral sense. In the Old Testament the term *flesh* is used to denote man in his independence of, and rebellion against, God. That independence is most easily to be seen in outrageous sinners; but just as often, perhaps more frequently, it disguises itself in the clothes of decency and religion. Independent man likes to maintain his sense of independence and self-achievement even in his relations with God. He does not like to admit his spiritual bankruptcy. He would scorn accepting his weekly groceries as a gift of charity from the grocer: he can afford to buy them. And he resents the idea of receiving salvation as a gift even from God: he must, he can and will, so he thinks, pay for it, earn it. He feels that he has the resources to do so. But that is, in actual fact, trust in the flesh.

Paul was himself an example of this same thing; and for him conversion meant abandoning the perverted use of circumcision, and coming to see, and to conform to, its inner spiritual meaning. Let him tell his story in his own words:

> Watch out for those dogs, those men who do evil, those mutilators of the flesh. For it is we who are the circumcision, we who worship by the Spirit of God, who glory in Christ Jesus, and who put no confidence in the flesh—though I myself have reasons for such confidence. If anyone else thinks he has reasons to put confidence in the flesh I more: circumcised on the eighth day, of the people of Israel . . . as for legalistic righteousness, faultless. But whatever was for my profit I now consider loss for the sake of Christ . . . that I may gain Christ and be found in him, not having a righteousness of my own that comes from the law, but that which is through faith in Christ—the righteousness that comes from God and is by faith. (Phil 3:2–9)

Circumcision, at this level, then signifies that radical repentance and change of attitude when someone renounces all trust in his or her own efforts, law-keeping, observance of rituals and all else, and instead trusts solely in Christ, accepting as a gift the righteousness that God, and God alone, can give.

Spiritual circumcision

There is one further and deeper significance given to circumcision in the New Testament. To understand it, we should first go back to the Old Testament and to one of its metaphorical uses of the term. The happy description of Israel's restoration in Deuteronomy 30 includes this promise: 'And the LORD your God will circumcise your heart, and the heart of your seed, to love the LORD your God with all your heart, and with all your soul, that you may live' (Deut 30:6).

The demand that we love the Lord our God with all our heart, mind, soul and strength is the first and greatest of all the commandments. But Israel's long history has shown that unregenerate man, 'man-in-the-flesh', cannot fulfil the law's demand. That is as true of us Gentiles as it is of the Jews; and in God's mercy Israel's history of sinful disobedience, disloyalty, rebellion, unfaithfulness, exile and discipline under God's chastisement serves as a vivid and salutary demonstration designed to convince the whole world of the fact that the law cannot save us: it can only condemn us (Rom 3:19).

Nor can the unregenerate change their own hearts and make themselves love God. If ever they are to love God as they should, they will first have to be cut free from their roots in the flesh, and be transferred into the Spirit (Rom 8:4–9). That is an operation that only God can perform. No ritualistic, ceremonial knife could reach the deep-seated trouble, no human hand wield the knife efficiently enough to deal with the problem. But what we cannot do, God can. Here in Deuteronomy 30:6 he records his promise that he will do it; and in Colossians he tells us how he does it; through our union with Christ in his death, burial and resurrection.

> In him you were also circumcised with a circumcision not made with hands, in the putting off of the body of the flesh, in the

circumcision of Christ; having been buried with him in baptism, in which you were also raised with him through faith in the working of God who raised him from the dead. And to you, when you were dead through your offences and the uncircumcision of your flesh, he has given life in Christ. . . . (Col 2:11–13)

In both Old and New Testaments, then, circumcision carries significance not just at one, but at many levels; though normally, of course, at only one level on any one occasion. It would certainly be false to suppose that every possible significance of the rite was meant to be read into every mention of it in Scripture. But it would equally be false to suppose that a true interpretation of the Old Testament rite of circumcision must insist that it everywhere has only one and the same meaning.

17

Logical Thought-flow and Intentional Silence

For the purpose of this study we turn once more to the Epistle to the Hebrews. We shall there study first one example of the way in which its author bases his case on the precise order in which an Old Testament passage makes its statements. Then we shall move on to observe how he attaches significance not merely to what an Old Testament passage explicitly records but also to what it does not record.

Interpreting order

Our example comes from Hebrews 10. Here the main thrust of his general argument is to prove that the sacrifice of Christ is not only superior to the animal sacrifices commanded by the law: it has superseded them and rendered them obsolete. His argument up to this point runs as follows. The law, he says, can never by its sacrifices make those that offer them perfect, for if it could, the worshippers, having been cleansed completely once and for all, would feel no need to offer sacrifices any more, and the offering of sacrifices would then cease. As it is, however, in that system of animal sacrifices, the people's sins are judicially brought up against them every year (on the Day of Atonement) and further offerings of sacrifices are required. The reason for all this repeated offering is the basic impossibility and inability of the blood of animals actually to take away the guilt of human sins (Heb 10:1–4).

Our author then suggests that it is this unsatisfactoriness of animal sacrifices that lies behind the Messiah's prophetic words recorded in Psalm 40. These words, our author points out (Heb 10:5), explain the purpose of Messiah's coming into the world, and our author first quotes them in full:

> Sacrifice and offering you did not desire, but a body you pre-pared for me; with whole burnt offerings and sin offerings you were not pleased. Then I said, 'See I have come (it has been writ-ten about me in the scroll of the book) to do your will, O God.' (Ps 40:6–8 [in the Septuagint translation]; Heb 10:5–7)

But our author is not content to quote the passage in full and then to leave it to his readers to perceive, as best they can, how this passage supports the case he is arguing. Instead, he quotes the pas-sage again (Heb 10:8–9), this time with comments of his own, aimed at demonstrating:

1. that the passage contains not one but two distinct statements by Messiah;

2. that Messiah's second statement is spoken not merely *after* the first statement, but *in response to* the contents of the first statement;

3. that the fact that there are two statements and that the sec-ond is a response to the first is not an analysis arbitrarily im-posed on the psalm by our author: it is explicitly indicated by the psalm itself.

His words are:

> Saying above [i.e. at the beginning of the quotation Messiah be-gins his first statement by saying]: Sacrifices and offerings and whole burnt offerings and sacrifices for sin you did not desire, nor were you pleased with them [and here our author adds the explanatory comment:] which are offered according to the law. (Heb 10:8–9)

Then he has said (and this is Messiah's second statement, the 'Then I said' of Ps 40:7): 'See I have come to do Your will.' Notice at once the phrase 'Then he has said'. This is not a comment by our author, arbitrarily insisting that Messiah's speech can, and should be, divided into two statements. Our author is pointing out that in the psalm's own text Messiah himself begins his second statement with the words *'Then I said,* See I have come to do your will'. Messiah is thus indicating that his second statement is being made in direct response to God's dissatisfaction with animal sacrifices, expressed in the first statement. Instead of animal sacrifices that could never satisfy God, Messiah indicates that he has come to do God's will by offering to God his own body as a sacrifice for sin, to God's complete and eternal satisfaction.

It is our author's contention, then, that the very order of the Psalm's statements expresses Messiah's intention to set aside the first in order to establish the second (Heb 10:9), that is to do away with the Old Testament's animal sacrifices, and to replace them with the sacrifice of himself.

Interpreting the silences of biblical narrative

> For this Melchizedek, king of Salem, priest of God Most High, who met Abraham returning from the slaughter of the kings, and blessed him, to whom also Abraham divided a tenth part of all, (being first, by translation [i.e. of his name] king of righteousness, and then also king of Salem, which is, king of peace; without father, without mother, without genealogy, having neither beginning of days nor end of life, but made like unto the Son of God) abides a priest continually. (Heb 7:1–3)

The historical narrative concerning Melchizedek is to be found at Gen 14:18–20; but before we consider our author's interpretation of this passage, we ought to trace the route by which he came to think about this passage in the first place. Like all early Christians he began by believing that Jesus is the Son of God and accepting the historical facts of his death, resurrection, and ascension into heaven. Christ had also taught his disciples (see Matt 22:41–46) that Psalm 110:1 ('The LORD says to my Lord, Sit at my right hand until I make your enemies your footstool') referred to him and indicated his deity, his ascension, his session at God's right hand, and the interval that must transpire between his ascension and his second coming and final victory over all his enemies.

This verse, then, would have been foundational for our author's understanding of the gospel of Christ, as it was for other New Testament writers; and he quotes it in part or whole at Hebrews 1:3, 13; 8:1; 10:12–13; 12:2. It was natural for him, therefore, to pass from Psalm 110:1 to verse 4 of that same psalm, which declares: 'The LORD has sworn, and will not repent, You are a priest for ever after the order of Melchizedek'. Our author had no doubt that this too referred to the Lord Jesus; and he noticed that it made two statements about him. First, that God had appointed Christ to be a priest for ever, and had done so to the solemn accompaniment of an oath (see his comment at Heb 7:20–21); and, secondly, that Christ's priesthood was to be 'after the order of Melchizedek'. Naturally therefore our author turned to the biblical account of the ancient priest Melchizedek (Gen 14:18–20), to see how its details could illustrate, and help us to understand more fully, the priesthood of our Lord.

He noticed first the things that the record explicitly says about Melchizedek:

1. *He was priest of God Most High*, i.e. he was not a pagan priest of some idolatrous deity: he was priest of the one true God.

2. *He met Abraham as Abraham returned from the slaughter of the kings, and he (Melchizedek) blessed him (Abraham)*. From this our author deduces that Melchizedek was a greater personage than Abraham: for without any dispute the less is blessed by the greater (Heb 7:6–7).

3. *Abraham gave Melchizedek a tenth of all the spoils he had taken.* Now at this time Abraham had already been promised by God that he would be the father of a great nation. When, therefore, he gave tithes to the priest Melchizedek, he was acting as the founder and patriarch of Israel, and as the progenitor of the Levitical priesthood that should spring from him. From this our author argues that Melchizedek had superior status not only to that of Abraham himself but also to that of the subsequent Levitical priesthood (Heb 7:4–10).

4. The text gives the name of this king-priest as *Melchizedek*, and the name of his royal city as *Salem*. Our author obviously considers

these names significant, for he points out to his Greek-speaking readers that in Hebrew 'Melchizedek' means 'king of righteousness' and 'Salem' means 'peace'. Our author does not say what the significance is. Perhaps he thought it was too obvious (to Christian readers at least) to need explanation. True peace in any city depends on the righteousness of its government; but in one who served as a prefigurement of Christ and of the gospel, this combination of the terms 'righteousness' and 'peace' is highly appropriate. Compare this with Paul's statement of what we experience through Christ, our great high priest: 'Being justified by faith we have peace with God through our Lord Jesus Christ' (Rom 8:1).

So much then for our author's comments on what the Old Testament narrative actually says. But now he adds a further description of Melchizedek:

> Without father, without mother, without genealogy, having neither beginning of days nor end of life, but made like the Son of God, he remains a priest for ever. (Heb 7:3)

Here we must be careful to perceive what our author means. He is not claiming that the historical person Melchizedek actually had no human parents, existed for all eternity, and never died. Nor is he claiming that Melchizedek was a 'christophany', that is, a preincarnation appearance of the Son of God (as in Gen 32:24–30, and Judg 13:3–22). He is pointing out that in the biblical record of Melchizedek nothing is said about his parents, nothing about his genealogy or year of birth, and nothing is recorded about his death or when his priesthood ceased. He just appears on the page of Genesis without any intimation of his previous history, is announced as a priest, and after just three verses is not mentioned again (until Ps 110:4). As far as the record of Genesis is concerned, his priesthood continued indefinitely.

In our author's mind the absence of all these details from the biblical record is no accident. God who inspired the composer of Psalm 110:4 to write of Messiah: 'You are a priest for ever after the order of Melchizedek' had already inspired the author of Genesis in his description of Melchizedek, both in what he explicitly said of him, and in what he left out. The purpose of that inspiration was that when anyone subsequently read in Psalm 110:4 that Messiah was to be a priest for ever after the order of Melchizedek, and then looked back to Genesis 14 to see what 'after the order of Melchizedek' might mean, he might there discover a deliberately drawn prefigurement of Messiah's eternal priesthood, a prefigurement that *within the scriptural record* had been 'made to resemble the Son of God' both by the information it explicitly provided and by the information it withheld.

It was, then, belief in the divine inspiration and authority of Scripture that led our author to attach significance both to the statements and to the silences of this biblical record.

18

Internal Coherence as a Basis
for Expository Preaching

A CASE STUDY FOR this third implied feature that the New Testament utilizes can be found in Hebrews 3:7–4:16. Though part of the ongoing argument of the book, this passage contains what is virtually a sermon preached by the author of this epistle to his readers. The sermon is ultimately based on the historical facts of what happened when Moses led Israel to the border of the promised land and the great majority of the people refused to enter (see Num 13–14). And not only on those bare facts; for on that occasion God himself interpreted the spiritual significance of the people's refusal, and the author of Hebrews will from time to time refer to that interpretation.

But the author of Hebrews does not found his sermon directly on the historical narrative of Numbers 13–14. He founds it on a sermon preached by the poet who wrote Psalm 95 some centuries after Israel's refusal, but also centuries before the Epistle to the Hebrews was written. Our particular concern, therefore, is to observe the methods which the author of Hebrews uses to appropriate the message proclaimed by this psalm and to apply it to his readers.

Step one

First, he reminds his readers of the authority possessed by the verses he is about to quote from the psalm:

Wherefore, even as the Holy Spirit says . . . (Heb 3:7)

In other words, the exhortation which is to follow—'Today, if you hear his voice, do not harden your hearts . . .' is not, in our author's estimation, simply good advice from a religiously minded poet: it is the voice of the inspiring Spirit of God speaking directly to our author's readers; and they should accept it as such.

Not only so: for whereas in verses 1 to 8 of the psalm the poet refers to God in the third person '. . . *his* presence . . . unto *him* . . . in *his* hand . . . the sea is *his* . . . *he* is our God . . .', etc., from verse 9 to the end the psalm dramatically introduces God speaking directly in his own voice and referring to himself in the first person: 'Your fathers . . . saw *my* works . . . I was angry . . . I said . . . they have not known *my* ways . . . I swore in *my* wrath . . . they shall not enter *my* rest'.

The author of Hebrews, then, is not simply appealing to his own authority as an inspired writer of a New Testament epistle (though he had the right to do so): he is about to preach his readers a sermon based on an Old Testament passage, and so he begins by first reminding them of the divine authority of that passage.

Step two

His second step is to quote the passage in full. His intention is not arbitrarily to select a phrase or two from this psalm, and then, regardless of their original context, build around them a sermon composed largely of ideas that have little or nothing to do with their original context. His sermon will take the form of expository preaching. He will follow the passage's own progress of thought from the beginning to the end, successively emphasizing, or even repeating, its leading terms and phrases, elucidating its references to the historical event in Numbers, explaining its major concepts, and all the while justifying his application of the warning of this Old Testament psalm to his contemporary readers.

So let us here follow the author's example and quote the passage from the Psalms in full:

Today, if you hear his voice,
do not harden your hearts as in the rebellion,
on the day of testing in the wilderness,
when your fathers tested and tried me,
and saw my works forty years.
Therefore I was angry with that generation,
and said, 'They always go astray in their heart;
and they have not known my ways.'
As I swore in my wrath,
'They shall not enter my rest.' (Heb 3:7–11)

Step three

Now he begins to expound the actual text of Psalm 95, and he does
so by first summing up in his own words its major lesson. In this
way right from the start the main lesson will be fixed in his readers'
minds, then reinforced, and not be clouded, by his subsequent comments on the details: 'Take care, brothers, lest there shall be in any
one of you an evil heart of unbelief in falling away from the living
God' (Heb 3:12).

How fair to the psalm is this summary? The psalm itself rebukes
the Israelites for 'going astray in their hearts'; but it does not use the
term 'evil heart of unbelief', nor does it talk of 'falling away from the
living God'. Is our author unjustifiably introducing into his sermon
ideas of his own, thus exaggerating the warning given by the psalm
itself?

The answer is, No. He has consulted the historical record of
Israel's rebellion in the desert to which the psalm is referring (Num
14:1–11, 22–23). There he has found God commenting on Israel's
behaviour in these terms: 'How long will this people despise me?
And how long will they not believe in me . . . ?' (Num 14:11).

Here then is the basis of our author's warning against 'an evil
heart of unbelief'. And as for 'falling away from the living God',
the record shows that Israel did precisely that. God had redeemed
them out of Egypt, led them through the desert, brought them to
the borders of Canaan, all with the purpose of giving them Canaan
as their inheritance. But eventually they bitterly resented his ever

having redeemed them out of Egypt, and they proposed making themselves a captain and returning to Egypt, thus rejecting God's promised inheritance and reversing the effect of his redemption. And you cannot do that without falling away from the living God himself (Num 14:1–10). 'An evil heart of unbelief' and 'falling away from the living God', then, are precisely what the psalm is referring to when it warns its readers not to harden their hearts as Israel did.

Step four

Our author now returns to the opening words of the passage:

> Today, if you hear his voice,
> do not harden your hearts. . . . (Heb 3:13)

He notices that these opening words are a ringing exhortation. Accordingly, he, as a preacher, himself exhorts his readers, not merely to accept the Holy Spirit's exhortation, but themselves, in their turn, to exhort one another in unison with the Holy Spirit's exhortation (Heb 3:13). He notices, moreover, that in the psalm the Holy Spirit prefaces his exhortation with the word *today*; and as a careful exegete, he treats this time note as significant. 'Today', as he understands it, refers not to a particular day of twenty-four hours, but to a period (cf. a similar interpretation at 2 Cor 6:2). As long, then, as this 'today period' lasts, there is opportunity to hear God's word and to believe it. On the other hand, the very use of the word *today*, implies that *tomorrow* the opportunity may no longer be available. Hence the danger of hardening their hearts to the call of God during the 'today period'.

Understanding the implications of his text in this way, our author now applies it: 'But exhort one another day by day, so long as it is called today, lest any one of you be hardened by the deceitfulness of sin' (Heb 3:13).

Sin, he points out, is deceitful; and to see how deceitful it can be, one need only read the historical narrative of the exodus. When the nation first came out of Egypt and stood on the farther side of the Red Sea, they joined with Moses and Miriam enthusiastically singing praise to God for their deliverance (Exod 15). From that an observer might have concluded that they were all genuine believers. But the fact is they weren't, and never had been (Exod 12:38; Num 14:11, 22); and their continual complainings, their threats of rebellion (Exod 17:2–4) and their virtual apostasy at Mount Sinai (Exod 32) ought to have alerted them to that fact. But sin is deceitful: it hid the fact from them, lulled their consciences, and hardened their hearts until their basic unbelief eventually broke out in undisguised, direct rejection both of God and of his redemption.

Step five

Now a question arises; and we may illustrate what that question is by briefly recalling the Old Testament incident which we discussed in Chapter 13, namely Korah's rebellion against Moses and Aaron. If some preacher were to take the story of that rebellion and apply its solemn warnings to genuine modern believers, wholly loyal to the Lord Jesus, who have, nevertheless, disagreed with their church leaders over some small matter, it would surely be a serious misapplication of the Old Testament story (see our characterisation of Korah's rebellion in Chapter 13).

But now our author is taking another Old Testament story, namely that of Israel's rebellious refusal to enter Canaan, with all its solemn implications, and suggesting that some at least of his contemporary professing Christians were in danger of committing a similar rebellion. That, if true, would be very serious. He realises, therefore, that he must justify the implicit analogy which he is drawing between their behaviour and Israel's; otherwise his application of the psalm's warning will appear arbitrary, lose its cogency, and be offensive.

He now, therefore, sets out to justify the analogy by first stating what his readers' present spiritual situation is. Notice that that situation is not something he deduces from the Old Testament narrative. It is the situation proclaimed by the Christian gospel quite independently of whether the analogy he is about to draw from the Old Testament is valid or not.[1] And the situation is this: 'We have come to share in Christ, if we hold our original confidence firm to the end' (Heb 3:14).

The Christian gospel declares that it is no use having made a Christian profession some time in the past, if one does not hold it to the end. Indeed, the evidence that the original profession was genuine, is precisely that it is maintained to the end. Repudiate the profession and it casts doubt on whether the profession was ever genuine, on whether it ever had any root, and therefore on whether the one who made the profession ever did in reality come to share in Christ in the first place. (Cf. Christ's interpretation of the parable of the Sower, Luke 8:13–15.)[2]

That, then, is the Christian position. But now our author moves on and draws the analogy between Israel's behaviour in the desert and that of his contemporary readers. Or rather, he points out that it is the Holy Spirit who draws the comparison by saying—and here our author goes back to the beginning of the psalm passage and quotes it again—

> Today, if you hear his voice, do not harden your hearts *as in the rebellion*. (Heb 3:15)

In other words, here is the Holy Spirit recalling the rebellion in the desert, and explicitly citing it as a parallel case, exhibiting the same danger as our author's contemporaries are in.

Step six

But our author is not content to regard the analogy which the Holy Spirit draws as simply a broad, general analogy: he insists on examining the details of the Numbers narrative and on applying these details to his readers. And rightly so: for Psalm 95 likewise

---

1 It is, of course, valid: our author speaks under divine inspiration.
2 For a fuller exposition of this verse see Gooding, *An Unshakeable Kingdom*, 110.

includes in the analogy a number of the details involved in the rebellion. They are:

1. The fact that it was a rebellion
2. God's anger with the rebels for forty years
3. God's oath that they should not enter his rest.

Our author therefore takes each one of these details in turn and comments on it in such a way as to bring out its relevance to his readers and to the warning he is seeking to urge upon them.

Comment on Detail 1

> For who were they who, having heard, rebelled? Was it not all those who came out of Egypt by Moses? (Heb 3:16)

The question is rhetorical, and the implied answer is, Yes, all: all, that is, except a few individuals like Caleb and Joshua. The rebellion, then, was not a strange, rare aberration perpetrated by a few, altogether untypical, people, such that it would be grotesque to suggest that any of our author's readers could be guilty of a similar offence. If virtually the whole nation rebelled in Moses' day, it is not unthinkable that some, at least, of our author's hearers might be in danger of committing the same sin.

Comment on Detail 2

> And with whom was he displeased for forty years? Was it not with those who sinned whose carcasses fell in the wilderness? (Heb 3:17)

In other words, the rebellion was not a freak storm that suddenly blew up, and just as suddenly blew itself out, with no serious or permanent consequences. On the contrary, the seriousness of the rebellion was such, and its consequences so irreparable, that God relentlessly waited till all that rebellious generation had died out before he let the next generation enter the promised land (see Num 14:32–35; Deut 2:14–15).

Comment on Detail 3

> And to whom did he swear that they should not enter his rest,
> but to those that were disobedient? (Heb 3:18)

Here our author's concern is to define precisely what was the sin
involved in this rebellion. It was not a sudden temporary outburst
of, say, ill-temper brought on by frayed nerves. It was a case of
fundamental, persistent, unbelief. And our author draws the conclusion: 'So we see that they were unable to enter in because of
unbelief' (Heb 3:19).[3]

Step seven

At this point our author's exposition of the psalm strikes a more
positive note. Hitherto he has concentrated on those who because
of their deliberate and persistent unbelief were sentenced by God's
oath never to enter the promised land of Canaan, or, in the language of Psalm 95:11, never to 'enter my [i.e. God's] rest'. But now
our author asserts that the language of God's oath, taken in the
general context of the psalm, indicates that his sentence on the
rebels has not cancelled the promise in respect of everyone else.
Far from it. Those who, unlike the rebels, believe God's word and
do not harden their hearts still have open to them the possibility,
indeed the promise, of entering God's rest. Says our author:

> Therefore, since the promise of entering his rest still stands, let
> us fear lest any one of you should seem to have fallen short of
> it. (Heb 4:1).

Questions immediately arise, and the first one is this: Where
does the psalm explicitly say that this promise still stands open,

---

3 The Greek word-cluster translated as 'disobedient' (Heb 3:18), 'disobedience' (4:6,
11), is consistently used everywhere else in the New Testament to describe the attitude of those who deliberately reject the gospel and refuse to believe it. This group of
words is never used of true believers whose faith is weak or who temporarily fall into
some disobedience (see Gooding, *An Unshakeable Kingdom*, 113).

and open not only to the psalmist's immediate readers, but to our author's contemporaries—and even to us?

The answer is that the psalm nowhere states this explicitly; but our author contends that its general argument obviously implies it.

What grounds, then, can be put forward in support of his contention? In the first place one can call as witness the original historical narrative.

The context of God's oath in Numbers 14

When God swore his oath against the rebels, he simultaneously promised not one thing only but two:

1. The rebels would never enter the promised land.
2. But Caleb, their contemporary, would, and so would the rebels' children, who being under age, would not be held responsible for their parents' decision.

> Then the LORD said . . . None of the men who have seen my glory and my signs that I did in Egypt and in the wilderness, and yet have put me to the test these ten times and have not obeyed my voice, shall see the land that I swore to give to their fathers. And none of those who despised me shall see it. But my servant Caleb, because he has a different spirit and has followed me fully, I will bring him into the land . . . and his descendants shall possess it. . . . As I live, declares the LORD, what you have said in my hearing I will do to you: your dead bodies shall fall in this wilderness, and of all your number, listed in the census from twenty years old and upward, who have grumbled against me, not one shall come into the land where I swore that I would make you dwell, except Caleb . . . and Joshua. . . . But your little ones, who you said would become a prey, I will bring in, and they shall know the land that you have rejected. (Num 14:20–24, 28–31 ESV)

God had originally promised the nation's forefathers, Abraham, Isaac and Jacob, that he would bring their descendants into Canaan (Num 14:24, 31). The fact that God subsequently swore an oath that the rebels would never enter it, obviously did not cancel the original promise for everyone else. It left the promise still standing for Caleb and Joshua, the rebels' contemporaries, who were true believers, for their descendants, and even for the rebels' descendants.

The general context of God's oath in Psalm 95

With this we come back to Psalm 95 where the Holy Spirit points out to the 'today' generation that they can hear God's voice speaking to them as their forefathers did. He exhorts them, therefore, not to harden their hearts as the rebels did in the wilderness; and he strengthens his exhortation by reminding the 'today' people of what happened when their forefathers hardened their hearts: God swore an oath that they would never enter his rest. But what, we may well ask, would be the point of reminding the 'today' people of this solemn consequence of the rebels' refusal to believe, if no promise or possibility of entering God's rest (or any equivalent thereof) was left standing for the 'today' generation if they did not harden their hearts, but rather believed God's word? The very reminder of God's oath that the *unbelievers* would not enter his rest, surely implied that *believers* would.

Our author, therefore, is on solid ground when he argues that Psalm 95 leaves the promise of entering God's rest still standing for the people of 'today'. But he has an additional reason for declaring that the promise still stands open, as we shall now see.

Step eight

Our author now draws our attention to the analogy between the promise held out to believers by the Christian gospel and the promise given to the Israelites when they were redeemed from Egypt. He has already made use of this analogy earlier in his sermon; and we noticed there that he did not first state Israel's position and then deduce the Christian position from that. He first stated the Christian position, and then pointed to the similarity between it and the earlier experience of Israel in the wilderness. He follows the same order here in citing another detail in the same analogy:

Our present Christian position: 'for we are in the position of having had good news [i.e. the gospel] preached to us'.

The position of the ancient Israelites: 'just as they too [*scil.* were in the position of having had good news preached to them]'.

The parallel is obvious; but let us first recall what this Christian good news involves.[4] It tells the believer not only that he has been redeemed from the power of darkness and granted forgiveness of sins (Col 1:13–14), but that he has before him, as an integral part of his salvation, 'an inheritance incorruptible, and undefiled, and that fades not way, reserved in heaven' for him (1 Pet 1:3–4). In addition, he has the present possession of the Holy Spirit who is 'the guarantee of our inheritance until we acquire possession of it' (Eph 1:13–14). Neither part of this twofold gospel, 'this so great salvation' (Heb 2:3), is optional. The two parts are inseparable. Accept the first part, and you accept both. Refuse to believe and accept the second part, and you thereby reject the first part as well.

Hence the danger that our author's readers were in. They had professed to believe that Jesus was Messiah; but now some of them seemed to be reluctant to 'go on to maturity' (6:1), to enter into even that part of the great Christian inheritance that is open to a believer's present enjoyment — such as the benefits bestowed by our Lord's high-priesthood (Heb 7), the blessings conferred by the new covenant (Heb 8–9), and the privilege of present spiritual entrance into the Most Holy Place (Heb 10) — let alone entrance to the heavenly inheritance to come (10:35–39; 11:13–16; 12:22–29; 13:14).

This reluctance, therefore, on the part of our author's readers was ominous; and for that reason he calls attention once more to their ancestors' reluctance, indeed their refusal, to enter their physical and earthly inheritance. The parallel between their ancestors' behaviour and their own is so close, that as he now probes deeply into their ancestors' hearts to expose the cause and implications of their refusal, he is simultaneously inviting his readers to probe deeply into their own hearts to confront a possible cause of their own reluctance.

---

4 The Greek word εὐαγγελίζομαι (euangelizomai) = 'to have good news preached to one', is a member of that word-group which the New Testament consistently uses for 'the gospel'.

Why the gospel did not profit their ancestors

First, let us remind ourselves what 'good news' or 'gospel' it was that their ancestors received. It certainly included the good report which the two spies, Caleb and Joshua, brought back after they had reconnoitred the land and its giant inhabitants:

> The land which we passed through to spy it out, is an exceeding good land. If the Lord delight in us, then he will bring us into this land, and give it to us, a land which flows with milk and honey. Only rebel not against the Lord, neither fear the people of the land. (Num 14:7–9)

But that particular piece of good news which Caleb and Joshua reported to the people was not a separate, or additional, gospel: it was an integral part of the one gospel that God had originally preached to Israel right from the start when they were still in Egypt:

> I have come down to deliver them out of the hand of the Egyptians, and to bring them up out of that land unto a good land and a large, unto a land flowing with milk and honey. (Exod 3:8)

There never had been two gospels, one which promised them deliverance from Egypt, and then subsequently a second gospel which promised the land of Canaan as an optional extra to any who might care to go in for it. There were two parts to this gospel, but only one gospel.

Why then did this great gospel not profit them? Because, says our author, 'The message which they heard was not assimilated by faith on the part of the hearers' (Heb 4:2).

They all had heard the good news right from the start. Caleb and Joshua had believed it right from the start. But the majority of their contemporaries had simply gone along with it, and had never personally assimilated it or incorporated it into themselves by faith; and when it came to the test they were found never to have truly believed it.[5]

---

5 Some Greek mss have a slightly different reading, which can be translated: 'because they were not united by faith with those who (really) heard'. This would mean that, being unbelievers, they were not united with true believers like Caleb and Joshua.

They were like ships which rested alongside the quay, without ever having been securely tied up to the quayside; and when the storm came, they drifted away and were swept onto the rocks (see Heb 2:1, and by contrast 6:18–20).

A positive contrast

By this detailed analysis of their ancestors' basic unbelief, our author has probed his readers' hearts very deeply in order to lead them to make sure that in spite of apparent inconsistencies between their initial profession of faith and their present practice they are truly believers, and will by God's help correct those inconsistencies. Initial faith may be weak; however, we are not saved by the strength of our faith but by the Saviour in whom our faith has been placed. In all likelihood the persecutions they had recently suffered (10:32–35) had grievously assaulted their faith; and our author had no intention of undermining still further what little faith they had, but rather of assuring them that genuine faith in Christ, however weak, is enough to secure salvation and the promised inheritance. Once more, therefore, he now enunciates clearly and simply what is required for entering God's rest. Says he: 'We enter that rest, *we who did believe*' (4:3).

We should notice at once that the Greek participle, here translated 'did believe', is in a tense that points backwards to the time of our initial faith, when first we personally put our trust in Christ. It is true that initial faith, if genuine, will endure and give good evidence of itself—Christ our intercessor will see to that (Luke 22:31–32; Heb 7:23–25), but initial faith brings us immediately into that rest which Christ offers to all who come to him (Matt 11:28); into that rest which we experience when we believe the good news that acceptance with God depends not on the meritorious works that we do, but on the work that Christ has done for us (Rom 3:21–28; Eph 2:7–10). Such initial faith, we remember, was enough to secure for the dying thief, when he believed, immediate access into the rest of the eternal paradise of God (Luke 23:42–43); and so it will be for all who put their faith in Christ.

Step nine

But now a question arises about the wording of the psalm which our author is expounding; and we had better settle this question before we continue with our author's exposition. The question is this. In Numbers, God's oath against the rebels is 'surely they shall not see the land' (Num 14:23), or 'surely you shall not come into the land' (14:30). But when in Psalm 95 the Holy Spirit refers to this oath, he rephrases it as 'they shall not *enter my rest*'. Why?

Because, in the first place, Psalm 95:11 is addressed to the 'to-day generation' of Israel, when the nation had been in the promised land for centuries. It would, therefore, make no sense to warn them that if they rejected God's gospel as their ancestors did, they would never see or enter the promised land. What they were in danger of missing was not entry into the promised land, but something far more important, namely, entry into God's rest.

This but raises another question. If 'entry into God's rest' is not the same as 'entry into the promised land', why does the Holy Spirit give the impression in Psalm 95:11 that 'never enter my rest' was the phrase used in God's oath against the rebels in the desert?

Two things come into consideration here. First, when the believing Israelites entered the promised land, they did experience, at one level, a God-given rest: 'The land had rest from war', says Joshua 11:23; and 22:4 adds, 'And now the LORD your God has given rest to your brethren'. Moreover, centuries later, God who, to use his own words, had 'not dwelt in a house since the day that I brought up Israel out of Egypt, even unto this day, but have walked in a tent and in a tabernacle' (2 Sam 7:6), allowed Solomon to build him a permanent stone house, and entered into his resting-place (2 Chr 6:41). For the time being, God had achieved his purpose in bringing Israel out of Egypt and into the promised land. God could now cease from his 'walking', and enter his resting place.

There is, then, a certain similarity between the goal of ancient Israel's redemption, namely, a God-given rest which, in some sense, God himself shared, and the rest which in Psalm 95 God holds out to the 'today generation'. That justifies the use of the same word 'rest' to describe both. On the other hand, they are not the same. The rest which Israel eventually entered was impermanent and often interrupted; the rest which God holds out in Psalm 95 is eternal. Israel's God-given rest in Canaan was, then, a prototype of the far greater rest which God offers the 'today generation'; but it was not exactly the same thing.

So the rebels in the desert certainly missed the God-given rest in Canaan. But they missed much more than that. For God's rest of which the Holy Spirit speaks in Psalm 95 had been available from the very creation of the world to all those who put their faith in God and his word (Heb 4:3). But the rebels in the desert rejected God's word, rejected God's gospel, and in the end turned their backs on God. So doing, they were condemned never to enter, not only Canaan, but the eternal rest of God. And what that rest is we must let our author explain as he takes the next step in his sermon.

Step ten

> ... even as he has said, 'As I swore in my wrath, They shall not enter into my rest', although the works were finished from the foundation of the world. For he has said somewhere of the seventh day on this wise, 'And God rested on the seventh day from all his works'; and in this place again, 'They shall not enter into my rest'. (Heb 4:3–5)

It is, then, our author's contention that when in the psalm God uses the phrase 'my rest', he is referring to the rest which he himself began when the work of creation was finished, and he 'rested from all his work which God had created and made' (Gen 2:3). The created universe of heaven and earth and of life within it, carried both potential for development and the possibility of redemption and renewal when man, its chief steward, should by his disloyalty and disobedience threaten the achievement of God's original purpose in creation. But the fact that God put his hand to creating the universe, and brought the work of creation to completion, was the guarantee that his purpose in creating it would eventually be achieved. Creation was not left half-done, nor would it be left to fall back into the nothingness out of which it was created. The achievement of its end-purpose was already implied in the fact that God initiated and then completed the work of creation; and in that divine certainty God rested.

The entry of the nation of Israel into the promised land was but one of the purposes God had in mind when he created the world; and the fact that he purposed it, was the guarantee that it would be fulfilled. By faith Caleb and Joshua accepted the utter certainty of that fulfilment, and thus entered into God's own rest of heart about the outcome even before all the necessary battles were won and they had rest from war (Num 14:6–9). Their contemporaries had no such faith in the certainty of the fulfilment of God's purpose, and in consequence they did not enjoy God's rest of heart as they faced the battles ahead. So they refused to enter the promised land and never enjoyed the subsequent rest from war.

Step eleven

But now our author envisages a possible objection from his readers: all God's promises to give Israel rest were completely fulfilled when Joshua finally conquered all the kings of Canaan, and the Israelites had rest from war. Therefore, no similar, subsequent rest is held out for us; and we need not worry as to whether we have entered, or ever will enter, that rest.

In answer our author simply points out that Psalm 95 with its offer to the 'today generation' of entrance into God's rest, was written centuries after the rest which Joshua achieved for Israel in Canaan. Joshua's rest was obviously not the fulfilment of the rest held out in the psalm. 'There remains therefore', he concludes, 'a rest for the people of God' (Heb 4:9). It is a 'keeping of sabbath' (Greek: σαββατισμός, sabbatismos, Heb 4:9); it is the same as the rest which God enjoyed when he ceased from his work of creating: 'for he who has entered into his [God's] rest, has himself also rested from his works as God did from his' (Heb 4:10).

We naturally ask: When do we cease from our own works and enter this rest? The answer is twofold:

Initial rest

This can be known by experience here and now when we respond to Christ's personal invitation:

> Come to me, all you who labour and are heavy laden and I will give you rest. Take my yoke upon you, and learn from me, for I am gentle and lowly in heart, and you will find rest for your souls. (Matt 11:28–29 ESV)

From him we learn that for justification and peace with God we must abandon all faith in our own works, and rest entirely on the work of propitiation that Christ has done and finished for us (Rom 3:19–31). And though there are many battles ahead, we can, like Joshua and Caleb, enjoy the rest of God in our hearts, knowing that our final salvation is secure (Rom 5:1–11; 8:31–39).

Final rest

This we will know at our physical death, when we depart from our body and are present with the Lord (2 Cor 5:1–8; Rev 14:13); or, if we are alive at the second coming, when the Lord Jesus returns, changes us and takes us with our resurrected fellow believers to be for ever with the Lord (1 Thess 4:13–18; 2 Thess 1:7–12).

Step twelve

And now our author's expository sermon nears its end; but like a faithful pastor he will not conclude without a solemn exhortation and then a word of strong encouragement. The living and powerful word of God on which his sermon has been based has searched, and will continue to search, the very depths of their hearts. They should not try to avoid the cutting edge of its thrust, but rather make sure that they do not miss God's rest through disobeying God's gospel (Heb 4:11–13).

In recent times, it is true, they may have behaved inconsistently with their professed faith. But they have no need to abandon their confession of faith, for in Christ they have a faithful, merciful, compassionate and understanding high priest. Let them then 'come boldly to the throne of grace, and they will receive mercy and find grace to help in time of need' (Heb 4:14–16).

CATEGORY FIVE

Typological Shadows

19

The Tabernacle as a Shadow
of the Heavenly Things

IT HAS TO be confessed that among academic theologians during the last hundred years typological interpretation of the Old Testament has not always enjoyed great favour. This has been due in part to a feeling that such interpretation does not mesh well with the rational grammatico-historical approach to the text, which is on all sides considered basic to a proper understanding of the Old Testament. It is also due to the manifestly arbitrary meanings sometimes imposed on the text by some practitioners of typology. Typological interpretation, it is felt, relies too much on creative imagination, rather than on rational exegesis and exposition. Moreover, it is suggested that this superimposing of a typical meaning on the text tends to devalue its primary, original meaning.

In the last thirty years or so, however, a marked swing in favour of typological interpretation has been taking place, due in large part to the publication in English of a book by the liberal scholar, Leonhard Goppelt.[1] In it he demonstrated that typological interpretation of the Old Testament is not only legitimate: in the New Testament it is of central importance. His work has been widely influential as has the more recent work of G. K. Beale who has convincingly advocated the legitimacy of typology.[2]

1 *Typos*, published in German in 1939; English translation 1982.
2 See Beale's collection of articles by various scholars, both against and for typology,

In this second part of our book, we have left discussion of typology to the last—deliberately. It is not that we wish to disparage typological interpretation. It is that we intended to emphasise the fact that typology (strictly so called) is only one of the devices that the New Testament uses to mine the wealth of the Old. Some expositors and preachers, convinced that the New Testament writers themselves were justified in employing typological interpretation, are nevertheless averse to our treatment of any features of the Old Testament as types other than those which the New Testament writers, under divine inspiration, authoritatively declare to be types. The caution of these expositors and preachers is excessive, as Beale points out. But even they are not faced with a stark choice: either the plain, straightforward, literal meaning of the text (along with any moral or spiritual implications it might have had for its original readers, and so perhaps for us) or a typological interpretation. The New Testament's own treatment of the Old demonstrates, as we have attempted to show, that other interpretational categories are open to us: simile, formal comparison, metaphor, legal paradigm, analogy, and fulfilment, not only of predictions, but also of prototypes.[3] Therefore, with the encouragement received from our studies thus far, and not dismissing the concerns of our friends, we shall now seek to discover how we ought to understand the tabernacle as a type.

The word *type* in English has many connotations as any detailed dictionary will show. The Greek word τύπος (*typos*), from which the English word is derived, likewise has several connotations; and, as

which he has edited in his *Right Doctrine from Wrong Texts?* Notice in particular his ringing vindication (p. 404) of our right to follow the example of the New Testament writers and to engage, with all due care, in expounding the Old Testament ourselves typologically. See also the massive volume, covering the whole of the New Testament, co-edited with Carson, *Commentary on the NT Use of OT*.

3 Many scholars work with a broader definition of typology which includes some, at least, of these categories, especially prototypes. We shall not quarrel with their classification, for it is merely a question of lexical semantics. For ourselves we simply prefer to use the term 'type' of things which God designed for no other purpose than to function as types.

we noticed in Chapter 7, when it is used in the Greek New Testament, it carries different senses in different contexts.

In popular biblical English, however, *type* has come to be used of any Old Testament person, institution, ceremony, or event that in some way, to a greater or lesser degree, foreshadows a New Testament counterpart. So, for instance, Joseph in some of his experiences is well said to be a *type* (in the popular sense) of Christ; and Samson, in some, but certainly not in all, respects is likewise, but not so well, said to be a type of Christ.

It may, therefore, take a little effort on our part to grasp in what sense the Greek word *typos* and its correlative ἀντίτυπος, *antitypos* are used in Scripture in connection with the tabernacle. To start with, it will involve distinguishing the two similar, but significantly different, functions that God designed the tabernacle to fulfil. In this chapter we shall consider its function as a shadow of the heavenly things and, in Chapter 20, its function as a shadow of the good things to come. Chapter 21 will conclude this part of our study by looking at the tabernacle symbolism in the scenes in heaven recorded in the Revelation.

God's temporary dwelling place among his people

Said God to Moses, 'Let them [the Israelites] make me a sanctuary that I may dwell among them' (Exod 25:8). But God did not leave it to Moses—still less to the Israelites—to construct what they thought might be a suitable sanctuary for God to dwell in. Not only did he give Moses detailed, verbal specifications for its structure and furniture: he also gave him a visual representation—what the Hebrew calls a תַּבְנִית (*tabnīth*)—both of the tabernacle itself and of its furniture (25:9). He then commanded Moses: 'See to it that you make them according to their *tabnīth* which you have been shown [literally 'have been caused to see'] on the mountain' (25:40).

What exactly, then, does the Hebrew word, *tabnīth* mean? Opinions differ. It is a noun formed from the verb בָּנָה, *bānāh*, 'to build', 'to construct'. This led F. F. Bruce to consider that the *tabnīth* must have been 'something like a scale model of the sanctuary that was to be erected'.[4] B. K. Waltke prefers 'plan' or 'blueprint'.[5] At Exodus 25:40 the Septuagint translates *tabnīth* not by the Greek word παράδειγμα *(paradeigma)* as at 25:9, but by *typos*, for which most English versions put 'pattern'.

But whatever the exact meaning of *tabnīth*, the logical thought-flow in Hebrews 8:1–5 shows that the New Testament regards it as having been some kind of figurative, visual representation of the heavenly sanctuary. For this paragraph asserts that the Mosaic tabernacle, built strictly according to this *typos* (=*tabnīth*), was, as a result, a 'copy and shadow of the heavenly things' (Heb 8:5). It was not—obviously not—'the true tabernacle', that is, 'the real thing', 'God's heavenly sanctuary'; for Moses didn't build that: God did (8:2). Moses' tabernacle was, as Hebrews 9:23 once more repeats, only a copy of 'the things in the heavens'. But at the same time it was a real, God-devised, copy of those heavenly things. Its holy places, as Hebrews 9:24 points out, were unlike the heavenly sanctuary, in this respect that they were made by human hands; nevertheless they were, to quote the KJV, 'like in pattern to the true'. The Greek word this time is *antitypos*. Moses' tabernacle answered exactly to the *typos* God showed him on the mountain. It was therefore itself, in the Greek sense of the word, a *typos* of heaven; and it (along with the temples that succeeded it, up to and including Herod's temple) served as such for centuries.

We, therefore, should not underestimate the significance of the historical tabernacle (and its successors). There was only one (genuine) such building at any one time.[6] Eventually there came to be many Jewish synagogues both in Palestine and in countries where expatriate Jews lived. But they were not repeat versions of the tabernacle. Only in the tabernacle did the invisible God presence

4 *Hebrews*, 165, n. 27. This is a possible meaning, for the Septuagint at this point (Heb 25:9) has *paradeigma* which can mean 'an architect's model'.
5 *TWOT*, 1:118.
6 Unlike the hundreds of temples to Zeus (Jupiter) or Artemis (Diana) that were built all over the Middle East.

himself above the cherubim on the ark. Only at the tabernacle (temple) could sacrifices for sin be offered and accepted.[7] The tabernacle was unique.

Granted, moreover, that its furniture and rituals were only symbolic, shadows, 'types' of the great eternal realities; yet they served for centuries as a means of God's self-revelation to his people. They communicated eternal truth through symbols which people at the time could understand. Just as the abstract truths of arithmetic are sometimes taught to small children by the use of differently coloured bricks, so God used those material 'copies and shadows' to inculcate in his people certain fundamental principles of life, atonement, forgiveness and holiness on which fellowship with the God of heaven, who now condescended to dwell among them, depended (see Ch. 3).

Take, for example, the three sacred vessels that stood in the first compartment of the tabernacle, called the Holy Place: the Lampstand, the Table of the Bread of the Presence, and the Golden Altar. All three were vessels of presentation. The practical function of the Lampstand was primarily to uphold seven lamps so that they might shine before the Lord continually (Lev 24:1–4), as well as providing light for the priests. Similarly the Table presented twelve loaves of bread before the Lord continually (Lev 24:5–9). And on the Golden Altar the high priest had regularly to burn incense before the Lord (Exod 30:6–8). But even in those far off days, all three had profound significance beyond their practical function.

The Lampstand (Exod 25:31–40)

Important as its practical function was, the Lampstand was not made in a minimalist, merely functional, style. It was superbly crafted, beautifully attractive and symbolically eloquent. For it was

---

7 As an analogy we may cite the fact that when the Word became flesh and 'tabernacled among us', as God incarnate, there was only one of him: he was unique. He was not, as some seem to think, simply a notable instance of how God has dwelled in every man and woman that has ever lived.

made to resemble, in great detail, a living almond tree. It had a base, or 'thigh' as the Hebrew puts it, representing the lower part of a tree where its roots become visible as they begin to descend into the ground. Then it had a shaft, representing the trunk of the tree. Extending from the trunk were six branches, three on each side. The goldsmiths were strictly instructed: these branches must not be joined on to the trunk mechanically. They must be 'of one piece with the trunk', beaten out of the basic lump of gold at the same time as the trunk, so as to give the lifelike appearance of having grown naturally out of the trunk, sharing its life (Exod 25:32, 35–36). In addition, exquisitely patterned in the gold of both the branches and the trunk were representations of features which a living almond tree displays each year as it goes through its processes of producing fruit. In nature, of course, these features follow one another; in the golden tree that formed the Lampstand all three were present simultaneously.

Now admittedly there is difficulty in deciding the exact meanings of the ancient Hebrew botanical terms which are used to denote these features. One can see this by simply comparing a few English translations;[8] however, we shall reserve a detailed discussion of this difficulty for the Appendix at the end of this book. In spite of this uncertainty about the exact meaning of the terms, it is clear that what the Hebrew text describes and what the Lampstand displayed were features by which a living almond tree expresses its nature as it goes through its annual processes of producing fruit.

The practical function, then, of the Lampstand was to carry and present the light; but—and here is the important thing—it was itself a symbolic 'tree of life'. It displayed that life first of all in the sheer beauty of its blossoms: in Israel the almond tree was the first to blossom after the deadness of winter, carrying hope of new life, and more than a hint of resurrection life. And then the tree displayed its

8 Exod 25:33 reads in KJV 'Three bowls made like unto almonds, with a knop and a flower'; in RV 'Three cups made like almond-blossoms . . . a knop and a flower'; in NIV Study Bible 'Three cups shaped like almond flowers with buds and blossoms', and in a footnote 'The cups of the lampstand resemble either the calyx (outer covering of the flower) or the almond nut'.

life also in various representations, worked by the goldsmiths into its trunk and branches, of its fruit-bearing processes.[9]

What then could this tree of life mean to a Jewish priest who served in the first division of the tabernacle where the Lampstand stood? If he knew his book of Genesis, it would surely have reminded him of the fall, and of how Adam and Eve were driven out of the garden of Eden so that they could no longer 'reach out their hands and take also of the tree of life, and eat, and live for ever'; and of how God had then stationed cherubim at the east end of the garden, and a flaming sword that flashed in every direction to guard the way to the tree of life (Gen 3:22–24).

Yet here now the priest was standing in the Holy Place. In front of him hung the Veil that carried representations of cherubim all over it. So did the roof above him and the walls on either side.[10] Cherubim above him, then, and cherubim all round him. Yet here he stood in the presence of this tree of life, so near that if he pleased he could put out his hand and touch it; if he were the high priest he would in fact have had to touch it as he tended its lamps daily (Exod 30:7).

It was, we know (and presumably the priest did too), only a symbolic tree of life, a mere shadow, an antitype of a heavenly reality.[11] For the time had not yet come when our Saviour, Jesus Christ, would abolish death and bring life and incorruption to light through the gospel (2 Tim 1:10). Yet God was not tantalising his faithful priests in those far off days with what for them could never be more than an empty symbol. Rather, God was indicating through this symbol that there was already the beginning of a way back to

9 In the next chapter we shall consider this 'Tree-of-Life-that-carried-the-Light' in its second function, as 'a shadow of the good things to come' (Heb 10:1). We shall then perceive what an eloquent type it was of the eternal Word of whom John's Gospel states (1:3–4): 'All things were made by him. . . In him was life, and that life was the light of men.' But for the moment we are still studying the Lampstand in its first function as a copy, for the Israelites in times BC, of the things in heaven.
10 Roof and walls were formed by the ten curtains that composed the tabernacle (strictly so called, cf. Exod 26); and the cherubim on the walls would have been visible through the interstices in the wooden frames that formed the rigid structures that upheld the curtains.
11 See Rev 2:7.

the tree of life, reversing man's original exclusion from Eden's paradise (cf. Rev 2:7).

Moreover, only a shadow of heavenly things though it was, the symbol reminded generations of Israel's priests that the one, true, living God, who had revealed himself to Israel and was now dwelling among them in the tabernacle, was the sole source, Creator and maintainer of life, physical and spiritual, with all its temporal and eternal potentials. This was a helpful and necessary reminder for priests who had to guard their fellow-Israelites from the (sometimes attractive) idolatry of the surrounding nations. These nations had long since suppressed the knowledge of the one true God (Rom 1:18–23), and had made for themselves substitute gods by deifying the forces of nature, as do our modern atheistic evolutionists.

King David sang to God: 'For with you is the fountain of life; in your light do we see light' (Ps 36:9 ESV). There is no evidence that David was thinking of the Lampstand when he composed this psalm. But his poetry well expresses what was typified by the Tree-of-Life-that-Carried-the-Light.

The Table of the Bread of the Presence (Exod 25:23–30)

The Table's function

Like the Lampstand we have just studied, the Table, which stood opposite it on the other side of the Holy Place, was a vessel of presentation. Its function was to hold up and present twelve loaves of bread and a quantity of incense before the presence of the Lord continually (Exod 25:30; 40:23; Lev 24:6–8). Every Sabbath the priests, acting on behalf of the people, had to arrange new loaves on the Table; an everlasting covenant obliged them to do so (Lev 24:9). Even when the camp was on the move, the loaves had still to be on the Table (Num 4:7). Each Sabbath, when new loaves were placed on the Table, the priests were allowed to eat the old loaves. But they had to eat them in a holy place. It was not a common meal (Lev 24:9).

The significance of the twelve loaves

Many commentators vigorously insist that the loaves on the Table represented God's gracious provision for his people: not their provision for God. The motivation behind this insistence is sound: for it seeks to guard the institution of the Bread of the Presence from the modernistic suggestion that it was a hangover from an earlier stage in the evolution of religion, in which Israel, like other nations, felt that they had to feed their gods, and that these anthropomorphic gods physically ate the sacrifices offered to them. So Professor J. I. Durham writes:

> Any idea of food being provided for Yahweh ... is surely as removed from this provision as from the offering of sacrifices; whatever primitive people may think about food for their gods, the people of Israel cannot by any stretch of the socio-theological imagination be put into such a category.[12]

To which we add our own 'certainly they cannot'.

On the other hand, we who frequently use metaphors ourselves must surely allow God to use metaphors himself if he so chooses. When the Old Testament says of the burnt offering that it was 'an offering made by fire, an aroma pleasing to the Lord' (Lev 1:9, 13, 17), it no more implies that God has a physical nose than the New Testament does when it remarks that Christ gave himself up for us as a sacrifice to God for an odour of a sweet smell (Eph 5:2). Amid the moral and spiritual stench that instigated the crucifixion of Christ and surrounded his cross, the fact that Christ was willingly giving himself up for us sinners as a sacrifice to God rose up to God as a delightful fragrance. Sometimes, God's metaphors strongly express his personal interest in Israel's sacrifices: '*My* offering, *my* food for *my* offerings made by fire, *my* pleasing aroma, you shall be careful to offer to *me* at their due time' (Num 28:2).[13]

In any case, the twelve loaves were not the only things laid on the Table before the Lord. The twelve loaves themselves were arranged

12 *Exodus*, 362.
13 Cf. esv, and the translation given by Allen, *EBC*, 2:948.

in two rows (or in two piles: the translation is uncertain); but in addition to the loaves pure frankincense had to be placed along the two rows (or, on top of the two piles). And there it stayed, like the loaves, before the Lord until, at the end of each week, it was offered on the big altar in the court 'as a memorial portion to represent the bread and to be an offering made to the LORD by fire' (Lev 24:7 NIV).[14]

The loaves and the frankincense together, then, were a special form of the grain (or, cereal) offering—which accounts for its similarities with the regulations for the grain offering in Leviticus 2. If, for instance, the grain offering was of fine flour, oil and frankincense, then a part of it, namely a handful of the flour and oil and all the frankincense, had first to be offered on the altar as the 'memorial' of it, as an offering made by fire of a pleasing aroma to the Lord; and then the rest of the offering was given to Aaron and his sons: a thing most holy of the offerings of the Lord made by fire (Lev 2:1–3). Similarly the directions for the Bread of the Presence given in Leviticus 24:5–9, first make the point, as we have just seen, that the frankincense was an offering made by fire to the Lord (24:7). And then they stress the fact that the same must be said about the loaves: Aaron and his sons must eat them 'in a holy place: since it is for him a most holy portion out of the offerings unto the LORD made by fire' (24:9).

We conclude, then, that the twelve loaves represented the twelve tribes, and that they were presented before the Lord continually, primarily for his satisfaction and pleasure.[15] This was no primitive pagan superstition. The twelve loaves were only a symbol; and any Israelite would soon learn what the priests saw at first hand, that God never literally ate the loaves, nor miraculously removed them.[16] The twelve loaves presented perpetually before the Lord represented

14 RV = 'that it may be to the bread for a memorial, even an offering made by fire unto the Lord'. See the discussion of the term 'memorial portion' (Hebrew אַזְכָּרָה ['azkārāh]) by Wenham, Leviticus, 68, n. 3.
15 It can hardly be said that they represented God's provision for the twelve tribes; for the twelve tribes never got near eating any of them. Only the priests were allowed to do that.
16 When the risen Christ says that if any one opens the door, he will come in and eat with him (Rev 3:20), he doesn't mean literal eating either.

the realisation of God's purpose in redeeming Israel: 'You have seen what I did to the Egyptians, and how I carried you on eagles' wings and brought you to myself. . . . you shall be my treasured possession . . .' (Exod 19:4–5). And again, 'The Lord's portion is his people' (Deut 32:9).

Moreover, the fact that the ingredients of the loaves came from the twelve tribes (cf. Lev 24:8) as an offering made by fire to the Lord does not mean that they thought that by this sacrifice they were gaining atonement and forgiveness. It was not a sin offering, but a cereal offering. Moved by the mercy of God in redeeming them from Egypt and in granting them a great inheritance, the tribes were symbolically presenting themselves a living sacrifice to God (cf. Rom 12:1). Together with the frankincense it was an odour of a sweet smell, a sacrifice acceptable, well pleasing to God (cf. Phil 4:18).

The grandeur of the Table

The twelve loaves, then, represented the twelve tribes of Israel; but the Table that upheld them and presented them before the Lord did not represent them. Only look at its grandeur.

It was made of acacia wood and then overlaid with gold. But not with just any grade of gold: it had to be pure gold, that is gold of the highest purity obtainable.[17] Round the top of the table ran a moulding of gold. This, apparently, was of solid gold, that is, not wood overlaid with gold. Encircling the table (whether vertically or horizontally is not clear) was a border a hand-breadth deep, and that too had a moulding of solid gold. When the tabernacle was on the move, the Table had to be carried. For this purpose four rings were attached, one each on the outside of the four legs, so that two carrying poles could be inserted through them along the length of the Table. Even these rings had to be of gold, and the wooden carrying poles had to be overlaid with gold. Then the Table had to be equipped with various utensils to be used in the service of the Table. There were plates and dishes, pitchers and bowls: and all

17 In modern terms approaching as near as possible to 24 carats.

these too had to be of pure gold, no less. No wonder the Table is referred to as 'the pure Table' (Lev 24:6) just as the Lampstand is called 'the pure Lampstand' (Lev 24:4).

This, then, was no ordinary table of merely functional design. It was sumptuously grand in its every detail. It was in fact God's own provision for upholding and presenting his people before his presence for his own satisfaction and delight. That loaves made of common-though-fine-flour should be placed on such a majestic table is for its very contrast striking enough. But that these loaves should by God's own choice symbolically represent the twelve tribes of his redeemed, but often erring, people bespeaks a wealth of divine grace that is uncountable.

And to this was added yet another grace: God's priests were allowed at the end of each week to come to that same table, eat the twelve loaves, and in a holy place, share symbolically in God's satisfaction in his people.[18]

The Golden Altar of Incense (Exod 30:1–10; 40:26–27)

Both the Lampstand and the Table, as we have seen, were vessels of presentation. So, in a sense, was the third piece of furniture that stood in the Holy Place; for on it Aaron had to burn incense before the Lord twice every day: in the morning when he dressed the lamps, and in the evening when he lit them (Exod 30:7–8). Unlike the other two, however, this piece of furniture was an altar, with four horns, one at each corner, like the big Bronze Altar in the court (Exod 27:1–2; 30:2, 10).

Moreover, it had a ritually significant relationship with the Bronze Altar. The coals of fire which burned the incense and released its fragrance were taken from the Bronze Altar where the burnt offerings and sin offerings were immolated (cf. Lev 16:12; Num 16:35). And the blood of the sacrifices of atonement, shed at

18 The lavish use of gold in the tabernacle is not legendary exaggeration. See Kitchen, *Reliability of the Old Testament*, 280; and for Solomon's temple, see Millard, *Treasures*, 70–3.

the Bronze Altar, was smeared on the horns of the Golden Altar. This happened once a year on the Day of Atonement (Exod 30:10), and also on those occasions when a sin offering was offered for a priest or for the whole congregation (Lev 4:7, 18; Heb 5:1–3). The incense presupposed basic atonement.

On the other hand, the Golden Altar differed from the Bronze Altar in that no burnt offering, sin offering, cereal offering or drink offering was ever offered on it: only a very special kind of incense, designed solely for the Lord's satisfaction. Its use for the pleasure of any human being was strictly prohibited (Exod 30:9, 38).

Incense could, however, be burned elsewhere than on the Golden Altar. Two notable instances of this are in fact recorded in some detail in the Pentateuch, and study of these two occasions will help us perceive the significance of the twice daily burning of incense on the Golden Altar. For all three involved direct encounter with the living God.

The first instance

The first instance was occasioned by a case of deliberate persistence in self-willed rebellion against God in religious affairs. Korah had disputed the authority of God's appointed apostle, Moses, and God's high priest, Aaron.[19] In spite of God's signal judgment on Korah, the people as a whole continued their opposition to Moses and Aaron. Whereupon the cloud covered the tent of meeting and the glory of the Lord appeared. Realising that this was God's response to the people's rebellion, and what this direct encounter with God would mean, Moses said to Aaron:

> 'Take your censer, and put fire on it from the altar and lay incense on it and carry it quickly to the congregation and make atonement for them, for wrath has gone out from the Lord; the plague has begun. So Aaron . . . ran into the midst of the assembly. . . . And he put on the incense and made atonement for the people. And he stood between the dead and the living, and the plague was stopped. (Num 16:46–49 ESV)

19 For a full discussion, see Ch. 13, pp. 204–7.

The people, as people will, had got caught up in the rebellion of their eloquent religious demagogues, and now sullenly resented God's judgment on those demagogues as being excessive. They must be taught the gravity of rebellious criticism of God. Hence the beginning of the plague. But that same God, who in judgment remembers mercy, directed Aaron, the very high priest they had criticised, to burn incense before him on their behalf and so make propitiation for them. And the plague was stayed.

The second instance
The second instance was part of the annual ceremonies designed to 'make atonement for the Holy Place because of the uncleannesses of the children of Israel, and because of their transgressions, even all their sins; and so shall he [Aaron] do for the tent of meeting which dwells with them in the midst of their uncleannesses' (Lev 16:16).

Israel were no worse than the rest of us; but when God came to dwell among them, it was no afterthought on his part that the very presence of Israel round his dwelling place would defile it. Hence God's provision for them of the Day of Atonement sacrifices. The blood of those sacrifices would cleanse the tabernacle and its sacred vessels (cf. Heb 9:22).

But there was a problem. The blood of the atonement sacrifices had to be taken into the Most Holy Place and sprinkled on the front of the mercy seat eastward; and the people's representative, Aaron, their high priest, had to take it in and sprinkle it. But he was a sinner himself! His own presence defiled the tabernacle as did the people's! How could he possibly pull the Veil aside, enter the Most Holy Place, and appear before the mercy seat, which was the precise point at which God had promised Moses to 'meet with you . . . from above the mercy seat, from between the two cherubim which are on the ark of the testimony' (Exod 25:22 ESV)?

Well, first of all Aaron had to offer a sacrifice of atonement for himself and take its blood and sprinkle it on the front of the mercy seat. Even so, as soon as he pulled the Veil aside and entered the Holiest to have this direct encounter with God, even before he had time to sprinkle the blood on the front of the mercy seat he had immediately to burn incense on the fire in his censer before the Lord, 'that the cloud of the incense may cover the mercy seat that is over the testimony, so that he does not die' (Lev 16:13 ESV).

Commentators say that the cloud had to cover the mercy seat where God presenced himself, to prevent Aaron from seeing God for 'no man shall see [God] and live' (Exod 33:20). And that is probably so. But the incense would have cast its fragrance, which was designed for God's pleasure alone (Exod 30:37–38), all over the mercy seat. And in God's eyes that fragrant cloud would have covered Aaron too; and his presence would have been welcomed.

The twice daily burning of incense (Exod 30:7–8)

This took place in the first tabernacle on the Golden Altar of Incense, and necessarily outside the Veil, because on ordinary days Aaron was not allowed to enter the second tabernacle. But the positioning of the Altar of Incense was highly significant. 'You shall put it before the veil that is by the ark of the testimony, before the mercy seat that is over the testimony, where I will meet with you' (Exod 30:6). So although Aaron had to stay outside the Veil, yet when he came to burn incense on this altar, he had to come as near as possible — with only the Veil between — to the exact spot where God had undertaken to meet with man. It was a direct encounter with God.

This same point is emphasised in the instructions for the making of the special incense that Aaron had to burn daily: 'You shall grind some of it very small and put it before the testimony in the tent of meeting, where I will meet with you' (30:36). Aaron must never be short of an adequate supply of incense for these encounters with God on behalf of the people.

The reason for the daily burning of incense

Aaron had to burn incense twice a day: in the morning when he dressed the lamps, and again in the evening when he lit them. Now the oil for the lamps was extracted from olives by beating them. Then the oil had to be refined to remove any particles of the skin or flesh of the olives that may have fallen into the oil (Lev 24:2). Even so, the trimming of wicks when they were burnt and greasy would have been a smelly business; and a new wick, when it is lit can at first emit more fumes than light. This was, of course, a natural weakness inherent in the use of oil lamps in the ceremonial service of God. Some have suggested, therefore, that the twice daily burning of incense was originally intended to cover the unpleasant smell from the lamps that otherwise would be unacceptable in the presence of God, and perhaps offensive to him.

Others might object to this explanation on the grounds that it would reduce the God of Israel to the level of pagan deities who were imagined as physically liking good smells and disliking bad ones. Dogmatism on the matter is unnecessary and unjustified. Scripture does not explain why the burning of the incense had to coincide with the trimming and lighting of the lamps.

But of this we can be sure: God was pleased with the fragrance of the incense; for it was he who specified its ingredients, and commanded it to be made for his pleasure and no one else's (Exod 30:34–38). It is not inconceivable that in the years of Israel's spiritual childhood (cf. Gal 4:1–3), the fragrance of the incense could have carried a metaphorical, if not a symbolical, meaning. We know from God's explicit statements elsewhere that God dislikes bad smells, both moral and ceremonial; and he is not afraid to express his disgust in metaphorical language: he warns Israel that should their physically sweet-smelling sacrifices be accompanied by lives of immorality and religious infidelity 'I will make your sanctuaries desolate, and I will not smell your pleasing aromas' (Lev 26:31 ESV).

Again, when Israel adopted pagan rituals with their pseudo-recipes for holiness, God's disgust was outspoken: 'These are a smoke in my nose, a fire that burns all the day' (Isa 65:5).

This carries a voice for us even today. Not all forms of worship are acceptable to God. On the other hand, sacrificial giving in the cause of Christ is 'an odour of a sweet smell, a sacrifice acceptable, well-pleasing to God' (Phil 4:18). God still likes nice smells!

God's gracious gift to Israel of a high priest

In view then of Israel's waywardness, uncleanness and the weakness and inherent imperfection of their worship, it was merciful of God to provide them with a high priest and representative who could intervene between them and God and offer incense on their behalf before God. A thin plate of gold which Aaron had to wear on his forehead carried the words: 'Holy to the LORD'. Their significance was this:

> Aaron shall bear any guilt from the holy things that the people of Israel consecrate as their holy gifts. It shall regularly be on his forehead, that they may be accepted before the LORD. (Exod 28:36–38 ESV)

These were not idle words. Early on in Aaron's ministry, two of his sons

> each took his censer and put fire in it and laid incense on it and offered unauthorised fire before the Lord which he had not commanded them. And fire came out from before the Lord and consumed them, and they died before the Lord. Then Moses said to Aaron, 'This is what the Lord has said, "Among those who are near me I will be sanctified, and before all the people I will be glorified."' (Lev 10:1–3 ESV)

To modern sensibilities this may sound barbarous; but that is because our modern western world has lost awareness of the infinite glory and holiness of God. If an otherwise sane person were to imagine he could improve a painting by Rembrandt by dabbing paint on it, the art-loving world would be outraged. The living God is 'a consuming fire'; and we must learn to offer service to him with reverence and awe (Heb 12:28–29). We lose that sense of awe at our peril.

Aaron himself eventually failed. At Sinai he was too lenient with the people (Exod 32:1–5, 21). Later he misrepresented God and paid the penalty (Num 20:12–13, 23–29). It did but emphasise the need for another priest to arise, not after the Aaronic order, but after the order of Melchizedek.

20

The Tabernacle as a Shadow
of the Good Things to Come

So FAR WE have studied three examples of the tabernacle's first function as a shadow, or *typos* (or *antitypos*) of the heavenly things. Now we move on to consider its second function as 'a shadow of the good things to come'. Those good things were the glorious benefits to be brought to us by our Lord Jesus Christ. But the New Testament shows that those good things were not all to be brought to us at exactly one and the same time. We must therefore expect to find that the shadows-of-these-good-things-to-come were fulfilled:

1. some of them by his incarnation and earthly ministry;
2. others by his death and sacrifice on our behalf;
3. others by his resurrection, ascension and present ministry;
4. others at his second coming; and
5. still others by his gracious joining of his people to himself as his body.

God's dwelling place: the *mishkān*

The literal meaning of the term, 'tabernacle'

Said God to Moses: 'Let them [the Israelites] make me a sanctuary that I may dwell among them' (Exod 25:8); and the verb God used for 'dwell' was the Hebrew word שָׁכַן (*shākan*). The resultant dwelling place for God is called in Hebrew the מִשְׁכָּן (*mishkān*), a noun derived from the verb *shākan* (Exod 25:9). In the Septuagint of this passage *mishkān* is translated by the Greek word σκηνή *(skēnē)* which means 'a tent', or 'tabernacle'; and one can scarcely fail to notice how similar the Hebrew and Greek words are: the Hebrew with its three consonants, *sh-k-n*, and the Greek with its three consonants, *s-k-n*.[1]

When for the first time Moses erected this dwelling place for God, we are told that 'the cloud covered the tent of meeting, and the glory of the Lord filled the tabernacle'. That was spectacular indeed, awesomely powerful, so that Moses was not able to enter into the tent of meeting, because the cloud settled on it, and the glory of the Lord filled the tabernacle (Exod 40:34–35).

The presence of God was real; but the tabernacle was only a shadow, insubstantial, temporary, evanescent, compared with the great permanent reality to which it pointed. The Apostle John witnessed that great reality at first hand, and he describes it thus: 'The Word became flesh and dwelt among us, full of grace and truth'; and the word he uses for 'dwelt' is the Greek word ἐσκήνωσεν *(eskēnōsen)* with its three basic consonants, *s, k, n,* based on the Greek word for 'tent', or 'tabernacle'. Some have translated the sentence 'The Word became flesh and tabernacled among us'.

Then John adds: 'And we contemplated his glory, glory as of the one and only Son from the Father, full of grace and truth' (John 1:14). The Word, who in the beginning already existed, who was with God and was God, now, without ceasing to be God, became truly human, with a real human body. That body was crucified and buried. But the third day he rose from the dead, and during the forty days before he ascended, he gave his disciples unmistakable evidence that he still had a real human, though now glorified, body of flesh and bone. That body he will have for all eternity; and one day we too shall see him and contemplate his glory. 'In him dwells all the fullness of deity bodily' (Col 2:9).

---

1 We need not stay to discuss the linguistic history behind this similarity.

The stricter meaning of the term 'tabernacle'

The term *tabernacle* (*mishkān*) is sometimes used in Scripture, as in common parlance, to refer to the whole building that Moses constructed.[2] But in its stricter meaning the term *tabernacle* refers not to the whole building, still less to its contents, but to the ten linen curtains described in Exodus 26:1–6. These ten curtains, strictly speaking, were the tabernacle, the *mishkān*, the dwelling place of God. And in this context this stricter meaning is used consistently.

For instance, when the building was erected, these curtains were spread over gold-covered frames at the sides and at the back. These frames are said to be 'frames for the tabernacle' (Exod 26:15). They upheld the ten curtains, the *mishkān*, and thus allowed them to function as God's dwelling place. But the frames were not the tabernacle: the curtains were.

Then it is explained in detail how these originally separate curtains, though many, came to form one *mishkān*. First they were made into two sets. Five curtains were placed side by side and sewn together; and then the other five similarly. Next, each set was equipped with fifty loops of blue material along one of its selvedges.[3] Then fifty golden clasps were put through the fifty loops on the one selvedge and the fifty loops on the other selvedge, clamping the two sets together so that 'the tabernacle [the *mishkān*] shall be one' (Exod 26:6).[4]

God's ancient dwelling place, the *mishkān*, was thus a plurality in unity; and it may well be that this elaborate system was devised for some practical purpose—such as making it easier to pack and store

2 Cf. Exod 40:34–35.

3 'The edge of a piece of woven material finished in such a manner as to prevent the ravelling out of the weft. Also, a narrow strip or list at the edge of a web of cloth, which is not finished like the rest of the cloth, being intended to be cut off or covered by the seam when the material is made up.' (*Oxford English Dictionary*, 2nd ed., 1989, s.v. 'selvedge').

4 This stricter meaning is maintained when the following verses make provision for a series of eleven goat hair curtains to act as a 'tent' (Heb. אֹהֶל, *'ōhel*) over the 'tabernacle' (*mishkān*). Like the ten linen tabernacle curtains, the eleven goat hair curtains were arranged in two sets, one of five and the other of six. Then the two sets were each fitted with fifty loops and clamped together with fifty bronze clasps: and so 'You shall couple the tent together that it may be one' (Exod 26:11).

them when in transport—and that it had no additional significance as a shadow of the good things to come.

But it can do us no harm at this point simply to recall the actual fact that the present dwelling place of God is likewise a plurality in unity. For on the day of Pentecost he who during his life on earth 'tabernacled' among us, baptised his people in the Holy Spirit and thus formed them into one body:

> For as the [human] body is one, and has many members, and all the members of the body, being many, are one body, so also is the Christ. For in one Spirit were we all baptised into one body, whether Jew or Greek, whether bond or free. . . . (1 Cor 12:12–13)

And later Paul adds that of the two, Jew and Gentile, Christ has created in himself one new man, and is building this newly effected unity together for a dwelling place of God in the Spirit.[5]

The Veil: the *pārōketh*

In Hebrews 9:3 the פָּרֹכֶת (*pārōketh*) is called 'the second veil', to distinguish it from the screen (Heb.: מָסָךְ, *māsāk*) that hung at the entrance to the tabernacle building. The *pārōketh* by contrast hung two-thirds the way down the interior of the building. The *māsāk* screened the Holy Place, with its Table, Lampstand and Golden Altar, from the eyes of the general public. What the *pārōketh* screened was nothing less than the Ark and Mercy Seat, the presence and the symbolic throne of God; and screened it from the eyes even of the priests.[6]

The priests came inside the *māsāk* every day of the week; inside the *pārōketh* no one ever came except the high priest, and he on the yearly Day of Atonement only.

It was the counterpart of this *pārōketh* in Herod's temple that at Christ's death was rent in two from the top to the bottom (Matt 27:51).

---

5 Eph 2:15–16, 21–22. In this passage the metaphor is changed from a movable tabernacle to a permanent temple built on a foundation. But the basic meaning remains the same.

6 The function of the *pārōketh* as a screen makes the older translation, 'the Veil', preferable to the modern one, 'the Curtain'.

The effect of the Veil

Architecturally, the effect of the Veil was to divide the interior of the tabernacle into two separate compartments, normally called 'the Holy Place', and 'the Most Holy Place'.[7] But in Hebrews 9:2, 3, 8 the first compartment is called 'the first tabernacle', and the second compartment 'the second tabernacle'.

It is important, then, to grasp the meaning of these technical terms. When Hebrews refers to 'the first tabernacle' it does not mean the tabernacle that Moses built as distinct from later copies. All later copies, including Herod's temple, had a Veil that divided the building into two compartments, and gave the first tabernacle, the Holy Place, separate status from 'the second tabernacle', the Most Holy Place. By its term, 'the first tabernacle', Hebrews is referring to the first compartment in the Mosaic tabernacle and in all subsequent copies.

Using these terms, then, Hebrews makes the point that as long as the first tabernacle has separate status the way into the Holiest has not yet been made visibly open.[8] Obviously not! For the thing that gave the first tabernacle its separate status from the second tabernacle was the Veil. As long as it hung there, the way into the Holiest was obviously not open. Remove the Veil, however, and the first tabernacle would no longer have separate status. The whole interior of the building would be one undivided compartment. The way into the Most Holy Place would be completely open.

The significance of the Veil

Why, we may ask, did the Holy Spirit ordain that there should be this Veil in the tabernacle barring for centuries the way into the Most Holy Place? The answer is that Israel's sacrifices were inadequate: none of them could perfect the worshipper's conscience (Heb 9:9). When an Israelite in true repentance and faith brought a

---

7 In contexts where it is obvious which Holy Place is meant, Scripture often refers to the Most Holy Place simply as the Holy Place, e.g. Lev 16:2; Heb 9:8; 10:19.

8 Note the perfect tense. Herod's temple was still standing when the Epistle to Hebrews was written; and it still had a veil.

prescribed sacrifice, his particular sin, or sins, were forgiven (Lev 4:20). But when he sinned again, he had to bring another sacrifice. There was no finality. A believer's conscience could not rest in the assurance that the guilt of all his sin had been once and for all atoned for. Hence there was no entry for him into the Holiest. Even King David, who expressed the blessedness of being forgiven (Ps 32), would not have dared to enter the Most Holy Place.

Now from the Epistle to the Hebrews it would seem that some of its intended readers were still hankering after the Jerusalem temple, its priesthood and ceremonies. The writer therefore reminds them that the very temple they hankered after still had a Veil barring the way into the Holiest and thereby still advertised the inadequacy of its sacrifices (Heb 9:9); whereas Christ's one sacrifice for sins for ever fitted them for entry into the Most Holy Place, and that not merely in an earthly temple, but into heaven itself (Heb 10:12–22).

A problem with the Veil

The verse that describes the way into the Holiest which Christ has inaugurated for us has proved a problem for some commentators. In the RV it runs:

> . . . boldness to enter into the holy place by the blood of Jesus, by the way that he dedicated for us, a new and living way, through the veil, that is to say his flesh. . . . (Heb 10:19–20 RV)

This verse appears to say that the Veil too was a shadow of a good thing to come, namely Christ's flesh, that is his human nature and his human body. But the famous bishop and scholar, B. F. Westcott, could not accept that Scripture would speak of Christ's flesh 'as a veil, an obstacle, to the vision of God in a place where stress is laid on his humanity'.[9] He therefore interpreted the verse so as to identify our Lord's flesh not with the Veil, but with the new and living way through the Veil. The NEB's translation does similarly: '. . . the new and living way which he has opened for us through the curtain, the way of his flesh'.

9 *Hebrews*, 32.

But this difficulty seems to overlook the fact that the Veil was a merciful provision. It certainly barred access into the immediate presence of God; and yet it allowed the priests to come at least into the Holy Place, to the Lampstand, the Table, and the Golden Altar of Incense and to all that they stood for. If there had been no Veil, they could not have entered even the Holy Place; for without the Veil, the Holy Place too would have been in the immediate presence of God. Whereas with the Veil there, they could not only enter the Holy Place, but also come right up to the Veil, inspect all its colours, figures and symbolism, and thereby learn something of the majesty of God.

The Veil, then, was a wonderful foreshadowing of Christ in his incarnation, his life and ministry on earth. The crowds could come right up to him, sinners could touch him, little children nestle in his arms. Yet all the fullness of deity dwelled in him bodily. Indeed, he so expressed the Father that he could say: 'he who has seen me has seen the Father' (John 12:45; 14:9).

That was inexpressibly wonderful, but more wonderful still is the fact that he no longer acts as a Veil. That same Jesus, still truly human and with a real human body, rent with the nails and the spear-thrust, has entered into heaven itself, into the immediate presence of God as our precursor, representative and high priest. In so doing he has inaugurated a new and living way for us ourselves to enter the immediate presence of God; and we may even now enter there in spirit as boldly as one day we shall do so in bodies re-fashioned and conformed to the body of his glory.

The Altar and the Laver in the Court

Two vessels stood in the tabernacle court: the first, the large Bronze Altar, the second the Laver. Both offered cleansing: the Altar by blood, the Laver by water.[10] As shadows of the good things to come they prompt us to ask whether the Christian gospel likewise offers cleansing both by blood and by water. The answer is, Yes. 1 John

10 Exod 27:1–8; 30:17–21; 38:8; 40:6–12.

1:7 declares that the blood of Jesus, his Son, cleanses us from all sin; and Ephesians 5:25–26 states that 'Christ also loved the church and gave himself up for her, that he might sanctify her, having cleansed her by the washing of water by the word'.

This raises a second question: why do we need two cleansings? Why is our cleansing by the blood of Christ not enough by itself? The answer to this question is to be found by examining first what it is that the blood cleanses, then what the water cleanses, and then the difference between the two.

The cleansing by blood

Blood cleanses the conscience. Says Hebrews 9:13–14:

> For if the blood of goats and bulls, and the ashes of a heifer sprinkling those who have been defiled, sanctify unto the cleanness of the flesh, how much more shall the blood of Christ, who through the eternal Spirit offered himself without blemish unto God, cleanse your conscience from dead works to serve the living God?

Dead works, that is, works that lead to death and alienate human beings from God, burden and defile the conscience, and thus unfit a person for fellowship with the all-holy God. Not until the conscience is cleansed from its awareness of guilt could anyone enjoy entry, let alone peace, in the presence of God. The blood of Christ cleanses the conscience, not as though it were some detergent, but because it stands for his death which paid the penalty that the wrath of God pronounced on our sins. The result is that the believer's conscience is cleared of guilt, he has peace with God, and access into his presence: the very effect that the tabernacle sacrifices and ceremonies could not achieve (Heb 9:9).

But if the blood of Christ is so effective, why do we need cleansing by water as well?

The cleansing by water

The metaphorical language of Ephesians 5:25–27 is helpful here. It is based on a husband's love and care for his wife. Now if through speeding and careless driving a wife wrecked her husband's new car, she would doubtless say sorry, and seek his forgiveness, which he would readily—or eventually—give. But should his wife develop ugly sores or pimples on her face, he would not say 'I forgive you for it': forgiveness would be inept and uncalled for. On the other hand, his love for her would demand that he got her the very best treatment to remove these blemishes.

When, therefore, Christ in his love for the church cleanses her that he might present her to himself 'without spot or wrinkle or any such thing', what, in literal terms, do these spots and wrinkles represent? Not sin that needs to be forgiven, but character defects that need to be removed: selfishness, envy, jealousy, pride, spite and such like things. If character defects should drive us to commit sinful actions, then, of course, these actions would need forgiveness through the blood of Christ. But the defects themselves are not cleansed by the blood of Christ. How then?

The washing of regeneration

Paul's advice to Titus casts light on this question. He reminds Titus that Cretans of that time were, on their own admission, 'liars, evil beasts, lazy gluttons' (Titus 1:12). But Paul cannot forget that 'we ourselves were once foolish, disobedient, led astray, slaves to various passions and pleasures, passing our days in malice and envy, hated by others and hating one another' (3:3 ESV). Evil characters had led to evil life style and behaviour.

But when Paul proceeds to describe how they were saved, it is noticeable that in this context he does not mention the atoning blood of Christ. Instead he concentrates on the other main element in salvation. God, he says, in his goodness and loving-kindness saved us 'by the washing of regeneration and renewal of the Holy Spirit, whom he poured out on us richly through Jesus Christ our Saviour' (3:5–6 ESV). The new birth, then, and the renewal of the mind (Rom 12:2), are both performed by the Holy Spirit.[11]

11 NB the water metaphors: 'washing' and 'poured out'.

So the blood of Christ purges our guilt and brings us peace with God. But we are not thereafter left to struggle against our character defects the best we can. God is no pharaoh. He does not expect us to make bricks without straw. He offers us not only forgiveness, but along with it new life with its new nature and new powers.

The once-for-all and the repeated washing

The tabernacle Laver provided the priests with water for washing, and stood conveniently between the two points to which their duties called them, namely between the Bronze Altar and the tent of meeting (Exod 30:19–21).

At their induction the priests were brought to the door (to the *māsāk*) of the tent of meeting and there bathed all over. This was a ceremonial once-for-all washing that prepared them for their ministry (Exod 29:4). Thereafter they had repeatedly to wash their hands and feet whenever they entered the tent of meeting or ministered at the Bronze Altar (Exod 30:19–21).

If, then, these washings in water also were 'shadows of the good things to come', we may rightly ask whether the Christian gospel offers two washings in water, one once-for-all and the other constantly repeated. The answer is, Yes; and our Lord himself in the upper room used literal water to illustrate the spiritual cleansing which these tabernacle ceremonies foreshadowed (John 13:1–11).[12]

Peter in a moment of excessive zeal suggested that the Lord wash not only his feet but his hands and his head as well. Christ replied: 'The one who has been bathed all over, only needs to wash his feet. Otherwise he is completely clean' (13:8–10).

Christ's metaphor was based, as a long line of commentators have observed, on the customs of the time. Invited to a feast, a man would first take a bath in his own house, and then walk to the feast. When he arrived at his host's house, he would not need to bathe all over again, but simply to wash the dust of the road off his feet.

12 Christ also used his washing of the disciples' feet as a vivid example to them of their duty to perform humble acts of service to one another.

Normally his host would direct one of his own servants to do this for the guest.

But if that is the basis of the metaphor, what do its terms mean at the spiritual level?

The bathing all over

This surely is what our Lord had earlier referred to as 'being born again [or, from above] of water and the spirit' (3:5). This is the initial basic condition for entry into the kingdom. Without this new birth none can enter. But once experienced, it does not need to be repeated. It is a once-for-all event. One cannot be born again and again repeatedly, and does not need to be, in spiritual life any more than in natural life.

The repeated washing

Once born again of God's Spirit, however, we need constantly to 'cleanse ourselves from every defilement of body and spirit, bringing holiness to completion in the fear of God' (2 Cor 7:1 ESV). We need 'by the Spirit to mortify the deeds of the body' (Rom 8:13).

The necessary preparation for entry into the Holiest

To sum up, we may notice what, according to the Epistle to the Hebrews, is the double cleansing (10:22), by blood and by water, provided to prepare us for our entry into the Holiest of All. We are to draw near boldly:

1. 'with a true heart in fullness of faith',
2. 'having our hearts sprinkled [i.e. with blood] from an evil conscience' (see Heb 9:14),
3. 'and our body having been bathed all over with pure water'.[13]

---

13 The whole of our Lord's enacted parable in John 13 was based on cleansing by water. It is a curiosity of exposition that some, otherwise careful, expositors suggest that the bathing-all-over in the parable represents our initial cleansing by the *blood* of Christ.

The Lampstand, the Table and the Incense Altar

In the previous chapter we studied these three vessels as 'shadows of the heavenly things'. Now we must consider what they pointed to as shadows of the good things to come.

The Lampstand and its lamps

If the Lampstand was a shadow of the good things to come, there is no doubt whom it foreshadowed. For as we earlier saw, the Lampstand was a symbolic tree of life and at the same time it carried the light. It eloquently pointed to him of whom John says 'In him was life, and that life was the light of men' (John 1:4).

Now in saying 'in him was life', John is not merely saying the obvious, that our Lord, the eternal Word, who was with God and was God, was himself alive. John means that the Word was the source of all created life: 'All things were made through him and nothing of all that was made was made without him.' If we ask where he got the life from to create the almost infinite number of living things in the universe, the answer is, he didn't get it from anywhere. He himself was its source.

And when John adds: 'and that light was the light of men', he is, strictly speaking, still referring to created life. If you were walking along a dark road at night and suddenly a beam of light shone through the hedge across your path, you would naturally ask where this light came from. You would not be content to think that it didn't come from anywhere: it 'just was'. Light has to have a source. Similarly with life. If we are to discover its significance both in ourselves and in the world at large, we must trace it to its source: the personal, self-existent, eternal Word, in whom, through whom and for whom the universe was made; and who gives to all created life its ultimate meaning and purpose.

He did not cease to be the source of life when he became flesh and tabernacled among us. To his contemporaries he explained: 'As the Father has life in himself, even so he gave to the Son also to have life in himself' (John 5:26). In consequence he could give eternal life instantaneously there and then to any who believed in him (5:24–25). Anticipating his 'going away' he assured his disciples that he would continue to be the source and maintainer of their spiritual life: 'Because I live, you shall live also' (14:19). And even when he was still on earth he claimed to be the resurrection and the life (11:25); and he called Lazarus out of the tomb to prove it (11:43). The hour would come, he said, when 'all that are in the tombs shall hear his voice, and shall come forth' (5:28–29).

Not for nothing was the Lampstand made to resemble an almond tree, the first tree in Israel to blossom after the deadness of winter. Not for nothing did it carry the light of seven lamps. It was deliberately designed to point to him who said:

> I am the light of the world; whoever follows me shall not walk in darkness, but shall have the light of life. . . . If anyone keeps my word, he shall never see death. (John 8:12, 51)

The Table of the Bread of the Presence

Here we recall what we saw earlier (p. 288): that the twelve loaves on this table represented the twelve tribes of Israel; that they were placed there primarily for God's satisfaction; that nevertheless at the end of each week the priests were invited to eat this bread in a holy place. Already, then, in the centuries before Christ this table bespoke an amazing fellowship: a table at which both God and man found satisfaction.

As we now make the transition to thinking about this table and its twelve loaves as a shadow of the good things to come, Isaiah's concept of Messiah as the true Israel can help us. From chapter 40 onwards in Isaiah's prophecy God addresses the whole nation of Israel, as 'Israel, my servant' (Isa 41:8). But when God bids us contemplate his servant (52:13), it is evident that he is talking not of the nation as a whole, but of an individual. The nation had transgressed and deserved God's punishment. But this Servant 'would be stricken for the transgression of my people' (53:8); his death would be as a sin offering (53:10). 'By his knowledge shall my righteous one, my servant, make many to be accounted righteous, and he shall bear their iniquities' (53:11 ESV). Such statements can only apply to one individual, that is, Christ.

We conclude that Christ was God's perfect servant. He was all that Israel should have been and more besides. He was the ideal Israel in whom God's soul delighted, at whose baptism the voice out of heaven proclaimed: 'This is my beloved Son, in whom I am well pleased' (Matt 3:17).

As a shadow of the good things to come, then, the twelve loaves on the Table of the Bread of the Presence point in the first place, to Christ. But just as the priests at the end of each week were allowed to eat the loaves that had been placed on the table primarily for God's satisfaction, so nowadays believers are called to share with God in his infinite satisfaction in Christ. Let the Apostle John explain.

He writes first of 'that eternal life that was with the Father' (1 John 1:2). In Greek the grammatical case that John uses for the noun (the Father) after the preposition *with*, is normally used of relationship between persons. It is the usage John employs in the similar passage in his Gospel: 'the Word was *with* God' (John 1:1). So the phrase 'the eternal life that was *with* the Father' bespeaks a personal fellowship of infinite and eternal satisfaction between the Father and the Son.

'And', continues John, 'that life was manifested'. He is referring to our Lord's incarnation and life on earth; and he adds 'that which we have seen and heard we declare to you also, that you also may have fellowship with us [apostles]; and indeed our fellowship is with the Father and with his Son Jesus Christ' (1 John 1:2–3).

Now in biblical terminology 'to have fellowship with someone' means to have something in common with that someone. What is it, then, that John invites us to share in with him, with the other apostles, and indeed with the Father and with his Son? It is nothing less than that eternal life which was with the Father (1:3).

The condition for enjoying this fellowship
It is the simple historical fact that in the Holy Place in the tabernacle the Lampstand stood directly opposite the Table. When, therefore, a

priest walked to the Table to share in the bread with God, all seven lamps on the Lampstand would be blazing on him. In other words, to have fellowship with God, he had to 'walk in the light'.

As then, so now. Let John explain once more:

> God is light, and in him is no darkness at all. If we say we have fellowship with him, and walk in the darkness, we lie, and do not the truth. But if we walk in the light as he is in the light, we have fellowship one with another. (1 John 1:5–7)

Inevitably, if we walk in that light, it will expose our shortcomings and sins. But God has made provision for our predicament: 'the blood of Jesus his Son cleanses us from all sin' (1:7). We need not try to hide our sins; on the contrary we are commanded to confess them. And when we do, 'he is faithful and just to forgive us our sins, and to cleanse us from all unrighteousness' (1:9).

What is more, John says, 'if anyone sins, we have an advocate with the Father, Jesus Christ the righteous. And he is the propitiation for our sins' (2:1–2). But thinking about Christ's advocacy on our behalf will lead us directly to the third sacred vessel that stood in the Holy Place.

The Golden Altar of Incense

In the course of history the burning of incense on the Golden Altar came to be associated with prayer. Some suggest that this was because the burning of incense inside the temple coincided with the offering of the תָּמִיד (tāmîd), the daily perpetual sacrifice morning and evening, outside the temple; at which time people would gather outside and pray.

Already David prays: 'May my prayer be set before you like the incense; may the lifting up of my hands be like the evening sacrifice' (Ps 141:2 NIV).

Later, in New Testament times, a priest named Zechariah—father of John the Baptist—'was chosen by lot to enter the temple of the Lord and burn incense', again in connection with the people's prayers:

And the whole multitude of the people were praying outside at the hour of incense. And there appeared to him an angel of the Lord, standing on the right side of the altar of incense . . . the angel said . . . 'Fear not, Zechariah, because your prayer has been heard.' (Luke 1:10–13)

It takes no great leap of the imagination, therefore, to see that the Golden Altar with its incense, and priestly prayers, foreshadowed the intercessions of our high priest (Heb 7:25–28) and his ministry as our advocate with the Father (1 John 2:1). Moreover on the Day of Atonement the blood of the propitiatory sacrifice, enacted at the Bronze Altar in the tabernacle court, was smeared on the horns of the Golden Altar that was before the Lord (Lev 16:18; see also 4:7, 18). Accordingly we are told that our advocate with the Father 'is the propitiation for our sins' (1 John 2:2). In other words, the power and effectiveness of Christ's advocacy on our behalf stems from the sufficiency of his propitiatory sacrifice for our sins at Calvary.

Incense as a shadow of the good things to come
In Revelation 8 John uses the symbolism of the tabernacle's Golden Altar to picture for us the spiritual transactions that he witnesses in heaven:

> And another angel came and stood at the altar with a golden censer, and he was given much incense to offer with the prayers of all the saints on the golden altar before the throne, and the smoke of the incense with the prayers of the saints, rose before God from the hand of the angel. (Rev 8:3–5 ESV)

From what follows it is clear that with the addition of the incense the saints' prayers became effective.

This too was a shadow of the good things to come. We today need no physically fragrant incense to make our prayers effective before God. We pray in the name of the Lord Jesus; and that name is a potent and unfading fragrance before the Father (cf. John 14:13–14; 16:23–24).

Another layer of meaning

We saw in the previous chapter that both the Table and the Lampstand were vessels of presentation: the Table presented twelve loaves of bread before the Lord for his pleasure continually; and the Lampstand upheld seven lamps to shine before the Lord, likewise continually. In this their common function both vessels foreshadowed Christ. In Ephesians we read: God has raised Christ from the dead and made him to sit at his own right hand. But not him alone. For it was God's good pleasure 'that we should be holy and blameless *before him*' (Eph 1:4 ESV). And that God has already achieved— and will in the future achieve it even more fully. 'He has raised us up with Christ and seated us with him in the heavenly places in Christ Jesus' (Eph 2:6 ESV). Christ upholds and presents us before the Father to the Father's eternal satisfaction.

The Lampstand was composed of a central trunk and six branches. It foreshadowed Christ in whom was life and that life was the light of men. But Christ has shined on us, so that we are 'light in the Lord' (Eph 5:8). Not only so. Christ has imparted his life to us. We are 'in him'; and by his Spirit he upholds and energises us in the ministries he has given us: we shine as lights for God in this perverted world (Phil 2:15). We are also a means of enlightenment to the rulers and authorities in the heavenly places, as now through the church God makes known to them his multifaceted wisdom (Eph 3:9–10). Above all, Christ enables us to fulfil the prime function for which we were created, and have been redeemed and gifted, namely, to shine before the Lord continually for his delight, now in the church, and hereafter in heaven.[14] And it is to that realm that we will now turn our attention. From these glorious benefits, foreshadowed in the tabernacle and brought to us by our Lord Jesus Christ, we move on to consider a final, special case of the New Testament's use of the tabernacle's symbolism.

14 For a study of the Ark and Mercy Seat see pp. 62–5.

21

The Tabernacle as a Key to the Interpretation of the Revelation

THE FOUR CENTRAL sections of the book of the Revelation record John's visions of successive scenes in heaven. On each occasion a description of some feature of the tabernacle sets the scene and defines the significance of the ensuing events.

Section 1 – A door is opened in heaven (Rev 4:1 — 7:17). John is summoned to enter and sees God's throne, the equivalent of the Ark in the tabernacle. There follows a detailed description of the throne, including its four 'living creatures', otherwise known as *cherubim* (see Ezek 10:20), reminiscent of the two cherubim on the mercy seat on the Ark, where God 'sits enthroned' (1 Chr 13:6 ESV). Compare also the throne and its occupant above the cherubim in Ezekiel's vision (Ezek 1:26).

Section 2 – The seventh seal is opened (Rev 8:1–11:18). And there follows a silence in heaven for half an hour. Then there comes an angel with a gold censer. Much incense is given to him to offer with the prayers of all the saints on the golden altar before the throne. Then the censer is filled with fire from the altar and emptied out on the earth.

Section 3 – God's temple in heaven is opened (Rev 11:19–15:4). And the ark of his covenant is seen within the temple. There are flashes of lightning, rumblings, peals of thunder, an earthquake and heavy hail.

Section 4 – The temple of the tabernacle of testimony in heaven is opened (Rev 15:5–19:10). And out of the temple come seven angels with the seven plagues . . . and one of the living creatures gives to the seven angels seven golden bowls full of the wrath of God . . . and the temple is filled with smoke from the glory of God and from his power, and no one can enter the temple until the seven plagues of the seven angels are finished.

Now this use of tabernacle symbolism in the Revelation takes us back to the first function of the tabernacle, which was to be 'a copy and shadow of the heavenly things'. And 'things in heaven' was precisely what John was given to see and what he records. He makes no attempt to explain the symbolism or to interpret it as 'a shadow of the good things to come'. He is describing what for him was a present reality. In describing heaven, even in this Christian era, much of the description must necessarily continue to be in metaphorical and symbolic terms.

Every section begins with something being opened in heaven. That is obvious. What perhaps is not so obvious is that the particular feature of the tabernacle that is then mentioned at the beginning of each section sets the scene for the divine judgments that fall on earth in the course of that section. And not only sets the scene, but explains why that set of judgments must fall on earth and on its inhabitants.

Section 1 (Rev 4:1–7:17)

In Section 1, then, we see the throne. It is the throne of the Creator and his creatorial rights are explicitly expounded:

> Worthy art thou, our Lord and our God, to receive the glory and the honour and the power: for Thou didst create all things, and because of thy will they are, and were created. (Rev 4:11)

The universe has no other raison d'être than to serve the Creator's will. But mankind has rebelled against that will and insisted on serving their own will. The result: spiritual, moral, and often physical, chaos.

But the Creator is not prepared to tolerate this state of affairs for ever. He has purposes for the redevelopment of earth, and eventually for a new heaven and a new earth, in which the Creator's will shall be done on earth even as it is in heaven. Hence the inevitability of God's judgments to prepare for the redevelopment. Redemption is provided for the repentant by the sacrifice of the Lamb (Rev 5); but judgment must eventually fall on the recalcitrant. The rights of the Creator's throne demand it.

Then at the end of the section, when the judgments are past, an innumerable throng of the saved comes into view, their garments washed in the blood of the Lamb. The blessings that attend them are then described consistently with the dominant theme in this section, the throne of the Creator:

> Therefore they are before the throne of God; and they serve him day and night in his temple. And he who sits on the throne shall spread his tabernacle over them. They shall hunger no more, neither thirst any more; neither shall the sun strike upon them, nor any heat. For the Lamb who is in the midst of the throne shall be their shepherd, and shall guide them unto fountains of waters of life; and God shall wipe away every tear from their eyes. (Rev 7:15–17)

The Creator's throne will see to it that his creation shall never again hurt any of his redeemed people.

Section 2 (Rev 8:1 – 11:18)

In Section 2 the piece of tabernacle furniture that sets the scene for what follows is the Golden Altar of Incense. Now in Moses' tabernacle the Golden Altar was functionally related to the Ark 'which is called by the name of the LORD who sits enthroned above the cherubim' (1 Chr 13:6 ESV). Though the Veil had necessarily to hang between them, the Golden Altar was deliberately stationed directly opposite the Ark (Exod 30:6). When, therefore, the priest stood at the Golden Altar burning incense before the Lord and praying, he was directly addressing God who sat enthroned the other side of the Veil. Indeed, if you believed that, how wouldn't you pray and expect answers to your prayers?

But this raises in thoughtful minds the age-long problem of evil. Atheists will say: if there is a throne in heaven occupied by a God who cares for justice and hears the prayers of the persecuted, why does he allow atrocities to be perpetrated on innocent people? Why does he not intervene and put a stop to it? Why is he silent in the face of evil? It is not only atheists that ask such questions. The problem has vexed many believers throughout the centuries. Psalm 94 long ago voiced their anguished perplexity:

> O LORD, God of vengeance . . . shine forth. Rise up, O judge of the earth; repay to the proud what they deserve! O LORD, how long shall the wicked . . . exult. . . . They crush your people. . . . They kill the widow . . . and murder the fatherless; and they say The LORD does not see . . . (Ps 94:1–7)[1]

Christ himself dealt with this problem in the parable of the Widow and the Unjust Judge (Luke 18:1–8). He told the parable in order to exhort us never to give up pleading with God to avenge his people. The parable itself tells of a widow who pleaded with a judge to avenge her of her adversary. For a while the judge refused. But the widow persisted pleading. So the judge, unjust though he was, at last relented and saw to it that justice was done. Said Christ: 'And shall not God avenge his elect who cry to him day and night', even though (it seems as if) he is dilatory towards them? (18:7).[2]

This apparent delay in God's intervention to do justice for his people is likewise strikingly brought out in the great drama that John was allowed to witness. John watched the Lamb open the first four seals (Rev 6:1–8), and immediately after each opening a divine judgment fell on earth. When the fifth seal was opened, the souls of those martyred for their faith cried out (like the author of Psalm 94):

1 'Vengeance' in passages such as these does not mean 'revenge'. It means the act or process of seeing to it that justice is done.
2 For a discussion of this last phrase see Marshall, *Luke*, 674–5.

'How long, O Master, the holy and the true, dost thou not judge and avenge our blood on them that dwell on earth?' (Rev 6:10).

They were told they must wait a little while yet. Then at the opening of the sixth seal catastrophic judgments fall on the world and bring this series to its climax (6:12–17).

But all is not yet over. The seventh seal is not yet opened; and when it is, another series of judgments will fall. So the seventh seal is opened, and then . . . nothing happens, nothing at all! Instead there is silence in heaven for about half an hour. If through John's eyes we too are watching the drama unfold, we shall be wondering: When will this silence be broken, and what will break it?

To start with, the seven angels that stand before God are each given a trumpet (8:2). But still no sound is heard. Then another angel is given much incense to add it to the prayers of all the saints upon the Golden Altar which is before the throne; and as the smoke of the incense rises up before God, their prayers become effective. The angel takes the censer, fills it with the fire of the altar, and casts it on the earth: and there follow thunders, and voices, and lightnings, and an earthquake (8:3–5). The silence is at last over. In answer to the prayers of all the saints, collected over many centuries, God now arises to avenge his own.

As this Section 2 proceeds, the timing of God's intervention continues to be a dominant theme. In chapter 10 a mighty angel comes down from heaven and swears an oath that there shall be delay no longer, but that in the days of the trumpet call by the seventh angel, the mystery of God will be fulfilled just as he announced to his servants the prophets (10:1–7).

The same theme pervades the climax of the section, as the twenty-four elders give God worshipful thanks, because the time has come:

> . . . for the dead to be judged, and for rewarding your servants, the prophets and the saints, and those who fear your name . . . and for destroying those who destroy the earth. (Rev 11:18)

Section 3 (Rev 11:19—15:4)

Just as the references to the symbolism of the tabernacle at the beginnings of Sections 1 and 2 proved to be functionally related, so too will the references to the tabernacle at the beginnings of Sections 3 and 4. This can be seen at once from the similarity of their language.

Says Section 3: 'And there was opened the temple of God that is in heaven' (11:19).

Section 4 will say: 'the temple of the tabernacle of the testimony in heaven was opened' (15:5).

Thus far the language is almost identical. But there are significant differences in what follows; and it is these differences that reveal in each case the relevance of the particular chosen piece of tabernacle symbolism to the events that are subsequently described.

When the temple is opened in Section 3, there is seen God's Ark. This time, however, it is not viewed as God's throne, as it was in Section 1. Instead it is referred to as 'the ark of his covenant'. This emphasises the fact that the ark contained the two stone tablets on which were engraved the Ten Commandments; they formed the basis of the covenant God made with Israel (Exod 24:1–8). The first two stipulations of that covenant were:

> You shall have no other gods before me. (Exod 20:3)

And

> You shall not make for yourself a carved image, or any likeness of anything that is in heaven above, or that is in the earth beneath, or that is in the water under the earth. You shall not bow down to them, nor serve them; for I the LORD your God am a jealous God. (Exod 20:4–5)

It is easy to see how a sight of the Ark of the Covenant sets the scene for the judgments that follow; for we shall read in this section of a time when its basic terms will be blasphemously defied by the leading world empire of the day.

> And they worshipped the dragon, because he gave his authority to the beast. And they worshipped the beast, saying, Who is like

unto the beast. . . . And he opened his mouth for blasphemies against God, to blaspheme his name and his tabernacle. . . .

[Then another beast will arise, and] he makes the earth and its inhabitants to worship the first beast . . . that they should make an image to the beast . . . and worship the image. (Rev 13:4, 6, 11–12, 14–15)

Refusal will mean execution; and those who do not accept the mark of the beast on hand or forehead will not be able to buy or sell.

In spite of this God will maintain loyalty to himself and to his covenant on the part of thousands of men and women. All these shall have the name of the Lamb and of his Father written on their foreheads. Subsequent verses explain how this loyalty is achieved: the Lamb 'buys them', not with money or goods, but with his life's blood (14:1–5). And at its conclusion the section triumphantly records the songs of those that come victorious from the beast and from his image and from the number of his name; and it predicts the time when all nations will come and worship God (15:2–4).

Section 4 (Rev 15:5 — 19:10)

Like the three preceding sections Section 4 begins with something opened in heaven. But this time John sees no piece of tabernacle furniture: not the throne, nor the Golden Altar of Incense, nor the Ark of the Covenant. Instead John sees seven angels come out of the temple with seven golden bowls full of the wrath of God (15:7). True, the temple out of which they come is called 'the tabernacle of the testimony', and the 'testimony' is the Ten Commandments that formed the basis of God's covenant with Israel mentioned in Section 3. But in Section 4 no mention is made of the Ark that housed the Ten Commandments. Rather we are confronted with the glory of God himself whose personal testimony those commandments were. 'God spoke all these words' (Exod 20:1). They were the expression of the character and will of the living God.

When he descended on Sinai to announce them to Israel, the mountain top 'was wrapped in smoke because the LORD had descended on it in fire. The smoke of it went up like the smoke of a kiln' (Exod 19:18 ESV). But now the blatant unholiness about to be described in this Section 4 has not only disobeyed commandments written on stone tablets: it has constituted a personal affront to God himself. Hence the wrath that fills the bowls of the seven angels is

> the wrath of God that lives for ever and ever. And the temple was filled with smoke from the glory of God and from his power; and no one was able to enter the temple until the seven plagues of the seven angels should be finished. (Rev 15:7–8)

The special objects of that wrath are two symbolic women, both called Babylon. One (Rev 17) seems to represent the perversion of religion—in the Old Testament Babylon was notorious for its idolatry. The other (Rev 18) seems to stand for the perversion of commerce. It is described in similar terms as is Tyre in Ezekiel 26 and 27; and Tyre's empire was built on trade.

The figurative language in which the charge is brought against these two women is drawn from the Old Testament. There Judah's original relationship to God is described as having been that of a virgin to her lover, as a wife loyal to her husband.[3] But Judah went wildly astray through religious and political compromise. She is denounced in Ezekiel 16 and 23 in vivid oriental imagery as a dissolute harlot worse than Samaria and Sodom. Her infidelity has not only broken the commandments: it has wounded and enraged the heart of God.

The first woman (Rev 17)

The first woman, in Revelation 17, then, has prostituted her God-given feminine beauty in an unholy alliance with the dominant world empire of the day. That empire is described as a beast 'full of names of blasphemy' (17:3). Yet this woman is sitting on the beast, lending it her religious influence in an attempt to wield power herself and control the political beast and its allies. For that purpose

---

3 Cf. Jer 2:2 where God says: 'I remember the devotion of your youth, your love as a bride, how you followed me in the wilderness' (ESV). Cf. also 2 Cor 11:2–3 where a similar figure of speech is applied to the church.

she has also connived with the beast in the execution of the saints and those that bore faithful testimony to Jesus, that is, the martyrs (17:6).

By her infidelity she has not only wounded the heart of God: she has declared war on him. Says James:

> You adulterous people, don't you know that friendship with the world is hostility towards God? Whoever, therefore, chooses to be a friend of the world, constitutes himself an enemy of God. (Jas 4:4)

John is invited to witness God's judgment on this great harlot. Her own sinful infidelity brings her to disaster: the Beast and his political allies eventually tire of her interference, and destroy her (Rev 17:1, 16–17).

The second woman (Rev 18)
The second woman is very different from the first. She is not primarily religious or political, but commercial. Witness the long list of luxury goods which she sells to the merchants for them to make themselves rich:

> . . . gold, silver, jewels, pearls, fine linen, purple cloth, silk, scarlet cloth, all kinds of scented wood, all kinds of articles of ivory, all kinds of articles of costly wood, bronze, iron and marble, cinnamon, spice, incense, myrrh, frankincense, wine, oil, fine flour, wheat, cattle and sheep, horses and chariots. (Rev 18:12–13 ESV)

Now all these goods are innocent enough in themselves. Indeed, they are the love-gifts to mankind by the Creator who gives us richly all things to enjoy (1 Tim 6:17). But accumulation of great wealth has induced in this woman, not a grateful dependence on, and love for, God, but an idolatrous self-confidence and arrogant independence of God. Her heart attitude is 'I sit as a queen, I am no widow, and mourning I shall never see' (Rev 18:7 ESV). She doesn't need to curry favour with the world's political authorities. She has more financial resources than most of them. It is they who come to her, seeking her favours, which, like the harlot she is, she sells to them and to merchants worldwide.

Moreover, obsessed with excessive wealth, she has lost the in-trinsic value of human beings made in the image of God. She has treated them as mere commodities and sold them as slaves for profit (18:13). Prophets and saints that have protested against her iniqui-ties she has secretly had murdered (18:24). And by the magic spell of her glittering consumerism all the nations of the earth have been deceived as to life's true values (18:23).

She is a powerful example of what John means when he says:

> Do not love the world or the things in the world. If anyone loves the world, the love of the Father is not in him. For all that is in the world—the desires of the flesh and the desires of the eyes and pride in possessions—is not from the Father but is from the world. And the world is passing away. . . . (1 John 2:15–17 ESV)[4]

The striking thing about God's judgment on this woman and on the system she represented was the suddenness with which it all collapsed: 'for in a single hour all this wealth has been laid waste' (Rev 18:17 ESV).

A third woman (Rev 19:1–8)

If the disloyalty of the first two women so provoked the wrath of God that no one could enter the temple until the plagues on them were finished, the loyalty of the third woman occasions great out-bursts of triumphant hallelujahs in heaven:

> Let us rejoice and be exceeding glad, and let us give the glory to God: for the marriage of the Lamb has come and his wife has made herself ready. And it was given to her to array herself in fine linen, bright and pure: for the fine linen is the righteous acts of the saints. (Rev 19: 7)

The New Testament's interpretation of the tabernacle as a type

May we not rightly conclude from the Revelation's view of these scenes in heaven that the theme of the tabernacle which we have

4 See pp. 212–19 for a more complete discussion of 'the world'.

been studying in these last three chapters is of eternal significance? It is certainly and gloriously so. But let one final reference to the tabernacle in Revelation assure us of the answer:

> And I saw the holy city, new Jerusalem, coming down out of heaven from God, made ready as a bride for her husband. And I heard a great voice out of the throne saying, Behold the tabernacle of God is with men and he shall dwell with them, and they shall be his people, and God himself shall be with them, and be their God. (Rev 21:2–3)

PART THREE

Guidelines for our own Interpretation
of Old Testament Narrative

22

The Need for Guidelines

The Purpose of Part Three

In Part One we studied the New Testament's general relation to the Old Testament. In Part Two we investigated many different components of five major thought categories of interpretation which it uses to extract the wealth of the Old Testament and apply it for our benefit. Now in Part Three we shall attempt to formulate some guidelines for our own interpretation of Old Testament narratives on which the New Testament either does not comment at all, or else does so only in part.

The need for such guidelines was discussed in Chapter 5. There we cited two specific examples: David's behaviour as king in the second half of 2 Samuel, and Abraham's sacrifice of his son in Genesis 22. Many more such examples could be quoted. We need guidelines, therefore, both to direct our thinking and also to provide some control to test the validity of the interpretations we eventually arrive at. That is why in Part Two we set out to discover what help we could find from the New Testament's own example in its detailed exposition and application of the Old.

It would be tiresome to list here again all the lessons we learned in Part Two; but some basic principles are worth emphasising at this point by way of reminder.

The simplistic idea that our interpretation must be either literal or typological is false for a number of reasons:

1. Between the two extremes (literal or typological) the New Testament uses many other interpretational categories, such as simile, metaphor, prototype, and analogy; and we may follow the New Testament's example in this.

2. Typology, to be valid, must in the first place start from a correct understanding of the literal and historical meaning of the thing, person, ritual or event in question. Otherwise it is invalid.

3. Moreover it is often not a question of *either* literal *or* typological interpretation and application, but of *both* literal *and* typological. Witness the New Testament's treatment of the story of Adam and Eve (see Chapter 16).

The nature of the analogy must be considered

All kinds of figurative language depend on some analogy between themselves and the literal entity on which they are based.[1] But sometimes the New Testament claims an analogy between two things neither of which is figurative; both are equally literal. When Abraham believed God and it was counted to him for righteousness (Gen 15:6), what he believed God about was God's promise to give him a son. When we believe God and it is counted to us for righteousness, we are not asked to believe that God will give us a son. Yet Paul in Romans 4:16–25 claims that there is a strict analogy between our faith and Abraham's. Abraham's faith was in God who gives life to the dead (4:17), ours is in God who 'raised our Lord Jesus from the dead, who was delivered up for our trespasses and was raised for our justification'. It is not a question of Abraham's faith being a 'type' of our faith; nor is our faith a simile or a metaphor based on his literal faith, nor a fulfilment of his prototypical faith. Our faith and Abraham's are simply instances of the same thing, of literal people putting literal faith of the same kind

---

1 e.g. simile: she ran like the wind; metaphor: he enjoyed being in the limelight; prototype: Christ our Passover was sacrificed for us.

in the same God who gives life to the dead. The analogy, then, is between two literal things of the same quality (see the discussion in Chapter 8, pp. 135–6).

The ethical effect of Christ's doctrine of the two comings of the Messiah should not be overlooked

We refer to this doctrine again here (we have already discussed it in Chapter 6) because of the direct effect it was intended to have on the practical lessons for our own behaviour that we as Christians draw from certain Old Testament narratives.

Joshua, for example, was commissioned by God to execute the wrath of God on the corrupt culture of the Canaanites, and to do so by force of arms. Christ did not dispute that fact. But throughout his earthly ministry he was at pains to distinguish between the purpose of his first coming and that of his second. At his first coming he insisted that he was not sent to judge the world or to execute the wrath of God on sinners. That solemn task he would perform at his second coming. The sole purpose of his first coming was, at the cost of his own suffering and death, to seek and to save those who were lost (John 3:17; Luke 19:10).

Moreover, he strictly forbade his disciples to use the sword, or violence of any kind, either to further, or protect, his kingdom (Matt 26:51–52; John 18:36–37). It has been a sad misrepresentation of Christ and a direct disobedience to his prohibition, when Christians have felt free to copy Joshua and use armed force to protect or to further Christ's kingdom.

Now with these preliminary reminders we must set about our task of formulating guidelines for our own interpretations. But let us make things as easy for ourselves as we can, by first studying in detail a narrative on which the New Testament makes extensive though not complete comment, namely, Abraham's sacrifice of Isaac. After that we can tackle narratives on which the New Testament makes no comment at all.

23

Abraham's Sacrifice of Isaac

A̲t least seven guidelines for interpreting Old Testament narratives can be formulated from the New Testament's interpretation of this well-known incident and the issues arising.

GUIDELINE 1:
> *If the New Testament interprets some Old Testament narrative,*
> *we should regard its interpretation as authoritative and should*
> *follow its lead*

Now according to James, Abraham's offering up of Isaac teaches us the necessity of justification by works: 'Was not Abraham our father justified by works, in that he offered up Isaac his son upon the altar?' (Jas 2:21). There can be no doubt about it: according to the New Testament this is the primary meaning of the narrative.

GUIDELINE 2:
> *No explanation of the New Testament's interpretation of an Old*
> *Testament narrative can be sound, if that explanation ignores,*
> *or conflicts with, the Old Testament narrative on which the*
> *interpretation is based*

Superficially, there appears to be a contradiction between Paul's doctrine of justification by faith (Gen 15:6 and Rom 4:1–5) and James' doctrine of justification by works (Gen 22). One attempt to resolve this apparent contradiction is the explanation: we are justified by faith before God; but before men we are justified by works.

But this explanation contradicts the narrative of Genesis 22. When Abraham climbed Mount Moriah, there were no men there, except himself and Isaac; and Isaac did not know he was going to be sacrificed until he was actually laid on the altar (Gen 22:7–8). Even Abraham's servants were told to stay at the foot of the mountain; and further that Abraham and Isaac were going to the top of the mountain to worship, and both would return (22:5). It is doubtful whether even Sarah knew of the intended sacrifice of her son; and there is no record that the local Philistines were aware of it. There were, therefore, no men there before whom Abraham could be justified by his works in offering up Isaac.

By contrast, the explicitly stated fact is that, when Abraham had laid Isaac on the altar and had raised the knife to slay him, the Angel of the Lord called to him out of heaven and said: 'Now *I* know that you fear God, seeing you have not withheld your son, your only son, from me' (22:12 ESV). The voice of the Angel of the Lord, was the voice of the Lord himself (cf. Exod 3:2–8). Abraham was being justified before God by his works.

It is useless to protest that God did not need Abraham to sacrifice his son, before he could know that Abraham's faith was genuine, since God surely knew that already. If God calls out of heaven and says to Abraham, '*now* [after what has happened] I know that you fear me, seeing you have not withheld your son from me', we must accept what God says. It is God who requires us to justify our faith before him by our works.[1]

---

1 We can, if we wish, ponder different kinds of knowledge. I myself, for instance, know that it is freezingly cold at the South Pole. I know it mentally. I can see that it must be so, considering its position, etc. But I don't know it by experience: I have never been there. God knew from all eternity that one day I should be born and live out my days on earth. I am glad he was not content with that kind of knowledge, but insisted on my actually being born, thus making it possible for me in my physical life on earth to know him, and for him to know me, experientially. And we may further wonder (if we are given to imagining impossible things) what God would have said, if, when he tested Abraham, Abraham had replied: 'Lord, you already know that I love and fear you, and you already know the future, and what I shall do; so I don't see why I should have to offer up Isaac to prove it to you.'

GUIDELINE 3:
*The New Testament implies that one Old Testament narrative
does not contradict another*
In other words Genesis is not a chance collection of stories which
some compiler stuck together, with little or no regard for their mutual consistency, simply because he happened to find them in various sources. So James is aware that he cannot interpret Genesis 22
regardless of whether his interpretation agrees or disagrees with
the statement in Genesis 15:6. He must explain how Genesis 15:6 is
related to Genesis 22. In fact he offers two explanations: one of the
relationship between the two Scriptures, and the other of the two
stages in Abraham's faith.

The two Scriptures
The Scripture in Genesis 15:6 that 'Abraham believed God and it
was counted to him for righteousness' *was fulfilled* by what happened on Mount Moriah (Jas 2:23). The use of the verb 'was fulfilled' does not imply that Genesis 15:6 was simply a prediction,
or promise: Abraham believed God and much later on, when he
had offered up Isaac, his initial faith was taken into account and
it was then, but only then, that the promise was fulfilled that it
was counted to him for righteousness. No! Genesis 15:6 records a
fact: Abraham believed God and it was there and then counted to
him for righteousness. He was at that time justified by faith. When
James says that Genesis 15:6 was fulfilled in Genesis 22, he is using
the term 'fulfil' in the sense that Christ used it when he said he
had not come to abolish the law but to fulfil it (see the discussion
in Chapter 7, pp. 114–15).

The two stages of Abraham's faith
'Faith worked with [and thereby aided] his works, and by works
his faith was brought to full expression' (Jas 2:22).[2] His faith was
already real when he believed God in Genesis 15:6. But real faith
will express itself in works. And real faith will grow and mature.

2 See Arndt and Gingrich, 'τελειόω', 809–810.

On Mount Moriah it was Abraham's faith that worked with, that is, supported and aided his works. Without that faith, the work of laying Isaac on the altar would never have been accomplished. Simultaneously, by this work of offering up Isaac his faith was brought to full expression.

It has to be admitted—and it is Genesis itself that tells us—that after Abraham initially believed God's promise, that he would give him a son, Abraham behaved inconsistently with his faith, and fathered Ishmael by Hagar. But at Mount Moriah Abraham's faith triumphed.

Genesis 22, therefore, does not contradict Genesis 15:6. On the other hand it does not simply repeat Genesis 15:6. The Genesis narrative is a record of the progression of Abraham's faith up until its triumph.

GUIDELINE 4:

If the New Testament comments on the same Old Testament narrative in more than one place, our interpretation, to be complete, must take all these places into consideration

It so happens that the writer to the Hebrews also mentions Genesis 22. His contribution is that he analyses in detail the nature and the significance of the works that Abraham was called upon to do so as to be justified by his works. Here is what he says:

> By faith Abraham, when he was tested, offered up Isaac, and he who had received the promises was in the act of offering up his only son, of whom it was said, 'Through Isaac shall your offspring be named.' He considered that God was able even to raise him from the dead, from which, figuratively speaking, he did receive him back. (Heb 11:17–19 ESV)

From this it is clear that it was not just any good work—such as giving money to charity, or feeding the poor—that Abraham was called upon to do. It was a work, designed by God, to test his faith. Abraham had originally complained to God that God had not given him a son to be his heir; and that, in consequence, when he died, his mere servant would inherit everything (Gen 15:1–4). God thereupon promised Abraham to give him a son and heir, and through that son multitudes of descendants. And Abraham believed God and it was counted to him for righteousness.

But the fulfilment of the promises was a long time in coming. And when at last it was about to happen, Sarah was still barren as she had always been; but now in addition she was old. And as far as fathering a child was concerned, Abraham was as good as dead. Isaac's birth then was a miracle. And when the boy began to grow Sarah expressed what for her, and for Abraham too, was the all important question which Abraham had originally raised with God: who should be Abraham's heir, when he died? Ishmael and his mother were therefore expelled: 'the son of this slave woman', said Sarah, 'shall not be heir with my son Isaac' (Gen 21:10 ESV).

And then, before Isaac was old enough to be married and have a son to begin the long line of promised descendants, God came to Abraham with the demand that he offer up Isaac as a burnt offering. It was a stunning challenge to Abraham's faith. All his hopes for the future were vested in Isaac. If Isaac were now sacrificed, Abraham would never have any descendants of the God-promised line (cf. Gen 17:18–21). At his age he would not hope to become a father again.[3]

The question that God's testing of Abraham raised was: when it came to his hopes for the future, was his faith in Isaac or in God? And the event showed beyond doubt that his faith was solely and utterly in God. Hebrews sums up the issue at stake exactly:

> . . . he who had received the promises was in the act of offering up his only son, of whom it was said, 'Through Isaac shall your offspring be named.' He considered that God was able to raise him from the dead, from which, figuratively speaking, he did receive him back. (Heb 11:17–19 ESV)

The work, then, by which Abraham was justified, was a work

---

3 The fact that Genesis 25 mentions that Abraham took another wife and begat several children, does not automatically imply that he did so after Sarah's death. 'It seems more likely that he had married Keturah earlier, perhaps after divorcing Hagar.' (Wenham, *New Bible Commentary*, 77).

which demonstrated that his faith was in God alone. God had originally made the promises, and those promises, on God's own insistence, were vested in Isaac, not in Ishmael. If God was now demanding that he sacrifice Isaac, Abraham would sacrifice him. But God couldn't lie or break his promises. God would have to, and God would, raise Isaac from the dead, that's all.

Now Abraham was a wealthy nomad, a sheikh. If God had asked him to give away his herds to the poor, and Abraham had done so, that would certainly have been a good work. It would also have satisfied James' demand that faith must not content itself with mere words, but show its reality by works (Jas 2:14–17). Nonetheless, it would not have demonstrated that his faith was in God alone, in quite the same way, and to the same extent, as his offering up of Isaac did.

GUIDELINE 5:
When the New Testament cites certain parts of an Old Testament narrative and then applies its lesson to us, it is a good thing to study the narrative in its immediate context to perceive how appropriate the application is

The writer to the Hebrews also cites from Genesis 22 the tremendous blessing that God pronounced on Abraham. He then draws two lessons from this citation, one regarding Abraham himself, and the other regarding the heirs of the promise, including us. The citation is as follows:

> For when God made a promise to Abraham, since he had no one greater by whom to swear, he swore by himself, saying, 'Surely I will bless you and multiply you.' (Heb 6:13–14 ESV)

The writer presumes his readers will remember the introduction to this blessing in the Genesis narrative: 'And the angel of the LORD called to Abraham a second time from heaven and said: "By myself I have sworn, declares the LORD, because you have done this and have not withheld your son, your only son . . ."' (Gen 22:15–16). And it is in the light of this, that the writer makes his two observations.

First observation
It was regarding the time in his life that Abraham received this promise from God and the circumstances in which he received it.

The writer's words are: 'And thus having waited patiently for a long time, he got the promise' (Heb 6:15). Not only a repetition of the promise he initially received in Genesis 15, but the first beginnings of its fulfilment in the 'resurrection' of Isaac from the dead.

The need to follow Abraham's example of patience is appropriately urged on the writer's first readers. They had some time ago made a profession of faith in Christ; but more recently their behaviour could have given the impression that they had abandoned their profession under the heat of persecution (Heb 6:1–12). They needed to observe, and then follow, the example of their ancestor Abraham who had to wait patiently and endure much testing before he received this mighty blessing from God (cf. Heb 6:11–12; 10:35–36).

Second observation
God's swearing of an oath was for the benefit of all the heirs of the promise, including ourselves. It guarantees to them anchor-like security (6:17–20).

Now if we do what Guideline 5 has suggested, we shall find that this question of security is not a theme that the writer to the Hebrews has arbitrarily deduced from these few verses about God's oath. This is in fact the third time that the question of security has surfaced in the immediate context in Genesis.

In Genesis 21:8–12 Sarah, with a mother's instinct to secure her true son Isaac's inheritance against any potential competition on the part of Ishmael and his descendants, declared: 'the son of this slave woman shall not be heir with my son, Isaac'. She demanded that Abraham should cast out Hagar and her son; and God told Abraham to do what Sarah demanded. And God explained to Abraham why: God was determined to secure that Abraham's descendants would come through Isaac, the son God had promised Abraham, and through him alone. God would make a nation of Ishmael too, because he was Abraham's son. But he was not the son that God had promised to Isaac. Only through Isaac would God's purpose for the blessing and salvation of the world be secured.

In Genesis 21:22–34 the Philistine King Abimelech with a father's concern for the security of his son, and therefore of his dynasty, asked Abraham to make a treaty with him. Abimelech was afraid that after his death Abraham would renege on the unwritten treaty of mutual benevolence they had between them, and attack his son and successors.

Abraham willingly gave Abimelech the treaty he asked for to guarantee his son's security. Both Abraham and Abimelech swore an oath to confirm the treaty; and after that Abimelech and his escort went home. But Abraham planted a tree at the place and called it Beersheba. It means 'the Well of the Oath', and was so called because of the oath that both he and Abimelech had sworn to guarantee the security of Abimelech's son. And there Abraham called on the name of the Lord, the everlasting God.

Security, then, for Sarah's son. And security for Abimelech's son. But what about security for Abraham's son and his descendants? Where would he find that?

He found it eventually in God's oath; and in the unforgettable memory of that oath, he came down the mountain and dwelt in a place called Beersheba (22:19).[4] It means once more 'the Well of the Oath'; but this time, God's oath.

But the focus of Genesis 22 is the process by which Abraham discovered that security. By God's own leading he stood, an old man on the top of a mountain, with his son in whom all the promises and all his hopes had been vested, now bound on the altar, and with the knife raised in his own hand about—at God's own demand—to slay his son, and be left, as far as he knew, with nothing, with no hope for the future, nothing but God and his promises and his faith in those promises.

But, in this changing world there is no greater security to be found than, bereft of all hope in all else, to be left with nothing but God and faith in him and his promises. That is eternal security.

4 Whether this is the same as the one mentioned in Genesis 21 or not, is immaterial.

GUIDELINE 6:
The whole of an Old Testament narrative is inspired by God,
and not just those features which the New Testament quotes.
We should, therefore, treat the whole narrative seriously as
being a narrative in its own right

That means we should pay attention to its dramatic structure and the effect this structure has on the development of thought throughout the story. We should mark its climaxes, both its minor ones and its major ones. We should take pains to understand the exact meaning of its technical terms and should allow ourselves to feel the emotional charge of its phrases. And above all we should allow the various characters in the story to tell us the significance of the events as they experienced them.

Four major parts to the narrative
First comes God's call to Abraham to offer up Isaac as a burnt offering to God; and Abraham's response up to the dramatic point where he raises the knife to slay his son (Gen 22:1–10).

Then the Angel of the Lord calls out of heaven telling Abraham to desist from actually slaying his son, for 'now I know that you fear God, seeing you have not withheld your son, your only son, from me' (22:11–12 ESV).

Thirdly, looking around, Abraham spies a ram caught in a thicket by its horns, and offers it up as a burnt offering in the stead of his son. And he calls the name of the place 'The LORD will provide'; and it is said to this day, 'On the mount of the LORD it shall be provided' (22:13–14).

Finally, the Angel of the Lord calls out of heaven the second time, announcing God's response to Abraham's action in not withholding his son from God. The response was the promise of God's blessing guaranteed by God's oath (22:15–19).

We may ask why the Angel had to call out of heaven twice. Why could he not have said all he had to say the first time?

The first simple answer is that he had to call the first time at the precise moment he did, for otherwise five seconds later Isaac would have been dead. And the second simple answer is that what Abraham did between the first call and the second must have been so important and necessary, that without it the second call could not have been made. The more thoughtful answer would be that the issues at stake summed up by the Angel's first call were different from the issues summed up by the second call.

The issues at stake in the first call
The fact, announced by the Angel, was that having ordered Abraham to offer up his son as a burnt offering, God was content to accept Abraham's heart-attitude, his firm decision to offer up his son to God, evinced by the arduous practical steps he took to effect the sacrifice. God did not allow him actually to slay his son.

Here we find answers to some of the questions we raised in Chapter 5. Why did God tell Abraham to do what elsewhere the Old Testament forbids, namely to offer human sacrifice? The first simple answer is that God did not allow Abraham actually to slay his son. He stopped him doing so.

Does that mean that God only pretended that he wanted Abraham to sacrifice his son? No, it would not be true to put it that way.

First of all, all we have that is any good is from God. God has the right to ask us to surrender it back to him. This is on a par with what Christ demanded: 'If anyone comes to me and hates not his own father, and mother, and wife, and children, and brothers, and sisters, yes and his own life also, he cannot be my disciple' (Luke 14:26).[5]

Secondly, for Abraham's good, God had to teach him, as we have seen, to place all his faith and hopes for the future in God rather than in Isaac.

Now God could have come to Abraham and said, Would you, if I asked you, surrender your son to me? And Abraham might well have said, Yes, of course. But how realistic would that response have

5 'Hate' here must be understood not in its modern western sense, but in its ancient Semitic sense: 'to give second, not first, place to'. Cf. Gen 29:31. We must put Christ before all other relationships.

been? The genuineness of Abraham's heart-attitude could be demonstrated, only when he was faced with the real life situation and was prepared to take the necessary practical steps.

But that demonstrated heart-attitude was enough for God, said the Angel's first call, without the physical act of slaying his son.

The issues at stake in the second call

Desisting at the Angel's call from sacrificing his son, Abraham looked round and saw a ram. He took it and offered it up as a sacrifice to God. But at this point we must notice our technical terms. Abraham did not offer the ram as a thank offering to God for sparing him the agony of sacrificing his son. He offered it as a burnt offering in the stead of Isaac.

That is highly significant. God's original demand was that he should offer up Isaac as a burnt offering. The demand was no pretence. The sacrifice could not simply be aborted. It had to be carried out fully, and was in fact carried out to completion by Abraham's offering up the ram in the stead of his son, that is as a substitute for Isaac (Gen 22:13). And it dawned on Abraham that this substitute for Isaac was God's provision, the provision in fact of the very God who had set him the test in the first place (22:1). And it was this that he called attention to when he named the place so that future generations might know the significance of what happened there. For he did not call it 'the place of my triumphant faith', or any such thing that would commemorate his spiritual attainment. He called it 'Jehovah Jireh', 'the LORD will provide', a promise based on his experience of God's provision of a substitute for his son, Isaac. Let all who are subsequently tested by God lay hold of this promise (cf. 1 Cor 10:13).

GUIDELINE 7:
After studying its immediate context, we should consider the
narrative's possible prototypical significance

This provision of an animal to be sacrificed as a substitute for a human being adds yet another level of meaning to the narrative.

No animal could ultimately be a sufficient substitute for a human being. Such Old Testament substitutionary sacrifices were but shadows pointing forward prototypically to the sacrifice of Christ. The Christian instinct that the story of Abraham's sacrifice of his son somehow or other foreshadowed Christ our great substitute is certainly true; but we must let the story as a whole determine in what sense it is true. According to the New Testament the prime significance of the story is Abraham's justification by works; and we must not brush aside the New Testament's interpretation in order to establish our own typological interpretation. What, then, has the sacrifice of Christ to do with our justification by works?

In answer, we should first inquire what standard God requires our works to meet, if we are to be justified by our works. Who would dare to answer: seventy-five per cent will do, or even less? Will God be satisfied with sub-standard works? Hardly! Christ, for instance, says 'I tell you, everyone who confesses me before men, the Son of Man also will confess before the angels of God; but the one who denies me before men will be denied before the angels of God' (Luke 12:8–9). Shall we turn round and say it doesn't really matter, if from time to time we deny him?

Believers normally desire to show by their works and devotion to Christ that they are true believers. Mostly they succeed. But sometimes they behave like the eleven disciples. The apostles in general, and Peter in particular, insisted that they would follow Christ wherever he went, even to prison and to death—and they meant it. But when they came to Gethsemane and were bidden to watch with Christ, weakness prevailed and they fell asleep.

Did this lapse in devotion matter? Of course, it mattered; and Christ chided them for it, and bade them 'wake up and pray, that you may not enter into temptation. The spirit indeed is willing, but the flesh is weak' (Matt 26:41). Yet they fell asleep again; and as a result Peter, all-unprepared, entered the high priest's court, was tested, failed miserably, and denied the Lord.

Christ, so Luke tells us, had foreseen it, and had prayed for Peter that in spite of this his faith should not fail; and Peter was eventually restored (Luke 22:31–34, 54–62). But this short-fall in his devotion was a grievous sin before God, and had to be paid for. And it was paid for. Indeed, in that very moment in Gethsemane when Peter's and the others' devotion fell short, Christ in absolute devotion to God prayed: 'Not my will but thine be done.' And thus prepared by prayer, he offered himself to God on the cross as their substitute to cover not only their pre-conversion sins, but the post-conversion shortfall in their works. And so he does for every true believer.

24

The Story of David and Goliath

Now, AT LAST, we come to study an Old Testament narrative on which the New Testament makes no detailed comment. We are, so to speak, on our own. How then shall we go about its exposition? How correctly deduce the lesson it was intended to teach us? And when we have arrived at our interpretation, how can we feel sure it is valid?

More or less obvious lessons

Some people's reaction to these questions may well be that they are excessively cautious, or even unnecessary. The story, they claim, carries its major lesson on its face: David's exemplary courage founded on his faith in God.

That is true, so far as it goes. The New Testament agrees. It does not explicitly mention David's fight with Goliath; but it lists David's name among that 'great cloud of witnesses' who testify that we too are called upon to show the same kind of faith, courage and persistence as they did (Heb 11:32; 12:1). How then can there be any problem with the exposition of the story and its application to ourselves?

Moreover the story carries another practical lesson on its face. It has David explaining to Saul how he came to have the astonishing faith that made him volunteer to face Goliath in battle to the death (1 Sam 17:33–37). It wasn't that the appearance of Goliath suddenly sparked off in David a bout of unaccustomed faith and courage. That could have been, as David's eldest brother suggested, nothing more than teenage foolhardiness (1 Sam 17:28). The opposite was true. David's courage and faith had developed over some years in the practicalities of daily life, looking after the family's sheep. When wild beasts attacked the flock, he had trusted God to give him the strength to attack and slay them. He then found that faith in God worked; and it had become a settled attitude of heart. Faith in God would work again, if Saul permitted him to take up Goliath's challenge.

We require no deep, expert analysis of this story to perceive what lesson it has to teach us.

Lessons from analogical interpretation

At the end of Chapter 8 we found that analogy is not only a valid means of applying an Old Testament lesson to ourselves: it is a means that the New Testament itself uses. We can therefore have no necessary objection to the use of analogy for applying to ourselves the example of David's fight with Goliath.

David fought the Philistine giant: we have to fight the 'principalities, powers, the world rulers of this darkness, and spiritual forces of wickedness in heavenly places'.

The form of warfare that David fought was different from ours. He fought with material weapons: we with spiritual. But our warfare is as real as his; and the metaphors that are used to describe our equipment for the fight are based on the literal weapons that any soldier in the ancient world would have used (Eph 6:10–20).

Lessons from typological interpretation

Some go further. They suggest that David's victory over Goliath foreshadows Christ's triumph over the devil. They base their suggestion on the similarity between the way in which David dispatched the giant, and the way in which Christ is said to have destroyed the devil (Heb 2:14–15). Having foiled Goliath, David used Goliath's own sword to cut off Goliath's head (1 Sam 17:51):

so in Hebrews 2:14–15 the devil is said to have the power of death, and Christ destroyed him by dying.

Questions concerning these lessons

Both the analogical and the typological interpretation take Goliath as representing, or foreshadowing, the devil himself or his demonic powers. But we could reasonably ask whether these interpretations arise naturally out of the particular form of ancient military warfare that is described in such detail in the narrative. Perhaps they do, perhaps they don't. But our conclusions would be safer if we first went back to the beginning again, and started our exposition by studying the literal, historical elements in the story.

Then, while we are at it, we could ask what significance the duel between David and Goliath had for the inspired author of 1 Samuel. Was it for him a brilliant, but one-off, incident with little, or no, connection with what had gone before? Or was it the climax of a movement of thought begun in the previous chapters?

GUIDELINE 8:
Start with the Old Testament story's literal, historical meaning

A special form of ancient warfare

The contest between David and Goliath was a special form of ancient warfare known as single-hero combat. It is the only instance of it recorded in the Old Testament, but other examples can be found in the literature of other nations at widely different times and places. The Greek poet, Homer, records at some length the duel between the Trojan hero, Paris, and the Greek hero, Menelaus, and a similar duel between Hector, the Trojan, and Ajax, the Greek (*Iliad*, Book 3 and Book 7, respectively). The much later Irish epic, *The Táin*, likewise describes many such duels between Cúchulainn, the Ulster hero, and individual heroes sent against him by the armies of the other provinces of Ireland, and finally the famous duel, lasting several days, between Cúchulainn and Ferdia. All these duels, in *The Iliad* and *The Táin*, are instances of single-hero combat.

The special features of single-hero combat

1. When two armies were fighting each other, it was open to either army to call a halt to the battle, to put forward one of their leading warriors and challenge the other side likewise to put forward one of their warriors, so that the two warriors could fight a duel, each as the representative of his own side.

2. The challenge having been made, both armies had to cease fighting and lay down their arms. A truce would then be proclaimed. During the truce no one from either side was allowed to shoot at the opposite side, and least of all at its proposed hero; for that would be to break the sacred truce.

3. Sometimes the warrior selected by the side that issued the challenge was so mighty that the other side had great difficulty in finding in their own ranks a warrior strong enough and courageous enough to go out and fight the enemy's hero.

4. Meanwhile the warrior from the challenging side was free to walk right up to the enemy's lines and taunt them, without fear of being shot at, since the truce was in force.

5. If the second army accepted the challenge of the other side, the conditions of the duel would be declared and agreed in terms of what the army whose warrior was defeated in the duel must in consequence do or suffer.

6. Then the two warriors would emerge each from his own army into no man's land and approach his opponent until the both of them were within earshot. Then they would pause while the challenging hero would denounce his opponent and warn him of the dire destruction he would suffer. And when he had finished his denunciation, his opponent would have his turn, and threaten his enemy with similarly dire destruction and even worse.

7. That done, they would close in on each other and fight with an assortment of weapons, which are generally described in the records in some detail since the choice of armour and weapons and the skill with which the weapons were wielded would vitally affect the result.

8. The fight would continue until one of the heroes was killed (or

occasionally when one of the heroes and the army he represented admitted defeat).

The story of David and Goliath exhibits all these elements

1. The Philistine army and the Israelite army were drawn up ready for battle, when the Philistines put forward their champion warrior, Goliath, who challenged the Israelites to choose a warrior of their own to fight with him in single-hero combat (1 Sam 17:1–10, 21, cf. element 1 above).

2. Goliath's physique, armour and weapons are described in detail (1 Sam 17:4–7, cf. element 7 above).

3. The terms on which the duel is to be fought are proclaimed: if the Israelite hero defeats the Philistine hero, all the Philistines will become servants to the Israelites. If Goliath defeats the Israelite hero, all the Israelites will become servants to the Philistines (1 Sam 17:8–10, cf. element 5 above).

4. On hearing Goliath's challenge, the Israelites are terror-stricken. None of them, not even Saul or Jonathan, is prepared to take up the challenge (1 Sam 17:11, 24, cf. element 3 above).

5. The challenge having been issued and followed by a truce, the Philistine hero is free to come right up to the Israelite lines without fear of being attacked (1 Sam 17:23, cf. element 4 above).

6. When David volunteers to go out and fight with Goliath, much emphasis is laid on David's choice of armour and weapons (1 Sam 17:38–40, 43, cf. element 7 above), and then on how he used his weapon in the contest (17:48–50).

7. David and Goliath emerge from their respective camps and advance towards each other until they are within earshot (1 Sam 17:40–41). Then they stop, and Goliath denounces and curses David (17:42–44), and David in turn announces Goliath's imminent death (17:45–47) (see element 6 above).

8. The two heroes close in on each other, and David swiftly dispatches Goliath (1 Sam 17:48–51).

The peculiar feature of the David–Goliath duel

We are now in a position to understand the ancient form of warfare known as single-hero combat. We can also see that the story of David and Goliath adheres to this ancient form of warfare—except in one crucial feature: the two combatants are not equally matched. On the one side the Philistine giant, a huge man in any case, with long military experience, and in addition armed with extraordinarily powerful weapons, and a helper to carry his shield into the bargain. On the other side a mere stripling of a youth, with little or no military experience, and armed simply with a staff and a sling.

When the Philistine caught sight of David, he felt insulted. He could scarce contain his anger at Israel's impertinence in sending him such a contemptible opponent, virtually unarmed, and with absurdly weak weapons. But David explained to him the true issue at stake in the duel: 'You come to me with a sword and with a spear and with a javelin; but I come to you in the name of the LORD of hosts, the God of the armies of Israel, whom you have defied' (1 Sam 17:45 ESV). It was not a question of who was the bigger man, the more experienced fighter, the better armed, and the more skilful tactician. 'The battle was the LORD's' (1 Sam 17:47).

One thing can be said at once: single-hero combat pointed up what the issue at stake was with far greater clarity than a pitched-battle could have done.

GUIDELINE 9:
Investigate indications of the author's intention in the thought-flow of the surrounding narrative

The duel between David and Goliath is the climax of the storyline that begins in 1 Samuel 8. In that chapter the nation's elders approach Samuel and demand that he appoint someone to be a king over them. Their motives were mixed. Samuel had been a very honest and faithful judge. But his sons, who succeeded him as judges, were corrupt. It was understandable therefore that the elders should reject them. But they were not content simply to replace these corrupt men with better and more honest judges. They proposed to do away with the office of judge altogether and to replace it with a monarchy. Samuel, who as a judge had served them well for many years, took their proposal as a slight upon himself and his office, and was deeply offended (1 Sam 8:6).

But the elders had other motives as well, as Samuel subsequently pointed out (1 Sam 12:6–13). The situation up till that time had been that, when Israel were oppressed in Egypt, they cried to the Lord and he sent Moses and Aaron to deliver them out of Egypt. When in the promised land they from time to time forgot the Lord and compromised with idolatry, God allowed their enemies to overcome and dominate them. Then they would cry to the Lord again, and he would hear their cries and raise them up a succession of deliverers.

But eventually they got tired of that process. To have to cry to the Lord when they had a hostile army breathing down their neck and threatening to enslave them, and to have to depend on God to raise up a deliverer—that was, apparently, too nerve-racking. So when the Ammonite King Nahash began to threaten them they demanded Samuel to set up an hereditary monarchy. That way, when an enemy attacked them, they would have a king already organised and in place to defend them, and would not have the uncertainty of having to cry to the Lord and wait for him to raise up a deliverer.

God read this demand as a rejection of himself (1 Sam 8:7–9). It was not that he disapproved of the idea of an hereditary monarch in and of itself. Chapter 16 of this very same book will tell how God sent Samuel to anoint David as king, and 2 Samuel 7 will record God's covenant which guaranteed the future of David's royal dynasty. It was the motive that lay behind the elders' demand that God disapproved of. Any organisation, any institution, that is devised to obviate the necessity of depending on God is fatally flawed.

To Samuel's surprise, however, God instructed Samuel to accede to the elders' request. He was to anoint Saul and to present him to the people as their king. God was about to teach the people a very salutary lesson. On the other hand, he did not force his choice upon the people against their will or better judgment. When the people saw Saul, they were delighted with God's choice: for

Saul was a very big man. He towered above everyone: 'he was higher than any of the people from his shoulders and upwards' (1 Sam 10:23). And truth to tell, when he was first appointed, Saul achieved some notable military successes against the people's enemies (11:1–15), as big men are apt to do.

But putting one's faith in a big man rather than in God has a fatal weakness: a big man will do very well until a bigger man comes on the scene. And one day there came out of the enemy camp a veritable giant of a man, Goliath (17:4–7); and he challenged Israel to single-hero combat. At the very sight of him, big man Saul along with the rest of the Israelites was panic-stricken (17:11).

Then David appeared on the scene and volunteered to go out and fight Goliath. Saul protested that this suggestion was utterly unrealistic: David was a mere cadet, Goliath was the Philistines' leading champion with years of experience. But David persisted. It was, he explained, simply a matter of faith in God. He had had plenty of experience of trust in God to deliver him from lions and bears as he guarded his flocks. God would similarly deliver him from the Philistine (17:33–37). At that Saul consented to let David fight Goliath. But now the choice of armour and weapons became all important. Saul urged David to use Saul's armour and sword. But the suggestion was stupid: Goliath's spear was so long and heavy that had David tried to use Saul's sword, Goliath would have speared him before David got anywhere near him. David rejected Saul's armour and weapons and instead took with him simply his staff and sling.

When Goliath caught sight of David his professional pride was injured. For Israel to send out a mere youth to engage in single-hero combat with the great Philistine hero was an insult. When he then caught sight of David's weaponry, he exploded with anger. 'Am I a dog', he shouted, 'that you come to fight me with a stick such as someone might use to chase a dog out of his backyard?' David's 'weapons' were contemptibly weak, his armour non-existent. Goliath cursed David by his gods (17:40–44).

But David, when his turn to speak came, explained to Goliath what the real issue at stake was in their duel, and why he had deliberately chosen such apparently weak weapons:

> You come to me with a sword, and with a spear, and with a javelin; but I come to you in the name of the Lord of hosts, the God of the armies of Israel, whom you have defied. Today the Lord will deliver you into my hand . . . that all the earth may know that there is a God in Israel; and that all this assembly may know that the Lord saves not with sword and spear; for the battle is the Lord's, and he will give you into our hand. (1 Sam 17:45–47)

With that David whirled his sling and its stone felled Goliath to the ground. Whereupon David ran and taking Goliath's own sword — for David had none himself — struck off his head.

On this showing, then, the story of David and Goliath exposes Israel's folly in ceasing to put their faith altogether in God, and in putting it instead in the 'big man' Saul. At the same time it displays the wisdom and power of God's tactics in using David's weak and apparently foolish weapons to bring the giant-man, Goliath, crashing to the ground, thus delivering his people from their oppressors, and directing their faith back to God.

Guideline 10:

*We should question the comparative importance of the lesson we
propose to draw from the Old Testament narrative*

Let us sum up our study so far. To decide what lessons the story of David and Goliath is meant to teach us, we have taken two steps:

1. We have tried to take seriously all the details of the narrative and to understand them in their historical context.

2. We have studied the story in its larger narrative context, and have tried to understand how it is related to one, at least, of the themes which the author of 1 Samuel has himself emphasised.

But there are two further questions we should ask:

3. Is the lesson which we think we have discerned in this story important enough to have occupied so large a portion of inspired Scripture? Or is it small and commonplace, such that it could be drawn from almost any passage in the Old Testament?

4. Is there any passage in the New Testament that teaches this same lesson in detail as its main, deliberate theme?

The answer to this fourth question is, Yes. The first chapter of 1 Corinthians (and much of the following three chapters) consists of the Holy Spirit's protest through Paul that the Corinthian Christians were beginning to make the fundamental mistake of placing their basic confidence in certain 'big men', certain famous preachers, like Paul, Cephas and Apollos, instead of in God. Now Paul, Cephas and Apollos were all three of them noble servants of Christ. Paul and Cephas, moreover, were apostles; and the Corinthians, like ourselves today, were required to accept and believe the words and writing of our Lord's apostles. But the Corinthians were going far beyond that. Each was claiming one of the three as his champion, boasting in him, and putting their faith in him, to the exclusion of the champions that others chose to glory in (1 Cor 1:11–13; 3:1–9; 4:6).

But to boast in man, as if salvation depended on man and not on God, is fundamentally false and ruinous. 'Was Paul crucified for you?' demands Paul indignantly (1:13). As the Old Testament elsewhere protests:

> Thus says the LORD, 'Let not the wise man boast in his wisdom, let not the mighty man boast in his might, let not the rich man boast in his riches, but let him that boasts boast in this, that he understands, and knows me. . . .' (Jer 9:23–24 ESV)

To boast in man, Paul argues, is to act clean contrary to God's strategy of the cross. To save man God had to break this false confidence in man, and to lead him to place his confidence solely in God. Hence, Paul explains, God deliberately chose to use what to the world seem utterly weak and scandalously foolish strategies, tactics and weapons:

> For the word of the cross is folly to those who are perishing, but to us who are being saved it is the power of God. . . . For since, in the wisdom of God, the world did not know God through wisdom, it pleased God through the folly of what we preach to save those who believe. . . . For the foolishness of God is wiser than men, and the weakness of God is stronger than men. . . . God chose what is foolish in the world to shame the strong. God

chose what is low and despised in the world, even things that are not, to bring to nothing things that are so that no human being might boast in the presence of God. . . . Therefore, as it is written, 'Let the one who boasts, boast in the Lord' . . . that your faith might not rest in the wisdom of men, but in the power of God. . . . So let no one boast in men. (1 Cor 1:18–31; 2:5; 3:21)

Conclusion

We conclude, then, that the New Testament reinforces the lesson which we have suggested is taught by 1 Samuel 17: Israel's faith in Saul, big man though he was, was misplaced. Saul could not save them. Only God could do that. And to make that point clear to Israel, God deliberately used not the big man, Saul, but the armourless, youthful, shepherd David and his impossibly weak and apparently foolish weapons to defeat the giant-man, Goliath, and to direct Israel's faith back to God.

Once more, then, the Christian instinct that this particular Old Testament story somehow or other points forward to Christ has proved true. But our study has helped us to understand more precisely in what sense it is true; and then to see what practical lesson it has to teach us.

25

The Case of the Gibeonites

WE NOW COME to study another Old Testament narrative on which the New Testament makes no direct comment and about which there is a greater level of disagreement. For many people—indeed for the great majority of expositors—the story of the Gibeonites carries an explicit, undeniable lesson. It records that at a crucial time in their history the Israelites failed to ask counsel from the Lord. As a result they were deceived into disobeying one of the Lord's strictest commands, and thereby suffered unfortunate, irreversible consequences for centuries thereafter.[1] The lesson for us is obvious: we should never become so confident in our own intelligence that we fail to seek guidance from the Lord. So runs the majority view.

Let us begin, then, by surveying the basic facts of the story.

The basic facts and the majority view

Before Israel's entry into Canaan, Moses had briefed them on how they were to treat the various cities they would encounter in the land. They must totally destroy the population in all the cities that would be near at hand to Israel's settlements. By contrast, cities that were far off were to be offered more merciful terms (Deut 20:10–18).

Now the citizens of Gibeon apparently heard of Moses' instructions through the grapevine; and they panicked, because they

1 Josh 9:1–10:27 and especially 9:14.

would be near Israel once Israel settled in. They decided that their only hope of avoiding total destruction would be to send a deputation to the Israelites before the latter discovered the true location of their city; and they would try to convince them that the city they came from was very far away. For that purpose they invented an elaborate hoax to make it easier for Israel to swallow their lie.

For this deception the Gibeonites are, of course, castigated by the commentators. But the narrative points out that at no point in these negotiations did Joshua and the princes of Israel 'ask counsel of the LORD' (Josh 9:14); and for this the Israelites are castigated by the commentators even more severely than the Gibeonites. Had the Israelites asked counsel of the Lord, he most surely would have exposed the Gibeonites' deceit. And then, so Israel's critics surmise, the Lord would have told them to obey Moses' command and destroy all the inhabitants of Gibeon and their satellite towns (9:17). But as a result of not asking counsel of the Lord, the Israelites were deceived into doing what Scripture explicitly forbade, namely making a covenant with the inhabitants of a nearby city, and allowing them to live.

Many feel, therefore, that the case against Israel is indisputable. Indeed we could add to the charge against them if we were inclined to do so. They not merely made an agreement with the Gibeonites: without seeking the Lord's directive or permission, they 'swore an oath by the LORD, the God of Israel', to 'let them live' (9:15, 18, 19, 20). That adds arrogance to the charge of careless disobedience.

Three days later, however, they heard that the Gibeonites were their near neighbours; and, taking the whole army with them, Joshua and the princes went to visit the Gibeonites on their own territory (9:17). The army grew restless. They wanted Joshua and the princes to renounce the covenant and destroy the Gibeonites forthwith (9:18). Legally, Joshua could have done so on the grounds that the Gibeonites had secured the covenant on false pretences. It was therefore invalid, and Israel was not bound to it. But Joshua and the princes argued that having sworn an oath in the name of God, they could not now go back on it; for, if they did, they were afraid that wrath from God would fall upon them (9:18–20).

It was certainly a difficult situation to be in. If the prosecution's case against Israel is correct, Joshua and the princes had already incurred the wrath of God for disobeying his command through Moses to destroy the Gibeonites. Now they were afraid that they would incur his wrath if they reversed their behaviour and obeyed his command through Moses. Faced with these difficult results of not having consulted the Lord in the first place, why did they not at least now consult the Lord? He surely would have solved their dilemma.

But once more Joshua and the princes did not consult the Lord — at least there is no record of their having done so. They decided to solve the dilemma by themselves. Contrary to what the army wanted, they insisted that they must keep the oath and not destroy the Gibeonites, even though it disobeyed Moses' command. On the other hand, to satisfy their own consciences, they modified the original terms of their covenant, and imposed a curse on the Gibeonites to the effect that they must for ever after be servants to the Israelites (9:18–27). It was the best compromise that Joshua and the princes could think of in the circumstances.

Thus far, then, the prosecution's case against Israel; and on this basis many devotional commentators draw out a warning lesson for us all. The Israelites, they point out, had recently experienced two great victories, first at Jericho, and then, after much prayer, confession of sin, and waiting upon God, at Ai (Joshua 6–8). Flushed with this success, however, they became too self-confident. When the Gibeonites arrived, they mistakenly felt no need to wait on God in prayer. They could, they thought, deal with this matter themselves: the facts of the situation were so clear, and the right action to take obvious. They were thus deceived into serious disobedience to God's word. Thereafter the only way they could extricate themselves was to adopt compromises, which landed them in a second-best and embarrassing situation for centuries to come.

Taught by their unfortunate example, we are then warned not to let past success remove our sense of constant need for prayer, dependence on God, knowledge of his word and scrupulous obedience to it.

Let it be said at once that in itself this advice is certainly good, wholesome and necessary. Nothing in the rest of this chapter will dispute or undermine it. But whether this is the lesson that the story of the Gibeonites was meant to teach us is, at the very least, doubtful. To start with, consider the theological implications of this interpretation, were it true.

GUIDELINE 11:
Consider the theological implications of any suggested interpretation

When the king of Jerusalem heard that the Gibeonites had made peace with Israel and were among them, he was alarmed. Gibeon was a great city, like one of the royal cities (10:2), a mother city to a number of satellite towns. He therefore organised a confederacy of all the southern kings and marched their armies, not against the Israelites, but against Gibeon. His intention was to destroy the Gibeonites root and branch for their defection to Israel; and with that in mind they besieged the city.

And now, had the Lord so wished, he could have allowed the Southern Confederacy of kings to do what (according to the majority interpretation) he wanted the Israelites to do, namely to destroy the Gibeonites. Instead, he intervened spectacularly to save them.

First, the Gibeonites managed to get a message through the enemies' lines to Joshua at Gilgal, pleading with him to come to their aid; and Joshua started to go. At that point God stepped in and encouraged Joshua: 'Do not fear them, for I have given them into your hands. Not a man of them shall stand before you.'

So Joshua led his army on a forced march all through the night and sprang a surprise attack on the besieging forces early the next day (10:6–9). And then,

> ... the LORD threw them [the besiegers] into a panic before Israel ... and as they fled ... the LORD threw down large stones from heaven on them ... There were more who died because of the hailstones than the sons of Israel killed with the sword. (Josh 10:10–11 ESV)

Finally, we read of Joshua speaking to the Lord:

> Joshua spoke to the LORD . . . and he said in the sight of Israel,
> 'Sun, stand still at Gibeon and moon, in the Valley of Aijalon.'
> And the sun stood still, and the moon stopped, until the nation
> took vengeance on their enemies. . . . There has been no day like
> it before or since, when the LORD listened to the voice of a man,
> for the LORD fought for Israel. (Josh 10:12–14 ESV)

Well, that certainly relieved the siege of Gibeon, and rescued
the Gibeonites from imminent destruction. But how, then, are we
to construe the story as a whole? Are we to think that God, left to
himself so to speak, never wanted to save the Gibeonites? Rather
he wanted Israel to destroy them according to Moses' command
(Deut 20:15–18); and if only Israel had consulted him, when the
Gibeonites first approached them, he would have told the Israelites
to destroy them. But Israel did not consult him. What is worse,
without his permission and against his will, they on their own initiative swore an oath in his name not to destroy the Gibeonites, but
to let them live (Josh 9:15). Are we to conclude, then, that through
the Israelites' folly and rank disobedience God was obliged to save
the Gibeonites when all the while he did not want to?

This surely is an unlikely interpretation, theologically speaking.
It would be easier to think that somehow God all the while intended
to show mercy on the Gibeonites, rather than that the Gibeonites
owed their salvation to Israel's forcing God's hand by swearing an
oath in his name without his permission and against his will and
intention.

An unsatisfactory explanation
It would be possible to argue—and many do—that though God disapproved of Israel's failure to execute his wrath on the Gibeonites,
yet in his mercy he overruled that disobedience for good: at least it
led to an opportunity for Israel to defeat the armies of the Southern
Confederacy. Yet such an explanation would seem to clash incon-
gruously with a major emphasis in the three chapters immediately
preceding the story of the Gibeonites (Josh 6–8).

The ban pronounced by Moses on cities near at hand (Deut 20:16–18), and therefore on Gibeon, was similar to that pronounced on Jericho (Josh 6:17–21, 24). It was a very solemn thing, and not to be trifled with. In Jericho's case the Israelites were warned that the slightest infringement by anyone would bring the curse of the ban on to the whole of Israel.

In the event a certain Achan broke the ban; and although at the time it was unbeknown to Israel, God could not overlook it. So when Joshua sent a battalion against the next town, Ai, God allowed the troops to be repulsed with the loss of some thirty lives. Not until Israel had dissociated itself from Achan's sin by executing him, did God allow Israel to proceed to the conquest of Ai and of the rest of Canaan.

Now Achan was not deceived when he broke the ban: he did what he did with his eyes wide open—too wide open in fact. Israel, by contrast, were deceived into thinking that the Gibeonites came from a distant city; and therefore Israel probably felt that they were doing right when they swore an oath in God's name to let them live. But according to the majority view it was their own fault that they were deceived. If only they had inquired of the Lord, he would have exposed the Gibeonites' hoax, and then—according to the majority view—would have ordered the Israelites to destroy them. As it was, the breaking of the ban in Gibeon's case was the result of culpable, prayerless irresponsibility on the part of Joshua and the princes.

If, then, because of Achan's breaking of the ban on Jericho God held up any further conquest until Israel repented and executed Achan, how was God consistent in overlooking Israel's breaking of the ban on Gibeon? And not only overlooking it, but immediately and without reproving Israel, empowering them with spectacular miracles to save the Gibeonites?

A possible alternative explanation

Theologically speaking, the majority view thus runs into severe difficulties. Could it, then, be mistaken? It is to be noticed that it depends on an unspoken assumption. When Joshua 9:14 observes that 'the men of Israel did not ask counsel at the mouth of the LORD', the majority view rightly presumes that if only they had asked for God's guidance he would have exposed the Gibeonites' lie that they came from a distant city. But then the majority view goes on to presume that God would also have expected, if not commanded, them to carry out the ban pronounced on all nearby cities and to destroy the Gibeonites. But, in the light of what followed, this presumption might be wrong.

Suppose—and at this stage it can only be a supposition—that God had read what the Gibeonites did as an expression of repentance; an acknowledgement that they were liable to God's righteous judgment, and yet a genuine plea that his mercy which was to be extended to distant cities might be shown to them as well.

Someone will raise the objection: but they lied! And not only lied, but contrived a deceitful charade to get Israel to swallow their lie!

Yes, they certainly did. But they were not the only Canaanites that lied. A woman in another, much nearer, city also lied. Yet not only was she saved, but her action in protecting the Israelite spies— which was the reason for her telling lies (Josh 2:2–7)—is cited in the New Testament as an instance of justification by faith (Heb 11:31) and by works (Jas 2:25).

Maybe, however, our discussion at this stage is in danger of becoming enmeshed in complicated detail. So let's delay decision for a while and start afresh, following another guideline.

GUIDELINE 12:
> Examine the book as a whole to see whether it has a dominant,
> or repeated, theme or themes

Judged by similarity of phrase the following passages seem to constitute a dominant theme in Joshua:

Josh 2:12–13 — Rahab. 'Swear to me by the LORD . . . *that you will save alive* my father and my mother, and my brothers, and my sisters, and all that they have, and will *deliver our lives from death*.'

6:17 — 'Only Rahab the prostitute and all who are with her in her house *shall live*, because she hid the spies . . .'

6:25 — 'But Rahab the prostitute and her father's household and all that she had, did Joshua *save alive,* and she dwelt in the midst of Israel unto this day.'

9:15 — 'Joshua made peace with [the Gibeonites] and made a covenant with them *to let them live.'*

9:20 — 'This we will do to them and *let them live.'*

9:21 — 'And the princes said to them, *"Let them live."'*

14:10 — Caleb (in contrast to a whole generation of his contemporaries who had died in the wilderness under the judgment of God). 'And now, behold, the LORD has *kept me alive,* as he promised, these forty-five years . . .'

20:9 — The cities of refuge. 'These were the appointed cities . . . that anyone who killed a person accidentally and without intent could flee there, *so that he might not die* by the hand of the avenger of blood before standing trial before the congregation.'

The book of Joshua certainly records the severe judgments of God on the corrupt Canaanite society and even on Achan the Israelite. But the severity is not unrelieved. The repeated phraseology of these expressions of God's mercy forms a delightful counterpoint.

Moreover, it will be worthwhile to consider Rahab's case in some detail for it may cast light on God's treatment of the Gibeonites. Both Jericho and Gibeon were equally under God's ban. Yet at Jericho an exception was made in the case of Rahab and all her family, and at Gibeon the whole city and all its inhabitants were saved from the judgment passed on all nearby cities. Why, then, and on what grounds did Israel spare Rahab? The answer to this question might help to explain why God spared the Gibeonites.

The details of Rahab's case

The situation was this. Before Joshua committed his army and people to the crossing of Jordan, he sent spies across, not, of course, to spy out the land of Canaan (that he and Caleb had done forty years earlier) but to discover what the mood was like in Jericho. Was the king mobilising his army to rush out and attack the Israelites as they attempted to cross Jordan? Or was the king preparing the city to endure a siege? It would have been very dangerous for Israel if the king had been intending to attack Israel as they were scrambling out of the river. What the spies discovered was that the king was not intending any attack, but was preparing to endure a siege (Josh 6:1).

When the spies entered the city, however, they made for the house of a prostitute named Rahab. Strange men entering her house would not be anything unusual or suspicious. Someone, however, informed the king, who sent the police to investigate. But Rahab had hidden the spies. She admitted to the police that two strange men had in fact come to her house—she didn't know from where!—but at nightfall, just before the city gates were shut, the men had slipped out of the city! Where they were going to, she didn't know either! But she advised the police to hurry up and catch them.

When the immediate danger was past, she brought the men out of hiding, and pleaded with them to swear an oath in the name of Yahweh, that when the Israelites destroyed Jericho and slew its citizens—as she knew they would—they would save her and her family alive (2:12–13). And the two spies responded by swearing an oath to this effect.

Now this is surely remarkable. In the first place there is no doubt that it contravened the letter, at least, of Moses' prohibition of mercy on the inhabitants of any city near at hand, and also derogated from the ban that God had pronounced on Jericho. In the second place their swearing of their oath would implicate Joshua and the Israelites and bind them to honour the oath. Yet they did not first communicate with base and consult Joshua and the Israelite princes (in the circumstances it would have been impossible). They just went ahead and took it on themselves to swear an oath that guaranteed that Israel would save her and her family, without, apparently, even seeking counsel of the Lord!

Why did they do it?

They did it, in the first place, because Rahab had saved their lives. Rahab's plea was undeniable:

> . . . since I have been loyal to you [KJV, dealt kindly with] . . .
> [swear] that you will be loyal to my father's house . . . and save

alive my father, and my mother and my brothers and sisters and all that they have, and will deliver our lives from death. (Josh 2:12–13)

It would have been very difficult for the spies to say: 'Yes, you were very loyal to us when the police came just now and you saved our lives at the risk of your own. And we are grateful to you for providing us with a rope to escape with through your window and down the wall. But, sorry, when we come back we shall kill you nonetheless. Our religion says we must. We cannot show loyalty to you.'

But the spies had another, even more powerful, reason for swearing an oath in God's name that they would save her and family alive: Rahab, they found, was a converted woman! To borrow a New Testament phrase, she had 'turned to God from idols, to serve the living and true God ...' (1 Thess 1:9). Listen to her speaking to the spies:

> I know that the LORD has given you the land, and that your terror has fallen on us, and that all the inhabitants of the land melt away before you. For we have heard how the LORD dried up the water of the Red Sea before you, when you came out of Egypt, and what you did to the two kings of the Amorites, that were beyond Jordan, to Sihon and to Og, whom you utterly destroyed. As soon as we had heard it, our hearts melted, neither did there remain any more spirit in anyone because of you; for the LORD your God, he is God in heaven above, and on earth beneath. (Josh 2:9–11)

Then what about her professed faith in God: was it genuine? Here we have no option but to bow to the verdict of the New Testament: 'By faith the prostitute Rahab was not killed, along with those who were disobedient, because she received the spies with peace' (Heb 11:31).

And James adds that not only was her conversion to faith in God genuine, but she justified her faith by her works (even though to protect the spies she lied to the Jericho police). For when she helped the spies to escape through her window, she advised them what route to take so that they should not be caught by the police whom she had sent off to look for them (Josh 2:16): 'Was not Rahab the prostitute justified by works when she received the spies and sent them out by another way?' (Jas 2:25).

Rahab's behaviour, therefore, shows that the spies were justified in making an exception in her case, in not including her in the general ban on Jericho, but swearing an oath in God's name to let her and her family live.

Presently we shall have to ask whether a similar case can be made out in favour of God's treatment of the Gibeonites. But for the moment we should observe one more feature of Rahab's story, which also illustrates our next suggested guideline.

GUIDELINE 13:
Consider the proportions of the narrative

The book of Joshua devotes two chapters to Jericho. Chapter 2 relates the incidents that we have just recounted involving Rahab and the spies. In our English versions there are 24 verses in this chapter; and all 24 of them involve Rahab, her treatment of the Israelite officers and their oath in God's name to save her and her family when the city was destroyed.

Then comes chapter 6 which relates the actual destruction of Jericho. It contains 27 verses in all. But one half of verse 17, and the whole of verses 22, 23 and 25 are devoted to the salvation of Rahab and her family, that is 3½ verses, leaving 23½ verses to the destruction itself.

The proportions, then, between the record of God's judgment and that of his mercy in this case can be set out as follows:

God's judgment: 23½ verses
God's mercy: 24 + 3½ = 27½ verses

Now if the moral corruption of Jericho was such that in God's judgment the whole city was to be destroyed, never to be rebuilt, it is a wonder that God saved any of its inhabitants. That God should save Rahab and her whole family, and spend more space in the narrative telling us about his mercy to Rahab, than he spends on the destruction of the city, shows where God's preferences lie: 'Mercy exults over judgment' (Jas 2:13).

In light of this we should not be surprised if God decided to save the Gibeonites.[2]

Evidence for the possible alternative explanation

Let us now consider what evidence exists that would suggest that the Gibeonites' repentance and faith were genuine, and that is why God saved them. First, when the Gibeonites were finally sure that Joshua would not break his oath and destroy them, they felt free to explain why they had lied and deceived Israel (Josh 9:15, 18–27). They had heard 'how the LORD your God commanded his servant Moses to give you all the land, and to destroy all the inhabitants of the land . . . therefore we were sore afraid for our lives because of you, and have done this thing' (9:24).

But someone may raise the objection that it was on their own confession they did what they did out of fear for their lives, not out of true repentance. Perhaps so. But out of fear of the final judgment thousands have 'fled for refuge' to Christ for salvation. Was their repentance not genuine?

Secondly, the Gibeonites must also have heard of the peace that might be offered to distant cities, for that is why they devised their elaborate hoax to make Israel think they came from a faraway city. It follows that they must also have heard of the terms on which that peace was to be offered: they must be prepared to be subject to forced labour and be servants to Israel (Deut 20:10–11). The evidence is that they were perfectly ready to submit to these terms.

When they first arrived and asked Israel to make a covenant with them, and Israel demurred, thinking they might actually come from a nearby city, the Gibeonites said to Joshua, 'We are your servants' (9:8); and they affirmed that it was the united wish of all their fellow-countrymen and elders that they should make this declaration on their behalf: 'We are your servants' (Josh 9:11).

---

2 We should also remember that Jonah's initial refusal to preach coming judgment on Nineveh was that God was so merciful that he feared God might then save even the Ninevites, if they repented.

That, admittedly, was what they said before the oath guaranteeing their safety was sworn. But even after the covenant was made,
and they were sure that Israel would never go back on it, they made
no attempt to renege on their readiness to keep the terms. So when
Joshua explained that from now on and for ever they must become
cutters of wood and drawers for all the congregation (9:21), for the
house of God (9:23), and for the altar of the Lord (9:27), they readily
consented: 'we are in your hand; whatever you judge to be good
and right to do to us, do it' (9:25).

Thirdly, we must also take into account how the Gibeonites' fellow nationals assessed their behaviour. They heard 'that the inhabitants of Gibeon had made peace with Israel and were among them'
(10:1); and they took it very seriously. They assembled a confederacy of southern kings and attacked Gibeon precisely because it
had made peace with Israel (10:4). And God for his part took their
making peace with Israel very seriously too. In his estimation the
Gibeonites were not hypocrites. If they were being attacked for sincerely making peace with Israel, then God would defend them.

Fourthly, how long, then, did the Gibeonites maintain their service to Israel and to God? The author of the book of Joshua comments
that the Gibeonites were still serving in this way 'until this day'.[3]

Moreover, when centuries later, King Saul in a fit of chauvin-
ism put a number of Gibeonites to death, God took great offence
at this breaking of Israel's solemn oath to the Gibeonites. He sent
a famine on Israel which was removed only when the Gibeonites
were allowed to choose, and then execute, the penalty for this
grievous sin (2 Sam 21).

Fifthly and finally, the reason God originally gave for insisting
on the destruction of the inhabitants of nearby cities, was to prevent
them from influencing Israel, by their very proximity, to copy their
abominable religious practices, such as idolatry, cultic prostitution
and child sacrifice. (See Deut 20:17–18.)

We have no ground for questioning the justice of God's judgment in this case. God had waited four centuries before executing

3 Cf. the same phrase used in connection with Rahab (Josh 6:25).

his wrath on their vicious practices (Gen 15:16). But the time had come when the only thing that could be done was surgically to cut out this moral cancer. Longsuffering must give way to judgment.

Nor can we think that God's care for his people's protection from this moral and spiritual infection was excessive. The book of Judges points to the evil results that invariably followed Israel's compromises with pagan religion.

But the Gibeonites were different. God, who reads the heart, saw that their repentance and faith were genuine. He honoured Israel's oath and covenant with them, defended them himself, and allowed them to be servants to his altar. Thereafter there is no record in the Old Testament that they ever introduced corrupt religious practices into Israel.

It is certainly a pity, then, that Joshua and the elders did not ask counsel of the Lord when the Gibeonites first arrived. If only they had, God would have let them see through their external false charade to their true repentance and faith as God saw it. And then they could have sworn in God's name to let them live, with peace of mind, knowing that they were doing God's will in having mercy not only on Rahab, but even on the Gibeonites.

Conclusion

Here for convenience of reference we list the guidelines suggested in Part 3:

GUIDELINE 1:

If the New Testament interprets some Old Testament narrative, we should regard its interpretation as authoritative and should follow its lead.

GUIDELINE 2:

No explanation of the New Testament's interpretation of an Old Testament narrative can be sound, if that explanation ignores, or conflicts with, the Old Testament narrative on which the interpretation is based.

GUIDELINE 3:

The New Testament implies that one Old Testament narrative does not contradict another.

GUIDELINE 4:

If the New Testament comments on the same Old Testament narrative in more than one place, our interpretation, to be complete, must take all these places into consideration.

GUIDELINE 5:

When the New Testament cites certain parts of an Old Testament narrative and then applies its lesson to us, it is a good thing to study the narrative in its immediate context to perceive how appropriate the application is.

GUIDELINE 6:

The whole of an Old Testament narrative is inspired by God, and not just those features which the New Testament quotes. We should, therefore, treat the whole narrative seriously as being a narrative in its own right.

GUIDELINE 7:

Consider the narrative's possible prototypical significance.

GUIDELINE 8:

Start with the Old Testament story's literal, historical meaning.

GUIDELINE 9:

Investigate indications of the author's intention.

GUIDELINE 10:

Question the comparative importance of the lesson it is proposed to draw from the Old Testament narrative.

GUIDELINE 11:

After studying its immediate context, we should consider the theological implications of any suggested interpretation.

GUIDELINE 12:

Examine the book as a whole to see whether it has a dominant, or repeated, theme or themes.

GUIDELINE 13:

Consider the proportions of the narrative.

In addition we should not forget the many devices which the New Testament uses in its interpretation of the Old Testament and which we studied in Part Two: straight quotations, simile, extended comparison, metaphor, fulfilment, legal precedent, analogy, legal paradigm, allusion, prototype and type. All these are examples for us to follow in our own study of Old Testament narratives.

It bears repeating that the guidelines mentioned above are but suggestions from one student to any other students that may find them helpful. They are not offered as infallible rules which, if followed meticulously, guarantee correct results.

Above all, as Christ himself taught us, we are to look in all the Old Testament Scriptures for 'the things concerning himself'; and everywhere we are to remember that the Old Testament is the word of the living God who by his Spirit is prepared to speak his word again livingly to the mind and heart of those who diligently seek him.

A Concluding Word

The Personal Witness of the Holy Spirit

AT THE BEGINNING of our study we prepared ourselves for the task ahead by recalling our Lord's personal attitude to the Old Testament. And then, with a prayer in our hearts that we might show the same devotion to Scripture as he showed, we launched on our own examination of the Old Testament.

Our subsequent survey of the many different ways in which the New Testament uses the Old has involved us in applying our minds to long, concentrated, objective study of the text without much concern for the subjective effect of it all on our hearts. Now this objective study is, for the time being, at an end. But before we leave the topic, it is surely appropriate that we should open our hearts to the Holy Spirit's personal witness to us, through the Old Testament, at the subjective level.

Early on (Chapter 4, pp. 70–3) we learned how, and by what mechanisms, prophecies, uttered by prophets who were merely human beings, were nonetheless the Word of God: these human beings were 'borne along by the Holy Spirit' (2 Pet 1:21). The New Testament goes further. It gives us grounds for thinking that even at the moment when the Holy Spirit was speaking through those prophets centuries ago, he had his eye on us and was speaking primarily for our benefit.

In doing so he had two (among many other) purposes prominently in mind. The first was to confirm and strengthen our faith, in spite of the many trials which as Christians we encounter, that Jesus really is the Christ, the Son of God.

The second was to make sure that we enter fully and completely into all the benefits and blessings of the new covenant established by the Lord Jesus. He, the Holy Spirit, it was who prophesied that one day God would make this new covenant (Jer 31:31 ff.). Christ inaugurated it (Luke 22:20). But it is the Holy Spirit who, by his power, implements its terms in our subjective experience (2 Cor 3:3, 6, 17–18).

Purpose one

> Concerning this salvation, the prophets who prophesied about the grace that was to be yours searched and inquired carefully, inquiring what person or time the Spirit of Christ in them was indicating when he predicted the sufferings of Christ and the subsequent glories. It was revealed to them that they were serving not themselves but you, in the things that have now been announced to you through those who preached the good news to you by the Holy Spirit sent from heaven, things into which angels long to look. (1 Pet 1:10–12 ESV)

In this passage Peter is writing to people who were, as he puts it, 'reduced to grief through trials of many kinds' (1 Pet 1:6). Their suffering was particularly testing because they had recently put their faith in the Lord Jesus; and they might well have expected that if Jesus was in fact the Christ, the Son of God, then receiving him would bring them God's blessing and *freedom* from suffering. As it was, they were now suffering not merely after they had trusted in Christ, but because they had trusted in him (1 Pet 2:20; 3:17; 4:12–16). Had they then made a mistake? Was Jesus after all *not* the Christ, the Son of God? It would be altogether understandable if doubts like these had entered their minds.

To steady and strengthen their faith, and to assure them that they had not made a mistake, Peter points out to them that the Holy Spirit had long since foreseen how unsettling to their faith it might be when, so strangely, as it might seem to them, they were called upon to suffer. Anticipating their need, therefore, he had, centuries before, testified through the prophets what the programme of salvation would be, and in what order its various stages would be implemented. The Messiah would certainly fulfil all the glorious things that the Old Testament promised he would. But that would not be the first stage. The first stage would be the sufferings of Christ; and only after that would come the glories.

Now when the Spirit of Christ in the prophets testified this programme in advance, the prophets themselves understood, of course, what the words meant. What they did not immediately understand was to what person, and to what time and circumstances, these prophecies applied. They therefore made thorough investigation. In response the Holy Spirit revealed to them that, to use Peter's phrase, 'it was not to themselves that they ministered these things but to you' (1:12). In other words, the Holy Spirit was testifying through these prophets not primarily for the benefit of the prophets themselves and their contemporaries, but for the benefit of the first century AD Christians. The suffering and death of Christ, when it happened, would be a severe shock to many of them. But their faith would recover, when they realised that the sufferings of Christ were not something strange or unexpected: the Holy Spirit had been speaking about it for centuries. All this long time, moreover, he had had his eye on these first century AD believers and had built up Scripture after Scripture in order to protect and strengthen their faith when suffering eventually came not only on Christ himself but also on them. And, of course, the Holy Spirit's testimony through these Old Testament Scriptures serves the same practical purpose for us when we suffer, as it did for our first century fellow Christians.

Not only so. The Holy Spirit, sent down from heaven on the day of Pentecost, was, says Peter (1:12), the power and authority behind the early preachers of the gospel (and, of course, behind all true preachers of the gospel ever since) that demonstrated that God had 'raised Jesus from the dead and given him glory' (1:21), thus fulfilling the second part of the Old Testament prophecies that predicted 'the glories that should follow' (1:11).

And then, for good measure, the Holy Spirit himself is the earnest, in the heart of believers, of the eternal glories that await them beyond the temporary sufferings of this life (2 Cor 4:16–5:5).

Purpose two

> Consequently, when Christ came into the world, he said, 'Sacrifices and offerings you have not desired, but a body have you prepared for me; in burnt offerings and sin offerings you have taken no pleasure. Then I said, "Behold, I have come to do your will, O God, as it is written of me in the scroll of the book."' When he said above, 'You have neither desired nor taken pleasure in sacrifices and offerings and burnt offerings and sin offerings' (these are offered according to the law), then he added, 'Behold, I have come to do your will.' He abolishes the first in order to establish the second. And by that will we have been sanctified through the offering of the body of Jesus Christ once for all. And every priest stands daily at his service, offering repeatedly the same sacrifices, which can never take away sins. But when Christ had offered for all time a single sacrifice for sins, he sat down at the right hand of God, waiting from that time until his enemies should be made a footstool for his feet. For by a single offering he has perfected for all time those who are being sanctified. And the Holy Spirit also bears witness to us; for after saying, 'This is the covenant that I will make with them after those days, declares the Lord: I will put my laws on their hearts, and write them on their minds,' then he adds, 'I will remember their sins and their lawless deeds no more.' Where there is forgiveness of these, there is no longer any offering for sin. (Heb 10:5–18 ESV)

The first part of this passage (vv. 5–14) contains the declaration of Christ himself.[1] In it he announces the purpose of his incarnation and entry into the world. Citing the words of Psalm 40:6–8, he indicates his intention to put an end to the constantly repeated sacrifices prescribed in the Old Testament, and in their place to offer the sacrifice of his own body. This sacrifice, being perfect, would be sufficient for all time, to perfect the sanctification of all who put their faith in him. Once having offered it, therefore, he would sit down on the right hand of God, and never have to repeat this offering again.

1 For a further discussion see Chapter 17.

So far, then, this passage relates the statement of the Son of God, and it gives us the objective facts regarding the sacrifice of Christ. But the objective facts are one thing; people's subjective understanding of them and their enjoyment of their implications for their peace of mind and heart could be another.

At this point, therefore, the Holy Spirit adds his own personal witness (Heb 10:15–18). He had himself inspired the prophet Jeremiah to write down the terms of the new covenant (Jer 31:31 ff.). Now he cites these terms again and puts special emphasis on the last clause: 'I will remember their sins and their lawless deeds no more' (Heb 10:17). Here, then, is the Holy Spirit's assurance, given to all who put their faith in Christ, of complete and eternal forgiveness.

The conclusion then follows logically: where a person has and enjoys forgiveness so complete as this, he or she will never need to offer anything at all in order to get forgiveness of sins (Heb 10:18). There are, of course, many sacrifices of different kinds that we are called upon, as believers, to offer continually. Such are sacrifices of praise to God, and sacrifices of doing good, and sharing what we have with other people (Heb 13:15–16). Such sacrifices, moreover, can be costly in terms of time, energy, and money; and they should be repeated as long as life and resources shall last. But the process of offering a sacrifice for sin has long since ceased. Christ's sacrifice on our behalf was all sufficient. Having offered it, he has sat down. We need not, we cannot, add anything to it: and no repetition by us is required. We can enjoy peace with God. And on this basis the Holy Spirit pours God's love for us into our hearts (Rom 5:5), and does so by drawing out, with impeccable logic, the implications of the death of Christ on our behalf:

> For while we were still weak, at the right time Christ died for the ungodly. For one will scarcely die for a righteous person—though perhaps for a good person one would dare even to die—but God shows his love for us in that while we were still sinners, Christ died for us. Since, therefore, we have now been justified by his blood, much more shall we be saved by him from the wrath of God. For if while we were enemies we were reconciled

to God by the death of his Son, much more, now that we are reconciled, shall we be saved by his life. More than that, we also rejoice in God through our Lord Jesus Christ, through whom we have now received reconciliation. (Rom 5:6–11 ESV)

Thank God for the personal witness of the Holy Spirit!

And now may he who had mercy on the Gibeonites and allowed them to become servants for his altar, move us by his ever greater mercy to us to love him with all our mind and to yield our bodies a living sacrifice, holy, acceptable to God, which is our reasonable service.

Appendix

The Two-fold Difficulty in Ascertaining the Exact Meaning of the Decorative Details of the Lampstand

İN THE FIRST place we are dealing with ancient Hebrew botanical terms the exact meaning of which may now be lost to us. Moreover, some at least of these terms can mean different things in different contexts. Take, for example, the Hebrew noun פֶּרַח (perach). It comes from the verb פָּרַח (pārach), meaning 'to sprout'. It can therefore mean either 'a bud' or 'a blossom'; and we have to decide which meaning is appropriate in any given context.

In the second place these ancient botanical terms are, in our context, being used to describe not a natural almond tree, but a work of art in an altogether different medium: a gold, six-branched lampstand in which the practical functions of the lampstand itself and of its lamps must control, if not modify, our interpretation of its terms.

Let's help ourselves, therefore, by first taking a simpler case. Aaron's rod (Num 17:8 [v. 23 in Hebrew text]) was not a complicated thing like the lampstand, but a simple rod of, presumably, almond wood. The Hebrew terms that describe the results of the miracle performed on it are given in Table 5.

We should notice that *perach* (term 2) does not here mean 'blossom', for that is what term 3 mentions. Similarly *shĕqēdîm* (term 4)

1.	'it sprouted':	Hebrew פָּרַח, *pārach;*
2.	it produced 'buds', or 'spurs':	Hebrew פֶּרַח, *perach;*
3.	it 'flowered':	Hebrew וַיָּצֵץ צִיץ, *wayyātsēts tsîts;*
4.	it produced mature almonds:	Hebrew וַיִּגְמֹל שְׁקֵדִים, *wayyigmōl shĕqēdîm*

Table 5. Hebrew terms used to describe Aaron's rod

does not mean 'almond blossoms' (already mentioned as term 3) but the mature fruit. Maybe all four stages miraculously appeared simultaneously; but the order in which they are mentioned is the natural order of development. Moreover, 'mature almonds' here must presumably mean the whole fruit and not just the nut, or the kernel inside the nut, which is what we eat. The almond fruit is a drupe, that is, a fleshy or pulpy fruit (like a peach, olive, or plum). Daan Smit describes it thus:

> When the flowers have been pollinated, they form many ovaries which grow into almonds. The oval fruits are about 4 cm long and surrounded by a thick fleshy skin. The outside is covered in soft hair, rather like the stone of a peach. In about October, when the fruit is ripe, the flesh casing divides lengthways into two parts, and the nuts are visible. They are ready to harvest in November, and when they have been dried, the soft kernel can be removed from the nut using a hammer. This is the almond we eat.[1]

The three main decorative terms of the Lampstand

When now we come to the description of the Lampstand and its decorative motifs, we find once more three major elements in both the central shaft (or, trunk) and the six branches. They are:

1. Hebrew גְּבִעִים (*gĕbi'îm*) = cups, or shallow bowls
2. Hebrew כַּפְתֹּרִים (*kaphtôrîm*) = capitals (on the top of pillars)
3. Hebrew פְּרָחִים (*pĕrāchîm*) = blossoms.

1 *Plants of the Bible,* 136–7.

It is at once noticeable that only one of these terms (element 3) is the same as one of those used in the case of Aaron's rod; and there it meant 'buds', while here it may mean 'blossoms'. Moreover the cups (*gĕbi'îm*) are said in the text to be 'made like almonds'; and it is still disputed whether this means 'like almond-blossoms' or simply 'like almonds'. And the Hebrew word *kaphtôrîm* (element 2), when it occurs in Amos 9:1, is in modern versions generally rendered 'capitals'. But here in connection with the Lampstand most modern versions put 'calyxes' or 'bud-husks'.

Unsurprisingly, scholarly opinion remains divided; and dogmatism is inappropriate. What we shall do, therefore, is first to state the majority view, and then mention one or two of its details that other scholars find doubtful.

The majority view

There is much to be said for this view. At first glance the RV's translation of Exodus 25:33, 'Three cups made like almond-blossoms . . . a knop and a flower', might seem repetitious in mentioning 'the blossoms' and then 'the flower' which could be the same thing as the blossoms.[2] But the majority view understands the three terms, 'blossoms, knop and flower' as a triad, which can then be understood as 'almond-blossoms, that is to say, both its calyx and its flower'.

Secondly the 'cups' (Hebrew *gĕbi'îm*) are likely to have been not 'drinking cups' such as the one that Joseph drank out of (Gen 44:2–5) which the Greek there translates as κόνδυ (*kondy*), but rather 'shallow bowls' for which the Greek of Exodus 25:31 ff. puts κρατῆρες (*kratēres*) — 'mixing bowls'. This latter meaning is more probable because the bowls at the end of the branches and on top of the central shaft were required to support oil lamps. But in any case the suggestion that these cups were made like 'almond blossoms' is reasonable enough, for the five petals of an almond-blossom are said to form a cup-shaped flower.[3]

2 Unless it refers to the centre of the flower, made up, not of the petals, but of the pistil and stamens.
3 See Sterry, *British Trees*, 240.

Weaknesses in the majority view

Reasonable as the majority view is, it has two weaknesses. First, the translation 'cups made like almond blossoms' is not unquestionable. Carol L. Meyers insists that the Hebrew could mean 'cups made like almonds': 'one other possibility which must not be overlooked is that the word is a technical term referring to some sort of repoussée work or perhaps to a type of inlay work in the shape of almonds.'[4] And the NIV seems to allow this possibility. In its Study Bible, its footnote to Exodus 25:31 says: 'The cups of the lampstand resemble either the calyx [outer covering of the flower] or the almond nut.'

Second, the Hebrew term, *kaphtôr*, for which most modern versions use 'calyx' or 'bud-husk', is used elsewhere in connection with the main shaft, that is, the trunk of this 'almond tree'. There it is said that there shall be a *kaphtôr* under each of the three pairs of branches at the point where they come out of the central shaft (25:35). Botanically, it is perhaps unlikely that each set of two branches should be represented as sprouting out of a calyx, or bud-husk. At the practical level one might suppose that the *kaphtôrîm* were placed where they were to support the branches at the points in the central shaft where the lampstand was at its weakest. In that case each *kaphtôr*, being shaped like a capital, would more likely represent a spur (that is a thickened part of the trunk from which a branch emerges) rather than a calyx or a bud-husk.

What difference does all this make?

Mercifully, very little. If the majority view is right, the Lampstand represents the beauty and potential of new life; and since the almond tree in the Middle East is the first to blossom after the deadness of winter, it carries more than a hint of resurrection life.

But if, as others suggest, the Lampstand's decorative motifs included almond nuts, then this symbolic Tree of Life, displayed not only life's potentials, the buds, and life's beauty, the blossoms, but also life's mature fruit, the almond nuts, and all three stages simultaneously.

4 *Tabernacle Menorah*, 23.

Bibliography

Allen, Ronald B. 'Numbers.' In vol. 2 of *Expositor's Bible Commentary*. Edited by Frank E. Gaebelein. Grand Rapids: Zondervan, 1990.

Arndt, William, F. Wilbur Gingrich, Frederick W. Danker, and Walter Bauer. *A Greek-English Lexicon of the New Testament and Other Early Christian Literature*: A Translation and Adaptation of the Fourth Revised and Augmented Edition of Walter Bauer's *Griechisch-Deutsches Wörterbuch Zu Den Schriften Des Neuen Testaments Und Der Übrigen Urchristlichen Literatur*. Chicago: University of Chicago Press, 1979.

Beale, G. K. *The Right Doctrine from the Wrong Texts? Essays on the Use of the Old Testament in the New*. Grand Rapids: Baker Academic, 1994.

Beale, G. K. and D. A. Carson, eds. *Commentary on the New Testament Use of the Old Testament*. Grand Rapids: Baker Academic, 2007.

Bengel, J. A. *Gnomon of the New Testament*. 3d ed. Translated by James Bryce. Edinburgh: T. & T. Clark, 1890.

Bruce, F. F. *The Epistle to the Hebrews*. Grand Rapids: Eerdmans, 1964.

Carson, D. A. *Matthew*. The Expositor's Bible Commentary 8. Grand Rapids: Eerdmans, 1984.

Carson, D. A., et al. *New Bible Commentary: 21st Century Edition*. Leicester: IVP, 1994.

Carson, D. A. and John D. Woodbridge, eds. *Hermeneutics, Authority and Canon*. Leicester: IVP, 1986.

Daube, D. 'Rabbinic Methods of Interpretation and Hellenistic Rhetoric.' *Hebrew Union College Annual XXII* (1949), pp. 239–64.

Durham, J. I. *Exodus*. Word Biblical Commentary 3. Dallas: Word, 1987.

France, R. T. *The Gospel According To Matthew: An Introduction and Commentary*. Tyndale New Testament Commentaries. Leicester: IVP, 1985.

Gooding, David W. *An Unshakeable Kingdom*. Leicester: IVP, 1989.

Goppelt, Leonhard. *Typos: The Typological Interpretation of the Old Testament in the New*. Translated by Donald H. Madvig. Grand Rapids: Eerdmans, 1982. trans. of *Typos: die typologische Deutung des Alten Testaments im Neuen* (Gütersloh: C. Bertelsmann, 1939).

Bibliography

Harris, R Laird, et al. *Theological Wordbook of the Old Testament*. Chicago: Moody Press, 1980.

Kierkegaard, Søren, *Fear and Trembling; Repetition*. Princeton: Princeton Unifversity Press, 1983.

Kitchen, K. A. *On the Reliability of the Old Testament*. Grand Rapids: Eerdmans, 2003.

Lightfoot, J. B. *Saint Paul's Epistle to the Galatians*. London: MacMillan, 1890.

Marshall, I. Howard. *The Gospel of Luke*. Exeter: Paternoster Press, 1978.

Meyers, Carol L. *The Tabernacle Menorah*. American Schools of Oriental Research Dissertation Series, No. 2. Missoula: Scholars Press, 1976.

Millard, A. R. *Treasures from Bible Times*. Oxford: Lion Publishing, 1991.

Moo, Douglas J. 'The Problem of Sensus Plenior'. Pages 175–212 in *Hermeneutics, Authority and Canon*. Edited by D. A. Carson and John D. Woodbridge. Leicester: IVP, 1986.

Oxford English Dictionary, 2d ed. Oxford: University Press, 1989.

Smit, Daan. *Plants of the Bible*. Oxford: Lion Publishing, 1992.

Sterry, Paul, *Collins Complete Guide to British Trees*. London: Harper Collins, 2007.

Wenham, Gordon J. *Genesis 16–50*. Word Biblical Commentary 2. Dallas: Word, 1994.

———. *The Book of Leviticus*. New International Commentary on the Old Testament. Grand Rapids: Eerdmans, 1979.

Westcott, B. F. *The Epistle to the Hebrews*. London: MacMillan, 1903.

Publications by David Gooding

Doctoral dissertation

'The Greek Deuteronomy', PhD thesis, University of Cambridge, 1954.

Books

Recensions of the Septuagint Pentateuch. Cambridge: Tyndale Press, 1955.

The Account of the Tabernacle: Translation and Textual Problems of the Greek Exodus. Texts and Studies: Contributions to Biblical and Patristic Literature, ed. C. H. Dodd, no. 6. Cambridge: Cambridge University Press, 1959.

edited *The Text of the Septuagint: Its Corruptions and Their Emendation* by Peter Walters (formerly Katz). Cambridge: Cambridge University Press, 1973.

Studies in Luke's Gospel. Bible Study and Discussion Papers 1–3. Dublin: Biblical Studies Institute, 1973.

An Unshakeable Kingdom: The Letter to the Hebrews for Today. Scarborough, Ontario: Everyday Publications, 1975; [in German] *Ein unerschütterliches Reich: 10 Studien über d. Hebräerbrief.* Dillenburg: Christliche Verlagsgesellschaft, 1987; rev. ed. Leicester: Inter-Varsity Press/ Grand Rapids: Eerdmans, 1989; repr. Port Colborne, Ontario: Gospel Folio Press, 1989; repr. Coleraine, N. Ireland: Myrtlefield House, 2013.

Relics of Ancient Exegesis: A Study of the Miscellanies in 3 Reigns 2. Society for Old Testament Study Monograph Series, 4. Cambridge: Cambridge University Press, 1976.

According to Luke: A new exposition of the Third Gospel. Leicester: Inter-Varsity Press, 1987; [in Polish] *Według Łukasza: nowe spojrzenie na Trzecią Ewangelię.* tr. Witold Gorecki. Wydawnictwo Ewangeliczne, 1992; [in Spanish] *Según Lucas: una nueva exposición del tercer Evangelio.* Editorial Clie/Publicaciones Andamio, 1996; repr. Port Colborne, Ontario: Gospel Folio Press, 2002; repr. Eugene, Origen: Wipf and Stock, 2005; repr. as *According to Luke: The Third Gospel's Ordered Historical Narrative.* Coleraine, N. Ireland: Myrtlefield House, 2013.

True to the Faith: A fresh approach to the Acts of the Apostles. London: Hodder & Stoughton, 1990; [in Spanish] *Según Hechos: permaneciendo fiel a la fe.* Editiorial Clie/Publicaciones Andamio, 1990; repr. Port Colborne, Ontario: Gospel Folio Press, 1995; repr as *True to the Faith: Defining and Defending the Gospel.* Coleraine, N. Ireland: Myrtlefield House, 2013.
In the School of Christ: A Study of Christ's Teaching on Holiness. John 13–17. Port Colborne, Ontario: Gospel Folio Press, 1995, 2001; [in Polish] *W szkole Chrystusa: studium nauczania Chrystusa na temat świętości, Ewangelia Jana 13-17.* tr. Adam Mariuk. Areopag, 2010; [in Burmese] 2013; repr. as *In the School of Christ: Lessons on Holiness in John 13–17.* Coleraine, N. Ireland: Myrtlefield House, 2013.
Windows on Paradise. Port Colborne, Ontario: Gospel Folio Press, 1998, 2001; [in Spanish] *Ventanas al paraíso: Estudios en el evangelio de Lucas.* Talleres Gráficos de la M.C.E. 1982.
The Riches of Divine Wisdom: The New Testament's Use of the Old Testament. Coleraine, N. Ireland: Myrtlefield House, 2013.

Books published with John Lennox
Christianity: Opium or Truth? Port Colborne, Ontario: Gospel Folio Press, 1997; [in German] *Opium fürs Volk?* Bielefeld: Christliche Literature-Verbreitung, 2012; [in Portuguese] *Cristianismo: Ópio do Povo?* Porto Alegre: A. Verdada, 2013.
Worldview I: The Human Quest for Significance: Forming a Worldview. [in Russian] Minsk, 1999.
The Definition of Christianity. Port Colborne, Ontario: Gospel Folio Press, 2001; [in Polish] *Definicja chrześcijaństwa.* tr. Przemysław Janikowski. Areopag, 2001; [in Spanish] Una definición del cristianismo para el siglo XXI : un estudio basado en los hechos de los Apóstoles. Editiorial Clie.
Key Bible Concepts. Port Colborne, Ontario: Gospel Folio Press, 2001; [in Russian] Ключевые понятия Библии. 1997; [in Bulgarian] Ключови библейски Понятия. 1997, 2004; [in Malay] *Konsep Utama Dalam Alkitab*; [in Spanish] *Conceptos bíblicos fundamentales.* Barcelona: Editiorial Clie/Publicaciones Andamio, 2001; [in Polish] *Kluczowe koncepcje biblijne.* Areopag, 2001; [in German] *Schlüsselbegriffe der Bibel.* Bielefeld: Christliche Literatur-Verbreitung, 2013; [in Portuguese] *Conceitos-Chave da Bíblia.* Porto Alegre: A. Verdada, 2013.
Worldview II: The Search for Reality (1). [in Russian] Minsk, 2004.
Worldview III: The Search for Reality (2). [in Russian] Minsk, 2004.

The Bible and Ethics: Studies for Group and Individual Work. Coleraine, N. Ireland: Myrtlefield Trust, 2011; repr. Port Colborne, Ontario: Gospel Folio Press, 2011.

Published lectures and booklets
The inspiration and authority, canon and transmission of Holy Scripture. Edinburgh: Darien Press, 1961.
How to Teach the Tabernacle. Dublin: Merrion Press, 1970; repr. Port Colborne, Ontario: Everyday Publications, 1977; [in Spanish] *Cómo enseñar el tabernáculo.* Port Colborne, Ontario: Everyday Publications, 1977.
Current Problems and Methods in the Textual Criticism of the Old Testament. Belfast: Queen's University, 1979.
How? The Search for Spiritual Satisfaction. Leicester: Inter-Varsity Press, 1980.
Freedom under God. Bath: Echoes of Service, 1985.
Unfettered Faith: The Promotion of Spiritual Freedom. Coleraine, N. Ireland: Myrtlefield Trust, 1986.
Wer glaubt muß denken. Bielefeld: Christliche Literatur-Verbreitung, 1998.
Die Bibel—Mythos oder Wahrheit? Gibt es eine echte Erfüllung? Dillenburg: Christliche Verlagsgesellschaft, 1993; 2nd ed. Bielefeld: Christliche Literatur-Verbreitung, 2001.
The Bible: Myth or Truth. [in Bulgarian: Библията: мит или истина] Coleraine, N. Ireland: Myrtlefield Trust, 2001.
How about God? Four broadcast talks (Belfast: Graham & Heslip, n.d.).

Chapters and major articles
'The Text of the Psalms in two Durham Bibles.' *Scriptorium* 12:1 (1958): 94–6.
'Aristeas and Septuagint Origins: A review of recent studies.' *Vetus Testamentum* 13:4 (1963): 357–379.
'Ahab According to the Septuagint.' *ZAW* 76 (1964): 269–80.
'Pedantic Timetabling in 3rd Book of Reigns.' *Vetus Testamentum* 15:2 (1965): 153–66.
'The Septuagint's Version of Solomon's Misconduct.' *Vetus Testamentum* 15:3 (1965): 325–35.
'An Impossible Shrine.' *Vetus Testamentum* 15:4 (1965): 405–20.
'Temple Specifications: A Dispute in Logical Arrangement between the MT and the LXX.' *Vetus Testamentum* 17:2 (1967): 143–72.
'The Septuagint's Rival Versions of Jeroboam's Rise to Power.' *Vetus Testamentum* 17:2 (1967): 173–89.
'The Shimei Duplicate and its Satellite Miscellanies in 3 Reigns II.' *Journal of Semitic Studies* 13:1 (1968): 76–92.

Publications

'Problems of Text and Midrash in the Third Book of Reigns.' *Textus* 7 (1969): 11–13.
'Text-Sequence and Translation-Revision in 3 Reigns IX 10 – X 33.' *Vetus Testamentum* 19:4 (1969): 448–63.
'Observations on Certain Problems Connected with the So-called Septuagint.' *TSF Bulletin* 56 (1970): 8–13.
'Jeroboam's Rise to Power: A Rejoinder.' *Journal of Biblical Literature* 91:4 (1972): 529–33.
'Two possible examples of midrashic interpretation in the Septuagint Exodus' in *Wort, Lied, und Gottesspruch: Festschrift fur Joseph Ziegler* (ed. Josef Schreiner; Echter Verlag: Katholisches Bibelwerk, 1972), 39–48.
'On the use of the LXX for dating Midrashic elements in the Targums.' *Journal of Theological Studies* ns 25:1 (1974): 1–11.
'A Recent Popularisation of Professor F. M. Cross' Theories on the Text of the Old Testament.' *Tyndale Bulletin* 26 (1975): 113–32.
'An Appeal for a Stricter Terminology in the Textual Criticism of the Old Testament.' *Journal of Semitic Studies* 21 (1976): 15–25.
'Tradition of interpretation of the circumcision at Gilgal.' Jerusalem: World Union of Jewish Studies, 1977.
'Structure littéraire de Matthieu 13:53 à 18:35.' *Revue biblique* 85:2 (1978): 227–52.
'Demythologizing, Old and New, and Luke's Description of the Ascension: A Layman's Appraisal.' *Irish Biblical Studies* 2 (1980): 95–119.
'The Literary Structure of the Book of Daniel and its Implications' (The Tyndale Old Testament Lecture, 1980). *Tyndale Bulletin* 32 (1981): 43–79.
'Demythologizing the Ascension: A Reply by D. W. Gooding.' *Irish Biblical Studies* 3 (1981): 45–54.
'A Sketch of Current Septuagint Studies.' *Proceedings of the Irish Biblical Association* 5 (1981).
'The Composition of the Book of Judges.' *Eretz-Israel*, H. M. Orlinsky Volume. Jerusalem: 1982.
'Philo's Bible in the *De Gigantibus* and *Quod Deus*.' in *Two Treatises of Philo of Alexandria: A Commentary on De Gigantibus and Quod Deus Sit Immutabilis*, with V. Nikiprowetzky (ed. D. Winston and J. Dillon; BJS 25; Chico, Calif.: Scholars Press, 1983), 89–125.
'The Problem of Pain.' *Journal of the Irish Christian Study Centre* 1 (1983):63–9.
The Bible and Moral Education for Schools, with John Lennox. Moscow: Uchitelskaya Gazeta (Newspaper for Teachers), 1993–5; repr. as *The Bible and Ethics*.
Articles in *New Bible Dictionary* on 'Bezalel, Bezaleel'; 'Capital' [in tabernacle]; 'Censer'; 'Gershom, Gershon'; 'Kaiwan'; 'Kohath,

Kohathites'; 'Merari, Merarites'; 'Oholiab'; 'Rephan'; 'Snuffers'; 'Tabernacle'; 'Texts & Versions 2. The Septuagint'; 'Trays'. Leicester: Inter-Varsity Press, 1996.

'The tabernacle: no museum piece' in *The Perfect Saviour: Key themes in Hebrews* (ed. Jonathan Griffiths; Nottingham: Inter-Varsity Press, 2012), 69–88.

Review articles

Review of Ilmari Soisalon-Soininen, *Der Charakter der asterisierten Zusätze in der Septuaginta. Gnomon* 33:2 (1961): 143–8.

Review of Joost Smit Sibinga, *The Old Testament Text of Justin Martyr. Journal of Theological Studies* ns 16:1 (1965): 187–92.

Review of Ilmari Soisalon-Soininen, *Die Infinitive in der Septuaginta. Journal of Theological Studies* ns 18:2 (1967): 451–5.

Review of James Donald Shenkel, *Chronology and Recensional Development in the Greek Text of Kings viii. Journal of Theological Studies* ns 21:1 (1970): 118–31.

Review of Adrian Schenker, *Hexaplarische Psalmenbruchstucke: Die hexaplarischen Psalmenfragmente der Handschriften Vaticanus graecus 752 und Canonicianus graecus 62, Journal of Theological Studies* ns 27:2 (1976): 443–5.

Review of Raija Sollamo, *Renderings of Hebrew Semiprepositions in the Septuagint. Journal of Semitic Studies* 25:2 (1980): 261–3.

Review of John W. Olley, *"Righteousness" in the Septuagint of Isaiah: A Contextual Study. Journal of Theological Studies* ns 32:1 (1981): 204–12.

Review of J. H. Charlesworth, *The Pseudographa and Modern Research. Irish Biblical Studies* 4:1 (1982): 46-49.

Review of Anneli Aejmelaeus, *Parataxis in the Septuagint. Journal of Semitic Studies* 28:2 (1983): 369–71.

Short Notice on Joseph A. Fitzmyer, *An Introductory Bibliography for the Study of Scripture. Journal of Theological Studies* ns 34:2 (1983): 693.

Review of Homer Heater, *A Septuagint Translation Technique in the Book of Job. Journal of Theological Studies* ns 35:1 (1984): 169–77.

Review of Roger Beckwith, *The Old Testament Canon of the New Testament Church. Irish Biblical Studies* 8:4 (1986): 207-211.

Review of George Alexander Kennedy, Duane Frederick Watson (eds.), *Persuasive Artistry: Studies in New Testament Rhetoric in Honour of George A Kennedy. Evangelical Quarterly* 64 (1992): 264–8.

Popular articles

'The True Peacemaker and Benefactor of the People.' *Precious Seed* 3:7 (1950).

Publications

'Modern Translations—Their Use and Abuse.' *Precious Seed* 7:8 (1956).
'New Testament Word Studies.' *Precious Seed* 12:1–4 & 13:1–6 (1961–62).
'How do you relate and reconcile the teaching on women in 1 Corinthians
    11 and 14?' *The Word* (Belfast, 1994).
'Symbols of Headship and Glory.' *The Word* (Belfast, 1980); [in German]
    'Symbole oder Zeichen von Autoritat und Herrlichkeit' tr. von G.
    Giesler. *Verlegerbeilage zu Die Wegweisung* 6/87 (Dillenburg, Christ-
    liche Verlagsgesellschaft, 1987).

STUDY GUIDE

THESE QUESTIONS ARE intended for personal or group study. Individuals who use them are likely to find it helpful to refer to the questions as they come to each chapter, though some may wish to wait until they have read the entire book and then use the questions to review the material.

For Bible classes, seminars and home study groups, the following guidelines are offered as a suggested use of the questions:

1. Allow at least 45 minutes for discussion.
2. Read the questions briefly *before* you read the chapter in order to make yourself or your group familiar with the central issues raised.
3. Read the chapter, noting the main Bible passages it refers to.
4. Read the main Bible passages that were noted.
5. Consider each question in turn. In a group situation, the leader should ensure that each question is dealt with and that the discussion remains relevant.
6. In a group situation, it may be useful at the beginning of the session to assign a question to one or more members, who will then have the responsibility for leading that section of the discussion. The leader should ensure that time is efficiently allocated.

Study Guide

All who use these questions are encouraged to recall the exhortations and encouragements given in the book's Introduction and concluding chapter. The Holy Spirit calls us to be grown-ups in intellect and to use that intellect diligently as we come to the Scriptures (1 Cor 14:20). Yet we do not study unaided; our Lord himself opens his disciples' minds so that they might understand the Scriptures (Luke 24:45).

PART ONE

Questions on Chapter 1

1. 'The Christian gospel is not a collection of timeless truths nor a philosophical system.' What is it then?
2. How is the Old Testament relevant to the validity of Christianity's truth claims?
3. What is the significance of Matthew's claim that Jesus Christ is the son of David and the son of Abraham?
4. Matthew's genealogy of Christ covers three major periods of history. In what way and to what extent did each of those historical periods contribute to the preparation of Israel for the coming of Christ?

Questions on Chapter 2

1. In what major respects does the New Testament show continuity with the Old?
2. When the New Testament abrogates some of the divinely ordained institutions of the Old Testament, how does it justify that abrogation?
3. What is the main gist of Stephen's speech before the Council (Acts 7) and how is it relevant to the charge brought against him?
4. With the coming of Christ, and then the coming of the Holy Spirit at Pentecost, there dawned a new spiritual epoch. What were the leading features of that epoch?
5. Write an essay on the topic 'The New Testament's Discontinuities with the Old'.

Questions on Chapter 3

1. First Timothy 3:15–17 and 2 Peter 1:20–21 both assert the divine inspiration of the Old Testament; but what is the special emphasis in each of these passages?
2. In ancient Israel who carried the prime responsibility for teaching children the Bible?
3. In what way and to what extent is the Old Testament profitable for Christian evangelism?
4. What are the main features of the Old Testament's doctrine of creation?
5. To what Old Testament passages does the New Testament appeal to validate its doctrines of The Fall, Substitutionary Atonement, and Survival after Death?
6. Cite from the New Testament examples of our Lord's application of the Old Testament to his own conduct.
7. The New Testament shares the same hope for the future as does the Old Testament. Comment.
8. The Old Testament sacrifices are now obsolete, having been superseded by the sacrifice of Christ. Then what, if any, lessons can we learn from those Old Testament sacrifices?
9. 'Holiness and love are two of the major lessons taught by the book of Leviticus.' Use your knowledge of Leviticus to illustrate and validate this assertion.

Questions on Chapter 4

1. Contrast the apostles' understanding of the Old Testament before the death and resurrection of Christ and their understanding of it after the resurrection. How would you account for this difference?
2. In what way does the difference between Nathan's two messages to David (2 Sam 7) illustrate the negative and positive statements about divinely inspired prophecy in 2 Pet 1:21?

3. Write an essay entitled 'The apparent problem raised by the interpretation of 2 Sam 7:14 given by the writer to the Hebrews (1:5); and the solution of that problem'.

Part Two

Questions on Chapter 6

1. In the synagogue at Nazareth (Luke 4) Christ read from Isaiah 61. What significance do you see in the fact that he ended his reading where he did?
2. What does Isaiah mean by 'the day of vengeance'?
3. For what purpose did Christ cite Psalm 110:1 in Matthew 22:41–46?
4. Where else does the New Testament cite Psalm 110, and for what purposes?
5. What has Psalm 110:1 got in common with Matthew 13:30, 39?
6. What is the so-called Problem of Evil?

Questions on Chapter 7

1. Discuss, with examples, the different senses in which the New Testament uses the word *fulfil*.
2. In what sense is the term *prototype* used in this chapter?
3. At first sight Matthew's claim that Hosea 11:1 was fulfilled when the child Jesus was brought back from Egypt, presents a difficulty. What is that difficulty? And how does the concept *prototype* help to solve that difficulty?
4. Explain how a study of the contexts of Jeremiah 31:15 and Matthew 2:17–18 helps us to see the significance of the parallels between these two passages.

5. What is the full meaning of the term *Nazarene* as applied to Jesus at Matthew 2:23? Does it merely tell us where he lived for thirty years?
6. Discuss the various meanings of the Greek word *typos*, as used in the New Testament.
7. In what sense did Christ come to fulfil the Law and the Prophets?
8. 'Love is the fulfilment of the law.' What would you say to ethicists who argue that motivation by love towards others is a sufficient guide for ethics, and that we have no need of hard and fast restrictive laws like those of the Ten Commandments?
9. Discuss God's strategy of first making promises and then subsequently fulfilling them. Why does he make promises at all? Why does he not just do things without first announcing them, sometimes centuries beforehand?
10. What does 1 Timothy 4:8 mean when it says that godliness 'has *promise* of the life that now is'?

Questions on Chapter 8

1. What is the meaning of the term *justify* in Romans 3:19–4:5?
2. Why is it necessary that salvation should be effected on a sound legal basis?
3. Discuss Paul's appeal (Rom 4:2) to Abraham's case as reported in Genesis 15:6. What authority does it add to his argument in the preceding chapter (Rom 3:19–31)?
4. Paul obviously holds that the chronological order of the events recorded in Genesis 15–17 is reliable and legally significant. On what grounds does he hold this?
5. What was the nature of Abraham's faith?
6. What analogy is there between Abraham's faith and ours?

Questions on Chapter 9

1. How did Christ use inference to defend himself against the charge of blasphemy?
2. What do you understand by the Latin phrase *a minore ad maius*? Illustrate your answer by a New Testament example.
3. What had the law about the behaviour of Jewish priests in the temple on the Sabbath got to do with the behaviour of Christ's apostles?
4. How is the Old Testament law about oxen relevant to modern Christian workers?
5. What do you understand by the term *legal paradigm*?
6. Why is it important to understand the intention of a law? Is it possible to break a law by keeping it?

Questions on Chapter 10

1. Recall the two covenants of Gen 15 and Jer 34:8–22; and answer the following questions:
   (*a*) What do these two covenants have in common?
   (*b*) Why was it significant who 'walked between the pieces'?
2. What is the difference between a one party and a two party covenant?
3. What is the meaning of the term *promise*? Can it have two different meanings? If so, what are they, and why is it important to distinguish them?
4. To what contemporary sound legal practice does Paul appeal in Gal 3:15?
5. Why cannot the terms of the Sinai covenant simply be added to God's covenant with Abram and his seed?
6. Was the covenant God made with Israel at Sinai a one party covenant or a two party covenant? How would you decide?

7. What expectation had Moses that Israel's possession of the land under Joshua's leadership and on the terms of the Sinai-covenant would be permanent and final?

8. Was the restoration of Israel to the promised land under Ezra and Nehemiah permanent? If not, why not?

9. The term *seed* in the phrase 'Abraham and his seed' can have different meanings. What meaning does Paul say it has in God's covenant with Abraham (Gen 15)?

10. How and in what sense can all believers today, whether Jew or Gentile, be regarded as Abraham's seed?

11. Why is Paul's interpretation of the seed the only one that gives Abraham, Isaac and Jacob any hope of possessing the land that had been promised to them?

12. What functions did the law have in the period between God's covenant with Abraham and his seed, and the incarnation of Christ?

13. When Scripture says that all believers in Christ are 'heirs according to the promise' (Gal 3:29), what is the inheritance of which they are heirs?

14. When was the new covenant enacted?

15. What are the better promises on which the new covenant has been enacted?

16. Why is the new covenant more glorious than the old?

Questions on Chapter 11

1. The Hebrew Old Testament is composed of three parts: The Law (*Torah*), The Prophets (*Nebi'im*) and The Writings (*Kethubim*). Compile a list to show that the New Testament quotes from all three parts of the Old Testament.

2. Give at least one example in each category of quotation and citation other than the examples already given in this chapter.

3. Is it enough for us now that the New Testament writers were familiar with the Old Testament and told us what we need to know

about it? If we should seek to know the Old Testament well ourselves, how can we guard against misquoting it? Discuss.

Questions on Chapter 12

1. Classify the figures of speech used in 2 Cor 3:13–18. The background to this passage is to be found in Exod 34:29–35. Explain how an understanding of what happened in the Old Testament passage helps us to grasp what the New Testament passage is saying.
2. Write explanatory notes on the formal comparisons, similes and metaphors used in these passages:
   (a) 2 Cor 11:2–3
   (b) John 6:48–50, 58
3. What is the significance of the comparison between Christ and Jonah in Luke 11:29–30; Matt 12:39–40?
4. Explain the figures of speech used in 1 Cor 5:6–8. What practical lesson is Paul seeking to teach by these figures of speech?

Questions on Chapter 13

1. What do you understand by the term *allusion*? How does tracing the New Testament's allusions to the Old Testament help us to understand what the New Testament is saying?
2. What did Cain, Korah and Balaam have in common? In what did they differ?
3. Why did God accept Abel's sacrifice and not Cain's?
4. From chapter 11 onwards the book of Numbers records several rebellions against God. Identify them, and then say how many of them are cited and expounded in the New Testament. What lessons does the New Testament draw from these incidents and apply to its readers?

Questions on Chapter 14

1. What is 'an implicit allusion'? Give an example. What is the point and purpose of such allusions?
2. Discuss and expound Christ's promise 'To him who overcomes will I give to eat of the tree of life which is in the paradise of God' (Rev 2:7).
3. In what different senses does the Apostle John use the term 'the world' in his first epistle?
4. In what sense can Pharaoh's Egypt become for us a picture of the world and its prince?
5. Write, in your own words, an essay entitled 'The Book of Exodus as a Thought-Model for Understanding the Gospel of John'.

Questions on Chapter 15

1. What is normally meant by the term 'allegory'?
2. Why do many scholars not like allegorical interpretations of the Bible?
3. What is the straightforward meaning of the parable of the Good Samaritan?
4. What is an ad hominem argument? Is Gal 4:21–31 an example of such an argument? If not, why not?
5. What indication is there in Paul's interpretation of the Hagar–Ishmael–Sarah–Isaac story, that he regarded that story as history and not as an allegory?
6. What does Paul mean by the term *flesh*, when he says that Ishmael's birth was 'after the flesh'?
7. In what sense, according to Paul, are believers 'children of promise' (Gal 4:28)?
8. 'The difference between Paul's pre-conversion attitudes to salvation and his post-conversion attitude can be expressed in terms of flesh and spirit.' Comment.

9. What was Christ referring to when he spoke of Jerusalem's 'children' (Luke 13:34)? Literal, metaphorical, or allegorical children? What is the difference between metaphor and allegory?
10. What does Paul mean by saying that the Law given at Mount Sinai 'bears children unto slavery'? Is the fault in the Law, or in people's misuse of it (Gal 3:19, 21, 23–29; 4:1–7, 24)?
11. What temporary function did the Law fulfil in Israel's history (Gal 3:19; 4:1–7)?
12. What is meant by 'the Jerusalem which is above' (Gal 4:26)?
13. Express in your own words the contrast depicted in Heb 12:18–24, between Mount Sinai and the heavenly Jerusalem.
14. Why do some people persecute others who differ from them in their religious beliefs? Is it ever right for a Christian to do so?

Questions on Chapter 16

1. Why does Paul in Rom 4:10–12 attach so much importance to the timing of Abraham's circumcision?
2. 'For Abraham circumcision had a double significance.' Comment.
3. What was the basic significance of circumcision for Abraham's descendants and household?
4. At one level circumcision was a token. A token of what? Had the token any value in the absence of the reality which it betokened? What lessons can Christians learn from the function of circumcision at this level?
5. Expound in your own words the significance that Paul gives to circumcision in Phil 3:1–9.
6. What do you understand by the phrase 'the circumcision of Christ' (Col 2:11–13)?
7. 'The story of the creation of Eve is applied in the New Testament at two different levels.' Explain.

Questions on Chapter 17

1. What does the author of Hebrews conclude from the position of verses 7–8 of Psalm 40 in the sequence of thought expressed in its immediate context?
2. What, do you think, first drew the attention of the author of Hebrews to Ps 110:1–4?
3. What does the author of Hebrews mean by stating that Melchizedek, whose description is given in Genesis 14, 'has been made to resemble' the Son of God?

Questions on Chapter 18

1. Which two Old Testament passages form the basis of the message preached in Heb 3:7–4:16?
2. What view of the authority of the Old Testament underlies our author's application of these two Old Testament passages to his readers?
3. What possible parallel does our author see between the behaviour of the Israelites in the desert and that of his readers? To what detailed similarities does he appeal?
4. On what grounds does our author argue that Psalm 95 holds out to his readers the promise of entering God's rest?
5. In what terms does our author describe the cause of Israel's failure to enter their promised rest? What is the meaning of those terms?
6. On what ground does our author state that believers nowadays enter God's rest?
7. What does God mean by the phrase 'my rest' in Ps 95:11? Cf. Heb 4:3–5.
8. Is 'entering God's rest' a present or future experience?
9. What functions are verses 11–16 of Hebrews 4 meant to perform at the end of our author's sermon?

Questions on Chapter 19

1. What was the *typos* that God showed to Moses on Mount Sinai?
2. What is the meaning of the word *antitypos* in Heb 9:24?
3. The Lampstand in the tabernacle was made to look like a living tree. Do you agree that it was a symbolic Tree of Life? Is there a Tree of Life in heaven (Rev 2:7)?
4. What did the loaves on the Table of the Bread of the Presence represent? Why were there twelve, and why had they to be accompanied by incense?
5. What was the significance of burning incense before God?
6. Why had Aaron to burn incense when he dressed the lamps and when he lit them?
7. Why had the horns on the incense altar to be smeared with blood? What blood?

Questions on Chapter 20

1. How does the function of the tabernacle help us to understand John 1:14?
2. What is the strict meaning of the technical term 'the tabernacle'? What is meant by saying that it was a plurality in unity? Do you think it illustrates any modern spiritual reality?
3. What lesson did the Holy Spirit convey to Israel by the Veil?
4. In what sense was the Veil a merciful provision? Did Christ ever function as a Veil? Does he do so now?
5. The tabernacle offered cleansing by blood and cleansing by water. Does the Christian gospel do the same? Why do we need both kinds of cleansing?
6. In what ways does the Lampstand point to Christ?
7. The Table of the Bread of Presence was a place of fellowship between God and his priests. How does this illustrate 1 John 1:2–4?
8. The Table stood directly opposite the Lampstand. What practical effect did this have on the priests? Does it have a lesson for us?

9. Our advocate with the Father is the propitiation for our sins (1 John 2:1–2). Does this remind you of any ritual in the tabernacle?
10. The Lampstand and the Table presented lamps and loaves before God. Examine what the New Testament says about our being presented before God.

Questions on Chapter 21

1. What features of the tabernacle are mentioned at Rev 4:1–11; 8:1–5; 11:19; 15:5–8?
2. What is meant by claiming that on each occasion these features set the scene for what follows?
3. Do you agree that these features help to explain why the judgments of God must fall on earth and on its inhabitants?
4. What is meant by the phrase 'the creatorial rights of the throne'?
5. What do you understand by 'the problem of evil'? What has it to do with the prayers of the saints?
6. Is it right for Christians to pray that God will one day intervene and see that justice is done for his people?
7. What relevance has the title given to the Ark in Rev 11:19 to what follows?
8. Why is it that when the temple of the tabernacle is opened in Rev 15:5ff, no piece of tabernacle furniture is seen? What is the significance of the smoke?
9. What is unusual about the use of tabernacle symbolism in the Revelation?

PART THREE

Questions on Chapter 22

1. Explain, in your own words, why the idea that our interpretation must be either literal or typological is too simplistic.
2. What does it mean to say that 'the nature' of the analogy must be considered?
3. What is the intended ethical implication of Christ's teaching of the two comings of Messiah?

Questions on Chapter 23

1. What determines a narrative's primary meaning when the New Testament cites that narrative?
2. What is one sure sign that an explanation of the New Testament's interpretation of an Old Testament narrative is inadequate or unreliable?
3. Are there other examples you could give to show that the New Testament implies that one Old Testament narrative does not contradict another?
4. What must we take into account from the New Testament if our interpretation of an Old Testament passage is to be complete?
5. How can studying the original context of an Old Testament narrative that the New Testament cites and applies to us, enhance our understanding of the New Testament's application? Discuss other possible additional examples.
6. What does it mean when we say that we should treat the whole of an Old Testament narrative seriously as being a narrative in its own right?
7. Should we consider a narrative's potential prototypical significance? If so, at what point should that consideration come in our study?

Questions on Chapter 24

1. When trying to interpret an Old Testament narrative that the New Testament does not comment on, what should be our starting point?
2. In the story of David and Goliath, how does the thought-flow of the surrounding narrative help to indicate the author's intentions? Choose one other example of a well-known Old Testament story and consider how its surrounding context might do the same.
3. What does it mean to say that we should question the comparative importance of the lesson that we propose to draw from an Old Testament narrative?

Questions on Chapter 25

1. What are the theological implications of the majority interpretation of the case of the Gibeonites?
2. How can a survey of a book as a whole and the identification of dominant themes indicate whether our interpretation is correct?
3. Can the proportion of space given to various themes in a narrative indicate anything about our own interpretation of that narrative? If so, how?

Questions on A Concluding Word

1. When the Holy Spirit was speaking centuries ago through the prophets, what was the first great purpose he had in mind for us?
2. What was the Holy Spirit's second great purpose?
3. What are the implications of each of these purposes for our lives as Christians today?
4. Set aside time at this point to give thanks to God and to praise him for his Word.

Scripture Index

408

Leviticus

11:44 57
11:45 57
16 61, 64–5
16:2 300 n.
16:12 290
16:13 292
16:16 292
16:17 205
16:18 311
17:11 34
18:5 124, 234
19:2 57
19:18 54, 57
20:7 57
20:8 57
20:26 57
21:8 57
21:15 57
21:23 57
22:9 57
22:16 57
24:1–9 283
24:2 293
26:31 294

Numbers

4:7 286
11 202
11:4–35 190
12:6–8 204
12:7 180
13–14 202, 258–75
14:11 203
14:20–24 266
14:24 266
14:28–31 266
14:31 266
14:32–35 264
16–18 40
16–17 202–7

16 194
16:3 204
16:13 205
16:14 205
16:35 290
16:36–40 206
16:46–49 291
17:1–11 207
17:8 377
20:1–13 202
20:12–13 295
20:23–29 202, 295
21:4–9 182–5
22–24 194, 200–2
22:7 200
22:8–12 200
22:15–19 200
22:20 200
22:23–35 200
22:23 203
22:35 200, 201
22:37 200
23:1–3 201
23:5 200
23:16 200
23:20 200
23:26 200
24:4 200
24:10–13 200
25 202
25:1–15 137
25:1–9 201
25:1–2 200
25:1 203
25:6–8 203
25:11 203
28:2 287
31:8 202
31:15–16 200, 201
32 202

Deuteronomy

1:8 186
2:14–15 264
4:25–27 158
5:16 175
6:5 54, 59
6:6–7 50
6:13 54
6:16 54, 175
8:1 157
8:3 54
18:10 84 n.
18:15 37
20:10–18 354
20:10–11 365
20:15–18 358
20:16–18 359
20:17–18 366
25:1 123
25:4 141–3
27:26 125
28:15 157
28:63–64 157
29:1 157
30 250
30:1–5 159
30:6 250
31:16–17 158
31:29 158

Joshua

book 163
1:1–4 38
1:5 176
2 364
2:2–7 360
2:9–11 363
2:12–13 360, 362–3
2:16 363–4
6–8 356, 358
6 364

Index of Greek and Hebrew Words

General Index

I recall seeing a wine expert who successfully identified the province in France where the grapes were grown that yielded the bottles he sampled. He explained that the telltale taste and bouquet resulted from the distinctive soils in which the vintage grew. So I have discovered, through the discriminating palate of Professor Gooding, how the various writings of the Hebrew Scriptures have left their distinctive marks on the fruit borne by the writers of the New Testament. *The Riches of Divine Wisdom* is clearly a masterwork of scholarship but written so it makes available to any devoted Bible student a largely unexplored field of both profitable and enjoyable study.

   —**J. B. Nicholson**, President, Uplook Ministries, USA

What a treasure trove of spiritual riches—gleaned from a lifetime in searching the Scriptures. Read these books, and you will be nourished, stretched, and enlightened, as I was.

   —**Dr Lindsay Brown**, International Director of the Lausanne Movement

I would not use the word lightly, but this really is 'Vintage Gooding'. All the great characteristics are here: his very special ability to discern the literary structure of books and passages, his love of the Bible as the Word of God, his ability to express each nugget of truth with conciseness, clarity and helpfulness. If you do not have time to read this whole book, then don't open it. You will be gripped from page one, as I was. And I certainly would not have wished to miss a single sentence or page. Gooding subtitles his book 'The New Testament's Use of the Old Testament' but in fact has given us a comprehensive (and highly readable) account of the basic principles of biblical interpretation.

— **Alec Motyer,** formerly Principal of Trinity College, Bristol

I anticipate that this book will rapidly become an essential resource for those seeking to understand and enjoy the way in which the New Testament unfolds the meaning of the Old Testament. David Gooding's analysis of texts that are often found difficult is both penetrating and accessible. I have personally found the material contained here extraordinarily helpful.

— **John C Lennox,** Professor of Mathematics, University of Oxford; Fellow in Mathematics and Philosophy of Science, Green Templeton College

I carefully read two earlier books in this series, on Luke and Acts, from start to finish. I am doing the same with this book for the same reasons: the opportunity to gain deep insights into biblical truth which only a master of the Scriptures could give, and to be devotionally enriched while doing so. This book is particularly important because it clearly and skilfully addresses a key area of biblical interpretation which all sincere students of the Word should develop skills in handling. I am refining some of my views on how I should approach the Old Testament as I read this book, and I am learning, learning, learning . . . .

— **Ajith Fernando,** Teaching Director, Youth for Christ, Sri Lanka; Author, *Deuteronomy: Loving Obedience to a Loving God*

This book is vintage David Gooding — Christ-centred, scholarly yet immensely readable exposition. With verve and skill, he tackles one of the most challenging issues facing every Bible student, presenting many of the rich insights of his teaching ministry. This is a landmark contribution. I found my thinking stimulated and sharpened as I read it.

— **Alan Gamble,** Bible Teacher, Glasgow, Scotland

The Riches of Divine Wisdom is a tour de force. Many Christians fail to take the Old Testament seriously. Others find the New Testament's use of the Old problematic. In this work Professor Gooding offers sane guidance to both groups with eloquence and clarity. He shows how the New Testament itself instructs us in interpreting the Old. Teachers, preachers and all serious Bible students will find it an invaluable resource.

> — **Gordon J. Wenham,** Tutor in Old Testament, Trinity College, Bristol; Professor Emeritus of Old Testament, University of Gloucester

In this wide-ranging study we meet typology, allegory, and 'fulfilment', and the different levels at which fulfilment may take place. We are reminded that dogged adherence to either a literal-historical or a typological reading of Scripture risks selling it short. And that, whereas we must always begin our engagement with texts at the literal-historical (or grammatico-historical) level, that is often only the first step in the unfolding of what they have to convey. . . . David Gooding presents this splendid volume as a kind of manual on the interpretation of Scripture, and on how consideration of the interplay of the two Testaments may help inform our own attempts at interpretation and exposition.

> — **Robert P. Gordon,** Regius Professor of Hebrew Emeritus, University of Cambridge (from the Foreword)

In this exceptionally informative book, Prof. David Gooding addresses with outstanding clarity the challenging task of explaining how New Testament writers draw on the Old Testament. As a highly-gifted, experienced Bible teacher and academic scholar, he has produced a profoundly helpful, and yet remarkably accessible, guide to this complex topic. Fully focused on using Scripture to interpret Scripture, Prof. Gooding skilfully enables the diligent reader to see with greater clarity the 'riches of divine wisdom'. For anyone interested in understanding better the unity of the Bible, this book is essential reading.

> — **T. Desmond Alexander,** Senior Lecturer in Biblical Studies, Union Theological College, Belfast

The Riches of Divine Wisdom is full of careful analysis, very helpful outlines clearly presented and replete with examples. I know of no other work which is so complete and practical in its delineation of ways in which the New Testament uses the Old Testament and so how to expound the Old Testament today. The scholarship is evident but it is worn lightly so that the work is suitable for wide readership. All who read it and follow its guidelines will be enriched!

> — **John W. Olley,** Research Associate in Old Testament and formerly Principal of Vose Seminary, Perth

CPSIA information can be obtained at www.ICGtesting.com
Printed in the USA
LVOW05s2023091214

418015LV00028B/1328/P